ALCOHOL

& DRUG

PROBLEMS

A PRACTICAL GUIDE
FOR COUNSELLORS

EDITORS:

Betty-Anne M. Howard

Susan Harrison

Virginia Carver

Lynn Lightfoot

ARF — Addiction Research Foundation — Fondation de la recherche sur la toxicomanie

INTRODUCTION

The impetus for this book came from the experience of Betty-Anne Howard, then director of the Addiction Research Foundation's Kingston Area Office, who was providing consultation to addiction assessment and referral workers in Ontario. A number of clinical issues kept recurring, such as: how to help and involve family members; how to address the needs of women (should they be approached or treated differently?); how to help a person with a history of physical or sexual abuse, etc.

It became evident that there were individual counsellors scattered across the province with expertise in the various themes that kept recurring. This book attempts to respond to these issues and provide a practical and useful resource for addiction counsellors.

Another impetus for this book has been the need to provide a Canadian perspective on addictions. Universal health care has meant that treatment services and approaches in Canada have developed in a somewhat different way from the mainly entrepreneurial approach of our neighbors to the south. Also, both our social safety net and the smaller number of large metropolitan areas have resulted in our having, in general, less serious "epidemics" of problems related to the use of drugs such as heroin, crack, etc.

It will be apparent to the reader that there are a number of philosophical underpinnings in the counselling approaches described in the book. These include: the position that substance abuse problems exist on a continuum of severity, are not necessarily progressive, and require a variety of interventions matched as much as is currently possible to the client's individual needs, given our current state of knowledge in this area.

The editors hope that the structure of the book – beginning with a section of what we have called "Core Considerations," followed by sections addressing particular population groups, and ending with issues related to substance abuse – will provide an accessible format for the counsellor who may want to "pick and choose" what is appropriate to his or her work at any point in time.

The Editors
Ottawa, Ontario
July, 1993

TABLE OF CONTENTS

CORE CONSIDERATIONS

SPECIAL NEEDS OF PARTICULAR POPULATIONS

ADDRESSING RELATED ISSUES

Core Considerations

Ethics and Professional Issues

WAYNE SKINNER

*T*his is not a systematic treatment of ethical and professional issues in clinical work in addictions. It is an essay offered from a personal viewpoint. Rather than providing firm answers to key questions, it is intended to encourage reflection and promote (and provoke) discussion and dialogue about the ethics of addictions treatment.

Clinical practice in addictions lacks a unified view of key ethical and professional issues. This is not surprising, given that addictions workers have so many different professional and life-experiential points of origin. Some of us have professional clinical training – in social work, nursing, or psychology, for instance; some of us have come to the helping role through the process of our own recoveries. Some of us have little professional training, but are rich in practical experience; some of us are just the opposite, theoretically strong but not well grounded in clinical practice. Some of us have specific training in addictions; some of us rely on general knowledge about human biopsychosocial functioning.

In short, addictions counsellors are a very diverse group. Our views about the nature of substance use problems, and our practices – our interventive methods – are varied, and at times conflict with each other. These differences need not be seen as problems to be eliminated, of course; they deserve to be appreciated and celebrated. But when it comes to establishing consensus and setting up clear-cut and broadly supported ways of acting and conducting ourselves, we do not face an easy task.

Conduct is at the heart of ethics and professional roles. How do I behave? How should I behave? For those who belong to a helping profession with a code of ethics, there already exists a framework within which conduct will be evaluated. Agencies also have policies and procedures that guide the actions of their staff. Additionally, there are legal statutes and regulations that govern confidentiality, reporting of abuse and neglect, and the duty to take action regarding imminent client self-harm or threats to others. From one perspective, the field may seem quite bare of unifying standards and guidelines; from another, there are many regulations and rules guiding and shaping the conduct of the helper.

Our challenge is to see the diversity of people who work within the field of addictions treatment as one of its fundamental realities, one of its special strengths.

Between the two poles of the volunteer and the trained professional is a great array of individuals of varied skills and experience, linked by a shared intention to make a positive difference in the lives of people with problems related to substance use.

The fertile diversity of the addictions treatment field ensures that even the most basic beliefs and attitudes are not uniformly held and are often contested and debated. One may ask, "what is addiction?" only to receive a dizzying barrage of answers, many of which contradict each other. Some will call addiction a disease. Others will say that it is genetically based or a learned behavior. Still others will insist that it is a socially constructed concept. Whatever the answer, each specific response will guide decisively how we understand the nature of substance use problems and what should be done about them. Indeed, our notions of the helping role and of what constitutes proper, ethical conduct will be shaped by the beliefs and attitudes we hold about human beings and human behavior.

So, let that be our first point here: professional conduct and ethical standards are themselves formed (though not totally determined) by what we take to be human nature, by how we see addiction problems, and by what we think needs to be done about them. It is easy to see why having a single set of facts, a single set of procedures, a single set of beliefs, and a single point of view would be appealing. It helps to quiet the voices of doubt that might otherwise rise within us or be heard in the questions of others. It eliminates the otherwise necessary struggle we have to engage in when, in a particular situation, we have to sort out the right thing to do.

Perhaps the most ethical position a helper can hold today is one that is open to critical self-reflection and self-evaluation. Such a helper is prepared to assess the intention and measure the effectiveness of what he or she is doing. Intentions in helping are often the very best, but intentions alone are a poor measure. The history of medical practice shows the harm that can be unwittingly inflicted by the well-intentioned helper. Surgery without respect for the need for aseptic procedures, blood transfusions that contain undetected contaminants, use of medication with side effects that outweigh potential benefits: these are just a few examples. Many methods that were the standards of care and treatment in the past would be flagrantly unethical today. What will the practitioners of the future have to say about the addictions interventions that we practise today?

Members of formal disciplines with their own codes of ethics and professional values may think that they are exempt from the labors of reflection. But the ethical challenge itself consists of this: to be able to locate in a specific situation what is unique to it and what is universal. That determines when general rules should be applied or whether the particular circumstances are paramount. For example, confidentiality is a guiding principle of professional conduct among counsellors, but there are times when other considerations must be given precedence – where the safety of an individual from death or grievous harm is at stake, for example. The counsellor also has a legal obligation to report cases of suspected child abuse to the appropriate child protection agency. When orienting clients to the rules of the counselling relationship, it is important to spell out and define the boundaries and limits to the process.

How can the helper evaluate whether aspects of his or her conduct and duty (which is at least a double duty: to the individual and to the community) are ethically defensible and socially acceptable and, if they are not, what to do about it? Several types of dilemma commonly occur in clinical work. First, the conflict can occur totally within the helper's self. One way this happens is when the worker feels caught between "want to" and "ought to." Extreme, though not uncommon, examples would be feeling strongly attracted to or repulsed by a client. The helper is expected to be especially adept at recognizing the feelings that are evoked by contact with other people. Being able to work with feelings that usually undo or subvert ordinary relationships is the special hallmark of the counselling experience. But when the helper feels immobilized by or pulled towards behavior that opposes his or her sense of what he or she should be doing, then an ethical problem has emerged and must be addressed responsibly. "Responsibly" is a good word to use here, because it encourages us to recognize not only that there is conduct that is proper to being a helper and a counsellor, but also that the counsellor is "response-able": that is, able to make the ethically required response. The response can take a variety of forms. Feeling unable to talk to colleagues or a supervisor, or deliberately avoiding doing so, is a likely sign that the counsellor is avoiding a matter of professional responsibility. This does not mean that consultation is always required: careful evaluation often leads the worker to an ethically supportable decision about how to proceed. But consultation should always be an option that the helper is willing to pursue. Not being able to candidly discuss a dilemma with professional colleagues is itself a sign that factors other than professional conduct are guiding the helper's behavior.

One key to the helping relationship is the realization that it involves taking the client into our care, "our" meaning both the agency and helper. The enduring measure of the helping relationship is that we do not take advantage of the client, especially given the vulnerability and dependence that the helping relationship, to be effective, must sometimes permit. Even when the helper believes there is a mutual interest or consent between helper and client, there can be no suspension of ethical standards regarding relationships.

When attraction or repulsion is so strong as to interfere with the helper's tasks, it would seem to be in the best interests of the client (and the counsellor) to transfer the client to another counsellor. This must, of course, be done in a skilled and sensitive way, with care being taken to avoid projecting the helper's own conflicted dynamics onto the client. Many clients already tend to take too much responsibility for failed events.

Stereotypically, we think of the helper's attraction to a client and the problems it might bring. It is just as important to think of the subtle ways that the client's behavior may be objectionable, offensive, or a threat. Dealing with violence, aggression, or other negative behavior may offend the helper's beliefs and sensibilities, so that the helper may even resist finding ways of engaging the client, which can be crucial to therapeutic success. Clients with substance use problems may behave in ways that are socially ridiculed or forbidden. They may be stigmatized because of health problems frequently associated with marginalized lifestyles, such as prostitution. Cultural differences can sometimes alienate the helper from the client to the extent that it interferes with the professional obligation to offer care.

Besides an internal conflict between feelings and duties, between "want" and "ought," the worker may feel caught between two duties or ethical imperatives (two "oughts"). Confidentiality and duty to inform have already been mentioned. The work of exploring painful issues with the client can itself be thought of in ethical terms. The adage Primum non nolire (Above all, do no harm) is an old motto in medicine. In encouraging clients to address painful experiences, feelings and thoughts – sometimes confronting them – the helper should be very clear about why he or she is doing this. What effect, or result, is being sought? In what state does it leave the client? Working at close quarters with a vulnerable person carries with it the challenge to be purposeful and to know the limits as well as the possibilities of the helping experience. For example, therapists sometimes try to produce a breakthrough by getting a client to give up control over feelings. It is often easy to produce such effects. But again, the helper has to answer why it needed to be done, and how it affected the client.

Another ethical dilemma emerges when there is a conflict between helper and client about what should be done. The therapeutic relationship is, in terms of power, asymmetrical: the helper has more than the client. This is not to say that the client is totally powerless, but the advantages tend to favor the counsellor. The self-reflective helper should consider to what degree his or her behavior is an exercise in power and control, rather than a purposeful attempt to help the client. Ways in which power circulates in the counselling relationship can reinforce rather than release the client from the dynamics of dependence and feelings of inadequacy commonly encountered in the treatment of substance use problems. The issue is not for the helper to deny or to avoid the power of his or her position, but to see how it works and affects the helping process. The helper's goal could be to use the strategic advantages he or she enjoys in the relationship (e.g., the worker knows more about the client than the client knows about the worker; the worker can usually direct what is talked about, when meetings begin and end, etc.) to help empower the client toward his or her healthy possibilities.

Additionally, conflicts that align a client and worker against a community standard or value can be seen as an ethical issue. An important part of the helper's role is to advocate for the needs of the client, needs that sometimes can only be remedied at the societal level, and sometime conflict with public values. Examples in the world of addictions treatment are easy to find. Consider the need for harm reduction strategies for intravenous drug users. In this case, the formal social rule is that such behavior is illegal and therefore prohibited. Taking that stance alone, the only permissible intervention would be immediate cessation of the drug use behavior, followed by abstinence. Yet while counsellors in addiction programs help clients discontinue drug use, public health concerns have led to advocacy of harm reduction measures such as needle exchanges, free condoms, and methadone programs. The goal expands beyond discontinuing unwanted behavior to the reduction or avoidance of harmful consequences. This alliance of client and therapeutic interest opposes public opinion (and established therapeutic philosophies, in some cases).

In the belief that ethical issues are an inherent part of all helping relationships, I have identified and illustrated three forms of dilemma that have ethical implications for the helper: first, between what the helper wants to do and what he or she feels is the correct thing to do (between personal desire and personal duty); second, between what the client feels is right and what the worker believes (between you and me); and third, between what worker and client agree on and social standards or rules (between us and them). In each of these situations, the helper's beliefs about human beings, substance use problems, the helping role, prospects for treatment, as well as his or her thoughts, feelings and assumptions about the particular client – all of these, along with other factors, shape and define ethical issues that require responses that go beyond the routine. Not so long ago, corporal punishment might have been tolerated or even valued as signs of parents' dedicated attention to the proper upbringing of children – that is, as a form of ethical behavior. Now we see in this behavior a dynamic of victimization that has toxic intergenerational aspects. It has become a crime.

Ethics and professional roles are not items to consider tangentially in addictions treatment. Because values and beliefs are so central to the helping project itself, they are at the heart of the very routines and assumptions that we take for granted. Extraordinary situations bring the ethical dimension into particularly sharp relief, but an essential part of the professional role is a commitment to keeping the most commonplace actions and convictions open to scrutiny and challenge.

To conclude, consider some very simple questions that a helper could ask in trying to see if his or her conduct meets an ethical standard. First, are there aspects of my work with a particular client that I would be embarrassed to see appear on the clinical record? If the details of my work with clients are accurately presented in the file, then I am being open about my work and prepared to have it evaluated by my peers. If I am holding back information regarding in-session events and my personal conduct, is it something that a detached and objective observer would be able to understand and accept?

Second, are there features of my work that I avoid sharing with my peers and in supervision? The mark of a competent helper is not that he or she knows all the answers but is always open to self-examination and in pursuit of self-improvement. Are there aspects of my work that I withhold because I know or suspect they are wrong, or because they would not pass review by my peers, or because I fear my work is of poor quality? Being able to seek out consultation, sharing information with colleagues, being open to different ways of doing things – these are signs of a helper who seeks most of all to be optimally helpful to clients.

Third, even (or especially) assuming that my intentions are of the highest order, what are the effects of my actions? Ultimately, ethics must be less concerned about why I do what I do than with the effects my actions have on others. What do I intend? And – more importantly – what is the result? For the ethical helper, there can be ultimately only two measures for this question of effects: the one given by the client and the one that is empirically (or factually) based.

Addictions is a field in which an inventory of specific ethical standards is not likely to be found. Instead, the process of helping is one that requires ongoing critical self-appraisal by the helper and openness to the word of the client and the work of the evaluator. Work that is clearly and honestly documented is the product of a responsible helper, as is an attitude of openness that seeks and invites dialogue and consultation about the demanding aspects of working with individuals with problems related to substance use.

Taking a person into our care is a task and a calling that puts the interests of the help-seeker first in ways that do not compromise our duty to enhance the safety and the health of the community. The ethics of clinical practice require us to recognize the balance – grounded in both meanings of the phrase "taking care" – that enables the client to heal and grow and the community to be safe and to evolve. The ethical helper is one who continuously and openly struggles with this challenge.

An Introduction to Health Care Law for Addiction Workers

R. M. SOLOMON AND S. J. USPRICH

INTRODUCTION

*T*he purpose of this chapter is to help addiction workers understand the basic legal principles governing assessment and treatment. Without question, the legal environment has become more challenging for all professionals. Those involved in health care are increasingly being sued, and called upon in disciplinary hearings and other legal contexts to explain and justify their conduct.[1] There has been a parallel trend towards recognizing and protecting the legal rights of clients, especially those who are young.[2] Despite the impression that may have been created by the media, the situation in Canada is not as troubling as it is in the United States. Nevertheless, legal issues will continue to play a greater role in the working lives of all health care professionals.

In addition to the legal issues inherent in any treatment relationship, several complicating factors can arise in the substance abuse field. First, a sizable percentage of clients may have only reluctantly entered treatment pursuant to a probation order or at the insistence of an employer, spouse, parent, or registrar of motor vehicles. What impact do such pressures have on the addiction worker's legal obligations to the client? Second, some clients may be under the provincial age of majority.[3] Nevertheless, the client may still have the legal capacity to give a valid consent to treatment. It may be difficult to determine in a specific case whether the particular underage client is competent to consent to the proposed treatment. Assuming that a client is capable of giving consent, how should a treatment professional respond to inquiries from parents, school officials, welfare workers, or police about the case? Third, alcohol and drug use frequently involves conduct that is not only illegal, but which may also endanger the client and others. Does a treatment professional have any legal obligation to inform the police of the criminal activities of his or her clients? Moreover, can a treatment professional be held civilly liable for failing to warn third parties of the dangers posed by a client?

These types of issues arise because substance abuse treatment can cut across the criminal justice, health care, child welfare, education, and employment systems. We cannot undertake an exhaustive legal analysis of these systems and their possible effects on treatment within the scope of this chapter. Rather, we focus on basic legal principles governing health care relationships and explain their special application to addiction workers.

Even in terms of the general principles, it is not possible to review the relevant statutes and cases in every jurisdiction in Canada. Consequently, we provide an overview of the major principles in the text, but give detailed references in the endnotes. The reader should understand that the exact legal rules vary from jurisdiction to jurisdiction to reflect differences in provincial case law and statutes.

This paper is divided into two major sections. In the first, we discuss the law governing consent to treatment, including: the general principles of consent; exceptions to the general principles; consent forms; competence to consent; substitute consent; and informed consent. The second section contains a detailed discussion of confidentiality, privilege, disclosure of client information, reporting obligations and the duty to warn.

SECTION 1: CONSENT TO TREATMENT

(A) INTRODUCTION

One hallmark of our legal system is the importance it attaches to the protection of the physical integrity of the individual.[4] Whether couched in terms of physical inviolability, autonomy, self-determination, or privacy, the basic interest is the same – namely, an individual's right to control his or her own body. This concept may be viewed as a double-edged sword. Whether the decision is wise or foolish, the law protects the individual's right to decide.

The law's concern with protecting the individual is clearly illustrated by the fact that virtually any physical interference with another may result in both criminal[5] and civil liability.[6] In the absence of consent, the defendant will be held liable unless he or she can establish explicit legal authority to justify the interference. In these situations, however, health care professionals are rarely charged with a criminal offence.[7] Rather, the issue of consent typically arises in determining whether there is a valid defence to a civil action for the tort (wrongful act) of battery.

Battery is defined as intentionally causing a harmful or socially offensive physical contact with another person.[8] The mere touching of another is sufficient to give rise to liability; the victim need not suffer any physical injury.[9] Any surgical procedure, administration of drugs or treatment that involves physical contact may constitute battery. Once the client establishes that there has been a physical contact, the burden of proof shifts to the treatment professional to establish a valid defence.[10] If the defendant cannot prove that the client consented, then the defendant will be held liable for all the consequences of the battery. In the vast majority of cases, the key issue is not whether there was a physical contact, but whether the treatment professional can establish the defence of consent.

The legal principles governing the defence of consent have developed almost exclusively from cases involving surgery and other physical interventions. However, the tort of battery is also relevant to alcohol and drug treatment programs that include physical examinations, the taking of blood samples, the administration of drugs, or other physical contact. It is equally clear that alcohol and drug treatment that involves only the taking of a history, questionnaires, counselling, or similar non-physical interactions cannot give rise to a battery claim. Nevertheless, the issue of consent and the principles governing it are still relevant in these situations.

(B) THE GENERAL PRINCIPLES OF CONSENT

As a general rule, a health care professional must obtain consent to initiate any physical examination, test, procedure, surgery, or counselling.[11] The consent should be obtained in advance and cover not only the intervention, but also any related issues regarding record-keeping, reporting and other disclosures of information. The consent must relate to the specific treatment or counselling that is undertaken.[12] If the client is competent to give a valid consent, then his or her consent alone is required.[13] As we shall discuss, the consent of the next-of-kin is only relevant if the client is incapable of consenting. Even in these circumstances, there are limits to the validity of substitute consents.[14]

To be valid, a consent must be given "voluntarily", in the sense that the client's decision is the product of his or her conscious mind.[15] The legal definition of volition is extremely broad. For example, clients who reluctantly consent to drug treatment because it is a term of probation, or because they have been threatened with being fired from a job or expelled from school will still be held to have "voluntarily" consented.

A client may consent implicitly or explicitly. The fact that a client comes for treatment provides some measure of implicit consent.[16] Clients may seek alcohol or drug treatment, and yet expressly limit the scope of their consent. An addiction worker may refuse to treat the client if these limitations are unreasonable. However, the worker cannot ignore a client's express prohibitions or override them.[17]

(C) INFORMED CONSENT

The consent must be based on a full and frank disclosure of the nature of the intervention and its risks. A client must be put in the position of being able to make an informed decision about whether to enter treatment, but need not be told of all the possible risks.[18] Rather, the courts have held that clients must be informed of the general nature of the treatment and any "material risks" associated with it.[19] A material risk includes a low probability of a serious consequence, such as a four per cent chance of death or a 10 per cent chance of a stroke. It also includes a high probability of a relatively minor consequence, such as a 35 per cent chance of infection. In addition, health care professionals have an obligation to disclose even non-material risks that they know or ought to know would be of concern to the particular client.[20]

Increasingly, the courts are requiring health care professionals to explain the proposed treatment and its risks in a broader context. This may include a discussion of alternative treatment, as well as the risks of leaving the condition untreated.[21]

A client may choose to rely on the addiction worker's judgment and decide to forgo being informed of the risks. However, the decision not to be fully informed is the client's and must be expressly communicated to the addiction worker. Health care professionals are also required to answer fully and honestly all of a client's questions, even if they relate to minor risks or relatively inconsequential aspects of the procedure.[22]

Addiction workers who do not meet these standards of disclosure are in breach of their duty and may be held liable in negligence. However, the client must also establish that this failure to inform caused or contributed to his or her injuries.[23] In effect, clients must prove that they would not have proceeded with the treatment if they had known of the risks.[24]

(D) EXCEPTIONS TO THE GENERAL PRINCIPLES OF CONSENT

The courts have relaxed the strict requirements of consent in three situations. First, in an unforeseen medical emergency where it is impossible to obtain consent, a health care professional is allowed to operate without consent to preserve the client's health or life.[25] This right is granted to health care professionals in order to save lives. It is on this basis that emergency room staff are permitted to operate on an unconscious accident victim.

The second exception to the consent requirement involves clients who have given a general consent to a course of therapy, treatment program or operation. In such situations, a client will be viewed as implicitly consenting to any subordinate tests, procedures or interventions that are necessarily incidental to the broader course of treatment.[26] However, this implied consent is negated if the client objects. While it may not be legally necessary, it is prudent to obtain a specific consent for any subordinate procedure that poses significant risks or involves sexually, legally or emotionally sensitive issues.

Third, the Canadian courts at one time held that health care professionals had a right to withhold information if its disclosure would undermine the client's morale or discourage him or her from having needed treatment.[27] However, the courts have become increasingly critical of this concept, and it now appears that clients must always be informed of the basic nature and risks of treatment or therapy.[28] Nevertheless, health care professionals do have some discretion in the way they inform a client, the technical matters they discuss and the emphasis placed on the relative risks of undergoing versus not undergoing the treatment.[29]

While it may be important to encourage a client to enter alcohol or drug treatment, staff cannot withhold information about the treatment or its risks, or exaggerate its benefits. Addiction workers may express their own views about the benefits of treatment in strong language, but they may not mislead clients.

(E) CONSENT FORMS AND THE BURDEN OF PROOF

Unless a statute provides otherwise, a client may give consent orally or in writing. Since the client's presence provides some measure of consent, it is not necessary to obtain written consent for routine treatment sessions. Nevertheless, it may be prudent to obtain written consent for treatment that involves significant risks, is complex or innovative, or entails potentially sensitive legal, sexual or emotional issues. Similarly, a written consent is advisable if the client is immature, unstable, rash, or lacks good judgment. Based on several of these criteria, a written consent should be obtained prior to undertaking ongoing alcohol or drug treatment.

A signed consent form does not provide conclusive proof of consent, but rather only some evidence of consent. The key issue is whether the client understood the basic nature of the procedures and their risks, and consented to them. A signed consent form is only as good as the information it contains and the circumstances in which it is presented to the client. A signed consent form will be of little value if: it is written in technical language that the client cannot understand;[30] it is presented as a mere technicality or in other circumstances where there is no opportunity to read it;[31] it is written in very general language that does not specifically identify the treatment and its risks; or the client is in severe pain, intoxicated or drugged when signing it.[32]

(F) COMPETENCE TO CONSENT

To be valid, consent must be given by a client who is legally competent. The general test of competence is defined in terms of whether the client has the ability to understand the general nature of the proposed treatment and its risks. This is a very low threshold test that is applied on a case-by-case basis.[33] As stated earlier, if the client is competent to consent, then his or her consent alone is relevant. Indeed, it would be inappropriate even to discuss a client's treatment with the next-of-kin without the client's consent, because this would involve a breach of confidence. Consequently, addiction workers should treat the assessment of a client's competence to consent as a preliminary issue of critical importance.

(i) Minors

General Principles: The age of majority varies across Canada. Moreover, this legislation typically does not govern the age of consent to treatment. In the absence of a statute to the contrary, the test of competence is the same whether the client is a minor or an adult. Generally, the court will assess whether the client is capable of understanding the nature of the proposed treatment and its risks. If a minor meets this test, then his or her consent is valid and parental consent is unnecessary. In some cases, the courts have relied on indications of independence as a guide to a minor's competence.[34] As the following cases illustrate, the Canadian courts are increasingly recognizing young clients' rights to make critically important treatment decisions on their own behalf.[35]

The Children's Aid Society of Toronto v. *LKD*[36]

The court upheld the decision of a 12-year-old Jehovah's Witness to refuse blood transfusions and chemotherapy to treat her acute leukemia. The judge emphasized that the girl was wise and mature beyond her years, and fully aware of the consequences. She had decided that she would prefer to die peacefully, rather than tolerate the side effects of chemotherapy or accept blood transfusions that violated her deeply-held religious convictions. The judge concluded that the girl was not a child in need of protection and refused the Society's application to compel her to have a blood transfusion. Clearly, the judge was influenced by the fact that the parents' and child's wishes were the same and that the dangers of the treatment were equal to those posed by the disease.

C. v. *Wren*[37]

The plaintiffs sought an injunction to prohibit a doctor from performing an abortion on their 16-year-old daughter. As was then required by the *Criminal Code*, the daughter had obtained approval from a therapeutic abortion committee. The court sympathized with both the parents and their daughter in this "painful dispute" over the ethics of the proposed abortion. However, the legal issue was clear – could this 16-year-old girl give a valid consent to a therapeutic abortion? The court concluded that the daughter understood the nature of the procedure and its risks, and therefore was competent to give a valid consent. Consequently, the parents' application for an injunction was dismissed.

Statutory Age of Consent Provisions: The general test of competence applies unless a statute provides otherwise. In any one jurisdiction, several statutes may impose specific age requirements for consent to treatment in particular circumstances. For example, in Ontario, the *Public Hospitals Act,*[38] *Human Tissues Gift Act,*[39] *Mental Health Act,*[40] and *Child and Family Services Act, 1984,*[41] all contain statutory age requirements that apply in certain stipulated circumstances. However, only the latter two acts are directly relevant to addiction workers. Since we cannot review all of the relevant provisions in each province,[42] we will focus on the Ontario *Mental Health Act* and *Child and Family Services Act, 1984* (*CFSA*) to illustrate the types of statutory age provisions.

The Ontario *Mental Health Act*, in effect, establishes 16 as the age of consent for treatment. Although the presumption is subject to review, a person under 16 is presumed to be "not mentally competent to consent."[43] Thus, a 15-year-old client in a mental health facility would be presumed to be incompetent to consent to alcohol or drug treatment. Unless this presumption were rebutted, the addiction worker would need to obtain a substitute consent. The act sets out elaborate procedures to obtain substitute consent if the client is incompetent.[44] The statutory provisions apply to an outpatient drug treatment program in a mental health facility, but not to an identical program operating out of a public hospital.

The *CFSA* contains perhaps the most relevant and complex statutory age provisions.[45] They apply to any "agencies", "societies", "licensees", and "persons" funded by the Ministry of Community and Social Services to provide "child development", "child treatment", "child welfare", "community support", "young offenders" and other "specified" services.[46] However, the *CFSA* apparently does not apply to any treatment provided pursuant to the *Public Hospitals Act, Mental Health Act* or *Health Disciplines Act*. Consequently, an addiction worker providing alcohol and drug treatment in an outpatient clinic of a public hospital would be governed by the common law's flexible test of competence. In contrast, the same social worker providing identical treatment in an agency funded by the Ministry of Community and Social Services would be subject to the consent provisions of the *CFSA*.

The complexity does not end even after one has determined that the *CFSA* applies. In a series of complicated provisions, the act establishes different age requirements for consent, depending on the type of treatment. Services may be provided to a child 16 years of age or older, solely on that child's consent.[47] For children under 16, parental consent (or that of the Children's Aid Society, if it has custody of the child) is required for residential services.[48] However, counselling services can be provided to a child who is 12 or older, based solely on that child's consent. A child under 16 must, however, be advised of the desirability of involving his or her parents.[49] The act also sets out a statutory test of capacity for determining the validity of a child's consent.[50]

Summary: Unless a statute provides otherwise, minors can give a valid consent to alcohol and drug treatment. The key issue is whether they are capable of understanding the nature of the proposed treatment and its risks. If the child is capable, then the consent of the parent or guardian is not required. As in Ontario, several provincial statutes may impose age-of-consent requirements for certain types of treatment in specific situations. In the end, the age of consent is governed by a complex tangle of common law and statutory provisions.[51]

(ii) Adults

The general test of competence is the same whether the client is a minor or an adult. The principles apply equally to those in custody or under other legal restraints, unless there is express statutory authority to the contrary.[52] If the person is competent,[53] his or her consent to treatment must be obtained.[54] Although a client's refusal to consent or accept treatment may constitute a breach of probation, another criminal offence or a violation of parole, that does not alter an addiction worker's obligation to abide by the client's decision.

The issue of an adult's competency may also arise in cases involving mentally ill, retarded or senile clients.[55] However, the mere fact that a client is, for example, mentally ill does not mean that he or she is incapable of giving a valid consent. Rather, addiction workers must assess the ability of each individual client to understand the nature of the proposed treatment and its risks. Although this principle is relatively easy to state, it may be extremely difficult to apply in many situations. For example, it may be perplexing to assess the understanding of an occasionally disoriented alcoholic.[56]

The role of health care professionals in treating those suspected of drinking and driving has caused some confusion. Although this issue is more relevant to hospital emergency staff than addiction workers, we will briefly summarize the current law. Health care professionals must refuse police requests to take blood samples[57] or conduct other tests on unwilling or unconscious suspects for enforcement purposes.[58] These situations must be distinguished from medical emergencies in which it is impossible to obtain the suspect's consent. In such cases, the staff may perform any medical procedures that are needed to save the life or preserve the health of the suspect.[59] Nevertheless, any blood samples or test results should not be given to the police.[60] Rather, the police must obtain a search warrant authorizing the seizure of that evidence.[61]

In 1985, Parliament introduced a special warrant that authorizes the taking of blood from unconscious drinking and driving suspects in limited circumstances.[62] A health care professional acting pursuant to this warrant is protected from both civil and criminal liability.[63] Nevertheless, the legislation permits health care professionals to refuse to participate in the procedure.[64]

(G) SUBSTITUTE CONSENT TO TREATMENT

The issue of substitute or next-of-kin consent arises only if the client is not competent to give or withhold consent. In such circumstances, the law permits the client's parents, guardians or next-of-kin to make treatment decisions on the client's behalf.[65] However, problems can arise in locating a parent, guardian or next-of-kin to exercise this authority in cases involving "skid-row" alcoholics, street youth or transients. Additional difficulties may occur if the parents or next-of-kin disagree on the appropriate course of action.[66]

The power to exercise substitute consent is not absolute. The decision to give or withhold such consent must be made in the client's best interests.[67] Thus, a court could invalidate a parental decision to refuse alcohol or drug treatment for their incompetent child, if the refusal was not in the child's best interests. The court could order that the child be given treatment or that the child be made a ward of the provincial child welfare agency.[68] In turn, the agency would ensure that the child received the needed treatment.

(H) FACTORS THAT INVALIDATE CONSENT

Once it is established that a client consented, it must be determined whether any factor would negate the consent. There are basically three factors that will have this effect: mistake, duress (coercion) and deceit (fraud). If the consent is negated, the addiction worker's legal position is the same as if there had been no consent.

The fact that the client consented to treatment under a mistaken belief will not invalidate the consent, unless the treatment professional was responsible for the client's misapprehension.[69] This issue would arise if an addiction worker inadvertently overstated the benefits of the treatment, or failed to answer adequately one of the client's questions. While it is important to encourage clients to have beneficial treatment, care must be taken not to overstate the case for treatment or understate its risks.

Consent that is obtained as a result of duress is invalid. However, the courts have defined duress as an immediate threat of physical force.[70] As long as the courts use this restrictive definition, the issue of duress is unlikely to arise in a typical alcohol or drug treatment situation. The fact that a client only reluctantly consented to avoid being thrown out of the house, expelled from school or charged with breach of probation does not constitute duress. In contrast, the issue of duress would arise if a client consented because of a threat of being physically restrained or drugged.

A client's consent will also be invalid if it was obtained as a result of deceit.[71] This issue would arise if an addiction worker *deliberately* overstated the benefits of treatment or understated its risks. Similarly, staff should not pass off experimental treatment as standard treatment, or mislead research subjects into believing that they are receiving an active drug when they are being given a placebo.

(I) CONCLUSION

Subject to a few limited exceptions, treatment relationships in our legal system are based on consent. Although consent issues usually arise in relation to medical procedures, they apply equally to psychological assessment, treatment and counselling. Therefore, prior to initiating treatment, addiction workers should ensure that they have obtained a valid consent. The following checklist is intended to assist in this task.

A Consent Checklist

_____ Is this an emergency situation in which the treatment professional is authorized to intervene without consent?

_____ If not, has the client explicitly consented to the proposed treatment?

_____ If not, has the client implicitly consented?

_____ Is the consent valid in the sense that it is based on a full and frank disclosure of the nature of the treatment and its risks?

_____ Is there adequate proof of consent? Is this a situation in which the consent should be in writing?

_____ Is the consent valid in that the client has the capacity to understand the nature of the procedure and its risks?

_____ If the client is incompetent, has a valid substitute consent been given?

_____ Are there any factors that will invalidate the consent? (i.e., mistake, duress, or deceit).

SECTION 2: CONFIDENTIALITY, DISCLOSURE AND RECORDKEEPING

(a) Introduction

This section begins with a discussion of confidentiality and the various legal repercussions that flow from breaching it. We next distinguish confidentiality from the legal term "privilege". While almost all information that addiction workers obtain in the course of treatment is confidential, little, if any, is privileged.

The real complexity, however, is not in determining what information is confidential, but in understanding when it is permissible to disclose confidential information. Accordingly, we discuss the circumstances in which client information may be disclosed, as well as those situations in which health care professionals are legally required to report information. Finally, we examine an addiction worker's potential civil liability for failing to control a client's behavior and warn others.

Most specific disclosure and reporting obligations are dictated by statutes. While there are numerous situations in which there are no clear statutory requirements, there are others in which more than one set of statutory provisions may apply.[72] Aside from problems with these gaps and overlaps, it may be extremely difficult even to find the governing provisions.

Even under the optimistic assumption that one can find the governing rules, it may be difficult to interpret and apply them. These different sets of rules developed independently, often on a piecemeal basis. When one puts them together, the result is statutory chaos.

The applicable statutory requirements may vary, depending on the professional affiliation of the person providing the treatment and where it takes place. For example, different rules may apply in a hospital, private clinic, school, or private agency. Given the broad spectrum of professionals working in the substance abuse field, it is impractical to describe all the relevant statutory provisions. We do not attempt to do so. Rather, we analyze the general principles and outline their specific application to common alcohol and drug treatment situations.

(b) Confidentiality

When used in a legal context, the term "confidentiality" refers to the obligation not to disclose voluntarily any information that has been received in confidence.[73] An obligation of confidentiality may be imposed on an individual by statute,[74] or an individual may assume it by promising to maintain confidentiality. Conversely, a client may indicate that information is being given "in confidence". However, even in the absence of an explicit statement, it is simply assumed in most professional relationships – such as those involving health care professionals, lawyers, and accountants – that all client or client information is confidential.[75]

Accordingly, addiction workers have a legal and ethical obligation to ensure that all information obtained during treatment remains confidential. This applies to information about the client and information that the client gives about others. As a general rule, addiction workers should not reveal any record or information to anyone, unless they are sure that they have the proper authority to do so. Depending on the circumstances, such authority may be based on the client's consent,[76] common law principles or statute. As we shall discuss, there are situations in which addiction workers may be legally compelled to disclose information. Since such disclosures are mandated by law and not made willingly, they do not constitute a breach of confidentiality.

A breach of confidentiality can lead to penal, civil or professional consequences. Many confidentiality obligations are defined by provincial legislation. For example, Ontario's *Mental Health Act* stipulates that, subject to specified exceptions, "no person shall disclose, transmit or examine" a client's clinical record.[77] A violation of this provision constitutes a provincial offence, punishable by a fine of up to $10,000.[78] The federal *Young Offenders Act*[79] (YOA) may also limit disclosures. For example, an addiction worker who reveals the name of, or a means of identifying, a young offender may unwittingly violate the privacy provisions of the *YOA*,[80] and thus may be subject to criminal prosecution.

In addition to possible prosecution, an addiction worker who breaches confidence may face civil liability. The client may be able to recover damages in a civil suit for breach of contract,[81] negligence, defamation,[82] or the emerging tort of breach of confidence.[83]

In the case of certain professionals, the client may also initiate disciplinary proceedings for a breach of confidence. The ethical codes[84] and laws[85] governing most professions provide that the wrongful disclosure of confidential information constitutes professional misconduct, and thus grounds for disciplinary proceedings.

(c) Privilege

The legal term "privilege" means the right to refuse to disclose confidential information when giving testimony or when faced with a subpoena ordering the production of documents.[86] As a rule, persons called as witnesses in court or before other legal tribunals must answer all relevant questions put to them. Privilege is an exception to that general rule. In the absence of privilege, a person who refuses to answer questions when required to do so may be found in contempt of court.

Traditionally, the only professional relationship to which privilege applied was that between solicitors and their clients.[87] The solicitor-client privilege is predicated on the view that the operation of our judicial system requires that clients speak freely with their lawyers, and this will only occur if such communications remain confidential. Although priests, journalists and health care professionals have claimed a comparable need for confidentiality, similar protection has rarely been granted.[88]

Despite frequent recommendation that privilege be extended,[89] the legislature and the courts have been reluctant to create further restrictions on the evidence available for trials. However, Quebec legislation provides that any information revealed to physicians in their professional capacity is privileged.[90] This privilege has been limited to civil trials and thus cannot be claimed by a physician testifying at a criminal trial.[91]

Even where legislation purports to provide privilege, the courts may interpret it narrowly on the basis that the interests of justice require admission of all relevant information.[92] For example, Ontario's *Education Act* states that a student record is "privileged" and not admissible in legal proceedings.[93] However in a case involving a 16-year-old student charged with a brutal murder, the court ruled that the record must be admitted and that the school officials must testify.[94]

In 1976, the Supreme Court of Canada recognized a new general category of privileged information,[95] but the requirements are stringent. To qualify as privileged, the information must meet all of the following conditions:

(1) it was given in confidence

(2) confidentiality is necessary to the relationship

(3) the relationship is one that society believes should be rigorously fostered

(4) the injury to the relationship from disclosure of the information is greater than the benefit of having a case decided on the basis of complete information.

Communications made in the course of most treatment and counselling relationships readily meet the first three requirements. First, clients expect that the information they give to health care professionals will be kept confidential. Second, successful treatment is said to depend upon maintaining confidentiality between the client and the counsellor. Third, society certainly has an interest in promoting successful treatment. The fourth criteria, however, is far more difficult to satisfy. If the information has a bearing on the case, the courts have required disclosure, ruling that the interests of justice outweigh the importance of maintaining confidentiality. For example, in a recent case involving a man charged with sexually molesting his stepdaughters, a psychiatrist was required to divulge statements that the accused had made during a family counselling session.[96]

While not tantamount to formal legal privilege, the courts have occasionally given certain professionals the practical benefits of privilege. A court can do this by simply declining to hold a witness in contempt when the witness refuses to disclose confidential information.[97] However, this occurs rarely and is usually confined to priest-penitent or psychiatrist-client relationships.[98]

In summary, while almost all information that addiction workers obtain in the course of treatment is confidential, little is privileged. Consequently, staff would be well-advised to adopt a working assumption that they and their records may be examined in court some day. This sobering thought should encourage staff to maintain complete records and adopt a professional tone in their preparation.

(d) Disclosure of Client Information

Addiction workers must understand the circumstances in which they are authorized to disclose client information. Treatment records do not belong to the client. Rather, they are the property of the agency and the professional providing the treatment.[99] Nevertheless, clients will usually be able to obtain access.

Various provincial statutes specify who may release information to whom and under what circumstances. The rules governing the disclosure of client information are complex. Interpreting these provisions can be a problem, but often the first difficulty is deciding which act is applicable. In some situations more than one statute applies, whereas in other situations there may be no governing statute.[100]

Some of this confusion may be alleviated by provincial freedom of information and protection of privacy legislation. Typically, these statutes provide a single comprehensive scheme governing confidential information and its disclosure. Such legislation is in force in Manitoba, New Brunswick, Newfoundland, Nova Scotia and Ontario.[101]

(i) Disclosure Dictated by Statute

Some statutory provisions give the client a right to the information contained in his or her own records. For example, the public hospitals legislation in Alberta, Ontario and Saskatchewan stipulates that a person with a signed request from a client may be given access to that client's medical record.[102] Presumably, this provision would permit a client to request access to his or her own record. However, the use of the word "may" indicates that disclosure is discretionary, not mandatory. The Alberta and Ontario mental health legislation provides that a client is generally entitled to examine his or her own clinical record.[103]

In Ontario, the record provisions of the *Child and Family Services Act, 1984* (*CFSA*) specifically exclude client records that are governed by the *Health Disciplines Act*, *Public Hospitals Act* or *Mental Health Act*.[104] Nevertheless, the *CFSA* applies to a broad range of agencies providing counselling or other treatment services that are funded by the Ministry of Community and Social Services.[105] Under the *CFSA*, a person 12 years or older generally has the right to access his or her own records.[106] As well, parents can access the records of their children under 16, unless the record relates to counselling.[107] Counselling records of a child 12 or older usually cannot be disclosed without the child's consent.[108] Once a child reaches 16, his or her records can generally be disclosed only with that child's consent.[109]

However, ascertaining the technical requirements of the appropriate statutory provisions may be an academic exercise. If a legal action is commenced, the rules of civil procedure typically enable the client to demand a copy of virtually all institutional and office records.[110]

(ii) Disclosure with Client's Consent

In the absence of a statutory provision to the contrary, health care professionals cannot, as a general rule, voluntarily disclose any client information without the client's consent – not even to family members, employers, probation officers, or the police.[111] Particularly in alcohol and drug treatment, the mere fact that a person is a client is highly sensitive. Consequently, even simple inquiries, such as whether a person is a client or has attended treatment, are best answered with an explanation that all client information is confidential.

Even if the client was examined at the request of a third party, such as an employer or a parent, the addiction worker must obtain the client's consent before disclosing any information to the third party.[112] If the counsellor thinks that the client's family should be involved, he or she should request the client's permission to involve them. Occasionally, there may be situations in which the client's consent to disclosure is implied, such as when an examination has been required as a prerequisite to obtaining employment or insurance. However, it is safest to obtain an explicit consent in all cases.

There is implied consent to share client information with other staff in order to provide proper treatment.[113] However, if there is any doubt as to whether information may be disclosed, the client's explicit consent should be sought. Any information shared with other staff imposes a confidentiality obligation on them. Consent to use client information in research publications may also be implied, provided the client's name is not used and the client is not recognizable from the information disclosed.[114]

There are often difficulties in establishing the existence and scope of an implied consent. For example, a young offender may sign a probation form stipulating that he or she is to obtain treatment. Does such a document provide an addiction worker with implicit consent to disclose information to the probation officer? Since health care professionals bear the burden of proving consent, it is in their interests to get the client's explicit consent for the release of any information. If the client refuses, then the probation officer can resolve this matter directly with the offender.

Consent may be given orally or in writing.[115] Although oral consent is sufficient, written consent provides greater protection in any future dispute. All such consents should be signed, dated, and stipulate to whom information may be given. The consent should be obtained at the outset of treatment, at which time the nature of the confidentiality obligation should be fully explained. The client then has the choice of refusing or accepting treatment on the terms under which it is being given.

However, addiction workers should not create the impression that confidential information will never be released without their consent. There is no such thing as "absolute" or "complete" confidentiality. Aside from disclosure through search warrants and court proceedings, various provincial laws require health care professionals to report certain types of information to provincial officials. Moreover, as we shall discuss, a health care professional may also face civil liability for failing to report certain information. It is far better to explain the limits of confidentiality at the outset, rather than to create false expectations that cannot be met.

(E) REPORTING OBLIGATIONS

(i) As Required By Provincial Statute

Provincial statutes impose several mandatory reporting obligations on health care professionals and others. The major reporting obligations are designed to help control communicable diseases, hazardous driving, and child abuse. In these situations, the perceived threat to the public is felt to outweigh the client's right to confidentiality, and thus justify the reporting obligation.

Most provinces have legislation that requires health care professionals and others to report clients with various diseases to public health officials. Physicians providing services to people who are not hospital clients may be required to report any client that they believe may have a communicable disease.[116] Hospital administrators have a similar reporting obligation with respect to clients.[117] School principals and teachers may also be required to report any pupils they suspect may have a communicable disease.[118] The list of diseases is extensive and typically includes AIDS, hepatitis, tuberculosis, venereal diseases, and various types of influenza.[119] Failure to report is an offence in some provinces and can result in fines and imprisonment.[120] Generally, no action or other proceeding may be brought against a person who makes the required report in good faith.[121]

Several provinces have motor vehicle legislation that requires physicians to report the name, address and clinical condition of any client of driving age who suffers from a condition that may make it dangerous to drive.[122] Although these provisions were probably intended to deal with medical conditions, such as failing eyesight, heart disease and epilepsy, they are broad enough to encompass habitual substance abusers.

In Ontario, for example, this reporting obligation is limited to medical practitioners and optometrists,[123] and thus would not apply to the vast majority of addiction workers. Consequently, they would have no legal obligation to report a client who admits to alcohol or drug-induced blackouts while driving. Indeed, if they were to report such a client, they might be in breach of their confidentiality obligations. Such "double bind" situations can occur in a variety of circumstances, and we will discuss approaches to handling these dilemmas later in the chapter.

The most comprehensive reporting obligations are contained in the provincial child protection legislation. For example, the Ontario *Child and Family Services Act, 1984* requires various professionals – including health care professionals, social workers, teachers and counsellors – to report to the local Children's Aid Society any case where they have reasonable grounds to suspect past or present abuse of a child under 16.[124] Child abuse is broadly defined to include: physical harm or sexual molestation for which a parent is responsible; lack of appropriate medical treatment; demonstrable emotional harm that is untreated; or a significant untreated mental, emotional or developmental condition.[125] This broad definition of abuse would likely include children who are not receiving treatment for their drug or alcohol problems. In any event, if facts emerge that indicate parental abuse, the addiction worker would be required to contact the local Children's Aid Society. Failure to report suspected child abuse constitutes a provincial offence that is punishable by a fine of up to $1,000.

In several provinces, these reporting obligations only cover abuse of children under 16. However, other provinces extend the obligation to report the suspected abuse of all minors. The child protection legislation generally takes precedence over any conflicting provisions of other provincial statutes.[126] Consequently, despite their confidentiality obligations, addiction workers would be required to report cases of suspected child abuse. Most provinces specifically provide that no civil action can be brought against a person for reporting as required.[127]

(ii) Obligation to Report Criminal Offences

Unless required by statute, people have no legal obligation to assist the police or answer their questions.[128] There is no general obligation under the *Criminal Code* to report an offence that one knows has been or, with the exception of treason,[129] is about to be committed.[130] Consequently, addiction workers need not report a client's illicit drug use to the police, nor even acknowledge that a client is seeking drug treatment. However, there is nothing preventing an addiction worker from reporting crimes, provided the information was not obtained in confidence.

Although a person may lawfully refuse to answer questions, someone who deliberately misleads the police or other criminal justice officials may be guilty of a criminal offence.[131] For example, a probation officer may ask whether a client has attended counselling as required by a probation order. While the addictions worker can appropriately reply that no information can be disclosed about a client, he or she cannot falsely state that the client attended. Staff who do so could be charged with obstructing justice.

(iii) Civil Liability For Failing to Control or Warn

Traditionally, the law did not require an individual to control the conduct of another person, whether to protect that person or others who might foreseeably be endangered.[132] Although the courts continue to pay lip service to the concept that "you are not your brother's keeper," they have recognized a growing number of special relationships in which one party will be held civilly liable for the conduct of another.[133] It is now well established that such a relationship exists between parents and children, teachers and pupils, and employers and employees. The courts are increasingly prepared to hold that a similar relationship exists between health care professionals and their clients.

Several challenging issues may arise in applying these principles to addiction workers. Consider a situation in which an intoxicated or "high" client attends a counselling session and causes a car accident while driving home. The counsellor may be sued for negligently allowing the client to leave in a condition that posed a foreseeable risk of injury to the client and others.[134] Such a case might succeed if the counsellor had been negligent in failing to recognize the client's intoxication, or had realized that the client was impaired but did not make a reasonable effort to stop him or her. Although the issue has not arisen concerning health care professionals, the Canadian courts have greatly expanded the scope of liability for failing to reasonably manage the intoxicated.[135]

A health care professional who learns of a client's plan to commit a serious crime may be held accountable for failing to warn or otherwise protect the intended victim. Although the Canadian courts have not yet addressed this issue, some American courts have imposed liability on health care professionals in these situations. In the leading case of *Tarasoff* v. *Regents of the University of California*,[136] a psychologist was held liable for failing to warn his client's intended victim. The client, who was being treated at the University Hospital, told his psychologist that he intended to kill his former girlfriend when she returned from her vacation. The psychologist concluded that the client was dangerous, and contacted the campus police. The client was picked up, briefly detained, and then released. Neither the woman nor her family were warned. When she returned, the client killed her. In imposing liability on the psychologist and the university for failing to warn, the court emphasized that the psychologist's confidentiality obligation to his client ended when the public peril began.[137]

An addiction worker may realize during treatment that a young client is endangered by his or her substance abuse, physical condition, or home situation. If the client is within the age limit of the particular province's child protection legislation, then the matter would have to be reported. In this case, there would be no technical violation of the confidentiality obligation, because the disclosure was mandated by law and not made voluntarily.

A more difficult situation arises if the client is older and there is no mandatory reporting obligation. If the worker breaches the client's confidence, it is possible that he or she may be sued or prosecuted. However, this is unlikely if the worker breached confidence in a reasonable effort to protect the client from serious harm. If the worker maintains confidentiality and the client is injured, then the worker *may* be sued for failing to protect the client.

As in *Tarasoff*, the situation becomes more complex when the choice is between maintaining the client's confidentiality and protecting an innocent third party. There have been several successful suits against American health care professionals for failing to act in these circumstances, but no comparable Canadian cases. Although there is no clear legal solution, it is best to intervene and err on the side of safety.

(f) Conclusion

Health care professionals should assume that all client information is confidential, but that nothing will be privileged. As a working guideline, information should not be disclosed without the client's consent, unless the professional is compelled by law to do so.

There are complex and varied statutory requirements governing disclosure and reporting. These may be supplemented by the rules that a particular agency or institution adopts. Moreover, additional requirements may be imposed by the governing body of the particular profession. We have canvassed the general principles and provided specific examples of common situations. However, it is incumbent on each addiction worker to ascertain the particular requirements pertinent to his or her own specific situation.

ENDNOTES

1. See for example, Ontario, <u>Report of the Commission of Inquiry into the Confidentiality of Health Information</u>, (1981), Mr. Justice Krever: Commissioner.

2. See for example, <u>Clark</u> v. <u>Clark</u> (1982), 40 O.R. (2d) 383 (Co. Ct.); R. Haliechuk, "Judge won't compel leukemia girl to have transfusions", <u>Ontario Lawyers Weekly</u>, Nov. 22, 1985, 20; and <u>C.</u> v. <u>Wren</u> (1986), 35 D.L.R. (4th) 419 (Alta. C.A.).

3. For examples of the age of majority provisions, see <u>Age of Majority Act</u>, R.S.A. 1980, c. A-4, s. 1; <u>Age of Majority Act</u>, R.S.B.C. 1979, c. 5, s. 1; <u>Age of Majority Act</u>, R.S.N.B. 1973, c. A-4, s. 1; <u>Age of Majority and Accountability Act</u>, R.S.O. 1980, c. 7, s. 1; and <u>Age of Majority Act</u>, R.S.P.E.I. 1974, c. A-3, s. 1.

4. See for example, <u>Cole</u> v. <u>Turner</u> (1705), 87 E.R. 907 (Nisi Prius); <u>R.</u> v. <u>Cotesworth</u> (1704), 87 E.R. 928; and <u>Green</u> v. <u>Goddard</u> (1704), 91 E.R. 540.

5. <u>Criminal Code</u>, R.S.C. 1985, c. C-46, s. 265(1).

6. Depending on the facts, a physical interference can give rise to one or more tort actions – battery (physical contact); assault (threat of immediate physical contact); and false imprisonment (imposition of a total restraint of movement).

7. But see <u>Bolduc</u> v. <u>R.</u> (1967), 63 D.L.R. (2d) 82 (S.C.C.).

8. <u>Bettel</u> v. <u>Yim</u> (1978), 20 O.R. (2d) 617 (Co. Ct.).

9. <u>Cole</u> v. <u>Turner</u> (1705), 87 E.R. 907 (Nisi Prius).

10. See <u>Allan</u> v. <u>New Mount Sinai Hospital</u> (1980), 28 O.R. (2d) 356 (H.C.), reversed on other grounds (1981), 33 O.R. (2d) 603 (C.A.); <u>McBain</u> v. <u>Laurentian Hospital</u> (1982), 35 C.P.C. 292 (Ont. H.C.); and E. Picard, "Onus of Proving Consent to Trespass to the Person: On Whom Does it Rest?" (1979), 17 <u>Alta. L. Rev.</u> 322.

11. For a review of the general principles of consent to treatment see G. Sharpe, <u>The Law and Medicine in Canada</u>, 2nd ed. (1987), 29-93; and E. Picard, <u>Legal Liability of Doctors and Hospitals in Canada</u>, 2nd ed. (1984), 41-147.

12. See Parmley v. Parmley and Yule, [1945] 4 D.L.R. 81 (S.C.C.); Schweizer v. Central Hospital (1974), 6 O.R. (2d) 606 (H.C.); and Brushett v. Cowan (1987), 42 C.C.L.T. 64 (Nfld. S.C.).

13. See Johnston v. Wellesley Hospital, [1971] 2 O.R. 103 (H.C.); Clark v. Clark (1982), 40 O.R. (2d) 383 (Co. Ct.); Gillick v. West Norfolk and Wisbech Area Health Authority, [1985] 3 All E.R. 402 (H.L.); and C. v. Wren (1986), 35 D.L.R. (4th) 419 (Alta. C.A.).

14. See In Re B (A Minor), [1981] 1 W.L.R. 1421 (C.A.); Re Superintendent of Family & Child Service and Dawson (1983), 145 D.L.R. (3d) 610 (B.C. S.C.); and "Eve" v. "Mrs. E." (1986), 2 S.C.R. 388.

15. This broad definition of volition is illustrated by Smith v. Stone (1647), 82 E.R. 533 (K.B.); and Gilbert v. Stone (1648), 82 E.R. 539 (K.B.). See also Norberg v. Wynrib (1988), 44 C.C.L.T. 184 (B.C. S.C.).

16. O'Brien v. Cunard SS. Co. Ltd. (1891), 28 N.E. 266 (S.J.C. Mass.). See also Reynen v. Antonenko (1975), 30 C.R.N.S. 135 (Alta. S.C.); and Strachan v. Simpson, [1979] 5 W.W.R. 315 (B.C. S.C.).

17. For a discussion of exceeding consent in a medical/surgical context see Mulloy v. Hop Sang, [1935] 1 W.W.R. 714 (Alta. S.C.); Allan v. New Mount Sinai Hospital (1980), 28 O.R. (2d) 356 (H.C.), reversed on other grounds (1981), O.R. (2d) 603 (C.A.). The same issues of exceeding consent may arise in addiction treatment situations.

18. Traditionally, a health care professional's failure to obtain consent was viewed as a basis for a battery action, whether the lack of consent was due to nondisclosure of risks, misrepresentation or oversight. In the late 1950s, the American courts began to analyze some, but not all, cases in which a doctor failed to disclose the risks of a procedure in terms of negligence – has the doctor failed to exercise reasonable care in advising the client of the nature of the procedure and its risks? Several Canadian courts adopted a similar approach. In Canada, as in the United States, this development created uncertainty as to the boundary between medical battery and medical negligence

In Reibl v. Hughes (1981), 114 D.L.R. (3d) 1, the Supreme Court of Canada finally resolved this issue by excluding from battery any claim based on a doctor's failure to disclose the risks of a procedure. Thus, once a client is aware of the general nature of a procedure and consents to it, he or she cannot sue for battery. A health care professional's failure to properly inform a client of the risks of a procedure can only give rise to a suit in negligence. Although this decision affects the client's remedy, it does not decrease the health care professional's need to obtain consent.

19.   Reibl v. Hughes (1981), 114 D.L.R. (3d) 1 (S.C.C.); and Hopp v. Lepp (1980), 112 D.L.R. (3d) 67 (S.C.C.). For recent applications of these cases, see Haughian v. Paine (1987), 40 C.C.L.T. 14 (Sask. C.A.); Mitchell v. Harris (1987), 40 C.C.L.T. 266 (Alta. Q.B.); Rocha v. Harris (1987), 36 D.L.R. (4th) 410 (B.C. C.A.); and Rayner v. Knickle (1988), 47 C.C.L.T. 141 (P.E.I. S.C.).

20.   Reibl v. Hughes (1981), 114 D.L.R. (3d) 1 (S.C.C.). For example, a health care professional may not have to disclose to a school teacher that a proposed treatment poses a 5% risk of causing minor long-term stiffness in her fingers. However, this risk would have to be disclosed to a concert pianist.

21.   For example, in Haughian v. Paine (1987), 40 C.C.L.T. 14 (Sask. C.A.), the surgeon's liability was based in part on his failure to explain the alternative non-surgical treatment and the risks of leaving the ailment untreated. In the court's words, "One cannot make an informed decision to undertake a risk without knowing the alternatives . . .". See also Kueper v. McMullin (1986), 37 C.C.L.T. 318 (N.B. C.A.); Coughlin v. Kuntz (1987), 42 C.C.L.T. 142 (B.C. S.C.); and Rayner v. Knickle (1988), 47 C.C.L.T. 141 (P.E.I. S.C.).

22.   Reibl v. Hughes (1981), 114 D.L.R. (3d) 1 (S.C.C.); and Sinclaire v. Boulton (1985), 33 C.C.L.T. 125 (B.C. S.C.).

23.   See Petty v. Mackay (1984), 31 C.C.L.T. 155 (B.C. C.A.); Ferguson v. Hamilton Civic Hospitals (1985), 50 O.R. (2d) 754 (C.A.); Kitchen v. McMullen (1989), 62 D.L.R. (4th) 481 (N.B. C.A.); and P. Osbourne, "Causation and the Emerging Doctrine of Informed Consent to Medical Treatment" (1985), 33 C.C.L.T. 131.

24.   For a review of the principles of informed consent, see G. Robertson, "Part One: Informed Consent in Canada: An Empirical Study" (1985), 18(1) Annals RCPSC 49; G. Robertson, "Part Two: Informed Consent in Canada: An Empirical Study" (1985), 18(2) Annals RCPSC 125; and G. Sharpe, The Law and Medicine in Canada, 2nd ed. (1987), 34-55.

25.   Marshall v. Curry, [1933] 3 D.L.R. 260 (N.S. S.C.). This right to proceed without consent has been narrowly defined. For example in Murray v. McMurchy, [1949] 2 D.L.R. 442 (B.C. S.C.), the defendant surgeon tied the plaintiff's fallopian tubes during a Caesarian section when he discovered tumours in the wall of her uterus. The court held that the health hazards that

the tumours might pose in a subsequent pregnancy did not warrant this drastic action and awarded the plaintiff $3,000 damages. See also <u>Parmley</u> v. <u>Parmley and Yule</u>, [1945] 4 D.L.R. 81 (S.C.C.); and <u>Boyer</u> v. <u>Grignon</u> (1988), 46 C.C.L.T. 47 (Que. S.C.).

26. See <u>Male</u> v. <u>Hopmans</u> (1967), 64 D.L.R. (2d) 105 (Ont. C.A.); and <u>Villeneuve</u> v. <u>Sisters of St. Joseph of Diocese of Sault St. Marie</u> (1971), 18 D.L.R. (3d) 537 (Ont. H.C.). The exact scope of this principle may be difficult to define in a specific case. Contrast the decision in <u>Pridham</u> v. <u>Nash</u> (1986), 57 O.R. (2d) 347 (H.C.) with that in <u>Brushett</u> v. <u>Cowan</u> (1987), 42 C.C.L.T. 64 (Nfld. S.C.).

27. <u>Kenny</u> v. <u>Lockwood</u>, [1932] 1 D.L.R. 507 (Ont. C.A.); and <u>Male</u> v. <u>Hopmans</u> (1967), 64 D.L.R. (2d) 105 (Ont. C.A.).

28. The exact scope of the privilege is difficult to define. In <u>Hopp</u> v. <u>Lepp</u> (1980), 112 D.L.R. (3d) 67, at 79 (S.C.C.), Chief Justice Laskin appeared to eliminate the privilege. Yet, in <u>Reibl</u> v. <u>Hughes</u> (1981), 114 D.L.R. (3d) 1, at 13, (S.C.C.), Laskin suggests that the client's emotional state is relevant to the doctor's obligation to disclose risks.

29. <u>Reibl</u> v. <u>Hughes</u> (1981), 114 D.L.R. (3d) 1 (S.C.C.); and <u>Hajgato</u> v. <u>London Health Association</u> (1982), 36 O.R. (2d) 669, affirmed 23 A.C.W.S. (2d) 54 (Ont. C.A.).

30. See for example, <u>Brushett</u> v. <u>Cowan</u> (1987), 42 C.C.L.T. 64 (Nfld. S.C.); and <u>Montaron</u> v. <u>Wagner</u> (1988), 43 C.C.L.T. 233 (Alta. Q.B.). See also <u>Casey</u> v. <u>Provan</u> (1984), 30 C.C.L.T. 169 (Ont. S.C.) and <u>Stamos</u> v. <u>Davies</u> (1985), 33 C.C.L.T. 1 (Ont. S.C.), in which the signed consent forms were held to be invalid, but the plaintiffs' claims were dismissed on other grounds.

31. See G. Sharpe, <u>The Law and Medicine in Canada</u>, 2nd ed. (1987), 85-90; and E. Picard, <u>Legal Liability of Doctors and Hospitals in Canada</u>, 2nd ed. (1984), 43-44.

32. See for example, <u>Beausoleil</u> v. <u>La Communaute Des Soeurs De La Charite De La Providence</u> (1964), D.L.R. (2d) 65 (Que. Q.B.).

33. See note 15.

34. See E. Picard, <u>Legal Liability of Doctors and Hospitals in Canada</u>, 2nd ed. (1984), 55-60.

35. Few medical issues have generated greater academic interest than the age of

consent. See for example, W. Wadlington, "Minors and Health Care: The Age of Consent" (1973), 11 <u>Osgoode Hall L.J.</u> 115; B. Tomkins, "Health Care For Minors: The Right to Consent" (1974-75), 40 <u>Saskatchewan L. Rev.</u> 41; and G. Thomson, "Minors and Medical Consent" (1981), 2 <u>Health Law in Canada</u> 76.

36.   See R. Haliechuk, "Judge won't compel leukaemia girl to have transfusions", <u>Ontario Lawyer's Weekly</u>, Nov. 22, 1985, 20. This decision stands in sharp contrast to that in <u>Pentland</u> v. <u>Pentland</u> (1978), 86 D.L.R. (3rd) 585 (Ont. H.C.), which reflects a much more paternalistic attitude towards young people. See also M. Haig, "Blood transfusions for infants upheld", <u>London Free Press</u>, Nov. 30, 1985, Al.

37.   (1986), 35 D.L.R. (4th) 419 (Alta. C.A.).

38.   R.S.O. 1980, c. 410.

39.   R.S.O. 1980, c. 210.

40.   R.S.O. 1980, c. 262.

41.   S.O. 1984, c. 55.

42.   However, see for example <u>Infants Act</u>, R.S.B.C. 1979, c. 196, s. 16; <u>Medical Consent of Minors Act</u>, S.N.B. 1976, c. M-6.1 ss. 2 and 3; and Sask. Reg. 331/79, s. 55.

43.   R.S.O. 1980, c. 262, s. 1d(1) and (2).

44.   <u>Ibid.</u>, s. 1a.

45.   S.O. 1984, c. 55, ss. 27 and 28.

46.   <u>Ibid.</u>, s. 3(1) 26 "service" and 27 "service provider".

47.   <u>Ibid.</u>, s. 27(1).

48.   <u>Ibid.</u>, s. 27(2).

49.   <u>Ibid.</u>, s. 28.

50.   <u>Ibid.</u>, s. 4.

51. In 1975, the Uniform Law Conference of Canada adopted <u>The Medical Consent of Minors Act</u> which provides a comprehensive statutory regime to govern the age of consent to medical treatment. However, to date only New Brunswick has enacted the necessary provincial legislation. See <u>The Medical Consent of Minors Act</u>, S.N.B. 1976, c. M-6.1.

52. Unfortunately, there is no comprehensive review of the federal or provincial statutes that authorize treatment in the absence of consent. See, however, <u>Attorney General of British Columbia</u> v. <u>Astaforoff</u>, [1984] 4 W.W.R. 385 (B.C. C.A.); and E. Carroll, "Forced Feeding of Prisoners: Mary Astaforoff, A Case in Point" (1983), 4 <u>Health Law in Canada</u>, 85.

53. For an interesting case on competency to refuse psychiatric treatment, see <u>Institut Philippe Pinel de Montreal</u> v. <u>Dion</u> (1983), 2 D.L.R. (4th) 234 (Que. S.C.).

54. See L. Vandervort, "Medical Treatment of Penitentiary Inmates" (1977), 3 <u>Queens L.J.</u> 368; and M. Somerville, "Refusal of Medical Treatment in Captive Circumstances" (1985), 63 <u>Can. Bar Rev.</u> 59. But see <u>Procureur Général du Canada c. Hopital Notre-Dame</u>, [1984] C.S. 426 (Que. S.C.).

55. See generally, M. Schiffer, <u>Mental Disorder and the Criminal Trial Process</u> (1978), 289-322; E. Liberman, "Mental Competency and Medical Treatment in Ontario" (1985), 6 <u>Health Law in Canada</u> 32; and H. Savage and C. McKague, <u>Mental Health Law in Canada</u> (1987), 95-129.

56. See <u>Kelly</u> v. <u>Hazlett</u> (1976), 1 C.C.L.T. 1 (Ont. H.C.); <u>MacKinnon</u> v. <u>Ignacio, Lamond and MacKeough</u> (1978), 29 N.S.R. (2d) 656 (S.C.); and <u>R.</u> v. <u>Smith</u> (1989), 6 W.C.B. (2d) 250 (Ont. Dist. Ct.).

57. <u>Pohoretsky</u> v. <u>The Queen</u> (1987), 33 C.C.C. (3d) 398 (S.C.C.); and <u>R.</u> v. <u>Dyment</u> (1988), 45 C.C.C. (3d) 244 (S.C.C.).

58. <u>Re Laporte and The Queen</u> (1972), 8 C.C.C. (2d) 343; <u>R.</u> v. <u>Truchanck</u> (1984), 39 C.R. (3d) 137 (B.C. Co. Ct.); and <u>R.</u> v. <u>Greffe</u> (April 12, 1990), unreported (S.C.C.).

59. See <u>R.</u> v. <u>Carter</u> (1982), 144 D.L.R. (3d) 301 (Ont. C.A.); and <u>R.</u> v. <u>Katsigiorgis</u> (1987), 39 C.C.C. (3d) 256 (Ont. C.A.).

60. <u>R.</u> v. <u>Dyment</u> (1988), 45 C.C.C. (3d) 244 (S.C.C.).

61. See note 59.

62. <u>Criminal Code</u>, R.S.C. 1985, c. C-46, s. 256.

63. <u>Ibid</u>., s. 257(2).

64. <u>Ibid</u>., s. 257(1).

65. See generally, B. Dickens, "The Role of the Family in Surrogate Medical Consent" (1980), 1 <u>Health Law in Canada</u> 49; and G. Sharpe, "Guardianship: Two Models for Reform" (1983), 4 <u>Health Law in Canada</u> 13.

66. See for example, <u>Pentland</u> v. <u>Pentland</u> (1978), 86 D.L.R. (3d) 585 (Ont. H.C.).

67. "<u>Eve</u>" v. "<u>Mrs E.</u>" (1986), 2 S.C.R. 388. But see <u>Re B</u>, [1987] 2 All E.R. 206 (H.L.). See also J. Magnet, "Neonatal Intensive Care: The Dilemma for Medical Law" (1981), 13 <u>Ottawa L.R.</u> 345; G. Ferguson, "The Right to Treatment: Re Stephen Dawson" (1986), 6 <u>Health Law in Canada</u> 55; and E. Keyserlingk, "Non-Treatment in the Best Interests of the Child: A Case Commentary of <u>Couture-Jacquet</u> v. <u>Montreal Children's Hospital</u>" (1987), 32 <u>McGill L.J.</u> 413.

68. For examples of the relevant provincial legislation, see: <u>Child Welfare Act</u>, S.A. 1984, c. C-81, s. 25; <u>Family and Child Services Act</u>, S.B.C. 1980, c. 11, s. 10(b); <u>Child and Family Services Act, 1984</u>, S.O. 1984, c. 55, s. 53; and <u>Family and Child Services Act</u>, S.P.E.I. 1981, c. 12, s. 34(2).

69. <u>Boase</u> v. <u>Paul</u>, [1931] 4 D.L.R. 435 (Ont. S.C.); <u>Parmley</u> v. <u>Parmley and Yule</u>, [1945] 4 D.L.R. 81 (S.C.C.); and <u>Guimond</u> v. <u>Laberge</u> (1956), 4 D.L.R. (2d) 559 (Ont. C.A.).

70. See <u>Latter</u> v. <u>Braddell</u> (1880), 50 L.J.Q.B. 166 (C.P.); and <u>Norberg</u> v. <u>Wynrib</u> (1988), 44 C.C.L.T. 184 (B.C.S.C.).

71. <u>R.</u> v. <u>Maurantonio</u> (1967), 65 D.L.R. (2d) 674 (Ont. C.A.); and <u>Bolduc</u> v. <u>R.</u> (1967), 63 D.L.R. (2d) 82 (S.C.C.).

72. For example, various statutory provisions would have to be considered in the case of a young offender who was diagnosed in a public hospital as having venereal disease. Overlapping provisions would govern the issues of consent, recordkeeping, confidentiality, and reporting.

73. For example, in <u>Fraser</u> v. <u>Evans</u>, [1969] 1 Q.B. 349 (C.A.), the court stated at 361:

> No person is permitted to divulge to the world information which he had received in confidence, unless he has just cause or excuse for doing so. Even if he comes by it innocently, nevertheless once he gets to know that it was originally given in confidence, he can be restrained from breaking that confidence.

See also Parry-Jones v. The Law Society and Others, [1968] 1 All E.R. 177 (C.A.); Tournier v. National Provincial and Union Bank of England, [1924] 1 K.B. 461 (C.A.); and Cronkwright v. Cronkwright (1971), 14 D.L.R. (3d) 168 (Ont. H.C.).

74. See for example Hospitals Act, C.S.N.S. 1979, c. H-19, s. 63; Hospitals Act, R.S.A. 1980, c. H-11, s. 40; Mental Health Act, R.S.O. 1980, c. 262, s. 29; and Education Act, R.S.O. 1980, c. 129, s. 237(2)(a) and (b).

75. See for example, A.G. v. Mulholland, [1963] 2 Q.B. 477, at 489-490 (C.A.).

76. It should be noted that the right to confidentiality belongs to the client. Generally, if the client requests that information be divulged, then the health care professional must comply. See C. v. C., [1946] 1 All E.R. 562 (P.D.A.).

77. R.S.O. 1980, c. 262, s. 29(2).

78. Ibid., s. 64.

79. R.S.C. 1985, c. Y-1.

80. Ibid., s. 38.

81. A contractual relationship generally exists between health care professionals and their clients. However, clients suing health care professionals often claim for both breach of contract and negligence in a single law suit. See Hughston v. Jost, [1943] O.W.N. 3 (H.C.); and Gibson v. Bagnall (No. 2) (1979), 24 O.R. (2d) 567 (H.C.).

82. For example, a health care professional who includes untrue defamatory comments in a client's record may be sued for libel. See Foran v. Richman (1975), 64 D.L.R. (3d) 230 (Ont. C.A.).

83. See H. Glasbeek, "Limitations on the Action of Breach of Confidence" in D. Gibson (ed.), Aspects of Privacy Law, (1980), 217; A. Vickery, "Breach of Confidence: An Emerging Tort" (1982), 82 Columbia L. Rev. 1426; and S. Rodgers-Magnet, "Common Law Remedies for Disclosure of Confidential

Medical Information" in F. Steel and S. Rodgers-Magnet (eds.), <u>Issues in Tort Law</u>, (1983), 265.

84. The ethical duty of confidentiality is broader than the legal duty at common law. See <u>Furniss</u> v. <u>Fitchett</u>, [1958] N.Z.L.R. 396 (S.C.).

85. See for example, <u>Medical Profession Act</u>, R.S.A. 1980, c. M-12, ss. 34 and 36; and <u>Health Disciplines Act</u>, R.S.O. 1980, c. 196, s. 60(3) and Reg. 448, R.R.O. 1980, s. 27(22).

86. For a comprehensive review of privilege, see P. McWilliams, <u>Canadian Criminal Evidence</u>, 2nd ed. (1984), 915-924 and 963-976.

87. <u>Ibid.</u> 920-924. See also B. McLachlin, "Confidential Communications and the Law of Privilege" (1977), 11 <u>U.B.C. L. Rev.</u> 266; and H. Glasbeek, "Limitations on the Action of Breach of Confidence" in D. Gibson (ed.), <u>Aspects of Privacy Law</u>, (1980), 217.

88. See for example, <u>Re Kryschuk and Zulynik</u> (1958), 14 D.L.R. (2d) 676 (Sask. P.M. Ct.) (social worker); <u>G.</u> v. <u>G.</u>, [1964] 1 O.R. 361 (H.C.) (marriage counsellor); and <u>R.</u> v. <u>Smith</u> (1985), 8 O.A.C. 241 (C.A.), leave to appeal dismissed (1985), 11 O.A.C. 317 (S.C.C.) (psychiatrist).

89. For example, the Law Reform Commission of Canada recommended that a qualified privilege be granted to professionals. The information would be privileged only if the court determined that the protection of privacy outweighed the public interest in the administration of justice. See <u>Report on Evidence</u>, (1975), 80.

90. <u>Medical Act</u>, R.S.Q. 1977, c. M-9, s. 42.

91. <u>R.</u> v. <u>Potvin</u> (1971), 16 C.R.N.S. 233 (Que. C.A.).

92. See <u>Cook</u> v. <u>Dufferin-Peel Roman Catholic Separate School Board</u> (1983), 34 C.P.C. 178 (Ont. S.C.); <u>R.</u> v. <u>B.</u> (1979), 2 Fam. L. Rev. 213 (Ont. Prov. Ct.); and <u>R.</u> v. <u>Snider</u>, [1954] S.C.R. 479.

93. <u>Education Act</u>, R.S.O. 1980, c. 129, s. 237(2).

94. <u>R.</u> v. <u>B.</u> (1979), 2 Fam. L. Rev. 213 (Ont. Prov. Ct.).

95. <u>Slavutych</u> v. <u>Baker</u>, [1976] 1 S.C.R. 254.

96. <u>R.</u> v. <u>R.S.</u> (1985), 19 C.C.C. (3d) 115 (Ont. C.A.).

97. See <u>Dembie</u> v. <u>Dembie</u> (1963), 21 R.F.L. 46 (Ont. H.C.).

98. See <u>G.</u> v. <u>G.</u>, [1964] 1 O.R. 361 (H.C.); and <u>R.</u> v. <u>Hawke</u> (1974), 3 O.R. (2d) 210 (H.C.).

99. See for example, <u>Public Hospitals Act</u>, R.S.O. 1980, c. 410, s. 11, which provides that the "medical record compiled in a hospital for a client or an out-client is the property of the hospital". See also Sask. Reg. 331/79, s. 16.

100. For example, if a ward of the Children's Aid Society is treated in a public hospital, then the record disclosure requirements of both the <u>Child and Family Services Act, 1984</u>, S.O. 1984, c. 55, s. 165 and O. Reg. 518/88, s. 21, apply.

101. <u>Freedom of Information Act</u>, S.M. 1985-86, c. 6; <u>Right to Information Act</u>, S.N.B. c. R-10.3; <u>Freedom of Information Act</u>, S.N. 1981, c. 5; <u>Freedom of Information Act</u>, S.N.S. 1977, c. 10; and <u>Freedom of Information and Protection of Privacy Act, 1987</u>, S.O. 1987, c. 25, s. 21. Both British Columbia and Saskatchewan have general privacy statutes, but they do not provide any specific protection of records. See <u>Privacy Act</u>, R.S.B.C. 1979, c. 336; and <u>Privacy Act</u>, R.S.S. 1978, c. P-24.

102. <u>Hospitals Act</u>, R.S.A. 1980, c. H-11, s. 40(5)(a); O. Reg. 518/88, s. 21(4)(c)(i); and Sask. Reg. 331/79, s. 16(2)(c).

103. <u>Mental Health Act</u> R.S.A. 1980, c. M-13, s. 37(6)(a); and <u>Mental Health Act</u>, R.S.O. 1980, c. 262, as amended, s. 29a.

104. <u>Child and Family Services Act, 1984</u>, S.O. 1984, c. 55, s. 163(2)(e),(f) and (g).

105. <u>Ibid.</u>, s. 162(b).

106. <u>Ibid.</u>, s. 167(1)(a).

107. <u>Ibid.</u>, s. 167(1)(b) and (2).

108. <u>Ibid.</u>, ss. 165(3) and 167(2).

109. <u>Ibid.</u>, s. 165(3).

110. See for example, <u>Rules of Civil Procedure</u>, O. Reg. 560/84, Rule 30.

111. For a discussion of release of information to family members, see G. Mason and R. McCall Smith, <u>Law and Medical Ethics</u> (1983), 101-104. For a discussion of disclosure to employers, see <u>Halls</u> v. <u>Mitchell</u>, [1928] S.C.R. 125; and <u>Miron</u> v. <u>Pohran</u> (1981), 8 A.C.W.S. (2d) 509 (Ont. Co. Ct.). Regarding disclosures to police, see G. Sharpe, <u>The Law and Medicine in Canada</u>, 2nd ed. (1987), 187-191.

112. See for example, <u>Mental Health Act</u>, R.S.A. 1980, c. M-13, s. 37(6); <u>Hospitals Act</u>, C.S.N.S. 1979, c. H-19, s. 63(1); and <u>Child and Family Services Act, 1984</u>, S.O. 1984, c. 55, s. 165.

113. However, some discretion must be exercised in disclosing confidential information even to colleagues. See <u>Re: Lavasseur and College of Nurses of Ontario</u> (1983), 18 A.C.W.S. (2d) 126 (Ont. H.C.); and <u>Halls</u> v. <u>Mitchell</u>, [1928] S.C.R. 125.

114. <u>Doe</u> v. <u>Roe</u> (1977), 400 N.Y.S. 2d 668 (S.C.).

115. Some statutes, however, require consent in writing. See note 35.

116. See for example: <u>Public Health Act</u>, C.S.A., c. P-27.1, s. 33(1); <u>Health Act</u>, R.S.B.C. 1979, c. 161, s. 88; <u>Communicable Diseases Act</u>, R.S.N. 1970, c. 52, s. 4(1); <u>Health Act</u>, R.S.N.S. 1967, c. 247, ss. 60(1), 76(1) and 93(1); and <u>Health Protection and Promotion Act, 1983</u>, S.O. 1983, c. 10, s. 28.

117. See for example: <u>Public Health Act</u>, C.S.A. c. P-27.1, s. 33(1); <u>Health Act</u>, R.S.B.C. 1979, c. 161, s. 3; <u>Communicable Diseases Act</u>, R.S.N. 1970, c. 52, s. 5(1); and <u>Health Protection and Promotion Act, 1983</u>, S.O. 1983, c. 10, s. 27(1).

118. See for example: <u>Public Health Act</u>, C.S.A. c. P-27.1, s. 33(1); <u>Health Act</u>, R.S.B.C. 1979, c. 161, s. 103; <u>Communicable Disease Act</u>, R.S.N. 1970, c. 52, s. 5(1); <u>Health Protection and Promotion Act, 1983</u>, S.O. 1983, c. 10, s. 28; and <u>Public Health Act</u>, S.P.E.I. 1980, c. 42, s. 12(2).

119. See for example: Alta. Reg. 238/85; B.C. Reg. 4/83; Man. Reg. 338/88; N.B. Reg. 88/200; and O. Reg. 161/84 .

120. Failure to report is not an offence in Manitoba, New Brunswick, Prince Edward Island, or Saskatchewan. However, in Ontario and Alberta, failure to report may result in a fine of up to $5,000. See <u>Health Protection and Promotion Act, 1983</u>, S.O. 1983, c. 10, ss. 99(2) and 100; <u>Public Health Act</u>, C.S.A., c. P-27.1, s. 81(3).

121. For example, see <u>Health Protection and Promotion Act, 1983</u>, S.O. 1983, c. 10, s. 94(4).

122. See for example: <u>Motor Vehicle Act</u>, R.S.B.C. 1979, c. 288, s. 221; <u>Highway Traffic Act</u>, S.M. 1985-86, c. 3, s. 157(1); and <u>Highway Traffic Act</u>, R.S.O. 1980, c. 198, s. 177(1). It is interesting to note that the requirement in Alberta is discretionary. See <u>Motor Vehicle Administration Act</u>, C.S.A., c. M-22, s. 14.

123. <u>Highway Traffic Act</u>, R.S.O. 1980, c. 198, ss. 177 and 178.

124. <u>Child and Family Services Act, 1984</u>, S.O. 1984, c. 55, s. 68(3).

125. <u>Ibid.</u>, ss. 68(1) and 37(2)(a),(c),(e),(f),(h).

126. See for example: <u>Child Welfare Act</u>, S.A. 1984, c. C-8.1, s. 3(2); <u>Family Services Act</u>, R.S.N.B 1973, c. F-2.2, s. 30(2); <u>Children's Services Act</u>, C.S.N.S., c. C-13, s. 77(1); and <u>Child and Family Services Act, 1984</u>, S.O. 1984, c. 55, s. 68(7).

127. See for example: <u>Child Welfare Act</u>, S.A. 1984, c. C-8.1, s. 3(4); <u>Child and Family Services Act</u>, S.M. 1985-86, c. 8, s. 18(3); <u>Family Services Act</u>, R.S.N.B. 1973, c. F-2.2, s. 30(5); <u>Children's Services Act</u>, C.S.N.S., c. C-13, s. 77(2); and <u>Child and Family Services Act, 1984</u>, S.O. 1984, c. 55, s. 68(7).

128. See for example, <u>Koechlin</u> v. <u>Waugh</u> (1957), 11 D.L.R. (2d) 447 (Ont. C.A.); <u>R.</u> v. <u>Carroll</u> (1959), 23 D.L.R. (2d) 271 (Ont. C.A.); <u>Rice</u> v. <u>Connolly</u>, [1966] 2 Q.B. 414; <u>Kenlin</u> v. <u>Gardiner</u>, [1967] 2 Q.B. 510; and <u>Colet</u> v. <u>The Queen</u>, [1981] 1 S.C.R. 2.

129. <u>Criminal Code</u>, R.S.C. 1985, c. C-42, s. 50(1)(b).

130. See A. Mewett and M. Manning, <u>Criminal Law</u>, 2nd ed. (1985), at 437.

131. In the case of the police, the charge would be "obstructing a peace officer in the execution of his duty." In the case of other officials, the charge would be "obstructing justice." See <u>Criminal Code</u>, R.S.C. 1985, c. C-42, ss. 129(a) and 139(2).

132. See C. Wright, "Negligent Acts or Omissions" (1941), 19 <u>Can. Bar Rev.</u> 465; and H. McNiece and J. Thornton, "Affirmative Duties in Tort" (1949), 58 <u>Yale L. J.</u> 1272.

133. See for example, <u>Jordan House Ltd</u>. v. <u>Menow and Honsberger</u>, [1974] S.C.R. 239; <u>Arnold</u> v. <u>Teno</u> (1978), 83 D.L.R. (3d) 609 (S.C.C.); and <u>Toews</u> v. <u>MacKenzie</u> (1980), 109 D.L.R. (3d) 473 (B.C. C.A.).

134. In the United States, the police have been held liable when they stopped, but failed to arrest, drunk drivers who subsequently were involved in accidents. See <u>Irwin</u> v. <u>Town of Ware</u> (1984), 392 Mass. 745; and <u>Weldy</u> v. <u>Town of Kingston</u> (1986), 514 A. 2d 1257 (N.H.).

135. See for example, <u>Smith</u> v. <u>B.C. (A.G.)</u> (1988), 30 B.C.L.R. 356 (B.C. C.A.); and <u>Hague</u> v. <u>Billings</u> (1989), 48 C.C.L.T. 192 (Ont. H.C.).

136. (1976), 17 Cal. (3d) 425 (Cal. S.C.).

137. For a discussion of the impact of <u>Tarasoff</u>, see D. Givelber, W. Bowers and C. Blitch, "<u>Tarasoff</u>, Myth and Reality: An Empirical Study of Private Law in Action", [1984] <u>Wisconsin L. Rev.</u> 443; and M. Lewis, "Duty to Warn Versus Duty to Maintain Confidentiality: Conflicting Demands on Mental Health Professionals" (1986), 20 <u>Suffolk U.L.R.</u> 579.

Motivational Interviewing Techniques

TERRY SODEN AND ROBERT MURRAY

INTRODUCTION

T he last 25 years have seen remarkable advances in the assessment and treatment of addictive disorders. These advances have given clinicians far more sophisticated methods of helping clients change their alcohol/drug-taking behavior. The theoretical foundation for these motivational counselling techniques is a more concrete and increasingly comprehensive understanding of human behavior as it relates to the use/abuse of substances. The importance of the addiction counsellor's underlying beliefs and attitudes (i.e., theoretical orientation) cannot be overstated. As Albert Einstein said "...the theory determines what we can observe," and what clinicians observe about their clients directly influences their counselling activities.

This chapter discusses the principles, guidelines and strategies emerging from this new theoretical framework of addictions and how people change. It presents a brief historical review of the biopsychosocial model of addictions and a new perspective of motivation. It then examines factors influencing motivation, and the change process, and provides a survey of motivational counselling approaches.

BIOPSYCHOSOCIAL MODEL OF ADDICTION

As we integrate different perspectives and develop more sophisticated conceptual models of substance abuse, the Biopsychosocial Model of Addictions (Donovan & Marlatt, 1988) has emerged as the cornerstone of a new and more comprehensive approach to the treatment of addictions. Qualified professional addictions counsellors now see substance abuse disorders as the result of various characteristics within an individual interacting with numerous environmental factors. This process may also lead to a variety of other compulsive behaviors, such as eating disorders, uncontrolled gambling, and sexual promiscuity.

From a biopsychosocial perspective, a substance use disorder is conceptualized as "...a complex, progressive pattern having biological, psychological, sociological, and behavioral components" (Donovan & Marlatt, 1988, p.5). Unlike the traditional view of "alcoholism" or "drug addiction", the Biopsychosocial Model maintains that substance abuse is the result of a multitude of factors. It also recognizes that substance abusers are a varied lot. They differ with respect to:

- patterns of consumption
- family history
- current environmental stressors
- self-esteem and self-efficacy
- coping skills
- employment status, educational achievements
- social supports
- financial resources
- physical and emotional health
- beliefs and attitudes, including those that pertain to their substance use.

In addition, the Biopsychosocial Model recognizes the possibility that problems related to the abuse of substances may develop in anyone (i.e., not confined to a single personality type), and may result in numerous and differing consequences. A variety of treatment options must therefore be considered and available so that treatment planning can match interventions to the needs, strengths and circumstance of each client (Pattison and Kaufman, 1982, in Lewis, Ch.1).

MOTIVATION: AN INTERACTIONAL PROCESS

Understanding motivation as the product of an interactional and/or interpersonal process is significantly different from the traditional attributional model. From the traditional perspective, motivation is a trait that reflects the underlying personality structure of an individual. Substance abusing clients are usually seen as unmotivated because they use defences such as denial, minimization, projection, and repression. Research has demonstrated, however, that

> "...motivation should not be thought of as a personality problem or as a trait that a person carries through the counsellor's doorway. Rather, motivation is a state of readiness or eagerness to change, which may fluctuate from one time or situation to another. This state is one that can be influenced" (Miller and Rollnick, 1991, p. 14).

This enlightened view emphasizes the complexity of change, and asserts that factors both external and internal to the substance abuser influence the change process. Three categories of factors have been identified:

- environmental/situational
- client
- therapist.

The creative use of the forces found within each of these categories can help the clinician and client bring about intentional change.

ENVIRONMENTAL/SITUATIONAL FACTORS

Research has uncovered three primary environmental/situational variables that affect the individual's desire to change or maintain the status quo. These variables include: time; geographical access; and social support.

TIME

Time reflects the inability of substance abusing clients to tolerate distress (especially that which results from acknowledging a substance abuse problem and/or its consequences) and the length of time it takes to receive assistance. Typically, substance abusers contact some component of the treatment system as a result of a crisis but then must wait lengthy periods of time for treatment.

The environmental/situational crises that trigger client contact take a variety of forms, such as loss or threat of loss of significant other(s), employment, or health. Many other critical incidents can prompt a person to seek assistance, including financial difficulties, emotional turmoil and legal problems. The capacity of the "continuum of care" to respond quickly to the substance abuser in crisis is a key factor in both initiating and reinforcing the desire to change (Leigh et al., 1984). Given the extensive time it takes for many people with substance use disorders to get support from the treatment system, it is imperative that agencies and workers develop mechanisms that help clients tolerate and adaptively manage their anxiety. If the system cannot respond to their needs while they are struggling to tolerate their anxiety, clients may be at risk to return to substance use and leave the treatment system.

One creative approach to this problem involves matching appropriate clients with healthy, mature members of mutual-aid/self-help groups, such as Alcoholics Anonymous or Narcotics Anonymous. The resulting relationship may give the client more of the daily support and encouragement he or she needs to cope with anxiety. Further, by observing the positive changes made by the recovered person, the client gains hope that change is possible. Simultaneously, this interaction reinforces the recovered person's sense of purpose in life; it also influences the client who believes that life is meaningless without his or her drug of choice. Witnessing the recovered person's healthy disengagement from substance abuse, the client may re-evaluate his or her expectations of what life might be like without drugs.

Many other strategies and/or resources could be used to help the client who is on a waiting list. Where appropriate, the worker may arrange for regular telephone contact, refer to a detoxification centre, or cultivate support of family members, friends, employer, colleagues, church members, etc. Research indicates that clients who have these types of support are significantly more likely to enter into, comply with, and successfully complete treatment (Leigh, Ogborne, & Cleland, 1984; Johnson & Pandina, 1991; Huselid, Self, & Gutierres, 1991).

GEOGRAPHICAL ACCESS

Travelling great distances to attend a treatment service can reduce motivation to enter treatment and engage in aftercare. Substance abusers often feel frustrated by inadequate transportation systems, lack of financial resources, and a sense of powerlessness to overcome these barriers to treatment.

Solutions to the above issue may include:

a) training existing health and social service providers to intervene effectively with substance abusing clients

b) developing local outreach treatment and aftercare programs by addiction-specific agencies

c) coordinating local services through strategic planning and community networking activities to better service substance abusers

d) enhancing the existing continuum of care in local communities.

SOCIAL SUPPORT

Social support has been shown in the research literature to influence the probability of the substance abuser entering into, engaging in, and successfully completing a process of positive change. It can be provided by family, friends and/or mutual-aid/self-help programs, etc.

To assess the potential impact of the client's present social milieu, the counsellor must ascertain the level of support that family or friends can provide, and the probability of their sabotaging the client's efforts. When indicated, the counsellor will need to work with members of the client's social network to ensure they support the substance abuser's efforts to change.

There are many issues that the counsellor may need to address with respect to the above. One of the most common is "enabling": when family members and friends unwittingly help the substance abuser avoid the consequences of his or her behavior, thereby encouraging it to continue. For example: the partner of a substance abuser with a hangover tells the employer that the person is home with the flu.

In such situations, the counsellor's task is: (a) to help the partner understand how "enabling" perpetuates substance abuse and (b) to help the partner find other responses that discourage substance abuse and bolster the development of motivation to change.

Surrogate support systems, such as the mutual-aid/self-help groups, are most effectively used when the counsellor actively helps the client make contact with the group. Sisson and Mallams (1981) found that when the clinician made the initial telephone call to a suitable AA member on behalf of the client, all of those clients followed through with the contact. When a group of clients were simply encouraged to attend AA and given a schedule of meetings, not one attended any meetings. When counsellors match clients with a compatible 12-Step member, the member can then support the client by explaining the program, informing him or her of meeting times, arranging to take the client to a first meeting, introducing others in the program, and guiding the client in the informal use of this support network.

CLIENT CHARACTERISTICS

The second category of factors that influence motivation are found within the individual and are often referred to as client characteristics. Miller (1986) found the following five major internal variables that affect motivation:
  1) the focus and level of *distress* experienced by the client
  2) the *severity* of the substance abuse problem
  3) *locus of control*
  4) *conceptual level*
  5) *stage of readiness to change.*

FOCUS AND LEVEL OF DISTRESS

The clinician must understand the source of the distress and its level of intensity. For example, if it originates from external pressure – a family member or employer threatening either the loss of a significant relationship or financial security – the client may resist any examination of his or her behavior. In such a case, the clinician is well advised to address the resistance through a non-punitive, motivational therapeutic approach. This can be done by understanding the nature or types of resistance. Munjack and Oziel (1978) suggest that resistance is the result of five different antecedents. These causes include: a) the client misunderstanding the counsellor; b) the client's lack of skills; c) the client being unable to see himself or herself succeeding; d) issues arising from previous counselling experiences, such as anxiety or guilt; and e) the rewards of the client's substance use/abuse.

Motivational interviewing strategies aimed at substance abusers who have been forced into treatment, should also include: a) encouraging the client to discuss his or her feelings about being forced to attend the interview; and b) uncovering the functions the substance serves, the level and pattern of consumption, and its social, emotional, physical, psychological, and spiritual consequences. This will increase the client's awareness of the impact of substance use on his or her life and therefore also provide a new focus for his or her distress.

As the focus shifts in this direction, the client's distress about this behavior often increases dramatically. This distress comes from recognizing that substance abuse interferes with the attainment of one's goals, adherence to one's intrinsic values, and/or progress toward the development of the "ideal self." The distress is further heightened by the threat of the loss of significant relationships, employment and/or health. Such a negative emotional state, coupled with low self-esteem (Perez, 1989), low self-efficacy (the belief that one does not have the skills required to make desired change occur; Annis, 1989), and the effects of withdrawal,[1] typically leads to an unbearable level of discomfort. This produces a pivotal period during which a client may either stop their substance abuse or continue it. It is referred to as the "window of opportunity," when the counsellor helps the client to "hit bottom" without necessarily having to "ride the garbage truck all the way to the dump."

Research shows that clients at this time are especially vulnerable to the influence of motivational strategies, delivered within the context of formal counselling or some other form of helping relationship. Regardless of the clients' point of contact with the treatment system – whatever therapeutic relationship they have – there is a significant increase in the probability that they will begin using adaptive behaviors that lead to positive changes. However, unless clients develop and use adaptive coping skills that increase their sense of self-efficacy and self-esteem, they are left extremely vulnerable to relapse or continued drug use. Motivational strategies designed to increase distress, while still maintaining a therapeutic relationship that builds client self-efficacy, will be discussed later in this chapter.

SEVERITY OF THE SUBSTANCE ABUSE PROBLEM

Level of Severity is another client characteristic identified by Miller and Rollnick (1991) that has implications not only for the direction of motivation but also the type and intensity of treatment required. Most current scientific authorities and treatment specialists in the field of addictions "view substance abuse problems on a continuum from non-problematic to problematic use, rather than as an either/or situation" (Lewis, 1988 p. 4). Level of severity is determined by the client's frequency and level of consumption, *combined with* life problems that have been identified through the assessment process.

The above-stated approach to substance abuse problems is relatively new. In the past, many counsellors considered consumption only when attempting to determine the severity of a problem. The Biopsychosocial Model has stimulated the development of a more comprehensive and multidimensional "severity continuum" that also considers the impact of substance abuse on various levels of the client's functioning (Prochaska and DiClemente, 1984, H. A. Skinner, 1981).

Regarding motivation, research has found that distress related to an individual perceiving himself or herself as having a severe substance abuse problem can *either* increase or decrease motivation to change. Distress experienced by the client, for example, can be so high as to paralyze the individual or be so low as to have little or no impact on willingness to change. The client who does not realistically assess the seriousness of his or her situation must be made aware of the consequences of substance abuse and its impact on affected life areas (Rogers & Newborn, 1976; Hingson et al., 1982). One way to do this is to give the client meaningful, constructive and personalized feedback.

Clients who are overly distressed by the perceived severity of their substance abuse problem must be encouraged to examine their strengths and past successes, thereby raising their self-efficacy and self-esteem. These clients also need help in evaluating what life might be like without substance use. Such motivational interventions reduce distress, and create hope and motivation to change (Prochaska & DiClemente, 1984).

Research also indicates that individuals with severe substance abuse problems have often made numerous attempts at treatment without success. This, according to Orford (1979), results in lower self-esteem and self-efficacy, leading to negative expectations of their capacity to benefit from treatment. Not surprisingly, this lowers motivation to enter the treatment system again because it seems futile.

A comprehensive assessment, done within the context of motivational interviewing, should enable the counsellor to accurately determine the severity of the substance abuse problem. With this information available to both the counsellor and the client, a negotiated decision can be made regarding a treatment plan that *matches* the client's needs and circumstances to the least intrusive but most effective form of treatment (McLellan et al., 1983). When comprehensive assessment and matching have not been followed, clients often receive inappropriate treatment and do not invest themselves in it. Because each unsuccessful treatment attempt leaves the client feeling that he or she has failed, it is vital to match the client with the least intrusive treatment that has the highest probability for success.

LOCUS OF CONTROL

The third factor found to influence motivation is Locus of Control (Rotter, 1966), a concept for understanding the extent of control an individual thinks he or she has over his or her environment. This concept pertains

> ...to the manner in which the individual perceives the value of his or her own efforts in having some impact on the environment. (Individuals with an internal locus of control) believe that their own skills and efforts are influential in achieving their goals, creating success, and having impact on the environment: clients feel that they are able to exercise control over their own lives, and acknowledge a sense of responsibility for themselves. (External locus of control

individuals) are more likely to believe in fate or luck... and that they are victims of circumstances and not responsible for themselves (Miller & Sovereign, 1989, p. 59).

Substance abusers often blame external factors for their consumption, their life situation, and their general sense of helplessness and malaise. This demonstrates a personality-perceptual-behavioral style common to individuals with an external locus of control. This orientation continues into the counselling relationship, with the client making numerous requests for guidance and direction. Even though the ultimate aim of counselling substance abusers is to help them take responsibility for their behavior, during the initial phases of motivational counselling the counsellor should provide consistent feedback that enhances the client's self-esteem while acknowledging that an "...external orientation is associated with higher anxiety and distress, which may in turn influence motivation for treatment" (Donovan & O'Leary, 1979).

CONCEPTUAL LEVEL

Conceptual level refers to a client's emotional maturity and interpersonal development. Just as locus of control is viewed as a continuum, so too is conceptual level. A substance abuser on the low side of the continuum tends to perceive his or her substance abuse problem in simplistic terms. Like a person who believes the external world determines the outcome of his or her behavior, the client on the low side of the conceptual continuum is highly dependent on authority figures for direction, and functions best in a structured environment with simple rules of conduct.

On the other hand, a "high conceptual level" client is cognitively complex, usually thinking in abstract terms. He or she tends to recognize the complexity of his or her problems and finds greatest satisfaction when functioning in an unstructured, flexible counselling situation that allows for independent thought, freedom to choose alternative treatment approaches, with a counsellor who sees his or her role as a facilitator and not an authoritative teacher.

The counsellor's responsibility is to differentially apply motivational counselling techniques, aware of the client's locus of control and conceptual level. In the authors' experience, individuals with a moderate to severe chronic substance use problem, when highly distressed, tend to initially present with an external locus of control, combined with a low conceptual level. These clients respond best to a counsellor who makes directive statements and recommends specific structured activities for the client to carry out.

An example of the above is found in many individuals who present at a detoxification centre and remain long enough to experience the pain and distress of withdrawal. They rely on the detoxification attendants for information, direction and nurturance, needing assurance that their present unpleasant experience of withdrawal will pass. This need compels such residents to seek out and accept advice without hesitation. However, as they begin to feel better, some of them shift to a higher conceptual level and a more internal locus of control. They become less interested in the advice and direction of others and more self-directed.

In the past, counsellors saw this as evidence of decreasing motivation to change and attempted to alter it by becoming increasingly more confrontive and directive. Although their intention was to be helpful, the outcome was usually resistance to any further help – resulting in the client dropping out of the treatment system. However, we now know that clients who shift from dependence on the counsellor to more self-directed, positive thinking and behavior may be manifesting higher self-efficacy. Research indicates that such individuals are most successful in changing their problematic behavior (Janis, 1982).

During this early phase of recovery, the counsellor should match his or her counselling strategies to the client's shifting dependence, conceptual level and locus of control, and not give in to the temptation to view the client as unmotivated. Instead, a more helpful approach is to support the client's need for independent decision-making and ownership of the therapeutic process.

STAGES OF READINESS TO CHANGE

The client's current readiness to change is the final and perhaps most important factor to consider when engaged in motivational interviewing. This multi-faceted variable is sufficiently complex to have been developed into a theory known as the Transtheoretical Model of Change, by James O. Prochaska and Carlo C. DiClemente. The theory provides an explanation of substance abusers as they go

Figure 1

WHEEL OF CHANGE

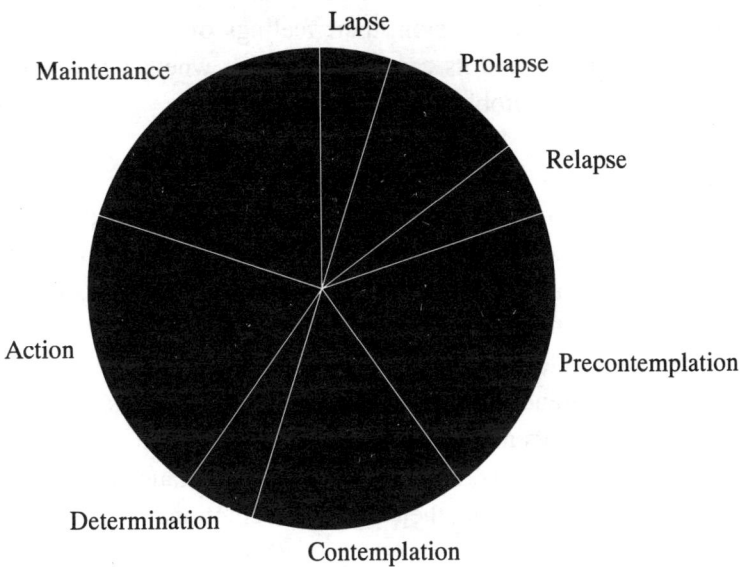

about the process of changing their behavior. It recognizes and acknowledges the difficulties and challenges inherent in altering substance use disorders and clearly describes the nature of recovery. Unlike other conceptual models of addictions and their treatment, which view change as a process of straight line growth, the Transtheoretical Model asserts that a "slip" or relapse is part and parcel of the cyclical nature of changing substance abuse behavior. This model is usually depicted as a "*wheel*" of change consisting of different stages.[2]

Precontemplation Stage

The first stage is known as "Precontemplation" – when others see the harm that the substance use is doing to the client, but the client does not. Not surprisingly, individuals in precontemplation who present at a counselling agency do so at the request or insistence of significant others, employers or the judicial system. It is therefore difficult to engage these clients in any meaningful dialogue about their substance use. Their resistance usually takes the form of: a) actual physical withdrawal from counselling, or b) superficial engagement in the assessment process, treatment planning, and the individualized therapeutic activities needed to bring about change.

Process-oriented research (Miller & Sovereign, 1989; Patterson & Forgatch, 1985) shows that the traditional confrontational approach creates a destructive dynamic with the vast majority of clients. For clients in the precontemplation stage, this situation is made worse when the counsellor attempts to use strategies more appropriate to clients at other stages of readiness. When clinical strategies and client stage of change are mismatched, clients often react in ways which have historically been interpreted as manifestations of "denial" and "resistance." In reality, however, these are responses to feeling accused, labelled, aggressively confronted, controlled, and not seen as a worthwhile human being with strengths and weaknesses, successes and failures, potential and resources. When working with clients in the precontemplation stage, the counsellor should try to uncover their reasons for coming to the counselling session, their feelings of being coerced, and how they view their consumption and its consequences, i.e., whether they see it as a problem or as a solution to other problems.

Contemplation Stage

The next stage of change, as outlined by Prochaska and DiClemente, is the "Contemplation Stage." Unlike substance abusers in precontemplation, clients in contemplation recognize some of the consequences of their alcohol/drug use but are ambivalent about altering it. The therapeutic task is to help these clients move beyond ambivalence to a feeling of cognitive dissonance (the internal conflict that results from an awareness that their substance use impedes the attainment of their life goals). These clients must also be helped to see how their drug use often clashes with their values and beliefs. For example, some substance abusers may idealize the role of parenthood, but neglect their children – emotionally, physically, spiritually or materially – when using substances. This neglect could include emotional non-responsiveness or intrusiveness, physical absence, poor role-modelling, or spending money on drugs instead of adequate food and clothing for the children.

Individuals in the contemplation stage are pulled in two directions. On the one hand, they are somewhat aware of the consequences of their substance use. On the other hand, substance use has a positive function in their lives. At the early phase of this stage, clients experience this ambivalence but don't believe they can change their situation. It is very important for the counsellor to help these clients understand their ambivalent feelings, and how their behavior is problematic, in order to move the change process forward.

Action Stage

According to Prochaska and DiClemente, the "Action Stage" is the shortest in duration, because it's the time when clients are the most enthusiastic and energetic. Such a peak level of effort can only be maintained for a limited period of time. Factors that help maintain the momentum of change throughout this stage include the increasing sense of self-esteem that results from clients "acting on their beliefs in personal self-efficacy", and the positive recognition received from others regarding dramatic changes in problematic behavior (Prochaska & DiClemente, 1984, p. 67). Clients who present in the action stage are eager to engage in activities that bring about immediate results – they may feel frustrated by therapists who spend a lot of time trying to understand the origin and complexity of the presenting problem.

Even though individuals in the action stage are "chomping at the bit," a comprehensive assessment is needed so that the counsellor and client both understand the nature of the client's problems and his or her strengths and weaknesses. Only in this way can realistic and achievable goals be set.

The "Action Stage" can be conceptualized as the time when "...the individual engages in a variety of processes intended to bring about a shift in direction" (Miller & Jackson, 1985, p.135), a shift that may be perceived by the client as slow and arduous. The client is sensitive, having lost an habitual pattern of behaving, and having to manage each day without a treasured coping mechanism.

Maintenance Stage

The next stage is one in which "...people work to continue the gains attained during action and to prevent relapse to their more troubled level of functioning" (Prochaska & DiClemente, 1984, p. 28). This "Maintenance Stage" continues the change process, with emphasis on assimilating and integrating the skills and abilities acquired during the action stage.

During the Maintenance Stage, the client typically experiences life, with all of its natural and unfolding joys, crises and challenges, while still lacking practice at coping with all that life has to offer. Successful maintenance is similar to what Alan F. Kleine (1974) describes as a healthy lifestyle containing three fundamental skills:

1. The ability to *learn how to relate oneself to others*. It means making and

maintaining rewarding human connections, mutual need-fulfillment, and satisfying communication. The ability to share affect with others is the *sine qua non* of social competence and also of personal need fulfillment. Such an experience is possible if trust has been established and authoritarian control [or perception of such] has been minimized.

2. The *capacity to choose*. The very essence of adaptation involves the making of successive choices. Decision-making rests upon the ability to make choices and to see the relationship between goals, values, means and end results.

3. The ability to *learn how to learn*. This is the essence of ego functioning. It includes reality-testing, value-testing and coping (p. 49-50).

The above three basic skills are quintessential elements of a stable sober lifestyle. In the authors' view, the capacity to effectively use these skills is essential to healthy human growth for ex-substance abusers in the maintenance stage. They are also the primary index of mental health.

Given the time-limited nature of most treatment services, a client's ability to function fully is usually developed following the active treatment phase. Because the supportive therapeutic relationship developed during the assessment process and action stage is now lost, the maintenance stage must include focused endeavors (discussed in detail later in this chapter) to help the client enjoy a balanced lifestyle and prevent relapse. Without the knowledge, skills and abilities to live life as it is, many individuals begin to dread facing reality and recall instead the rewards of using substances to cope with life situations. This places the client in grave danger of relapse, because it occurs at a time when the client has very little emotional memory of the consequences of such behavior.

Clients respond to this challenging period in a number of ways. First, they may be ambivalent about resuming drug use as a means of coping. This is experienced as an approach-avoidance conflict, filled with ambivalence, in which the client both wants and fears a return to drug use. Secondly, clients may use the defense mechanism known as "reaction formation." They act overconfident, pretending to believe in their ability to face any emerging life challenge without experiencing any temptation to use drugs. Lastly, clients may forget to use cognitive strategies, such as "remember when," thus fostering a susceptibility to relapse. If they forget the harmful effects of their previous drug abuse, they also lose the lessons learned from previous struggles. One consequence of such thinking is that the client gradually reduces the daily structure that helped them recover, and eventually misplaces the skills and strategies that helped him or her begin, continue and maintain a positive process of change.

Relapse

Discontinuing maintenance strategies signals the possible onset of the next stage, known as *relapse*, which should be viewed not as an event but as a cognitive/affective/behavioral dynamic process. As was mentioned earlier in this chapter, treatment of substance abuse has traditionally been viewed as a linear process, and relapse as equivalent to failure by the client. However, Prochaska and DiClemente view relapse as a stage in the cyclical change/recovery process. Thus, relapse should also be considered, by clinicians and clients alike, as an opportunity

> ...to foster a sense of objectivity or detachment... in which clients learn to perceive their addictive behavior [relapse] as something they do rather than as an indication of something they are. By adopting this objective and detached approach, clients may be able to free themselves from the guilt and defensiveness that would otherwise bias their view of their problem (Marlatt & Gordon, 1985, p. 51).

Seen this way, a relapse becomes a psycho-educational milestone from which the client gains information and feedback vital to the refinement of treatment goals, objectives and strategies. Understanding and using the dynamics and consequences of the relapse process can help them develop more comprehensive interventions that address those issues missed in previous treatment efforts.

The scientific literature indicates that the rate of relapse among substance abusers falls somewhere between 50 and 93 per cent (Marlatt & Gordon, 1985). Prochaska and DiClemente have found in their longitudinal studies that, "...85 per cent of these individuals [relapsers] are seriously considering making another attempt at changing the problematic behavior and could be considered contemplators" (Prochaska & DiClemente, 1984, p.29). They maintain that the remaining 15 per cent of relapsers re-enter the precontemplation stage.

We have a different perspective. Having worked with thousands of substance abusers from a variety of cultural, socio-economic, educational and ethnic backgrounds, it is our clinical experience that no one who has moved through the various stages in the "wheel of change" can ever forget what they learned about themselves and their negative experiences with substances. Anyone presently in relapse periodically experiences an approach/avoidance conflict, low self-efficacy, and ambivalence vis-à-vis maintaining their drug use/abuse versus changing it. This, by definition, places them in the "Contemplation Stage" and not "Precontemplation," and thus makes them more amenable to the influence of an empathic counsellor and the motivational interviewing approach.

THERAPIST CHARACTERISTICS

The last category of factors that influence client motivation are characteristics of the counsellor that become manifest in the "helping relationship" (Prochaska & DiClemente, 1984). They include the therapist's personal needs and resultant behavioral manifestations, and his or her feelings, expectations, and quality of empathy.

THERAPIST NEEDS AND THEIR BEHAVIORAL MANIFESTATIONS

The personal needs of the counsellor are crucial in determining the quality of interaction with the client. For example, Schorer (1965) found that clinicians with an intense need to see their efforts bring about change in their clients' consumption became over-involved with their clients, which resulted in increased client drop-out. This excessive need to realize "successful results" may reflect the counsellor's irrational belief that he or she is solely responsible for the client's behavior. One reason for this may be the counsellor's own self-esteem. His or her sense of self-confidence and professional competence may depend on the client's success or failure at meeting goals.

TRAPS THAT CATCH COUNSELLORS

Confrontational Trap

The Confrontation-Denial Trap is only one of a number of problematic dynamics identified by Miller and Rollnick (1991) that may ensue when the counsellors' needs to preserve or enhance their own self-esteem get played out in the helping relationship. The Confrontation-Denial Trap occurs when the clinician is so task-oriented that he or she gives little consideration to important process issues, such as the client's need to see himself or herself as owning the therapeutic process. The end result of this trap is that the professional becomes more directive and prescriptive, while the client becomes more entrenched and resistant (Miller & Sovereign, 1989).

Miller and Rollnick (1991) identified other traps that we view as manifestations of this same therapist need. These include The Expert Trap and The Premature-Focus Trap.

Expert Trap

In The Expert Trap, the clinician solves the client's problems and imposes "corrective" measures to rectify dysfunctional situations. As with the Confrontation-Denial Trap, the client's self-efficacy and self-esteem are not increased and may even be diminished. In a therapeutic relationship, highly-directive advice is appropriate with those clients who have a more external locus of control and tend toward the low end of the conceptual level continuum. However, when the client is contemplating a commitment to alter his or her behavior – or with clients who have an internal locus of control and a high conceptual level – less directive interventions are required. A nondirective but motivational approach tends to elicit self-motivational statements from the client, which generates a greater investment in the change process. Miller and Rollnick (1991) have identified four categories of self-motivational statements:

1. *Problem Recognition*, e.g., client says, "It never occurred to me that I was drinking so much."

2. *Expression of Concern*, e.g., client says, "I feel that my situation with drugs is really hopeless."

3. *Intention to Change*, e.g., client says, "It's about time that I did something about this."

4. *Optimism to Change*, e.g., client says, "I'm sure that I've got what it takes to stop drinking."

Premature-Focus Trap

As with the Expert Trap, the Premature-Focus Trap tends to inhibit the development of rapport, which is critical to the clarification and formulation of the client's strengths, problem areas, life situation and major concern(s). This trap occurs when the counsellor raises the issue of the client's alcohol/drug problem before the individual is prepared to discuss it. Clients then tend to use such defences as minimization, projection, intellectualization and outright denial to deal with their fear of entrapment and potential loss of control and self-esteem. To prevent this from happening, Miller and Rollnick (1991) say the clinician must "...avoid becoming engaged in a struggle about the proper topic for early discussion. Starting with the client's concerns, rather than those of the counsellor, will ensure that [falling into the Premature-Focus Trap] does not happen" (p. 70).

A clinician's need to be nurturing is another important factor in the development of clients' motivation to change. Research indicates that clinicians who have a high need to nurture retain a significantly greater number of clients throughout the therapeutic process than those clinicians with a low need to nurture (Schorer, 1965). Based on his study of interpersonal processes between clients and therapists, Coady (1991) found that "...a therapist stance that is nurturing, involving, and mildly influencing may be particularly important for achieving and sustaining a productive therapist-client relationship" (p. 132). Nurturing behavior can take many forms, including the following:

a) offering clients a beverage, such as coffee or juice, which symbolically satisfies the clients' need to be cared for

b) telephoning the client during the early stage of treatment to offer support between sessions

c) introducing the client (when appropriate) to a mutual-aid group member who understands and accepts the client's present situation and behavior, and is willing to provide daily support and encouragement

d) sending a personal note of concern, support and encouragement to clients who have missed an appointment.

Feelings of Therapist

The focus of the literature, vis-à-vis feelings, has been primarily limited to the therapist's warmth or hostility as they relate to the development and maintenance of the therapeutic relationship. Truax and Carkhuff (1967) comment that:

It is a rare human being who does not respond to warmth with warmth and to hostility with hostility. It is probably the most important principle for the beginning therapist to understand if he is to be successful in the therapeutic relationship (p. 42).

Many authors (P. Watzlawick et al., 1974; Anderson & Stewart, 1983; Zimberg et al., 1978; Rogers, 1965; Klein, 1974; Yalom, 1975; Kennedy, 1977) define warmth as a condition that exists in a sound therapeutic relationship. Warmth is the result of the therapist's strategic use of reflective counselling skills (attending, paraphrasing, reflection of feeling and summarizing). The effective use of these skills, combined with the counsellor's acceptance, understanding and positive feedback, encourages clients to disclose in depth their concerns and aspirations. This constitutes the essence of rapport – the most vital aspect of the therapeutic process.

The counsellor's hostility – even when masked – has significant negative impact upon motivation. Milmoe (1967) found that clinicians who conveyed hostility in their tone of voice, even if the content of their communication was not overtly hostile, had higher dropout rates among their clients.

Clinicians need to develop mechanisms that encourage ongoing monitoring of their emotional responses to clients. These could include regular clinical supervision/consultations that would provide support and opportunities to talk about the challenges inherent in working with this demanding population. Structures that provide clinical feedback and skills-training should also address any counter-transference issues that develop.

Expectations

The counsellor's expectations of the client's potential to succeed also affect motivation. Leake and King (1977) discovered that giving clients a "good" or "poor" prognostic label influenced the counsellor's view of the client and subsequent treatment outcome. For example, when clients received a randomly assigned "good" prognosis from an intake worker, the counsellor viewed both the client and the therapeutic relationship with greater optimism, and invested more energy in the treatment process (as observed in their behavior toward the client and their treatment intervention). Thomas et al. (1955) examined the clinician's expectations from the client's perspective. He found that clients' perception of the clinicians' expectations of their potential greatly influenced treatment outcome. In this research, clients who felt their counsellor believed in their capacity to change became more committed to treatment and remained in the therapeutic process, with a willingness to be influenced by the therapists' expertise and interventions.

Empathy

The founder of Client-Centred Therapy, Carl Rogers, maintained that the probability of clients changing within a therapeutic relationship increased dramatically when the therapist exhibited "accurate empathy," as well as non-possessive warmth and genuineness. He defined empathy as the counsellor experiencing accurate

...understanding of his client's private world, and is able to communicate some of the significant fragments of that understanding. To sense the client's inner world of private personal meanings as if it were your own, but without ever losing the 'as if' quality, this is empathy, and this seems essential to a growth-promoting relationship. To sense his confusion or his timidity or his anger or his feeling of being treated unfairly as if it were your own, yet without your own uncertainty or fear or anger or suspicion getting bound up in it, this is the condition I am endeavoring to describe. When the client's world is clear to the counsellor and he can move about in it freely, then he can both communicate his understanding of what is vaguely known to the client, and he can also voice meanings in the client's experience of which the client is scarcely aware. It is this kind of highly sensitive empathy which seems important in making it possible for a person to get close to himself and to learn, to change and develop (Rogers & Stevens, 1967, p. 92-3).

The higher and more accurate the level of empathy manifest in a therapist's behavior, the better the treatment outcome. The behavioral manifestations of high empathy include: a) focusing not only on problems and concerns but on clients' strengths and successes; b) clarifying discrepancies; and, c) providing non-judgmental, objective feedback.

Truax and Mitchell (1971) and Valle (1981) found that, among other variables, the use of accurate empathy was predictive of the rate and number of client relapses at six, 12, 18 and 24 months following conclusion of treatment.

Miller (1980) found that there is a relationship between therapist self-esteem and empathic interventions. This indicates that clinicians need high self-esteem to accurately empathize with their clients. Given that high empathy plays such a vital role in the treatment of drug problems, counsellors who have high self-esteem and exhibit accurate empathy are more likely to engage substance abusers in a therapeutic process of change.

The material covered to this point has focused on a variety of critical issues related to motivational interviewing of individuals with psychoactive substance use disorders. The first issue addressed was the importance of the Biopsychosocial Model of Addictions, which is shifting our perspective from one that is unidimensional to one that is multivariant. Next, we examined how motivation may be influenced by environment/situation, client, and therapist variables and characteristics. The remainder of this chapter will delineate specific motivational interviewing strategies designed to increase the probability of clients entering, complying, and successfully completing treatment.

GENERAL MOTIVATIONAL INTERVIEWING PRINCIPLES

William Miller (1991) has identified five broad clinical principles that can help counsellors assess and motivate substance abusing clients: 1) Express empathy; 2) Develop discrepancy; 3) Avoid argumentation; 4) Roll with resistance; and 5) Support self-efficacy.

EXPRESS EMPATHY

This first principle was partially addressed earlier in this chapter, under the heading of Therapist Characteristics. Empathy and its expression were identified in the work of Carl Rogers and others (Murgatroyd, 1986; Kennedy, 1977; Rogers, 1965; Anderson & Stewart, 1983; Priestly & McGuire, 1983; Turner, 1974). They maintained that reflecting an understanding of an individual's situation from his or her perspective, without judging, criticizing or blaming, is predictive of success in treating substance abusers.

> The attitude underlying this principle of empathy might be called 'acceptance' ... [which] is a respectful listening to the client with a desire to understand his or her perspectives. Paradoxically, this kind of acceptance of people as they are seems to free them to change, whereas insistent non-acceptance ("You're not O.K.: you have to change") can have the effect of keeping people as they are. This attitude of acceptance and respect also builds a working therapeutic alliance, and supports the client's self-esteem – an important condition for change (Miller & Rollnick, 1991 p. 5).

Expressing empathy can help reveal and heighten both sides of a client's ambivalence about change, thereby creating enough cognitive dissonance for the substance abuser to move through the contemplation stage to action.

DEVELOP DISCREPANCIES

Developing discrepancies allows the clinician "to create and amplify, in the client's mind, a discrepancy between present behavior and broader goals" (Miller & Rollnick, 1991, p. 56). Throughout the psychological literature, this phenomenon is referred to as creating cognitive dissonance. In layman's terms, it can be understood as the discrepancy between where you are and where you would like to be. This occurs when one becomes aware that "the cost of the bottle (or drug) exceeds the price on the label" (Soden, 1988) – that his or her substance use conflicts with personal goals, such as good health, vocational/financial success, healthy interpersonal relationships, positive self-image, and personal spiritual growth. Such awareness creates a motivating force that tips the balance of ambivalence in the direction of changing the recognized problem. As Miller and Rollnick (1991) state:

> A goal of motivational interviewing is to develop discrepancy – to make use of it, increase it, and amplify it until it overrides attachment to the present behavior. The strategies of motivational interviewing seek to do this in the client, [and] ...involves clarifying important goals for the client, and exploring the consequences or potential consequences of his or her present behavior which conflicts with those goals. When successfully done, motivational interviewing changes the client's perceptions (of discrepancy) without creating a feeling of being pressured or coerced...[resulting] in the client presenting the reasons for change (p. 57).

AVOID ARGUMENTS

Clinicians working with substance abusing clients have historically manifested their traditional view of motivation by engaging in a variety of interventions that included "labelling" (i.e., giving the client a diagnostic label such as "alcoholic" or "drug addict"). Although such confrontational strategies were used with the best intentions, they have always seemed, to some degree, an aggressive attack on clients' self-image and self-esteem. This invariably resulted in feelings of anger and shame, and a defensive reaction that often led traditional clinicians to say "the client is in denial." This is like hitting the client and then blaming them for saying "ouch." Research evidence validates the existence of this dynamic and the harm it may cause whenever used. Clients often respond to this painful and demeaning process by dropping out of treatment or through other avoidance behaviors, such as superficial compliance with the clinician's power and authority.

Even though motivational interviewing with clients in the "precontemplation" or "contemplation" stages involves helping them acknowledge their substance abuse problem, this process uses interventions that increase the client's awareness and ultimately reflect the client's desire to alter his or her problematic behavior. This is different from the confrontational approach, but similar to the self-labelling process inherent in the philosophy and writings of 12-step self-help programs. As Bill Wilson, the co-founder of Alcoholics Anonymous stated, "We do not like to pronounce any individual as alcoholic, but you can quickly diagnose yourself" (Alcoholics Anonymous, 1976, p. 31).

Clinicians must distinguish between motivational strategies that engage and enlighten the client, and behaviors that attempt to persuade clients to accept our authoritarian interpretation of their situation. One method of such self-evaluation is to continually monitor the client's response to us. Any indication of resistance or avoidance should prompt us to re-evaluate our behavior to determine whether we are using a destructive confrontational approach and, if so, consider shifting to a more empathic and constructive style that fits the motivational interviewing method.

ROLL WITH RESISTANCE

Mature 12-step self-help members understand and accept others' reluctance to alter behavior which, despite negative consequences, has helped them cope with reality. This philosophy is best embodied in their practice of telling newcomers "what happened to me as a practising substance abuser, my initial resistance to the program and, finally, how it has helped me." Through this process, the mature member conveys an understanding and acceptance of the cautious newcomer's resistance. This leads to a desire to associate with those empathic and inspiring members who have had similar experiences but are now in recovery.

Clinicians who are self-help members should *not* use this process as part of their professional repertoire because:

- it limits their potential to engage clients who find the self-help method unacceptable
- it limits the client's perspective of the "recovery process" to the pathway taken by the counsellor, even if it conflicts with the client's real needs. This is, in part, due to client's tendency to view the professional as having the answers to everything. Such a tendency diminishes the client's openness to other members' experience and interpretation of the self-help program
- it creates role confusion because the use of counselling communication skills should establish and maintain personal boundaries between the counsellor's membership in a self-help program and their role as a counsellor.

"Counsellor Self-Disclosure" differs from the self-help process of overcoming resistance in three major ways. First, the topic area of the self-disclosure should be limited to specific material being revealed by the client. Secondly, this strategy should be used only to illuminate the client's own situation, and not for the counsellor's benefit. Thirdly, the counsellor's self-disclosure should be consistently and directly related to the client's experience.

Counsellor Self-Disclosure and self-help "story telling" may promote similar outcome. Done correctly, Counsellor Self-Disclosure reduces the client's sense of uniqueness and isolation, just as the self-help members' story telling does. It also increases trust and rapport between the counsellor and the client, and promotes the expression of thoughts and feelings previously avoided. Counsellor Self-Disclosure lets the client see the counsellor as having struggled with similar issues, although not necessarily the problem of substance abuse. The client can then see the similarities between him/herself and the counsellor, as well as positive and negative feelings common to the human experience, thus promoting increased self-esteem and hope.

To overcome resistance, the counsellor must also encourage the client to take responsibility for any new perceptions of him or herself and any change in his or her behavior. This generates a recognition in both counsellor and client that the latter is truly the author of his or her own destiny – even within a therapeutic relationship. As Miller states, the counsellor offers, but does not impose, new perspectives of the client's behavior, and recognizes that "the client is a valuable resource in finding solutions to problems" (Miller & Rollnick, 1991, p. 60). When this empowering approach is consistently used by the counsellor, the client is encouraged to:

a) define and prioritize his or her problems (based on thoughtful consideration of the situation)

b) develop measurable, attainable goals

c) generate a variety of strategies to achieve these goals

d) select the most promising strategies and activities

e) undertake them, in spite of negative reactions from "drinking/drugging buddies" and/or co-dependents.

SUPPORT SELF-EFFICACY

The client's belief in his or her abilities to change their substance abuse is a key element in motivation to change and a good predictor of treatment outcome (Miller, 1981, p. 60-61). This principle is supported by scientific evidence of the potency of *belief-in-oneself* and *hope for the future* (Maddux et al., 1987): two variables that are critical motivators in changing substance abusers' destructive behavior. Consequently, counsellors who work with people with substance abuse problems must recognize the significance of timely empowerment of clients. Timely empowerment requires sensitivity not only to the client's need for nurturing and support, but also his or her need to nurture, feel autonomous and feel that they have the skills necessary to fully enjoy and live life without abusing substances.

Counsellors who support self-efficacy help clients accept that only they can change their behavior. "Motivational interviewing does not foster hope that the therapist will change the client" (Miller & Rollnick, 1991, p. 61). Instead, the client must recognize that the therapist's responsibility is to *help the client change him/herself.*

Counsellors may support self-efficacy in a number of ways:

a) by introducing the client to people who have overcome similar problems

b) by using strategies that encourage the client to recognize and acknowledge their past successes, along with their current strengths, skills and abilities

c) by negotiating therapeutic tasks and objectives that challenge the client's skills and abilities, but also have a high probability for success

d) by providing, within the therapeutic context, a range of approaches to changing substance abuse behavior, so that the client feels responsible for choosing and carrying out any of the alternatives available.

In effect, the counsellor is following a general philosophy "...that each person possesses a powerful potential for change. Your task as a therapist is to release that potential, to facilitate the natural change processes already inherent in the individual" (Miller & Rollnick, 1991, p. 62).

MOTIVATIONAL INTERVIEWING OF CLIENTS IN PRECONTEMPLATION

The pivotal process of change for precontemplators is called "consciousness raising." Consciousness raising makes the client aware of his or her substance use and how it interferes with: a) attaining his or her goals; b) adhering to his or her values and beliefs; and c) how the client wishes to be perceived by others. Consciousness raising is best accomplished through the use of motivational strategies that: i) develop a therapeutic relationship; ii) overcome resistance; and iii) uncover thoughts and feelings about the risks and reinforcers of the substance abuse.

MOTIVATIONAL STRATEGIES FOR PRECONTEMPLATIVE CLIENTS

USE OF REFLECTIVE SKILLS TO CONVEY INTEREST, EMPATHY AND A NON-JUDGMENTAL ATTITUDE

The four reflective skills are *Attending*, *Paraphrasing*, *Reflection of Feeling* and *Summarizing*. These skills involve responses that reproduce what the client is conveying, without the counsellor adding any information. The major purposes are: a) to allow the counsellor to understand what the client says and means; b) to ensure that the counsellor understands the messages or information that the client provides; c) to encourage the client to express thoughts and feelings that allow the counsellor to respond in a manner that conveys empathy and begins the process of building rapport; d) to reinforce certain aspects of what a client has said, thereby provoking the client to express self-motivational statements; and e) to foster exploration – a nondefensive response to resistance.

UNCOVER CLIENT'S PERCEPTION OF THE REASON FOR THE INTERVIEW AND THEIR UNDERLYING FEELINGS

Clients typically come to the initial interview with expectations and apprehension. An individual in precontemplation is usually very angry and/or resistant, because they have been pressured to attend by a significant other or person in authority. Rather than attempting to convince the individual in precontemplation of the value of the interview and their need for "treatment," the counsellor will achieve significantly better results by eliciting the client's perception of the interview, and accepting their accompanying emotional response without judgment. The purpose is not to manipulate the client, but to convey the message that the client and counsellor will collaboratively decide what occurs in the interview.

AVOID NEGATIVE LABELLING

The traditional confrontational approach to counselling clients with substance abuse problems emphasized the importance of convincing clients that they were "alcoholic." The futility of this activity was recognized by Bill Wilson, the co-founder of Alcoholics Anonymous, who wrote "We do not like to pronounce any individual as alcoholic..." (Alcoholics Anonymous, 1976, p. 31). This statement appeared to reflect the failure of his early attempts to motivate individuals to stop drinking by convincing them that they were "alcoholic." The futility of labelling others prompted him to influence Alcoholics Anonymous to adopt a philosophy of self-recognition in which the individual must determine the personal suitability of the label.

Rollnick (1991) supports this perspective: "From the beginning, it is important to avoid labelling, confrontation and giving advice. Ultimately, the clients are the ones who decide what is best. The goal is to encourage them to explore their substance use and possible reasons for concern, taking care to proceed at the client's own pace" (p. 205). Two clinical researchers, van Bilsen and van Emst (1986), also found that labelling caused real damage to the therapeutic relationship: "Our experience was that we were often fighting against our clients instead of motivating them to change" (p. 707). Research has also confirmed that labelling a client (whether as an alcoholic or drug addict) does not positively contribute to the outcome of treatment.

ORIENT THE CLIENT

Orienting clients to the therapeutic process is extremely important in preventing the development of avoidable resistance. It's easier to engage clients when the counsellor flexibly employs communication skills that convey creativity, confidence, caring and consideration (Zunin, 1972).

Areas to be covered when orienting clients include:
1. defining the general nature and goals of the service being provided;
2. determining and responding to the emotional state of the client;
3. ascertaining the client's expectations of the treatment agency/counsellor, and dealing with any misconceptions;

4. explaining the roles and responsibilities of both the client and the counsellor;
5. discussing such issues as fees, office hours, availability of the service provider, frequency of appointments, and client's rights.

TIMELY FOCUS ON CONSUMPTIVE BEHAVIORS AND THEIR CONSEQUENCES

The primary goal of the initial interview is to provide an atmosphere that will motivate the client to explore their situation and take appropriate action. Recognizing the need to start "where the client is," at some point the clinician will need to broach the subject of substance use/abuse if the client does not raise the issue. This can be effectively accomplished through a technique known as "funnelling" (Brekke, 1987), which is used to introduce sensitive topics and minimize any potential resistance. Typically, this involves starting with a general definition of the topic area to be explored with a rationale for such enquiry; e.g., the counsellor needs a complete understanding of the client and his or her situation. This enquiry initially focuses on a nonjudgmental exploration of the client's use of substances. The strategies employed include the reflective skills of attending, paraphrasing, reflection of feeling and summarizing, plus open-ended questions. The counsellor then gradually moves to a more specific probing of problems related to substance abuse, emphasizing the exploration of desired vs. actual outcomes of the client's behaviors.

EXPLORE THE CLIENT'S RESISTANCE, CONSIDER ITS POSSIBLE CAUSES, AND FLOW WITH IT

Experienced and effective counsellors understand and accept resistance as a natural component of any attempt to change habitual behaviors. Clients in precontemplation tend to exhibit one or more of the following forms of resistance:

Reluctance
A precontemplative client who exhibits this form of resistance shows a lack of understanding of significant others' concerns and disapproval of his or her substance abuse. The reluctant client's response to such "interference" is an unemotional direct or indirect statement that he or she does not see the need to examine or change behavior that others view as problematic; they typically do not become angry or hostile when responding.

One way to overcome this form of resistance is to provide personal and meaningful feedback, ensuring that it is done in a sensitive, empathic manner. When this occurs, the client usually does not react immediately, but considers the feedback for some time before accepting or rejecting it. The counsellor's understanding and sensitivity make the client feel free to consider the counsellor's opinion without fear of losing freedom of choice. This approach gives the client an opportunity to carefully weigh the information provided by the counsellor and come to an informed decision regarding their substance abuse.

Rebellion

Clients who employ this form of resistance appear to be heavily invested in the problem behavior. They also want to make their own decisions (internal locus of control). They tend to be hostile and defiant toward individuals who believe they have a substance abuse problem.

Examining a variety of interpretations of the "problematic behavior" can be helpful in overcoming rebellion. It is also important to provide the rebellious client with a number of options when negotiating a course of action.

Resignation

Clients in the precontemplation stage who use this form of resistance appear to have low self-efficacy and seem to feel overwhelmed by their substance abuse. They feel hopeless, believing that they would have little chance of changing their consumption, even if it was in their best interest to do so.

Resignation can be highly contagious, causing the counsellor to join clients in feeling overwhelmed by the complexity of their substance use. However, to be effective, counsellors must resist this tendency and maintain objectivity. They must instil hope and find ways to spark the client's belief that he or she can overcome their problems.

Rationalization

Counsellors who are very effective in overcoming other forms of resistance may nevertheless find the client who uses rationalization particularly troublesome. Rationalizing clients continually dispute the perspective or suggestions presented by the counsellor. In response, the counsellor may feel the need to preserve his or her position of authority and may unwittingly engage in a "point-counterpoint" verbal battle – which no one wins.

To manage this form of resistance, the counsellor must recognize and work through unresolved issues related to authority figures and self-esteem. Secondly, the counsellor needs to maintain an empathic and reflective stance toward the client. The use of "amplified reflection" can be particularly helpful. This is where the counsellor reflects in an amplified or exaggerated way what the client has said about his or her use of substances (taking care not to be sarcastic or too extreme, as this would probably produce a negative response). By so doing, the counsellor can encourage clients to re-evaluate their perspective without becoming defensive.

CLARIFY DISCREPANCIES

Negative forms of confrontation by the counsellor – such as labels and direct attacks – make clients combative and defensive. A significantly more effective alternative is to use other more therapeutic forms of confrontation which Soden (1988) has described as "discrepancy clarification." Discrepancy clarification allows the counsellor to maintain a neutral and empathic stance toward clients who are struggling with contradictory beliefs, attitudes, thoughts, feelings and behaviors. It helps clients become more congruent and establishes the counsellor as a role model in using *direct*, *honest* and *open communication*.

The counsellor deliberately uses a question or compound statement to encourage the client to consider a discrepancy he or she has unknowingly presented. The types of discrepancies or contradictions focused on by the counsellor may include those:

1. Between how the client sees himself or herself and how others see him or her (e.g., sees self as outgoing but is seen by others as quiet and reserved);
2. Between what the client says and how he or she behaves. (e.g., the client says he or she is not sad but is talking slowly with head down and tears rolling down their cheeks)
3. Between two statements made by the client. (e.g., the client says that the really important thing for him or her is to be treated for substance abuse, but later on in the interview states that the priority is reuniting with their spouse); and,
4. Between what the client says he or she believes and how he or she acts. (e.g., the client says that he or she believes it is inappropriate to attend a counselling session under the influence of alcohol, but smells of alcohol at the interview).

Discrepancy clarification should never include accusations, evaluations, or solutions to the client's problems. This approach should only be used for the benefit of the client and not as a vehicle for the counsellor to vent his or her frustrations. Its major purpose is to aid and strengthen the therapeutic process.

The following are two examples of counsellor statements that demonstrate discrepancy clarification:

"You have stated that you have had nothing to drink today, but I smell something remarkably similar to alcohol, and you seem to be slurring your words. This is very confusing to me. Help me understand how this could be?"

"You say that you aren't a reliable person, but you also have told me how you keep your kids' clothes clean, make sure they always have their meals on time and that you pay all of your bills on their due dates. In addition, you're never late for an appointment, and when you have to cancel, you always call to let me know. I'm a bit confused. How could an unreliable person act so responsibly and reliably?"

Effective use of discrepancy clarification requires counsellors to adhere to the following guidelines:

    a) Use it sparingly and only after a sound therapeutic relationship has been developed in which the client feels safe and secure.

    b) Always give positive feedback to the client who is able to clear up a discrepancy.

    c) If the client denies the contradiction, *do not* push it but instead reflect the client's feelings about the intervention and suggest that he or she think about it.

    d) If the client seems confused or concerned about the counsellor's discrepancy clarification, reflect that feeling, and work with the client on the emotional level until he or she is able to move on.

MOTIVATIONAL INTERVIEWING OF CLIENTS IN CONTEMPLATION

Clients in the contemplation stage will either change their problematic behavior or their new awareness of the behavior so that they no longer see it as a problem. The direction of change the client will take is determined by their level of self-efficacy (Bandura, 1977). Therefore, the counsellor, in addition to exploring the client's ambivalence, also needs to understand and work to increase the client's self-efficacy. To do so, the counsellor will need to use clinical strategies that activate certain processes in the contemplator: processes that have been identified by Prochaska and DiClemente (1983). These processes are:

SELF RE-EVALUATION

This involves an assessment of one's beliefs and values, and the level of congruency between them and one's thoughts, emotions and behaviors. Additionally, it includes an evaluation of the potential of what one could be without abusing substances.

SELF LIBERATION

This process involves making choices that will lead to self-efficacy. The choices are the result of accurate information processing, followed by effective problem solving. This process moves the client to actively take steps to change their substance abuse.

MOTIVATIONAL STRATEGIES FOR CONTEMPLATIVE CLIENTS

Strategies and techniques helpful for clients in the precontemplation stage can also help clients in contemplation.

Provide the client with objective feedback using the results of a structured assessment protocol.

Although feedback vital to promoting change can be given in an informal manner, conducting a structured assessment and providing its results can help build motivation to change. A comprehensive assessment in the context of a "helping relationship" allows the counsellor to gather information essential to the development of an individualized treatment plan. Objective results enable counsellors to provide feedback that is not expressed simply as personal opinion, which the client could easily reject, but as nonjudgmental feedback that allows the counsellor to be seen as the client's ally. This individualized approach also conveys a clear message that the counsellor understands the client's unique situation, which in turn causes the client to carefully consider the assessment results.

COMPLETE A DECISIONAL MATRIX

One strategy that assists in understanding both sides of a client's ambivalence, and which activates the process of "self re-evaluation," is the "decisional matrix."[3] This involves examining the short- and long-term advantages and disadvantages of both changing and maintaining the status quo.

Figure 2
_____

DECISIONAL MATRIX SHEET

	+	-	+	-
Substance use/abuse				
Non-use/abuse of substance(s)				

Short Term   Long Term

There are many benefits to the use of the decisional matrix:

1. "It often leads clients to realize that they need to obtain more information about consequences that they had not thought about before" (Janis, 1982, p.175).
2. It typically increases the clients' awareness of the need for detailed plans for any eventuality.
3. It helps clients to consider and evaluate positive alternatives to substance abuse.
4. It promotes rational decision making as an alternative to impulsive action (Janis, 1982).

The counsellor can use this procedure in three major ways. First, they can give the client a sheet similar to Figure 2, give them instructions on how to complete it, and then ask the client "to re-examine each cell, this time trying to think of additional pros and cons that might be important to consider, including consequences that might not be highly probable but could happen... the counsellor suggests that the client focuses especially on categories that have few or no entries..." (Janis, 1982, p. 172). Another approach is to have a significant other work on the decisional matrix with the client. The counsellor can then help both parties supplement the information in each cell. Finally, the counsellor may ask questions that elicit information for the completion of the decisional matrix. This is especially important for clients who have limited reading or language ability. Regardless of the format used to complete the decisional matrix, the focus of the counsellor should always be on the positive and negative consequences of substance abuse as they pertain to the client's psychological, physical, social and spiritual dimensions.

In summary, the decisional matrix sheet "...can be used with motivational interviewing to penetrate...ambivalence, to clarify the competing motivational factors, and to encourage the person to consider the possibility of change" (Miller & Rollnick, 1991, p. 41).

NEGOTIATE SHORT-TERM BEHAVIOR CHANGE CONTRACTS

Not surprisingly, clients in contemplation are not willing to make long-term commitments to substance use goals, and typically withdraw from treatment if goals are imposed on them. Motivation for change can be increased, however, if the counsellor negotiates with clients goals that involve relatively small or brief changes with a high probability of success. By putting this in terms of a "personal experiment," it frees the client to take a risk, meet the challenge and, if unsuccessful, return to the counsellor to review the results of the experiment without feeling that he or she has failed.

MOTIVATIONAL STRATEGIES FOR CLIENTS IN ACTION

The action stage begins with a client discontinuing his or her substance abuse. Most clients in this stage usually experience some initial discomfort associated with the "unknown," but also have enough self-efficacy to motivate them to follow through with activities outlined in the treatment plan. They continue or remain in counselling to "...make a public commitment to action; to get some external confirmation of the plan; to seek support; to gain greater self-efficacy; and finally to create artificial, external monitors of their activity" (DiClemente, 1991, p. 199).

Counsellors should affirm positive changes made by these clients and encourage them to take responsibility for any modifications to their behavior and/or lifestyle.

> Offering information about successful models (other successful clients or self-help members) can also help, as long as the models have used a variety of action plans. The purpose of the models is not to offer a rigid prescription for change (which would run counter to motivational interviewing principles), but to engender a sense that success is possible for people like this client (DiClemente, 1991, p. 199).

In the action stage, the processes used are not only those activated in the previous stages, i.e., "consciousness raising," "self re-evaluation" and "self liberation," but also "reinforcement management," "counter-conditioning" and "stimulus control." (For a comprehensive explanation of these processes, the authors refer the reader to Prochaska and DiClemente, 1984.)

MOTIVATIONAL STRATEGIES FOR CLIENTS IN MAINTENANCE

In the maintenance stage,

> ...the individual must work the hardest to maintain the commitment to change over time. It is during this stage that the person will be faced with a plethora of temptations, stressors, and the pull of powerful old habit patterns.... There are two ways of thinking about this stage. One approach is to consider the maintenance stage as a period following initial treatment during which the effects of the treatment program gradually wear off over time.... Like a new coat of paint, treatment effects look good at first and only gradually begin to fade as time passes (Marlatt & Gordon, 1985, p. 22-24).

This stage can also be seen as an opportunity for new learning. "The individual engages in a series of 'learning trials' in which new ways of responding to old temptation situations are gradually acquired" (Marlatt & Gordon, 1985, p. 25). From a motivational perspective, this is the most useful way of understanding the maintenance stage. Seeing it as an opportunity for new learning suggests that – as with any other endeavor to acquire new skills – one will periodically make errors. This trial and error process can increase the client's coping skills, with the greatest number of mistakes occurring in the early phase of the maintenance stage.

> Analysis of the relapse process over time with various addictive behaviors... shows that stabilization of the relapse rate begins approximately 90 days after the initiation of abstinence. Prior to this time, relapse rates are high, particularly within the first month. Beginning in the fourth month, however, the probability of remaining abstinent throughout the course of the year stabilizes (Marlatt & Gordon, 1985, p. 25-26).

Some motivational strategies for sustaining change during the maintenance stage are as follows:

1. Provide objectivity at times of despair: help clients see beyond their dark moment to the overall progress that they have made and the unlimited potential of the future.
2. When the client suffers self-doubt and low self-esteem, remind the client how he or she coped with similarly difficult past situations.
3. Encourage clients to celebrate anniversaries related to significant turning points.
4. Discuss and normalize the reality of life's challenges and natural crises.
5. Affirm the client's increased self-efficacy whenever he or she is faced with the challenge of such events as a career change, family crisis, or financial problem.
6. Teach the client a conceptual model for understanding the relapse process and techniques for managing it. *(For more information on relapse prevention, see Chapter 9.)*

CONCLUSION

This chapter has focused on the principles, guidelines and strategies emerging from the perspective of motivation as a state of readiness that is influenced by internal and external factors, including the characteristics, attitudes and behaviors of the counsellor. This new understanding of motivation, as it applies to individuals experiencing problems related to substance use/abuse, has as its underpinnings the tenets of the Biopsychosocial Theory of Addictions and the Transtheoretical Model of Change.

The approaches outlined in this chapter, when used with warmth, acceptance, positive regard, concreteness and immediacy, maximize the counsellor's ability to help his or her clients. However, we also recognize the reality of using motivational interviewing strategies. As clinicians, we can be *responsible to* our clients but *not responsible for* what they do. Because, in the final analysis, it is the clients who ultimately choose to maintain or change their problematic behavior. We must not only accept this reality but, when working with clients who want to change, we must also respect and protect their *right* to freely choose the type and intensity of treatment that they believe will best meet their needs.

Throughout this chapter, our primary consideration has been the conceptual, perceptual, and executable knowledge and skills required to influence the intensity and direction of clients' motivation. However, our clinical skills alone are not sufficient. We need to be ever mindful of the importance of our beliefs, attitudes, feelings, and expectations, vis-à-vis our clients. These factors, as they apply to our clients' strengths, resources and problems, are crucial to developing and maintaining a therapeutic relationship that ultimately engages clients in a process with the highest probability of resulting in successful change.

FOOTNOTES

1. Withdrawal is defined as the pain and anxiety an addicted person experiences when he or she stops using alcohol or drugs. It is a biopsychosocial phenomenon. "Part of the pain (of withdrawal) is created by physical damage and the body's need for the addictive substance. Part of the pain is caused by a psychological reaction to losing the primary method of coping with life – the use of addictive drugs. Part of the pain is social, caused by the separation from an addiction-centered lifestyle" (Gorski, 1986). The duration of the pain created by the body's need for the addictive substance depends on the type of substance that one is withdrawing from and the amount of time that the body has become accustomed to having it (Chaudron, in Watt, Saunders, Chaudron & Soden, 1988).

2. The wheel depicted in Figure 1 is an adaptation of the original wheel outlined by Prochaska and DiClemente (1984).

3. The decisional matrix depicted in Figure 2 is an adaptation of Janis and Mann's (1977) original notion of the decisional balance.

REFERENCES

Alcoholics Anonymous (1976). <u>Alcoholics Anonymous: The Story of How Many Thousands of Men and Women Have Recovered from Alcoholism</u>, New York: Alcoholics Anonymous.

Alcoholism and Drug Addiction Research Foundation (1984, revised 1990). <u>Assessment Handbook.</u> Toronto.

Alterman, A.I., O'Brien, C.P., & McLellan, A.T. (1991). "Differential Therapeutics for Substance Abuse". In Richard J. Frances and Sheldon I. Miller (Eds.) <u>Clinical Textbook of Addictive Disorders</u>. New York: The Guilford Press.

Anderson, C.M., & Stewart. S. (1983). <u>Mastering Resistance: A Practical Guide to Family Therapy</u>. New York: Guilford Press.

Annis, H.M., & Davis, C.D. (1989). "Relapse Prevention". In Hester & Miller (Eds) <u>Handbook Of Alcoholism Treatment Approaches</u>. New York: Pergamon Press.

Bandura, A. (1977). Self-efficacy: Toward a unifying theory of behavioral change. <u>Psychological Review</u>, 84, 191-215.

Brekke, J.S. (1987). "Detecting wife and child abuse in clinical settings". <u>Social Casework: The Journal of Contemporary Social Work</u> (June 1987), 332-338.

Coady, N.F. (1991). "The association between client and therapist interpersonal processes and outcomes in psychodynamic psychotherapy". <u>Research on Social Work Practice</u>, Vol.1 No. 2 122-138.

Daley, D.C. (1989). <u>Relapse Prevention: Treatment Alternatives and Counselling Aids</u>. Blue Ridge Summit, PA.: Tab Books Inc.

DiClemente, C.C. (1991). "Motivational Interviewing and the Stages of Change". In W. R. Miller, & S. Rollnick (Eds.) <u>Motivational Interviewing: Preparing People to Change Addictive Behavior</u>. New York: The Guilford Press.

Donovan, D.M., & O'Leary, M.R. (1979). "Control orientation among alcoholics: A cognitive social learning perspective." <u>American Journal of Drug and Alcohol Abuse</u>, 6, 487-499.

Donovan, D.M., & Marlatt, G.A. (1988). <u>Assessment of Addictive Behaviors</u>. New York: The Guilford Press.

Finney, J.W., & Moos, R.H. (1979). "Treatment and outcome for empirical subtypes of alcoholic patients". Journal of Consulting and Clinical Psychology, 47, 25-38.

Finney, J.W., Moos, R.H., & Newborn, C.R. (1980). "Posttreatment experiences and treatment outcome of alcoholic patients six months and two years after hospitalization". Journal of Consulting and Clinical Psychology, 48, 17-29.

Finney, J.W., & Moos, R.H. (1986). "Matching Patients with Treatments: Conceptual and Methodological Issues". Journal of Studies on Alcohol, Vol. 47, No. 2.

French, J.R., & Raven, B. (1959). "The Bases of Social Power". In D. Cartwright (Ed.), Studies in Social Power. Ann Arbor: University of Michigan Press.

Gorski, T.T. (1986). Staying Sober. Independence Missouri: Independence Press.

Gross, W.R., & Adler, L.O. (1970). "Aspects of alcoholics' self-concepts as measured by the Tennessee Self-Concept Scale". Psychology Report 27: 431-434.

Haley, J. (1963). Strategies of Psychotherapy. New York: Grune & Stratton.

Haley, J. (1987). Problem-solving Therapy. San Francisco: Jossey-Bass.

Hester, R.K. & Miller, W.R. (1989). Handbook of Alcoholism Treatment Approaches: Effective Alternatives. New York: Pergamon Press.

Huselid R.F., Self E.A., & Gutierres S.E. (1991). "Predictors of Successful Completion of a Halfway-House Program for Chemically-Dependent Women". Am. J. Drug Alcohol Abuse, 17(1), pp. 89-101.

Janis, I.L., & Mann, L. (1977). Decision-making: A psychological analysis of conflict, choice, and commitment. New York: Free Press.

Janis, I.L. (1982). Short-term Counseling: Guidelines Based on Recent Research. New Haven: Yale University Press.

Johnson V., & Pandina R.J. (1991). "Effects of the Family Environment on Adolescent Substance Use, Delinquency, and Coping Styles". Am. J. Drug Alcohol, 17(1), pp.71-88.

Katz A., & Bender, E.I. (1976). The strength in us: Self-help groups in the modern world. New York: Franklin Watts.

Kennedy, E. (1977). <u>On Becoming A Counselor: A Basic Guide for Non-Professional Counselors</u>. New York: The Seabury Press.

Kissin, B., Platz, A., & Su, W.H. (1971). "Selective factors in treatment choice and outcome in alcoholics". In N.K. Mello & J.H. Mendelson (Eds.), <u>Recent Advances in Studies of Alcoholism</u> (pp. 781-802). Washington, D.C.: Government Printing Office.

Klein, A.F. (1974). <u>Effective Group Work: An Introduction to Principle and Method</u>. New York: Association Press.

LaClave, L.J., & Brack, G. (1989). "Reframing to Deal with Patient Resistance: Practical Application", <u>Am. Journal Of Psychotherapy</u>, Vol. XLIII, No. 1, January.

Lawson, D.M. (1986). "Strategic Directives with Resistant Clients". <u>American Mental Health Counsellors Association Journal</u>, 8: 87-93.

Leake, G.J., & King, A.S. (1977). "Effect of Counselor Expectations on Alcoholic Recovery". <u>Alcohol Health and Research World</u>, 11(3), 16-22.

Leigh G., Ogborne A.C., & Cleland P. (1984). "Factors Associated with Patient Dropout from an Outpatient Alcoholism Treatment Service". <u>Journal of Studies on Alcohol</u>, Vol. 45, No. 4, 1984.

Lewis J.A., Dana R.Q., & Blevins, G.A. (Eds.) (1988). <u>Substance Abuse Counselling: An Individualized Approach</u>. California: Brooks/Cole Publishing Company.

Lieberman, M.A., & Borman, L.D. (1979). <u>Self-help groups for coping with crisis: Origins, members, processes and impact.</u> San Francisco: Jossey-Bass.

Maddux, J. E., Stanley, M.A., & Manning, M.M. (1987). "Self-Efficacy Theory and Research: Applications in Clinical and Counseling Psychology". In J.E. Maddux, C.D. Stoltenberg, & R. Rosenwein (Eds.) <u>Social Processes In Clinical and Counseling Psychology</u>. New York: Springer-Verlag.

Marlatt, G.A., & Gordon, J R. (1985). <u>Relapse Prevention</u>. New York: The Guilford Press

McLellan, A.T., Woody, G.E., Luborsky, L., O'Brien, C.P., & Druley, K.A. (1983). "Increased Effectiveness of Substance Abuse Treatment: A prospective study of patient treatment matching". <u>Drug and Alcohol Dependence</u>, 5, 189-195.

McLellan, A.T., Woody, G.E., Luborsky, L., O'Brien, C.P., & Druley, K.A. (1983). "Increased Effectiveness of Substance Abuse Treatment: A prospective study of patient treatment matching". The Journal Of Nervous and Mental Disease. 171, 597-605.

Miller, W.R. (Ed.) (1980). The Addictive Behaviors: Treatment of Alcoholism, Drug Abuse, Smoking, and Obesity. New York: Pergamon Press.

Miller, W.R. (1983). "Motivational interviewing with problem drinkers". Behavioral Psychology, I, 147-172.

Miller, W.R. (1985). Living As If. Philadephia: Westminster Press.

Miller, W.R., & Jackson, K.A. (1985). Practical Psychology For Pastors. Englewood Cliffs: Prentice-Hall Inc.

Miller, W.R., & Hester, R.K. (1986). "Inpatient Alcoholism Treatment". American Psychologist. July, Vol. 41, No. 7, 794-805.

Miller, W.R., & Hester, R.K. (1986). Treating Addictive Behaviors: Processes of Change. New York: Plenum Press.

Miller, W.R., & Sovereign, R.G. (1989). "The Check-up: A model for early intervention in addictive behaviors". In T. Loberg, W.R. Miller, P.E. Nathan, & G.A. Marlatt (Eds.), Addictive Behaviors: Prevention and Early Intervention (pgs. 219-231). Amsterdam: Swets & Zeitlinger.

Miller, W.R., & Rollnick, S. (1991). Motivational Interviewing: Preparing People to Change Addictive Behavior. New York: The Guilford Press.

Milmoe, S., Rosenthal, R., Blane, H.T., Chafetz, M. E., & Wolf, I. (1967). "The docter's voice: Postdictor of successful referral of alcoholic patients". Journal of Abnormal Psychology, 72, 78-84.

Mowrer, O.H. (1971). "Peer groups and meditation, the best 'therapy' for professional and layman alike". Psychotherapy: Theory, Research, and Practice, 8, 44-54.

Munjack, D.J., & Oziel, R.J. (1978). "Resistance in the behavioral treatment of sexual dysfunction". Journal of Sex and Marital Therapy. 4, 122-138.

Murgatroyd, S. (1986). Counselling and Helping. London: A. Wheaton & Co. Ltd.

Norcross, J., & Prochaska, J. (1983). "Clinicians' theoretical orientations: Selection, utilization, and efficacy". Professional Psychology: Research and Practice, 14, 197-208.

Orford, J., & Edwards, G. (1977). Alcoholism: A comparison of treatment and advice, with a study of the influence of marriage. Oxford: Oxford University Press.

Patterson, G.R., & Forgatch, M.S. (1985). "Therapist behavior as a determinant for client noncompliance: A paradox for the behavior modifier". Journal of Consulting and Clinical Psychology, 53, 846-851.

Pattison, E.M., & Kaufman, E. (1982). Encyclopedic Handbook of Alcoholism. New York: Gardner Press.

Perez, J.F. (1989). Counselling The Alcoholic Group. New York: Gardner Press Inc.

Perls, F.S., Hefferline, R.E., & Goodman, P. (1951). Gestalt Therapy: Excitement and Growth in the Human Personality. New York: Dell Publishing Co. Inc.

Priestley, P., & McGuire, J. (1983). Learning To Help. New York: Tavistock Publications.

Prochaska, J.O., & DiClemente, C.C. (1983). "Stages and processes of self-change of smoking: Toward an integrative model of change". Journal of Consulting and Clinical Psychology, 51, 390-395.

Prochaska, J.O., & DiClemente, C.C. (1984). The Transtheoretical Approach: Crossing the Traditional Boundaries of Therapy. Homewood, IL: Dow Jones/Irwin.

Prochaska, J.O., & DiClemente, C.C. (1986). "Toward a comprehensive model of change". In W.E. Miller & N. Heather (Eds.), Treating Addictive Behaviors: Processes of Change. New York: Plenum Press.

Robinson, D. (1989). "Mutual Aid in the Change Process" in Hester & Miller, (Eds.) Handbook of Alcoholism Treatment Approaches: Effective Alternatives. New York: Pergamon Press.

Rogers, C.R. (1965). Client-Centered Therapy. Boston: Houghton Mifflin Co.

Rogers, C.R., & Stevens, B. (1967). Person to Person: The Problem of Being Human. Walnut Creek, Cal.: Real People Press.

Rogers, R.W., & Mewborn, C.R. (1976). "Fear appeals and attitude change: Effects of a threat's noxious, probability of occurrence, and the efficacy of coping responses". Journal of Personality and Social Psychology, 34, 54-61.

Rogers, R.L., & McMillin, C.S. (1989). The Healing Bond: Treating Addictions in Groups. New York: W.W. Norton & Company.

Rotter, J.B. (1966). "Generalized expectancies for internal versus external control of reinforcement". Psychological Monographs, 80, whole No. 609.

Schorer, C.G. (1965). "Defiance and Healing". Comprehensive Psychiatry, 6, 184-190.

Sissons, R.W., & Mallams, J.H. (1981). "The use of systematic encouragement and community access procedures to increase attendance at Alcoholics Anonymous and Al-Anon meetings". Am. J. of Drug and Alcohol Abuse, 8, 371-376.

Skinner, H.A. (1984). "Assessing Alcohol Use by Patients in Treatment" in Smart and others (Eds.) Research Advances In Alcohol And Drug Problems, Vol. 8, Toronto: Plenum Press.

Soden, T.E. (1987). "Counselling Communication Skills", Native Addiction Training, Toronto: Whitehead Publishing.

Soden, T.E., & Murray, R.D. (1989). Microcounselling Skills Useful in Counselling Substance Abusers. (Unpublished Manuscript) Toronto: Addiction Research Foundation.

Soden, T.E., & Murray, R.D. (1990). Motivational Strategies Useful in Counselling Substance Abusers. (Unpublished Manuscript) Toronto: Addiction Research Foundation.

Soden, T.E., & Finlay, R. (1990). Motivation and Change. Training Video Package. Toronto: Addiction Research Foundation.

Thomas, E., Polansky, N., & Kounin, J. (1955). "The expected behavior of a potentially helpful person". Human Relations, 8, 165-174.

Thompson, F. (1985). Alcoholism Counselling: A Collection of Quotes and Comments. New York: Vantage Press.

Truax, C.B., & Carkuff, R.R. (1967). Toward Effective Counselling and Psychotherapy: Training and Practice. Chicago: Aldine.

Truax, C.B., & Mitchell, K.M. (1971). "Research on certain therapist interpersonal skills in relation to process and outcome". In A.E. Bergin & S.L. Garfield (Eds.), Handbook of Psychotherapy and Behavior Change: An Empirical Analysis (pp. 299-344). New York: Wiley.

Turner, F.J. (Ed.) (1974). <u>Social Work Treatment: Interlocking Theoretical Approaches</u>. New York: The Free Press.

Valle, S.K. (1981). "Interpersonal Functioning of Alcoholism Counsellors and Treatment Outcome", <u>Journal of Studies On Alcoholism</u>, Vol. 4, pp. 783-790.

Vaillant, G.E. (1988). "What can follow-up teach us about relapse?", <u>British Journal of Addiction</u>, 83, 1147-1157.

van Bilsen, H.P.J.G., & van Emst, A.J. (1986). "Heroin addiction and motivational milieu therapy." <u>International Journal of the Addictions</u>, 21(6), 707-714.

Watzlawick, P., Weakland, J.H., & Fisch, R. (1974). <u>Change: Principles of Problem Formation and Problem Resolution</u>. New York: W. W. Norton.

Watt, W.L., Saunders, S.J., Chaudron, C.D., & Soden, T.E. (1988). <u>Detox In Ontario</u>. Toronto: Alcoholism and Drug Addiction Research Foundation.

Walchtel, P.L. (1982). <u>Resistance: Psychodynamic and Behavioral Approaches</u>. New York: Plenum Press.

Yalom, I.D. (2nd. Edition 1975). <u>The Theory And Practice Of Group Psychotherapy</u>. New York: Basic Books Inc.

Zunin, L.M. (1972). <u>Contact: The First Four Minutes</u>. Toronto: Ballantine Books.

Zimberg, S., Wallace, J., & Blume, S.B. (1978). <u>Practical Approaches to Alcoholism Psychotherapy</u>. New York: Plenum Press.

Assessment, Case Management and Treatment Planning

CHRISTINE BOIS AND KATHRYN GRAHAM

*P*eople who seek help for substance abuse problems are likely to have a complex array of problems requiring assistance in more than one area of their lives. They come from all walks of life and all types of social contexts. The impact of substance abuse on their lives is complex and pervasive. To ensure that each person is linked to the range of services needed to assist in long-term recovery requires a careful assessment of his or her strengths and problem areas, treatment planning and referral, and ongoing support. These functions are the main components of case management.

The case manager is someone who can initiate and maintain a process that can help substance abusers identify and access the right interventions at the right time. The assumption of case management is that most people with substance abuse problems can best be served by access to a range of resources, rather than by a single counsellor/case manager trying to provide direct help with all the person's problems.

Case management has been implemented in many ways with varied groups of people, especially those with long-term chronic illness and disabilities (Austin, 1983). The importance of case management in the addictions field appears to have been recognized first in Ontario. In 1978, the Task Force Report on Treatment Services for Alcoholics in Ontario identified eight functions describing case management activities to support people in recovery (Marshman, 1978). In 1985, The Ontario Ministry of Health released an Addictions Service Policy that included nine descriptive functions of case management. Recently, the need for and value of case management have been recognized by researchers in the U.S. (Willenbring, Ridgely, Stinchfield, & Rose, 1991), and the influential report of the U.S. Institute of Medicine (Institute of Medicine, 1990) has strongly endorsed the role of case management in addictions treatment.

However, the field is still defining case management, and its actual applications are likely to differ, depending on the type of program that delivers it (Graham & Birchmore Timney, 1990). A recent survey of addictions programs in Ontario found that most provide some form of case management, but in the context of intensive treatment for addictions, it tends to be directed more towards one-on-one counselling and less towards systems-level roles of case management, such as referral and advocacy (Birchmore Timney & Graham, 1989).

In order for case managers to understand the potential for case management and to use it for the maximum benefits of clients, its various functions need to be described clearly and in clinical terms. This chapter provides brief guidelines for the five functions of clinical case management that were adopted by the Joint Commission on the Accreditation of Hospitals (1976) and are now commonly used in the general mental health field. These functions are defined as they apply in the context of helping addicted persons: (1) *assessment*: determining an individual's strengths, weaknesses and needs; (2) *planning*: developing a specific service plan for individuals to access resources in the most effective way; (3) *linking*: helping individuals to obtain required services; (4) *monitoring*: ongoing evaluation of progress and providing support and other interventions as needed; and (5) *advocacy*: interceding on behalf of an individual to ensure access to needed resources.

GENERAL ASPECTS OF CASE MANAGEMENT

The goal of case management is to help a person obtain needed services in a co-ordinated and effective way. It is a process that is intended to empower clients to act on their own behalf. There are basic principles which govern the way in which case management is conducted. These principles include:

(1) *empowerment*: The case management process is based on the idea that the client is involved in identifying his or her own needs and is actively involved in all aspects of the process. In order to ensure that the client is actively involved, the case manager must be adept at negotiation: a fundamental process of mutual exploration that empowers the client, helping him or her develop the power and resources to function independently.

(2) *individualized*: Every assessment and every treatment plan is different because each client is unique, with his or her own strengths and needs. The supports and services that a client requires will vary over time in intensity and type.

(3) *dynamic*: The case manager must constantly re-evaluate the client's treatment plan as more information becomes available, as the client and his or her environment change. The case manager must be flexible to allow the process to be dynamic.

(4) *least intrusive*: A treatment plan that requires the least amount of structural change in a client's life will be easiest for the client. Treatment should improve rather than disrupt the client's life.

A number of issues pertain to the overall delivery of case management, such as the appropriate training and education for case managers, the use of professionals versus paraprofessionals to deliver case management, and the role of case managers as change agents in the overall treatment system. These topics will not be addressed in this chapter but have been discussed in detail elsewhere (Graham & Birchmore Timney, 1990; Willenbring et al., 1991). Skills needed by case managers will be discussed, however, since some skills are critical to the appropriate delivery of clinical case management. First, case managers need to have the essential counselling skills that will enable them to listen to clients and build empathic rapport. They also need a good working knowledge of the range of services that could address the client's needs most efficiently. Because case managers spend considerable time and effort linking with other agencies, they need credibility with other agencies, as well as the ability to negotiate and communicate with staff of other agencies in a positive and productive way. Finally, the intricate processes involved in identifying problems that need to be addressed and making the best and most efficient use of the system of care in addressing these problems, requires excellent problem-solving skills.

The functions of case management will be described separately and in order; however, circumstances rarely allow for these functions to be carried out in a simple, orderly way. Theoretically, the process begins with assessment, then treatment planning, then referral; however, the nature of the client's needs will affect the order of functions and how they will be combined. For example, a client who wants help for withdrawal after being put out of the house by his or her spouse might be given an immediate referral to a detox and to a legal clinic. In this example, two referrals would have been made before a comprehensive assessment was completed. Thus, the case management process must be flexible in addressing functions so that the client is linked to appropriate services at the appropriate time.

ASSESSMENT

Assessment is the foundation of case management. Without an accurate, comprehensive assessment, case management activities could be misdirected and waste the client's and case manager's time. The assessment process includes identifying and defining a person's major strengths and problems. Its primary goal is to obtain information in order to refer clients to appropriate addictions treatment. This information is also needed to link clients to non-addictions services that will contribute to their overall recovery. It is important to use a structured interview format because this guarantees that consistent and comprehensive information will be collected.

For many people who abuse alcohol or other drugs, the assessment process provides their first opportunity to gain insight and objective feedback about the chaos of their lives. Sometimes, the assessment process itself may be the only intervention that some clients will want or need. Similarly, although the primary goal of assessment is to refer clients to addictions treatment, some clients will refuse addictions-specific treatment but will accept referrals to non-addictions agencies to resolve life problems that have led to or resulted from substance abuse. Experience has shown that the assessment process involves more than just matching a client to addictions treatment. It is therefore important that the assessment be conducted in a way that is most useful to the client. To do so, the case manager should not only obtain information about the client's strengths and problem areas, but also reflect this information back to the client in terms that are clear and unambiguous. For example, a client charged with a drinking and driving offence can feel devastated, but it may put things into perspective to point out that he or she has maintained a good employment record and provided for his or her family.

The assessment process is an opportunity for a client to learn about the association between his or her problems and substance use. For example, sleep disturbances, digestive problems or other physical problems can be linked to alcohol use. Making these links can reassure the client that he or she is not crazy. The client can see his or her problems with some perspective, which gives the client a sense that the problems can be managed. This education process not only provides hope that helps to motivate the client – it also provides a more objective evaluation of problems and a clear direction for addressing them.

The Assessment Process

The assessment process begins in an informal way when the client and case manager first meet. The formal part begins with the case manager explaining to the client the functions and procedures of assessment. It is useful to tell the client that the assessment is intended to benefit him or her by yielding information upon which decisions can be based. The client needs to know the kind of information that will be collected – such as alcohol and drug use, and functioning in life areas such as accommodation, marital/family relations, social relations, friends, leisure, education/employment, emotional and physical health, finances, and previous treatment history. Examples of the questions should be given to the client so that he or she can decide whether to participate.

At this point, the role of the case manager in the assessment process should be explained to the client. This role includes helping the client assess his or her strengths and problem areas, providing information about the service system, and helping the client develop and follow through on a treatment plan. The client needs to know whether the case manager will provide the intensive phase of addictions treatment or whether he or she will link the client to another addictions program as well as any other needed services. It is useful to explain how long the assessment process usually takes and that at any time the client may choose not to continue. It is crucial to explain, before the assessment begins, the limits to confidentiality (court subpoenas, medical emergencies, child abuse) and the provisions concerning consent forms*. Any costs associated with the service should also be discussed.

Many clients will commit to proceeding with the assessment; others will require additional support. Some clients might need to explore their fears and expectations about their drug use, particularly their fears about treatment. Others may need referrals to stabilize their lives and to start developing a support network

---

For more details on confidentiality and consent issues, see Chapter 2.

before the assessment can begin.

As a support to the substance user, the case manager may meet with family members to explain the assessment process and to provide them with information on how to support the client. It may be appropriate for troubled family members to become clients themselves. In such instances, they would independently receive case management, including being assessed for problem areas in their lives and their coping methods. When assessing family members, their own drug use should be fully explored.

Selecting Assessment Instruments

A variety of assessment instruments are available to the case manager. These have been described in recent publications (Alcohol Health & Research World, 1991; Annis & Davis, 1991; Donovan & Marlatt, 1988; Graham et al., 1993; Lettieri, 1988; Lettieri, Nelson & Sayers, 1984; NIAAA, 1991; Skinner, 1981; Sobell, Sobell & Nirenberg, 1988; Sobell, Toneatto, Sobell & Shillingford, in press) and need not be discussed in this chapter. We will, however, describe some of the considerations relevant to selecting assessment instruments.

First, the case manager needs to be familiar with the instruments chosen so that the assessment process can proceed in an orderly but comfortable fashion. In determining which instruments to use and when to use them, the case manager should consider characteristics of the client, such as age, sex, types of drugs used, or ethnic background. The case manager must be attuned to sensitive areas for each client and begin the assessment at a point that is comfortable for the client. Female clients, particularly those who are older, may be sensitive to the stigma against female drug users. With some clients, it may be best to begin with questions on less sensitive life areas; questions related to alcohol/other drug use can be addressed later on. On the other hand, youth may be sensitive to family issues, and rapport should be established before discussing them.

In conclusion, people who present for assessment have a range of substance-related problems and a variety of attitudes about disclosing problems in various life areas. The case manager needs to be knowledgeable about the typical concerns of various populations, including the elderly, youth, women, men, family members, natives, and those who have dual disorders, in order to be alert to areas of the assessment that are likely to be problematic. This knowledge can help the case manager ensure that the assessment process meets the needs of each particular client.

TREATMENT PLANNING[1]

The assessment process identifies strengths and problem areas for each client. This information is used to plan appropriate goals and interventions to aid the client's recovery. The planning process also uses information regarding the client's preference and service availability to determine an overall plan for recovery.

Although changes in the plan may occur over time, it provides a concrete focus and contract for case management.

The essence of treatment planning is the negotiation between client and case manager regarding specific interventions to address identified problem areas and to develop a manageable plan. The art of negotiation involves the ability to hear what the client wants, is capable of undertaking, and will carry out. Every treatment plan is unique, as is every client. It is critical that all aspects of the plan be acceptable to the client. For example, the most appropriate service might be in a large urban area, but a client from an isolated rural area may have had little exposure to cities and might find this option frightening and unacceptable. Treatment planning involves the following stages: prioritizing problem areas; exploring options with the client for addressing problem areas; matching services to the client's specific needs; identifying potential barriers to using particular services; and preparing the client for what is to follow.

Prioritizing Problem Areas

The first step in treatment planning is to prioritize the identified problems. In the assessment process, the case manager assesses severity of problems as well as the client's strengths in various life areas. These are compared to the client's perceptions. Sometimes both parties have similar perceptions of problems and priorities. At other times, discrepancies emerge and need to be discussed in order to develop an appropriate and acceptable treatment plan. For example, the case manager and the client may have different perceptions of the extent to which alcohol is causing problems in the client's life. In this situation, the case manager will need to determine with the client whether he or she is ready to set goals regarding alcohol use. If not, the case manager may need to employ motivational counselling techniques. Each problem area needs to be defined in active terms with clear goals. For example, for the area of marital problems, the goal for treatment planning could be improving marital communication. The planning would then focus on specific actions to address this goal.

Matching Services to the Client's Needs

Once problems and goals have been prioritized through negotiation, the client and the case manager begin discussing options for addressing problem areas. The plan must clearly identify the responsibilities both of the client and the counsellor. All activities in the plan need to have a time frame. If a client has decided to seek marital counselling to improve communication, then a date should be set by which the client will have made an appointment with a marital therapist, and so on.

At the heart of treatment planning is the concept of matching. No single treatment is suitable or effective for all persons who experience alcohol or drug problems. Some need outpatient care; some need inpatient care. Some benefit from mutual-aid groups such as AA; some do not. In their review, the Institute of Medicine (1990) concluded that matching clients on the variables of demographic factors, psychiatric diagnoses, personality factors, severity of alcohol problems and antecedents to drinking can improve treatment outcome significantly.

Therefore, matching involves selecting the treatments or alternatives that are most suited to the client's need and will be most likely to result in a positive outcome. Matching is a complex process because there are a number of client variables to be considered, including the client's preferences. Moreover, the selection of treatment options will depend on the kinds of services that are available.

The first thing to consider is the severity of the alcohol or drug problem. All other things being equal, clients with more severe problems require more intensive treatment. For example, outpatient treatment is usually appropriate for clients with moderate levels of dependence, while those with severe dependence may require day treatment or even a residential program. Gearing treatment to the severity of the problem is consistent with the principle of providing the least intrusive assistance. For some clients, especially those at an early stage of problem use, no addictions-specific treatment may be necessary. In these cases, the process of clarifying problems through assessment and the support of the case manager may provide sufficient intervention for the client to resolve alcohol or drug problems.

Matching is also a consideration when referring to non-addiction agencies. These referrals require ensuring that the client fits with other clients of the agency and the styles of particular service providers.

The case manager must have detailed knowledge about the other addictions treatment services and community agencies to which they are making referrals. It is important that case managers share information about changes in the existing resources, their accessibility, change of staff and any improvement or deterioration in service. These factors help determine the best treatment plan.

Identifying Potential Barriers

Part of developing a treatment plan is to identify barriers to following through on particular aspects of the plan. For example, there are some obvious barriers to attending certain treatment programs, such as lack of transportation, insufficient money, or need for adequate child care. There are also other equally important but less obvious barriers. These include: the client's belief about addictions (e.g., those who drink sherry are not alcoholics) and the client's attitude towards accepting counselling (e.g., men should be able to handle their own problems). For non-addictions services, a negative attitude on the part of service providers towards individuals who have alcohol and drug problems may prevent these clients from receiving adequate services from that agency. As well, the philosophy and mandate of agencies can be barriers to those with substance abuse problems. For example, some agencies will not provide services to clients unless they have achieved abstinence.

In directing clients to particular agencies, the case manager must know more about the agency than just the nature of services offered. The case manager also needs to know how the client is likely to experience the agency and its services. There are other important factors in the client's life that influence decisions to enter treatment and these need to be identified in developing the treatment plan. For example, entering treatment may mean giving up a job or an apartment. Such risks need to be identified, and both the costs and benefits of potential treatment options considered. The process of treatment planning can be completed in one session or could take several sessions, depending on the client's situation.

Preparing the Client for Treatment

The final stage of negotiating the treatment plan is preparing the client for treatment. The case manager provides knowledge and support to the client in maintaining sobriety before treatment begins. The client has an opportunity to express his or her fears about treatment and to receive accurate information about what will occur in the various types of therapy. This is especially helpful for those entering residential treatment. They will need specific information about visiting hours, weekend leaves, contact with family, rules about smoking, and suggestions regarding the kinds of things the client needs to take (e.g., stamps, writing paper, money). Making an appointment to see the client following treatment will provide reassurance about the continuity of care.

LINKING

Linking is the process of referring or transferring individuals to required services in the formal and informal care-giving systems. The exact steps taken in each referral will be determined by the client's need for support and his or her capabilities and resources. For a client who has a strong support system, and the knowledge and skills to access resources directly, linking may be as simple as giving the client the name, phone number and address of an agency. On the other hand, a client in distress, who lives in temporary housing and has limited literacy skills, may need the case manager to phone the referral destination directly and arrange transportation there.

The referral process is also affected by the characteristics of the referral destination. The case manager needs to know which route (phone call, letter, referral form) will gain access for the client. It is also useful to know whether referrals should be made only to certain workers. Other considerations about linking have been discussed in the previous section on treatment planning.

An important skill in case management is the ability to communicate with the referral destinations to ensure successful service access for the client. This means being familiar with the information requirements of the various agencies that accept referrals. For individual referrals, the case manager must provide information about the specific needs of the client, especially regarding any sensitivities the client may have (e.g., a woman experiencing the social stigma associated with alcohol problems). This process helps ensure a good match between the client and the service provider.

ADVOCACY

Advocacy involves interceding on behalf of an individual to assure access to needed resources and support. The counsellor may need to advocate on behalf of a client both with treatment agencies and non-treatment persons involved in the client's life, including family members, employer, and so on. Co-ordination, a function that is closely associated with advocacy, brings together support and services to enhance the client's treatment plan. Simply put, when advocating for a client, the case manager is obtaining something (a direct service, practical help, information or support) that directly benefits the client. Co-ordination involves activities such as sharing information or negotiating agency roles, which indirectly benefit the client.

The need for these functions varies according to treatment factors and client characteristics. Most advocacy occurs during the assessment stage, whereas co-ordination tends to occur during all phases of case management. The case manager needs to develop a large network of contacts to advocate for clients; and to successfully intervene in the system, the case manager needs negotiating skills. The case conference is a useful activity that the case manager can use to either advocate or co-ordinate services for the client. When a number of agencies are involved, a case conference can be used to define each agency's role and to ensure that the client's essential needs are being met.

MONITORING

Monitoring requires ongoing evaluation and then action as required. The term "evaluation" is used in two fairly distinct contexts. One context involves clinical case-level evaluation. The other is the evaluation of the program itself. The present discussion will focus on case-level evaluation. Program-level evaluation is a distinct area of study and the reader is referred to other documents for a description of this type of evaluation (Commission on Accreditation of Rehabilitation Facilities, 1988; Ellis, Reed & Barnsley, 1990; Graham, 1985; Graham & Birchmore Timney, 1989; Hawkins & Nederhood, 1987; McDermott, Pyett & Hamilton, 1991; Ogborne & Gavin, 1990; Rush & Ogborne, 1991). Case evaluation and program evaluation are linked in that the former usually forms the information base for the latter. The focus of the present discussion, however, is on case evaluation as part of *clinical* case management.

Case evaluation in case management is the process of collecting and interpreting information in order to monitor three main areas: the client's status/progress, actions taken by the case manager, and the role of other agencies in the case management process. Monitoring in each area is done for a specific reason. The client's status is monitored in order to intervene as needed or change the treatment plan as appropriate. Actions taken by the case manager are monitored to ensure that systematic care is provided to the client and for the case manager to assess which strategies most successfully address particular goals. The role of other agencies is monitored in order to assess: (a) the appropriateness of initial referrals made by other agencies to the case manager, and (b) how well agencies to which the client is referred meet expectations. As the agency network is constantly changing, monitoring the role of other agencies helps ensure that other services are used appropriately.

CLIENT MONITORING

Client monitoring can be done in both a formal and informal way. Informally, monitoring occurs at every contact with the client. The case manager initially notes the client's state through observation: Does he or she appear healthy? sober? anxious? and so on. Every contact with the client would likely include some general monitoring questions (e.g., How are you? How have things been going?), as well as some more specific questions relating to general problem areas (e.g., Have things been better with your wife/husband?) and follow-up on areas where particular actions were planned since the last contact (e.g., You were planning on attending this or that program since I last saw you. Were you successful with your strategies for avoiding alcohol?).

Monitoring helps the client focus on achieving his or her goals, and the treatment plan should be central to the monitoring process. The case manager must be careful not to fall into the trap of allowing the focus to be on general aspects of the person's life, rather than on systematic plans for change. With the treatment plan as the central core for discussion, the client can keep on track, and there is less risk of discouragement. Part of monitoring includes checking whether the client has followed through on referrals, and whether services received were appropriate. At the same time, and with the client's permission, feedback concerning progress can be obtained from service providers.

Another important function of monitoring is to collect information for revising the treatment plan. The case manager constantly needs to review the plan with the client and change it as new information becomes available, as different problems arise, and as goals are achieved. It is also important for the client and case manager to monitor the client's use of substances and identify situations in which he or she is at high risk of relapse. This allows the case manager to intervene and to either provide relapse prevention therapy, if needed, or refer the client as appropriate. Encouraging the client to maintain a realistic perspective is an essential component of monitoring; the client can be reminded of the progress that he or she has made. The case manager, where appropriate, can enhance the client's support network by providing (with consent) information about the client's plan and need for support to family members, friends or employer.

While monitoring the treatment plan, crises might occur at any time. These might include medical emergencies, suicide attempts, drug overdoses, emotional crises, housing needs or financial crises. Monitoring helps ensure that the case manager is available to help the client obtain the services that she or he may need as soon as possible.

These examples serve to illustrate the extent to which client evaluation is an integral part of the case management process. How the information is documented, however, will determine how useful monitoring can be in identifying and responding to patterns within a case. Methods of documentation will be discussed in the next section on monitoring case management.

Formal case evaluation involves using more standardized approaches to monitoring. These are used when a more objective or quantitative assessment in a life area is desired. Such measures are often used as part of reassessment, where a client's status at discharge or follow-up is compared to his or her status at initial assessment. For example, if a client has not abstained from alcohol during case management, it may be useful to administer standardized measures of recent alcohol consumption and consequences in order to assess with some accuracy the extent to which the client has improved. Such measures can be useful in revising the treatment plan and in discharge planning. When used as part of follow-up, they can provide information about the success of case management for that client and provide feedback to the case manager on long-term outcomes. Tools for case evaluation are described in a recent document developed by a working group of researchers and clinicians (Graham et al., in press).

MONITORING CASE MANAGEMENT

Case management is unstructured and flexible, driven by the needs of the client, the characteristics of available services and, to some extent, the personality of the case manager. The case manager engages in a complex array of activities, and it is important to document and evaluate these on an ongoing basis. Monitoring can help the case manager identify the strategies he or she finds most successful in a number of areas, such as reducing the rate of no-shows, motivating clients to accept addictions counselling, enlisting family support, and so on. Monitoring and documenting the case management process provides a way of evaluating whether the treatment plan has been followed and where revisions were necessary. An example of a basic template for monitoring case management is found in Appendix A. Such a template provides a log of interventions and events for quick review of the case. The template can be expanded to include other information relevant to the goals and practices of particular programs. It also organizes information so that data can be easily extracted for program description and evaluation.

AGENCY MONITORING

It is in the use and co-ordination of other agencies that the case management function differs from that of the primary therapist. The case manager must not only have good counselling skills but also must have an up-to-date working knowledge of a wide range of available services (including addictions-specific programs, legal, marital, social services, and so on). The case manager must keep abreast of eligibility requirements, culture and success rates of particular programs. New programs become available; existing programs close or change their mandates. Case evaluation is one of the main ways to continuously update knowledge. The case manager records every interaction with other agencies as part of recording the case management process. In addition, part of follow-up evaluation with clients includes their experiences with the programs to which they were referred. This information can be used to update knowledge about particular programs. It can also be done more systematically by reviewing agency roles as part of closing case files. The case manager should keep files on other relevant agencies. When a case is closed, experiences (both positive and negative) with agencies involved should be added to the agency file. This might include such information as waiting lists, client satisfaction, the names of the best contact persons at the agency, and so on. Effective use of other services is a key component of case management, and monitoring the role of other agencies is the best way to ensure that this component is implemented well.

In summary, case management is a complex process that gives clients structured support to address their problems. It is done in such a way as to provide the client with the help that he or she wants, when it is wanted. There are standard functions to guide the case manager, but the process is different for every client since each individual is unique.

Case management will be successful when the case manager has the ability to establish good rapport, has knowledge about substance abuse and the treatment network, and has genuine concern about the client.

FOOTNOTES

1. For a discussion of the use of community resources in treatment planning, see Chapter 8.

REFERENCES

Alcohol Health & Research World. (1991). Volume 15. Linking alcoholism treatment research with clinical practice.

Annis, H.M., & Davis, C.C. (1991). Drug use by adolescents: Identification, assessment and intervention. Toronto, Ontario: Addiction Research Foundation.

Austin, C.D. (1983). Case management in long-term care: Options and opportunities. Health and Social Work, 8(1), 16-30.

Birchmore Timney, C., & Graham, K. (1989). A survey of case management practices in addictions programs. Alcoholism Treatment Quarterly, 6(3/4), 103-127.

Commission on Accreditation of Rehabilitation Facilities. (1988). Program evaluation in alcoholism and drug abuse treatment programs. Tuscon, Arizona: Commission on Accreditation of Rehabilitation Facilities.

Ellis, D., Reid, G., & Barnsley, J. (1990). Keeping on track. An evaluation guide for community groups. Vancouver, B.C.: Women's Research Centre.

Donovan, D.M., & Marlatt, G.A. (Eds.) (1988). The assessment of addictive behaviours. New York: Guilford Press.

Graham, K. (1985). Evaluating case management: Asking the right questions. (ARF Internal Document No. 66) Toronto, Ontario: Addiction Research Foundation.

Graham, K., & Birchmore Timney, C. (1989). The problem of replicability in program evaluation. The component solution using the example of case management. Education and Program Planning, 179-187.

Graham, K., & Birchmore Timney, C. (1990). Case management in addictions treatment. Journal of Substance Abuse Treatment, 7, 181-188.

Graham, K., Price, B., Brett, P., Baker, A., Bois, C., Boyle, B., Chapman, L., Eliany, M., Gaskin, J., Martin, G., Sobell, L., & Thompson, J. (1993). Client outcome measures for use in addictions treatment. A directory of alternatives. Toronto, Ontario: Addiction Research Foundation.

Hawkins, J.D., & Nederhood, B., (1987). Handbook for evaluating drug and alcohol prevention programs. Rockville, Maryland: Office for Substance Abuse Prevention.

Institute of Medicine. (1990). Broadening the base of treatment for alcohol problems. Washington, D.C.: National Academy Press.

Joint Commission on Accreditation of Hospitals. (1976). Principles for accreditation of community mental health service programs. Chicago, Illinois: Joint Commission on Accreditation of Hospitals.

Lettieri, D.J. (Ed.) (1988). Research strategies in alcoholism treatment assessment. New York: Haworth Press.

Lettieri, D.J., Nelson, J.E., & Sayers, M.A. (1984). Alcoholism treatment assessment research instruments. NIAAA treatment handbook series. Rockville, Maryland: NIAAA.

McDermott, F., Pyett, P., & Hamilton, M. (1991). Evaluate yourself. A handbook for alcohol and other drug treatment agencies. Melborne, Australia.

Marshman, J.A. (1978). The treatment of alcoholics: An Ontario perspective. The report of the Task Force on Treatment Services for Alcoholics. (Prepared for the President, Addiction Research Foundation.) Toronto, Ontario: Addiction Research Foundation.

National Conference on Social Welfare. Case Management: State of the art. Final Report, Grant No. 54-P-71542/3-01, submitted to the Administration on Developmental Disabilities, U.S. Department of Health and Human Services, Washington, D.C., 1981.

NIAAA (National Institute on Alcohol Abuse and Alcoholism). (1991). Assessing alcoholism. Alcohol Alert, 12, 1-4.

Ogborne, A.C., & Gavin, M.T. (1990). Quality assurance in substance abuse treatment: Guidelines for practitioners. Toronto, Ontario: Addiction Research Foundation.

Ontario Ministry of Health. (1985). Addiction services policy. Toronto: Ministry of Health.

Rush, B. & Ogborne, A. (1991). Program logic models: Expanding their role and structure for program planning and evaluation. The Canadian Journal of Program Evaluation, 6, 93-105.

Skinner, H.A. (1981). Assessment of alcohol problems. Basic principles, critical issues, and future trends. In Y. Israel, F.B. Glaser, H. Kalant, R.R. Popham, W. Schmidt, & R.G. Smart (Eds.), Research advances in alcohol and drug problems, Vol. 6, (pp. 319-369). New York: Plenum Press.

Sobell, L.C., Sobell, M.B., & Nirenberg, T.D. (1988). Behavioral assessment and treatment planning with alcohol and drug abusers: A review with an emphasis on clinical application. Clinical Psychology Review, 8, 19-54.

Sobell, L.C., Toneatto, T., Sobell, M.B., & Shillingford, J.A. (in press). Alcohol problems: Diagnostic interviewing. In M. Hersen & S.M. Turner (Eds.), Diagnostic interviewing (2nd ed.). New York: Plenum Press.

Willenbring, M.L., Ridgely, M.S., Stinchfield, R., & Rose, M. (1991). Application of case management in alcohol and drug dependence: Matching techniques and populations. Rockville, Maryland: U.S. Department of Health and Human Services.

Client I.D. _____

Case Manager _____

APPENDIX A.

BASIC TEMPLATE FOR MONITORING CASE MANAGEMENT

Date	Location of contact 1. office 2. other (specify)	Duration of contact	Type of contact 1. in person 2. telephone 3. written 4. other (specify)	People involved in contact 1. client 2. other (specify)	Main areas addressed (and other info about the client's status)	Future plans

Physical Effects of Alcohol and Other Drugs

MELDON KAHAN

*A*lcohol and drug counsellors can play an important role in maintaining their clients' physical health. They are frequently called upon to explain the health risks of alcohol and drugs, and to inform clients of ways to minimize these risks. They often communicate with the client's family physician and other health care providers. They may be the first professionals to become aware of signs and symptoms of impending illness in a client. For these reasons, therapists need to be familiar with the physical effects of alcohol and drugs. This chapter presents a brief summary of the health effects of the main drugs of abuse.

ALCOHOL

Alcohol is a major cause of sickness and death in our society, outweighing the combined effects of all other drugs of abuse except tobacco. Following is a discussion of some common alcohol-related problems.

Gastritis

Gastritis is a common complication of heavy alcohol consumption. Alcohol causes irritation and erosion of the lining of the stomach, producing discomfort and pain in the upper abdominal area. Gastritis is potentially serious, because it can result in internal bleeding, the symptoms of which are bloody or dark-brown vomit, and bloody or black, tarry stools. Gastritis often heals quickly with abstinence. A wide variety of medications promote healing by reducing the production of acid in the stomach.

Alcohol also causes inflammation in the esophagus (esophagitis) and pancreas (pancreatitis). Symptoms of esophagitis include heartburn and vomiting. Pancreatitis causes severe abdominal pain and vomiting, often requiring hospitalization.

Alcoholic Liver Disease

Alcoholic liver disease occurs in three stages. The first is called "fatty liver," in which the liver accumulates fat and becomes enlarged. This stage is usually asymptomatic. The second stage is alcoholic hepatitis, or inflammation of the liver. This stage may be asymptomatic, but sometimes patients become seriously ill. They may develop jaundice, the signs of which are yellow skin, dark urine and whitish stools. They may also develop vomiting, fever, and pain in the liver area (right upper abdomen below the ribs).

Repeated episodes of alcoholic hepatitis lead to the third stage, cirrhosis, which is a major cause of death in Canada. In cirrhosis, large portions of the liver have died and been replaced by scar tissue. This may render the liver incapable of fully metabolizing dietary proteins, creating the buildup of intermediate chemicals that are toxic to the brain. This can lead to a condition called hepatic encephalopathy, in which patients become drowsy and forgetful, and eventually sink into a coma and die. Encephalopathy can be treated with a low protein diet and laxatives such as lactulose.

Cirrhosis also causes death through internal bleeding. Blood normally flows from the intestines into the portal vein, and from there into the liver. The scar tissue in the cirrhotic liver impedes the flow of blood in the portal vein, causing it to back up into veins in the esophagus. These veins then become swollen and engorged, a condition called "esophageal varices." Varices sometimes burst, causing profuse and often fatal bleeding. Ascites, a condition in which the abdomen fills with fluid and becomes protruberent, is also due in part to obstructed blood flow.

Clients with alcoholic liver disease should be told that fatty liver and alcoholic hepatitis are reversible with abstinence or reduced drinking; the liver has a tremendous capacity to heal itself. While cirrhosis is not reversible, clients often lead normal lives as long as they abstain completely from alcohol. Reduced drinking strategies are not recommended for patients with cirrhosis, since even moderate alcohol consumption may promote liver damage.

Trauma

Alcohol consumption is a major cause of trauma-related death and injury, including fatal motor vehicle accidents, work-related injuries, and violence (assaults and suicide).

Dementia*

Heavy drinking is associated with a number of neurological disorders. One common and serious disorder is dementia, defined as a global decrease in cognitive functioning. Alcoholic dementia differs from the most common form of dementia, Alzheimer's Disease, in that it is potentially reversible with abstinence (although only some recover, and recovery may only be partial). The cognitive changes of alcoholic dementia may be subtle, such as decreased ability to think abstractly. Counsellors who suspect dementia should refer the patient to a neurologist or psychologist for neuropsychological testing and possibly a brain (CT) scan. Patients should be advised of the diagnosis, and of the potential for recovery with abstinence.

---

*For more details on the cognitive effects of alcohol, see Chapter 5.

Cerebellar Disease

Alcohol can damage the cerebellum, a part of the brain that controls balance and equilibrium. Patients with cerebellar disease have tremors of the hands and walk with a wide-based gait, as if they were on a moving ship; sometimes they are unable to maintain their balance without a cane or walker.

Peripheral Neuropathy

Alcohol may damage the nerves in the feet and legs, causing a condition known as peripheral neuropathy. Patients with this syndrome have decreased sensation in their feet, and may experience painful burning sensations.

Wernicke-Korsakoff Syndrome

Heavy drinkers often eat poorly, and the metabolism of alcohol depletes the body's stores of the B vitamins. This can lead to a severe deficiency of vitamin B1 (thiamine), causing Wernicke-Korsakoff Syndrome. In the Wernicke's phase of this syndrome, patients become drowsy and unresponsive, and their walking and eye movements become unco-ordinated. Wernicke's is a medical emergency, requiring prompt administration of intravenous thiamine. If not treated in time, patients develop Korsakoff's, exhibiting marked impairment of short-term memory. Patients with Korsakoff's may not remember an event that occurred ten minutes earlier; to mask their confusion and make sense of their lives, they sometimes fabricate events ("confabulation"). Patients with Korsakoff's rarely recover, and frequently require institutionalization.

Blackouts

A blackout is a type of amnesia in which patients are unable to remember events that took place during the previous evening's drinking binge. Patients may on occasion behave in a bizarre or dangerous manner during a blackout.

Alcohol Withdrawal

Alcohol withdrawal can follow extended periods of heavy daily drinking. It begins 12 to 48 hours after the patient's last drink, and persists for up to seven days. Symptoms include tremor, sweating, fast pulse, high blood pressure, vomiting, and anxiety. Grand mal seizures are not uncommon. Other complications include irregular heartbeat, hallucinations, and delirium tremens (the DTs). Patients with delirium tremens become confused and disoriented, and may die of cardiovascular collapse.

Alcohol withdrawal is effectively treated by providing a calm, supportive environment and, if necessary, judicious use of benzodiazepines. Twenty milligrams of diazepam, administered orally every hour until symptoms subside, is the preferred drug treatment because it provides quick relief of symptoms, and it circumvents the need for take-home prescriptions of benzodiazepines.

Reproductive Effects

Cirrhosis of the liver causes a relative excess of estrogens in men, resulting in impotence, small testicles and breast enlargement (testicular feminization syndrome). Alcohol can cause irregular menstrual cycles in women, and infertility in both men and women.

Heavy drinking during pregnancy may result in Fetal Alcohol Syndrome, the features of which are delayed growth, cognitive impairment, and facial abnormalities such as short eye openings. FAS children have cognitive-behavioral problems such as hyperactivity, speech disorders and deficits in learning and memory. These problems persist into adolescence and adulthood. FAS is thought to be the leading preventable cause of mental retardation.

Not all children exhibit the full syndrome; some have only subtle cognitive deficits with no facial abnormalities, a condition known as Fetal Alcohol Effects, or FAE.

A safe level of alcohol consumption during pregnancy has not been established, and abstinence is the most prudent recommendation.

Cardiovascular Effects

Heavy drinkers are at risk of high blood pressure, stroke and irregular heart rhythms. Moderate drinkers may have a lower risk for heart attacks than non-drinkers, perhaps because alcohol has beneficial effects on cholesterol.

Psychiatric Effects

Heavy alcohol consumption can induce severe depression. Alcohol-induced depression usually resolves within two to four weeks of abstinence, distinguishing it from a primary affective disorder. Heavy drinkers are at substantially greater risk for suicide than the general population, partly because of alcohol-induced depression, and partly because of the impulsivity and emotional volatility associated with acute intoxication.

Safe Limits

A safe upper limit of alcohol consumption has not yet been firmly established, partly because of the widely varying effects of alcohol on the body; what may be safe for the heart may not be safe for the liver. Most recommendations set an upper limit of two to three standard drinks per day, and 12 to 14 drinks per week. Some recommendations suggest lower limits for women, because they are more prone to develop alcoholic liver disease than men. Other recommendations advise at least two days of abstinence per week, to give the liver a chance to recuperate and to diminish the strength of the drinking habit.

Effects of Alcohol on Blood Tests

Therapists are sometimes asked by their clients to interpret the results of blood tests taken by an alcohol treatment facility. One common abnormality in test results is an elevated level of gamma-glutamyl transferase (GGT), a liver enzyme. The liver increases production of this enzyme in response to heavy drinking. Also, liver cells damaged through alcoholic hepatitis become "leaky," allowing greater quantities of the enzyme to escape into the bloodstream. With abstinence or reduced drinking, GGT usually returns to normal within two to four weeks.

Alcohol causes red blood cells to increase in size, as measured by a test called mean cell volume (MCV). MCV returns to normal within one to two months of abstinence or reduced drinking.

Blood tests such as GGT and MCV are not as sensitive as a clinical interview in detecting alcohol problems. However, periodic tests can be used to confirm clients' self-reports of reduced alcohol intake.

Pharmacological Treatment of Alcohol Dependence

Disulfiram (Antabuse) and calcium carbamide (Temposil) act by inhibiting a liver enzyme that metabolizes alcohol, causing the build-up of a toxic metabolite called acetaldehyde. Patients who drink while on these drugs experience chest pain, headache, flushed face, vomiting, and an irregular heartbeat. The reaction is potentially fatal, because the blood pressure can drop precipitously and the heart can go into a dangerous rhythm. The patient should be instructed not to drink for at least seven days after taking Antabuse, and two days after taking Temposil.

Despite the fact that Antabuse has been available for many years, there is little convincing evidence that these drugs are effective in maintaining abstinence, and they should never be viewed as the sole treatment for alcohol dependence. They may be a useful treatment adjunct in patients who are motivated enough to take the medication every day, but do not feel confident in their ability to resist spontaneous impulses to drink. Temposil, which has a quicker onset of action than does Antabuse, has also been used in relapse prevention programs designed to increase patient self-efficacy; patients can use Temposil for short periods (a few days) when they expect to encounter high risk drinking situations.

Other medications that may prove useful in the future are the serotonin reuptake inhibitors such as fluoxetine (Prozac), and the opiate antagonist Naltrexone. These medications appear to decrease craving for alcohol and to lessen the severity of binge drinking.

OPIATES ("NARCOTICS")

Opiates act on receptors in brain cells to create a sense of euphoria and tranquility. Tolerance builds up quickly; chronic heroin users often report that the drug no longer gets them "high" but merely staves off withdrawal symptoms. Commonly abused oral opiates include oxycodone (contained in Percocet and Percodan), codeine (Tylenol 3), hydrocodone (cough syrups such as Tussionex and Hycodan), hydromorphone (Dilaudid), and morphine. Injectable opiates include morphine, meperidine (Demerol), and heroin.

Overdose

Opiates suppress the centres in the brain that control respiration and heartbeat, with potentially fatal results. Heroin users are at particular risk, because the purity of street heroin can vary widely.

Withdrawal

Opiate withdrawal is somewhat similar to a bad case of the flu. Patients experience sweating, muscle aches, runny nose and runny eyes, goose bumps, chills and nausea. Patients in opiate withdrawal are restless and uncomfortable, and they have strong cravings for opiates. Withdrawal peaks at two to three days after the last drug use, and resolves by five to seven days.

Opiate withdrawal is generally safe, and complications such as seizures do not occur. A major exception is withdrawal during pregnancy (see below). Opiate withdrawal can be treated over one to two weeks with tapering doses of methadone or with clonidine, a non-narcotic drug that blocks the nervous impulses in the brain that cause withdrawal symptoms. Treating withdrawal with opiates other than methadone should only be done if the risk of double-doctoring is remote, or if the patient is in a carefully supervised inpatient setting.

Methadone Maintenance

Methadone is a long-acting oral narcotic closely regulated by the Bureau of Dangerous Drugs. Patients in methadone maintenance programs drink a methadone solution daily in the presence of a nurse or pharmacist. They are required to provide regular supervised urine samples for drug testing, and to attend regular outpatient counselling sessions. Methadone maintenance programs have been convincingly shown to be the most effective treatment modality for chronic heroin addicts.

Reproductive Effects

Pregnant women addicted to heroin have a high infant mortality rate, due to delayed growth of the fetus and to premature labor. Opiate withdrawal during pregnancy can induce uterine contractions, causing miscarriage in the first trimester or premature labor during the third trimester.

To avoid these risks, pregnant women addicted to opiates should, as a rule, be offered methadone maintenance. Heroin-dependent women on methadone have better prenatal care, improved nutrition and substantially lower infant mortality rates than those not on methadone. However, they have higher infant mortality rates than women not using any drugs. Methadone crosses the placenta, and may inhibit the growth of the fetus.

Infants born to mothers using heroin or methadone may develop prolonged and severe withdrawal, often requiring several weeks of hospitalization. Seizures can occur during infant withdrawal.

COCAINE

Cocaine causes a rapid buildup of neurotransmitters in the brain to produce an intense euphoria and stimulation of the heart and nervous system. The euphoria usually lasts no more than 20 minutes, but the effects on the heart and nervous system last for hours. With time, the neurotransmitters become imbalanced, so that a chronic cocaine user may experience agitation and paranoia rather than euphoria following use.

Cocaine can be injected into the vein, smoked (in the form of "crack," a rock made by mixing cocaine with baking soda), or inhaled through the nose ("snorting"). The latter method irritates the lining of the nose and creates a milder euphoria than injecting or smoking, so heavy users tend inject or smoke the drug.

Withdrawal

Cocaine withdrawal occurs in three phases. The first phase is the "crash," in which patients who have completed a binge of cocaine sleep deeply for one to two days. This is followed by one or more weeks of intense cravings for cocaine, depression, insomnia with nightmares, and feelings of emptiness and irritability. Following this is the "extinction" phase, in which patients experience episodic cravings for cocaine that gradually diminish in intensity and frequency over a period of months. Whether these phases represent a true physiological withdrawal remains controversial.

Overdose

Cocaine overdose produces seizures, severe hypertension and rapid heartbeat, fever and delirium, and eventually coma and death.

Cardiovascular Effects

Cocaine can trigger a marked rise in blood pressure, a rapid and irregular heartbeat, and spasms of the blood vessels in the body. This can result in strokes, brain hemorrhages, heart attacks, and ruptured aneurysms. While patients with underlying hypertension or heart disease are at greatest risk for these dangerous complications, they have been reported to occur even in young healthy adults taking small doses of cocaine.

Reproductive Effects

Cocaine taken during pregnancy can cause separation of the placenta from the uterus, resulting in severe maternal hemorrhage and fetal death. Cocaine can also trigger premature labor. Regular use of cocaine during pregnancy may cause delayed growth of the fetus, due to poor blood supply through the placenta. Some studies suggest that cocaine causes birth defects of the kidneys. Infants born to heavy cocaine users tend to be irritable and to show impaired neurological and behavioral patterns such as disorganized response to environmental stimuli. The long-term significance of this is uncertain.

Other Physical Effects

Grand mal seizures are very common among cocaine users. Typically they occur within minutes of use, and last no more than one to two minutes. Like other stimulants, cocaine suppresses the appetite, leading to marked weight loss.

Psychiatric Effects

Cocaine can have profound psychiatric effects. Patients acutely intoxicated on cocaine display a wide variety of psychiatric symptoms, including delusions, paranoia, hallucinations (especially tactile), delirium, and severe anxiety. Paranoid delusional disorders and other types of psychoses have been linked with chronic cocaine use; they may persist for months after the cocaine use has ceased, and antipsychotic medication is often required. Cocaine can induce a severe depression, and heavy users are at high risk of suicide.

Stimulants other than cocaine, such as amphetamines, may result in similar problems. They differ mainly in the duration of intoxication: while a cocaine "high" typically lasts less than half an hour, amphetamine intoxication may persist for hours.

BENZODIAZEPINES

Benzodiazepines are among the most commonly prescribed of all drugs. Their main action is to diminish anxiety and induce sleep, but they are also used to treat alcohol withdrawal and prevent certain types of seizures. Patients do not necessarily develop tolerance to the anxiety-reducing or sleep-inducing effects of benzodiazepines.

A number of benzodiazepines are available on the market. They differ in their duration of action; for example, diazepam (Valium) and chlordiazepoxide (Librium) are long-acting, and triazolam (Halcion) and alprazolam (Xanax) are short-acting. They also differ in their dependence liability, that is, their ability to induce a pleasant euphoria that could tempt some patients to abuse them. Diazepam, triazolam, alprazolam and lorazepam (Ativan), for example, have higher dependence liabilities than oxazepam (Serax) or chlordiazepoxide.

Overdose

Benzodiazepines are relatively safe drugs, with little risk of lethal overdose, unless used in combination with other psychoactive drugs such as alcohol.

Withdrawal

Patients who abruptly stop their use of benzodiazepines are at risk for serious withdrawal if they have been using large amounts daily for prolonged periods (50 mg or more of diazepam, or the equivalent dose of another benzodiazepine, for more than one month). Seizures, confusion and hallucinations can occur.

Patients who suddenly stop taking therapeutic doses of benzodiazepines (30 mg or less of diazepam, or the equivalent dose of another benzodiazepine) tend to experience two groups of symptoms: Anxiety-related symptoms (emotional volatility, insomnia, irritability, poor concentration, panic attacks); and subtle neurological symptoms (mild visual distortions, or distortion of visual and auditory stimuli; blurry vision, unsteadiness of gait, déjà vu sensations). Serious complications of withdrawal, such as seizures, generally do not occur in patients stopping therapeutic doses. Nonetheless, withdrawal can be intensely uncomfortable, and may last weeks or months.

Because of its long duration of action, diazepam is the drug of choice in treating withdrawal. The patient should be given diazepam in a dose equivalent to that of their previous benzodiazepine, and this dose should be tapered slowly over a period of weeks or months (a maximum rate of 5 mg per week is suggested).

Many alcohol and drug programs and counsellors insist on total abstinence from benzodiazepines for all patients, even if they are not abusing them. This inflexible approach is not supported by the scientific literature and is potentially harmful to the patient. Because therapeutic doses of benzodiazepines do not generally result in severe social disruption or physical harm, and because withdrawal can be prolonged and difficult, the decision to withdraw a patient should be made only after a careful assessment of the risks and benefits (including psychiatric assessment if necessary). A program of therapeutic support must be in place before tapering is attempted.

Rebound Insomnia

Benzodiazepines suppress the deep and the rapid eye movement stages of the sleep cycle. When withdrawn suddenly, patients experience a fitful sleep interrupted by vivid dreams. This may take several weeks to resolve.

Other Effects

Benzodiazepine use increases the risk of motor vehicle accidents, and can cause falls and confusion in the elderly.

Psychiatric Effects

Benzodiazepines can contribute to depression, particularly in patients taking large doses and in patients with a pre-existing major affective disorder. Benzodiazepines can have a disinhibiting effect on patients with psychosis and with certain underlying personality disorders.

Patients who taper off benzodiazepines sometimes report feeling more alive, energetic, and clear-thinking. They may be more able to make important life decisions, and may benefit more from psychotherapy.

Sedative-Hypnotics

Sedative-hypnotics such as Placidyl, Noludar and Seconal have been largely replaced by benzodiazepines, although Fiorinal, a drug used to treat headaches, remains a common drug of abuse. Fiorinal is a combination of ASA, codeine, and a barbiturate known as butalbital.

Patients who abruptly stop high doses of sedative hypnotics occasionally develop a dangerous and potentially fatal withdrawal, with seizures, delirium, psychosis, and cardiovascular collapse. Chronic abusers of sedative-hypnotics should be advised not to discontinue them abruptly until they have been assessed by a physician knowledgeable in the management of withdrawal.

Sedative-hypnotics can also induce depression, and overdoses with these drugs are frequently fatal.

CANNABIS

Chronic daily users of cannabis often use the drug not for its mild hallucinogenic effects but for relief of anxiety, anger or boredom. Patients who suddenly stop cannabis use after taking high doses for long periods of time may experience a mild withdrawal consisting of one to two days of nausea, tremor, anxiety, and sleep disorders. Chronic users may miss its mood-stabilizing effect and experience anxiety and emotional volatility after stopping use.

Cannabis intoxication can trigger severe anxiety and rapid heartbeat. As with cocaine and hallucinogens, cannabis can induce psychosis.

HALLUCINOGENS

Hallucinogenic drugs such as LSD and "magic mushrooms" can cause a psychotic reaction that usually resolves once the drug has worn off, but may persist for months after use. Some users also experience "bad trips," during which they may be subject to extreme panic and other unpleasant sensations.

In the weeks and months after stopping use, a small percentage of users may experience "flashbacks," where they briefly relive past episodes of drug use. Though vivid and disturbing, flashbacks tend to last only minutes, and diminish in frequency and intensity over time.

RISK REDUCTION

Risk reduction is defined as the attempt to reduce serious risks to health in clients through strategies such as health education, immunization and screening. With the advent of HIV infection, risk reduction strategies should be viewed as an essential component of any alcohol and drug rehabilitation program.

Human Immunodeficiency Virus (HIV)*

The major risks of needle sharing are HIV and hepatitis B and C. Estimates of the prevalence of HIV among injection drug users in Canada vary between one and four per cent, considerably lower than in the United States and Western Europe. Counsellors have a responsibility to inform their clients about the risks of needle sharing and ways to reduce them. Myths are still common in the drug-using population; for example, while most clients are aware of the association between needle sharing and AIDS, some still think it is safe to share needles with sexual partners or close friends.

Clients should be informed about needle exchange programs in their area, and instructed on how to clean needles using household bleach (fill the syringe with bleach twice, then fill with water two or more times). Clients should be reassured that bleach will not enter their veins if this procedure is followed.

Some therapists express concern that giving such advice encourages or condones drug use. However the message to the patient is similar in intent to that given routinely to alcoholics: Don't drink, but if you do, make sure you don't drive.

Injection drug users should be tested for HIV, with their consent and only after receiving pre-test counselling. Although not curative, medication has been shown to prolong life and delay the onset of symptoms in asymptomatic HIV patients.

Hepatitis B

Hepatitis B is a virus that causes liver inflammation and damage. It is transmitted by needle sharing, sexual contact, and from mother to newborn. Most patients infected with hepatitis B recover within one to two months, but a small proportion become chronic carriers (that is, the virus persists indefinitely). Some of these patients develop liver cirrhosis later in life.

Patients entering a drug and alcohol treatment program should have their blood tested for hepatitis B. Injection drug users whose blood indicates that they have never been infected with hepatitis B should be offered vaccination, which is extremely safe and effective. hepatitis B carriers should have their sexual partners and household members vaccinated, and should be referred to a liver specialist. Interferon, a powerful antibiotic, can lead to improvement and, in some cases, cure.

Hepatitis C

This virus is similar to hepatitis B, except that it is transmitted primarily through needle sharing; sexual transmission is rare. It is estimated that 40 per cent of injection drug users are carriers, and up to 40 per cent of carriers will eventually develop cirrhosis.

Blood tests to detect hepatitis C are now available and should be ordered by the patient's physician whenever hepatitis C is suspected (for example, elevated liver enzymes). No vaccine is yet available to prevent hepatitis C, but it can be treated with Interferon.

See also Chapter 23, "AIDS and Substance Abuse"

Sexually Transmitted Diseases

Alcohol and drug users have high rates of sexually transmitted diseases such as chlamydia and gonorrhea. This reflects unsafe sexual practices and inadequate health care. Young women should be advised to see their physician or a health clinic for regular STD screenings and Pap tests. Both men and women should be given information on safe sex.

Unwanted Pregnancies

The drug-using population tends to use birth control sporadically. The irregular menstrual periods of women using alcohol or heroin may convince them that they are at little risk of becoming pregnant; with abstinence, however, they usually become fertile again. Both men and women should be counselled on the need for birth control.

Suicide

Patients with alcohol and drug problems are at extremely high risk for suicide. Patients who are intoxicated or in withdrawal may be at particular risk for an impulsive suicide attempt, and carefully supervised detoxification is required.

Impaired driving

All patients should be informed of the risks of driving while using any drug. Some patients believe that their driving is not affected if they don't feel intoxicated; they should be informed that even small amounts of alcohol or other drugs impair the ability to react quickly in complex driving situations.

CONCLUSION

Alcohol and drug abuse is associated with a wide variety of serious physical problems. Alcohol abuse can cause gastritis, liver disease, and damage to the brain and nervous system; it is a major factor in motor vehicle accidents and other forms of trauma. Alcohol, heroin and cocaine can harm the fetus. Cocaine has life-threatening cardiovascular complications. All drugs of abuse can have serious psychiatric complications. Intravenous drug use can transmit blood-borne infections such as HIV and hepatitis.

Counsellors should inform their clients of these health risks, and advise them of preventive practices and services such as immunization and needle exchanges. Counsellors also need to be alert to the symptoms and signs of physical and psychiatric illness in their clients.

ANNOTED BIBLIOGRAPHY

Andreasson, S., Allbeck, P., Romelsjo, A. Alcohol and mortality among young men: longitudinal study of Swedish conscripts. British Medical Journal 1988: 296, 1021-1025.

> A prospective study showing that heavy drinkers have a high mortality rate from suicide.

Camargo, C.A. Moderate Alcohol Consumption and Stroke: The Epidemiologic Evidence. Stroke 1989; 20: 1611-1626.

> A review of the relationship between alcohol consumption, hypertension and stroke.

Chasnoff, I.J., Griffith, D.R., MacGregor, S. et al. Temporal patterns of cocaine use in pregnancy: Perinatal outcome. Journal of the American Medical Association 1989: 261 (12), 1741-1744.

Chasnoff, I.J., Burns, W.J., Schnoll, S.H. et al. Cocaine use in pregnancy. New England Journal of Medicine 1985: 313 (11), 666-669.

Dombroski, M.P., Wolfe, H.M., Welch, R.A. et al. Cocaine abuse is associated with abruptio placentae and decreased birth weight, but not shorter labor. Obstetrics & Gynecology 1991: 77 (1), 139-141.

> The above three papers show that women using cocaine during pregnancy are more likely than normal controls to experience spontaneous abortion, abruptio placentae, and decreased birth weight. At birth, cocaine-exposed infants show impaired neurological and behavioral responses.

Cregler, L.L. & Mark, H. Medical complications of cocaine abuse. New England Journal of Medicine 1986; 315 (22): 1495-1500.

> Concise review of adverse physical effects of cocaine.

Finnegan, L.P. et al. The effects of maternal drug dependence on neonatal mortality. Drug and Alcohol Dependence 2 (1977): 131-140.

> This study shows that heroin-dependent mothers experience higher infant mortality rates than healthy controls, due to low birth weight and premature labor.

Freed, E.X. Changes in weekly self-ratings of depression by hospitalized alcoholics. Journal of Psychiatric Treatment and Evaluation 1981: 3, 451-454.

> In this clinical study, the depression of hospitalized alcoholics is resolved by four weeks of abstinence.

Frezza, M., Padova, C.D., Pozzato, G. et al. High blood alcohol levels in women. The role of decreased gastric alcohol dehydrogenase activity and first-pass metabolism. New England Journal of Medicine 1990: 322 (20), 95-99.

> This biochemical study suggests that women are more likely to develop alcoholic liver disease than men because they have lower levels of the enzyme needed to metabolize alcohol.

Fullilove, R.E., Fullilove, M.T., Bowser, B.P. et al. Risk of sexually transmitted disease among black adolescent crack users in Oakland and San Francisco, CA Journal of the American Medical Association 1990: 263 (6), 851-855.

> In this cross-sectional survey, the number of drugs used daily was associated with the number of risk behaviors (e.g., failure to use a condom, multiple sex partners).

Gawin, F.H. & Ellinwood, E.H. Cocaine and other stimulants: Actions, abuse, and treatment. New England Journal of Medicine 1988: 318 (8), 1173-1182.

> Reviews cocaine intoxication and withdrawal.

Griffiths, R.R. & Sannerud, C.A. Abuse of and dependence on benzodiazepines and other anxiolytic/sedative drugs. In: Psychopharmacology: The Third Generation of Progress, HY Meltzer (Ed), Raven Press, New York 1987.

> Excellent review of benzodiazepine dependence and withdrawal.

Loper, K.A. Clinical toxicology of cocaine. Medical Toxicology & Adverse Drug Experience 1989: 4(3), 174-185.

> Comprehensive review of adverse effects of cocaine.

Mihas, A.A. & Tavassoli, M. Laboratory markers of ethanol intake and abuse: A critical appraisal. American Journal of Medical Sciences 1992: 303 (6), 415-428.

> A good review of the effects of alcohol on blood tests.

Naranjo, C.A., Poulos, C.X., Bremner, K.E. & Lanctot, K.L. Citalopram decreases desirability, liking, and consumption of alcohol in alcohol-dependent drinkers. Clinical Pharmacology and Therapeutics 1992: 51/6, 729-739.

> A controlled study demonstrating that the serotonin reuptake inhibitor citralopram causes reductions in alcohol consumption.

National Institute on Alcohol Abuse and Alcoholism. Fetal Alcohol Syndrome. Alcohol Alert 1991: 13, 1-5.

> A readable summmary of current knowledge of FAS.

Rosett, H.L. & Weiner, L. Alcohol and the Fetus. Oxford University Press, New York, 1984. Pp. 41-64.
>A comprehensive review of research findings.

Sellers, E.M. & Kalant, H. Alcohol intoxication and withdrawal. New England Journal of Medicine 1976: 294, 757.
>Describes the use of diazepam to treat alcohol withdrawal.

Streissguth, A.P., Clarren, S.K. & Jones, K.L. Natural history of the fetal alcohol syndrome: A 10-year follow-up of eleven patients. Lancet 1985: 85-91.
>Shows that the physical and cognitive effects of FAS continue into adolescence, causing severe disability.

Williams, C.M. & Skinner, A.E.G. The cognitive effects of alcohol abuse: a controlled study. British Journal of Addiction 1990: 85, 911-917.
>Demonstrates cognitive impairment in heavy drinkers compared to light drinkers matched for age, social class and education.

Wright, C. & Moore, R.D. Disulfiram treatment of alcoholism. American Journal of Medicine 1990: 88, 647-655.
>Concludes that disulfiram may promote short-term abstinence but has no proven effect on long-term outcome; should not be used as sole treatment.

BOOKS

The following books are recommended because the non-physician will find them readable, yet informative and comprehensive.

Barnes, H.N., Aronson, M.D. & Delbanco, T.L. (Eds). Alcoholism: A Guide for the Primary Care Physician. Springer-Verlag, New York, 1987.

Cohen, S. & Kahan, B. Treating Alcohol Problems: The Family Physician's Guide. Saskatchewan Alcohol and Drug Abuse Commission, Regina, Sask., 1989.

Devenyi, P. & Saunders, S.J. (Eds). Physicians' Manual for Medical Management of Alcohol- and Drug-related Problems (5th Edition). Addiction Research Foundation, Toronto, Ontario, 1989.

Royal College of General Practitioners. Alcohol — A Balanced View. London, 1986.

The Implications of Alcohol-Produced Cognitive Deficits for Treatment Services

ED LARKIN

Cognitive and memory deficits are common among heavy consumers of alcohol. Extreme manifestations of alcohol abuse result in clinical conditions including Wernicke-Korsakoff Syndrome. This disorder is characterized by difficulty with or irregular walking, uncontrollable movements or paralysis of certain muscles, problems with recent memory, a general confusion and a tendency to confabulate or make up events to fill in memory loss. Such problems are typically the result of alcohol directly affecting nerve cells, vitamin deficiencies and head trauma as a result of accidents and falls. While such extreme confusion and memory loss is fairly well known as a result of the portrayal of extreme alcoholics in movies and on television, such problems are relatively rare among the alcohol-abusing population – i.e., five per cent or less (Schukitt, 1989). Less dramatic consequences occur before the effects of chronic alcohol abuse are evident to the causal observer; because of their effect and similarity to psychological problems, they may interfere with the provision of treatment.

Such cognitive deficits can develop to an advanced level before their effect is noticed in routine behavior. This is the case because, as a general rule, alcohol abuse initially reduces an individual's cognitive abilities in ways that are not immediately apparent during conversation or, more important, during clinical interviews. The verbal abilities of alcoholics – i.e., the ability to carry on a normal conversation and to comprehend the meaning of words – are amongst the last to show the effects of excessive consumption.

TESTING COGNITIVE ABILITIES OF ALCOHOLIC PATIENTS

A number of procedures are commonly used to measure cognitive functioning. Two simple tests that are widely available have been shown to be sensitive to these cognitive deficits. These are the Trail Making Tests, parts A & B (Reitan, 1986) and the Digit Symbol subtest of the Weschler Adult Intelligence Scale (Weschler, 1955).

The Trail Making Test, part B, requires the person to shift concepts: to go from one dimension (connecting dots between figures 1, 2, 3, 4, etc.) to a second dimension (connecting points to corresponding letters 1-a-2-b, etc.) Alcohol abuse typically reduces one's ability to shift concepts with the same speed and ability as non-alcohol abusers. Such abilities may return to normal levels a month or so after a person stops drinking. With regard to the Digit Symbol subtest of the Weschler Adult Intelligence Scale (WAIS), a comparison can be made between a well-learned ability, reflected by the vocabulary scores on the WAIS, and the ability to learn new material such as the Digit Symbol subtest of the scale. Usually, alcohol abusers are unable to learn immediately after becoming abstinent as well as their earlier abilities suggest they could – as measured by their vocabulary level. In summary, the performance of alcohol abusers on these structured tests reflects cognitive deficits in the ability to shift from concept to concept, to abstract information, and to learn new material.

Laine & Butters (1982), believe that the poor abstract reasoning ability is a function of inadequate abilities to generate hypothesis and testing strategies. Wetzig & Hardin (1990) conducted a study that supports the idea that alcoholics, particularly while intoxicated, use inefficient rehearsal strategies, rather than more elaborate mnemonic strategies to process and store new information. They continue to use this ineffective strategy when dealing with new information even after they become abstinent. In general then, many alcoholic clients have a reduced ability to deal in a systematic manner with new problems of an unstructured nature; and the more complicated the information processing a task requires, the more difficulties many alcoholics have.

Perhaps the most stable finding in the outpatient treatment of alcoholics is the dramatic dropout from treatment within the first month. Some investigators report that up to 80 per cent of all clients who enter a treatment program that relies on outpatient visits will have dropped out by the end of the fourth interview (Gerard & Saenger, 1966). This may be because many treatment techniques require abilities that these clients lack (Larkin, 1976).

COGNITIVE DEFICITS AND TREATMENT PROGRAMS

Unfortunately, many treatment programs require non-verbal abilities related to new learning and the processing of information. These *are* the abilities that are initially affected by excessive alcohol consumption. Few treatment programs take into account the fact that alcohol abusers, when recently abstinent, may continue to suffer from the cognitive effects that alcohol can produce. They may require a month or so of abstinence before they return to normal levels or thereabouts. It has been suggested (Solberg & Mateer, 1989) that many of the clinically relevant and frequently observed alcoholic behaviors (e.g., apathy, failure to learn from experience and perhaps most important, denial), may not *always* be the result of psychological defences or other mechanisms. In many cases, these problems may be due to recent excessive alcohol consumption resulting in reduced memory and learning ability. It has also been shown that the brain becomes smaller after alcohol abuse and that there is recovery in volume and ability after abstinence (Carlen, 1980). Research examining the relationship between cognitive deficits produced by alcohol abuse and the treatment process has only just begun. Becker and Jaffe (1984) tested the recall of information presented in a film on alcoholism to three groups of patients who had been abstinent for less than one week, one to two weeks and two to six weeks. They report that the recall of material with the two-to-six-week group was not significantly different from normal control subjects. The first group, abstinent less than one week, was impaired in the ability to recall information from the film and also in the ability to recognize correct answers.

To complicate the picture, it has recently been demonstrated that there are two types of cognitive recovery processes. Goldman (1983, 1986, 1987) and Goldman et al. (1983), while investigating the course of recovery of cognitive functions following abstinence from alcohol, have reported that retesting patients produced experience or practice effects. It appears that cognitive deficits associated with excessive alcohol consumption can improve with practice, and therefore may be amenable to rehabilitation by appropriately designed experience.

A therapist undertaking an initial assessment or treatment of the alcoholic client must take into account that up to three quarters of alcoholic clients entering treatment can be shown to suffer from alcohol-related cognitive deficits. Technically, such deficits are referred to as impairments in visuo-spatial and visual motor abilities, abstract reasoning, learning and memory skills. Pragmatically, such problems are demonstrated in the difficulty with learning new material, remembering new information and the ability to plan ahead or reason.

It should be noted that the traditional AA programs have alluded to these cognitive problems for over half a century in their self-help slogans such as "bring the body, the mind will follow" and "fifty miles into the woods, fifty miles out." The term "Mocus" has been used to describe the confused psychological state that alcoholics typically have when initially abstinent.

Several authors have investigated the recovery, both by time and experience, of these cognitive functions. Several have hypothesized on the difficulty they provide for treatment programs. For example, alcoholic clients' difficulties with past experiences, which could be explained in many cases by the effect of alcohol, may be interpreted clinically as denial (Gordon et al., 1988). From a treatment point of view, those treatment programs that rely heavily on information processing such as group educational sessions are doing so with a population that may not be able to benefit from such experience (Becker and Jaffe, 1984). Programs that rely on insight-based treatment also may have difficulty with clients with reduced ability to reason in the abstract.

In summary, up to 75 per cent of alcoholics, when measured using appropriate standardized tests, will show cognitive impairments that are not related to verbal abilities and therefore are not noticeable in clinical interviews. However, the types of difficulties that these clients have – i.e., a reduced ability to process new information, to store new information, and to shift from topic to topic – may be counterproductive both to the operation of the programs and to the outcome of treatment plans.

There are at least two ways to approach this programmatic problem. First, it is possible to organize treatment programs suited to the cognitive abilities of clients. Such structuring of information is not difficult, in principle, but seldom a facet in program planning. Secondly, there are early indications that the cognitive abilities of alcoholic clients can be restored by techniques initially designed for patients suffering from head trauma or strokes. Well thought out (and in some cases, computer-assisted) cognitive rehabilitation programs are available for general use and some have been shown to help alcoholic clients. For example: Gordon et al. (1988) describe an inpatient program that includes testing higher-risk patients and providing computer-assisted cognitive rehabilitation training when required.

An example of a cognitive rehabilitation program designed for the deficits of an alcoholic client are described in Larkin, Sinclair, Cleland and Parkinson-Heyes (1991). However, such sophisticated procedures from testing to remediation are not generally available at this time. Therefore, most practitioners involved in initial assessment in treatment of alcoholics should familiarize themselves with their clients' manifestations of alcohol-induced cognitive deficits and, where possible, match their treatment approaches to their clients' abilities.

SUGGESTED READINGS

Wilkinson, D.A. (1979). Cerebral deficits in alcoholism. Toronto: Addiction Research Foundation.

Becker, J.T. & Jaffe, J.H. (1984). Impaired memory for treatment-relevant information in inpatient men alcoholics. Journal of Studies on Alcohol, 45, (4).

Solberg, M.M. & Mateer, C.A. (1989). Introduction to cognitive rehabilitation: Theory and practice. New York: Guilford Press.

Wetzig, D.L. & Hardin, S.I. (1990). Neurocognitive deficits of alcoholism: An intervention. Journal of Clinical Psychology, 46 (2).

REFERENCES

Becker, J.T. & Jaffe, J.H. (1984). Impaired memory for treatment-relevant information in inpatient men alcoholics. Journal of Studies on Alcohol, 45, (4), 339-343.

Carlen, P.E. (1980). Reversible effects of chronic alcoholism on the human central nervous system: Possible biological mechanism. In D.A. Wilkinson (Ed.), Cerebral deficits in alcoholism. Addiction Research Foundation, 1980.

Gerard, D.L. & Saenger, G. (1966). Out-patient treatment of alcoholism. Toronto: University of Toronto Press.

Goldman, M.S. (1983). Cognitive impairment in chronic alcoholics: Some cause for optimism. American Psychologist, 10, 1045-1054.

Goldman, M.S. (1986). Neuropsychological recovery in alcoholics: Endogenous and exogenous processes. Alcoholism: Clinical and Experimental Research, 10, 136-144.

Goldman, M.S. (1987). The role of time and practice in recovery of function in alcoholics. In: Parsons, O.A., Butters, N. and Nathan, P.E. (Eds.), Neuropsychology of Alcoholism: Implications for Diagnosis and Treatment, (pp. 481-495), New York: Guilford Press.

Goldman, M.S., Williams, D.L. & Klisz, D.K. (1983). Recoverability of psychological functioning following alcohol abuse: Prolonged visual-spatial dysfunction in older alcoholics. Journal of Consulting and Clinical Psychology, 51, 370-378.

Gordon, S.M., Kennedy, B.P. & McPeake, J.D. (1988). Neuropsychologically impaired alcoholics: Assessment, treatment considerations, and rehabilitation. Journal of Substance Abuse, 5, 99-104.

Laine, M. & Butters, N. (1982). A preliminary study of the problem-solving strategies of detoxified long-term alcoholics. Drug and Alcohol Dependence, 10, 235-242.

Larkin, E.J. (1976). The treatment of alcoholism: Theory, practice and evaluation, Toronto: Addiction Research Foundation, 2nd Edition.

Larkin, E.J., Sinclair, L., Cleland, P. & Parkinson-Heyes, A. (in preparation). A program to reduce cognitive deficits in recovering alcoholics: A case study. Toronto: Addiction Research Foundation.

Reitan, R. Trail Making Test: Manual for Administration and Scoring. Tucson: Reitan Neuropsychology Laboratory, 1986.

Schukitt, M.A. (1989). Drug and Alcohol Abuse. New York: Plenum Medical Book Company.

Solberg, M.M. & Mateer, C.A. (1989). Introduction to cognitive rehabilitation: Theory and practice, New York: Guilford Press.

Weschler, D. Weschler Adult Intelligence Scale. New York: The psychological corporation, 1955.

Wetzig, D.L. & Hardin, S.I. (1990). Neurocognitive deficits of alcoholism: An intervention. Journal of Clinical Psychology, 46 (2), 219-228.

Wilkinson, D.A. (1979). Cerebral Deficits in Alcoholism. Toronto: Addiction Research Foundation.

Guidelines for Advising on the Goals of Treatment: Abstinence or Moderation

MARTHA SANCHEZ-CRAIG AND D. ADRIAN WILKINSON

INTRODUCTION

When treating clients for alcohol problems, the therapist has to decide whether to discuss a choice of goals with the client. Allowing clients to choose between abstinence and moderation is still anathema to many in the field of treatment. Others, with equal passion, see the denial of choice as a denial of the dignity and respect that they are ethically bound to accord their clients. This furious controversy has been portrayed as a clash of ideologies, or as a straightforward disagreement about the interpretation of scientific facts. Others have argued that, since this is a controversy only in certain cultural contexts, it must be largely sociocultural in origin. (Readers can review Duckert, Koski-Jannes & Ronnberg, 1989; Fingarette, 1988; Heather, 1989; Heather & Robertson, 1983; Kissin, 1983; MacAndrew & Edgerton, 1969; Peele, 1984, 1987; Sobell & Sobell, 1986/87; Wallace, 1987a, 1987b for varied treatments of these issues.)

We believe that all of the above interpretations of the controversy are valid:

1. There are differing conceptions of alcohol dependence, some consistent with choice of goal, others not (Chaudron & Wilkinson, 1988; Sobell & Sobell, 1986/87). These various conceptions often lead to definitional problems that preclude the possibility of a resolution. These are ideological differences.
2. Interpretations of the scientific data vary. Scientists have failed to reach consensus about valid empirical tests of the advisability of offering choice to clients, so there are varying interpretations of these data (Heather, 1989; Heather & Robertson, 1983; Sobell & Sobell, 1986/87).
3. There is considerable cultural variation in the perceived importance of the issue, so the importance of cultural context is clear (Miller, 1986; Peele, 1984, 1987).

This chapter makes no attempt to resolve any of these issues. It is a practical guide for those who already believe that most clients with alcohol-related problems should be encouraged to choose whether to aim for abstinence or moderation. Those who doubt the wisdom of offering such choice are referred to the extensive literature aimed at resolving such uncertainty. Those convinced of the rashness of encouraging choice must only deplore the inclusion of this chapter in a book such as this.

AIMS OF THE CHAPTER

Our aim is to review empirical and conceptual factors that have a direct bearing on the advice one should give to clients who are in the process of choosing their goal. Then we attempt to identify the information that should be brought to the client's attention, in the hopes of influencing the decision process. We offer guidelines to identify the minority of clients who, in our opinion, should not be offered choice. We also suggest a sequence that permits the most effective provision of advice to clients selecting their goals. Thus, most of the chapter is very practically oriented.

CLIENTS WHO SHOULD NOT BE ENCOURAGED TO CHOOSE THEIR GOAL

Broadly speaking, we identify two groups of clients who should not be offered the choice between abstaining or moderating their use of alcohol:

1. Clients should not be offered this choice if it is illegal for them to use alcohol. The legal prohibition might relate to the age of the client or to a court order, such as conditions of probation.

2. Clients may be judged mentally or developmentally incompetent to exercise responsible choice. Under this circumstance, it is a clear professional responsibility not to offer choice. In some jurisdictions, alcohol use might not be legally proscribed in the young, but their status as minors could nonetheless rule out discussion of alcohol use as an option. In addition, since alcohol use can result in serious cognitive impairment (Parsons, Butters, & Nathan, 1987), some alcohol-dependent persons may not be mentally fit to choose their goal responsibly. This state may be transitory for some clients, such as those who come to treatment sessions intoxicated, when the issue of goal choice would not be fruitfully addressed.

With these general exceptions, we believe clients should be encouraged to choose their goals. This does not, of course, mean that the therapist will not attempt to influence the choice. The therapist should have significant input into the decision process, sometimes actively recommending one option, on the basis of the considerations set out in the following sections.

INFORMATION TO BE REVIEWED AS A PRECURSOR OF CLIENT CHOICE

THE CLIENT'S MEDICAL STATUS

Certain medical conditions contraindicate any alcohol use by the client. Examples of such medical conditions would be: active liver disease or cirrhosis, pancreatitis, bleeding ulcers, or esophageal varices. Identifying these problems is a medical process. As a check against the existence of any such problem, clients should ask their physician whether they have any physical condition that would advise against any use of alcohol. The physician's opinion should be reviewed with the therapist in considering the goal. Therapists should strongly recommend abstinence for clients whose physicians advise them not to drink. If the client insists that he or she will continue to drink, the therapist should urge the most minimal levels of use, such as purely ceremonial use.

THE RISKS OF ALCOHOL CONSUMPTION

Clients should know the risks of alcohol consumption, both acute and chronic. We attempt to ensure that the clients know the risks of intoxication, the effects of varying doses of alcohol, and the long-term health risks of different levels of use. The relevance of individual differences (e.g., gender, physique) to the risks of drinking is also stressed. Our program stresses the theme that "All drinking has risks. If you want to avoid the risks, don't drink." This applies to the risks of intoxication and to chronic effects.

FAMILY HISTORY AND THE CHOICE OF GOAL

About 40 per cent of the clients in our programs report a history of alcohol dependence among first-degree relatives (a positive family history). We have found that clients with a positive family history have rates of successful outcome very similar to those with a negative family history (Sanchez-Craig, Wilkinson, & Walker, 1987). Clients with a positive family history are not more likely in our program to choose abstinence as their goal. However, in achieving moderate drinking they tend to use alcohol much less frequently than their successful counterparts with a negative family history. This research finding is now reviewed with our clients as something to consider when setting their own goal. We also inform them that another investigator has reported a positive family history to be predictive of abstinent outcome among clients in a program offering choice of goals (Miller & Joyce, 1979).

DRINKING HISTORY AND THE CHOICE OF GOAL

The client's lifetime history of drinking is discussed in the treatment sessions when considering the choice of goal. Our reason for doing so is conceptually, rather than empirically, based. If the client has an extensive history of problem-free drinking, or of problem-free drinking in well-specified circumstances (e.g., when drinking at home with the family), then the choice of moderation as the goal is more likely to be supported by the therapist. When the history involves problems associated with alcohol use from the outset of drinking, and almost all drinking episodes being of heavy consumption, then abstinence is more strongly recommended. The rationale for this position is that clients will probably be more successful in reacquiring old habits of moderation, or maintaining the habit of situationally specific moderation, than in acquiring a brand new pattern of alcohol use.

In addition, a history of intoxication on almost all occasions of drinking suggests that intoxication has been the sole purpose of alcohol use. *Clients aiming for moderation should do so to enjoy alcohol use for refreshment, to enhance food experiences, and to participate in ceremonial and social functions, but explicitly not for the purpose of intoxication.* Hence, if the sole attraction of alcohol has been intoxication, moderation, as conservatively recommended by ourselves, is likely to be an unattractive goal and is discouraged by the therapist. The cultural milieu of the client is likely to be particularly relevant to this consideration. In certain cultures, such as Scandinavian, intoxication is a fairly common objective of alcohol use, whereas other cultures, such as Italian and Spanish, strongly disapprove of intoxication. Canada, being multicultural, contains considerable local cultural variations in attitudes to alcohol use and intoxication. These variations should be borne in mind in working with clients.

An important further consideration when reviewing the client's history is how the client has acted in the past when intoxicated. If intoxication has been associated with marked changes in behavior, particularly antisocial behaviors or recklessness, then the risks associated with any drinking are increased. Hence, a history of such behavior changes when intoxicated would influence therapists to increase the strength of recommendations for abstinence as the goal.

HISTORY OF TREATMENT AND GOAL CHOICE

Many clients tell us that they have avoided seeking treatment because they were afraid that a goal of lifelong abstinence would be imposed upon them, and that treatment personnel would not consider them serious about change unless they accepted the imposed goal. With such clients, we stress that flexibility of goal choice is a feature of our approach.

Other clients tell us that they have experience with abstinence-based approaches, and that abstinence is their preferred route. We also see clients who have sampled "12-step" approaches and programs that insist on abstinence as the only appropriate goal, but who felt those concepts didn't apply to themselves. In each of the types of case presented here, the past history of treatment (or avoidance of treatment) quickly focuses the therapist on important aspects of the self-concept and probable goal preference of the client.

In addition to considering the client's attitudes to previous treatment efforts, it is important to review the outcomes. In our experience, clients with a history of lengthy periods of successful abstinence often want to return to that path, though preferring a new treatment approach with a different philosophical or theoretical basis. We have also seen some clients who have become determined to switch from successful abstinence to moderate drinking, and are looking for guidance on how to minimize the risks of the transition. We do not counsel clients to switch from long abstinence to moderation, but will assist those who have decided on their own to make the change and who ask for help. Recent long-term follow-up studies in Sweden show that many ex-patients successfully select this route without any therapeutic assistance (Nordström & Berglund, 1987).

A third type of outcome is reported by clients who have received traditional treatment, but rejected the idea of "loss of control over drinking." After participating in the previous program, these clients unsuccessfully attempted to moderate their drinking. They come to us seeking advice on how they can more effectively attempt moderation of alcohol use.

ALCOHOL DEPENDENCE AND CHOICE OF GOAL

One of the principal objectives of many programs incorporating flexibility of goals has been to encourage persons who are not severely dependent on alcohol to enter treatment. The rationale has been that such persons are often deterred from approaching treatment facilities for fear that abstinence will be the only legitimate goal of treatment (see e.g., Sanchez-Craig, Wilkinson & Walker, 1987; Sanchez-Craig & Wilkinson, 1986/87). Interviews with clients about their reasons for avoiding treatment for years (despite recognizing the problems caused by their use of alcohol) confirm the validity of this assumption in many cases. Thus, programs offering moderation are frequently targeted to clients who are not severely dependent on alcohol. Another reason for aiming for clients who are not severely dependent on alcohol has been the controversial nature of the goal of moderation. It is less contentious to offer choice when clients with severe alcohol dependence have been excluded from a study. Clients with severe alcohol dependence have a high incidence of illnesses (e.g., cirrhosis, esophageal varices) that contraindicate any drinking, and hence flexibility of goal choice is seen as less desirable for this group. Furthermore, many severely dependent drinkers have had numerous contacts with treatment agencies and self-help groups, and already believe that choice of goals is not a realistic option. Early studies also suggest that clients with relatively low levels of alcohol dependence were more likely to moderate drinking successfully, whereas abstinence was relatively more often achieved by the severely dependent drinkers (Orford, Oppenheimer & Edwards, 1976; for review see Sobell & Sobell, 1986/87).

GENDER AND CHOICE OF GOAL

It has been reported in a number of studies that women are more likely than men to achieve an outcome of successful moderate drinking after treatment (Miller & Caddy, 1977; Sanchez-Craig et al., 1989, 1991). This finding applies when the outcome criterion is an arbitrary definition of moderate drinking selected by the investigators. When reports of alcohol-related problems are the outcome measure, the gender difference is less likely to be observed. In addition, there appears to be a gender difference in the type of intervention to which males and females are most responsive (Sanchez-Craig et al., 1989, 1991). Hence, though there is some evidence that women are more likely to attain a consistent outcome of moderate drinking, we do not believe that current data warrant different advice to women and men about abstinence or moderation as their goal.

THE ROLE OF CLIENT PREFERENCES AND BELIEFS

It derives directly from the philosophical grounding of our approach (Sanchez-Craig, 1990) that client preferences and beliefs are among the most crucial data we consider when working with clients on the selection of their goals. However, this is not merely an ideological preference. There are data that are entirely consistent with the pragmatic value of this position, and we review them briefly here.

Among traditionalists, client preference for flexibility in treatment goals tends to be seen as evidence of "denial." This presumed symptom of the disease of alcoholism is considered part of the innate personality of the "alcoholic" (Miller & Sovereign, 1989), which must be challenged and overcome before treatment can succeed. It is certainly true that many alcohol-dependent persons minimize, trivialize and rationalize their dependence, but it does not necessarily follow that this is a symptom of disease. Alternatively, such denial may be viewed as a natural psychological reaction to the judgments of others about one's behavior and abilities. In line with an alternate formulation of denial is the evidence that directive, or confrontational, therapists generally tend to engender resistance in their clients (Patterson & Forgatch, 1984). Thus, the denial by traditionalists of autonomy for their clients can provoke a reactive denial of problems by the clients. This is not to say that excessive drinkers do not falsely deny that their drinking causes problems. The issue is how best to undercut such denial. In many cases, confrontation merely seems to strengthen it.

Miller (1983, 1985, 1987) has reviewed the literature on motivation for treatment and its relation to client goals, and concluded that:

> Personal goals are an important aspect of motivation for change. The provision of negotiable and alternative treatment goals can encourage early intervention, compliance with recovery related programs, and favorable treatment outcome. (1987, p. 133)

As a direct test of this conclusion, Miller and Sovereign (1989) varied the directiveness of feedback to clients who received their "Drinker's Check-Up," an assessment aimed at motivating heavy drinkers to change their drinking patterns. Clients who received directive feedback showed significantly greater resistance (arguing, interrupting, and changing the subject) and denial (minimizing the problem), than those who were given the same feedback in a non-confrontational non-directive manner. The resistant clients had poorer outcomes. Thus, therapist behavior engendered resistance and contributed to poorer outcome.

Orford & Keddie (1986) examined the relative importance of client preferences and beliefs versus level of dependence as predictors of outcome among clients offered a choice of goals. They found that client preferences and beliefs appear to be more strongly related to outcome than level of dependence.

Sanchez-Craig et al. (1984) randomly assigned problem drinkers to the goal of abstinence or to a condition allowing client choice of goal. Clients who were offered choice were more accepting of the assigned goal, were more successful in the initial phases of treatment, and required fewer elective counselling sessions during the aftercare phase of the program. Of particular importance was the subsequent discovery that the benefits of choice were most apparent among those clients who were the heaviest drinkers before treatment (Sanchez-Craig & Lei, 1986), and who had higher levels of alcohol dependence. In short, clients given choice were less resistant and more successful, particularly those with evidence of a more severe problem. Thus it appears that a preference for respecting the judgment of clients is more than just a philosophically-based value held by certain therapists. It has beneficial effects on the outcome of treatment.

Many therapists sincerely believe that giving any credence and respect to the opinions of "alcoholics" about their ability to moderate their drinking successfully is either naive or professionally irresponsible. Failure to confront alcoholic denial is considered by such clinicians to be "enabling the alcoholic's addiction." Our problem with this position is precisely that it represents a statement of belief by certain therapists. The assertion has not been scientifically or clinically tested. In our view, the "denial" of greatest concern here is the denial of appropriate services to persons with alcohol-related problems because of the untested beliefs of many treatment personnel. There is nothing wrong with having a diversity of treatment approaches for alcohol dependence, since we do not definitively know of an effective treatment, and there are strong theoretical and empirical reasons for expecting that there is no uniquely good approach (Cox, 1987; Miller & Heather, 1986). If one view of appropriate treatment prevails, and its disciples are able to suppress the offering of alternative approaches without scientific justification, then our clients and the public will be very poorly served. In the absence of evidence to the contrary, we urge that clients be given the dignity of being treated as if they are not self-deluded, which is the basic assertion of the construct of denial.

ENVIRONMENTAL CONSTRAINTS ON GOAL CHOICE

A number of environmental constraints mitigate against advising moderation as the goal of treatment in some cases. We review those most frequently encountered below.

FAMILY AND SOCIAL NETWORK

If attempting to moderate drinking is likely to cause serious tensions in the client's family, or with other close associates, then we tend to urge consideration of abstaining, at least in the medium term. Sometimes such tensions are based on other family members being successful graduates of programs stressing the disease concept of alcoholism, and the imperative for abstinence. In other cases, family members may have been frequently wounded (emotionally or physically) by the client's intoxicated behavior so that the prospect of any drinking is stressful enough to jeopardize the relationship.

LEGAL STATUS

If a client has been referred because of a legal problem caused by alcohol use, or involving intoxicated behavior, it may be imprudent to counsel a goal of moderation. This is clearly the case when drinking is precluded by the terms of probation. Sometimes abstinence is a strong recommendation of the client's legal counsel, and this again should weigh heavily. In general, if drinking has caused legal problems that are unresolved at the time of treatment, abstinence is likely to be a prudent goal.

OCCUPATIONAL FACTORS

Certain work environments promote drinking. Working in bars and restaurants on the service or the entertainment side frequently involves high availability of alcohol and considerable social pressure to imbibe. Because of these conditions, some of our clients who work in such establishments have opted for abstinence. Members of the armed forces often have access to alcohol at low prices through the various social clubs for military personnel. In such settings, social pressures to drink are quite often strong. Because of the combined pressures of high availability and strong social pressure, this occupational group may also prefer to abstain.

CULTURAL FACTORS

As we have previously discussed, in certain cultures moderate alcohol use in social gatherings is very much the norm, whereas in others occasional heavier use is more common (MacAndrew & Edgerton, 1969). When discussing treatment goals with clients, such variation in cultural background, and the influence it can have on the meaning of alcohol use, are relevant to goal selection.

Another "culture" that can influence the client's preparedness for moderate drinking is the "culture of youth." In Canada, in our experience, many young persons have most of their early drinking experiences outside the family with peers at parties where the objective of drinking is frequently intoxication. Consequently, many become "problem drinkers" with almost no experience of being a moderate user of alcohol. Thus, the history of almost exclusively immoderate use of alcohol suggests a longer period of abstinence before a goal of moderation is attempted, and a thorough examination by therapist and client of the personal meaning of alcohol use to the client.

MODERATE DRINKING: HOW MUCH IS TOO MUCH?

By moderate drinking we mean drinking at a level that does not jeopardize one's health, one's ability to carry out day-to-day responsibilities (at home, at work, or in the community), or one's safety or the safety of others. This definition implies that moderate drinking involves abstaining in a number of circumstances, such as before or during driving, or conducting hazardous tasks (at work or play), and when pregnant.

Note that this is not a prescription for "safe" or risk-free drinking. The only incontrovertibly safe level of drinking is abstinence. Many of our clients acknowledge that fact but still wish to attempt "low-risk" drinking. Then they ask what guidelines we can give them. We inform them of the levels of consumption that our clients have reported when they claim to suffer no adverse consequences of their drinking (Sanchez-Craig, 1986; Sanchez-Craig & Israel, 1985). In a number of studies, we have found that very few clients who stay within these guidelines report adverse consequences of their drinking. Some who drink over the guidelines also report no adverse consequences of drinking, but the risk increases as the levels of drinking increase.

Those who become moderate drinkers after attending our clinic have the following profile to their drinking:
- They have two or more abstinent days each week.
- They do not drink more than four standard drinks on any day. (We recommend a limit of three drinks for women because of their smaller physique, and apparently greater sensitivity to adverse effects of alcohol on physical health [see Hill, 1986].)

- They do not drink more than 12 standard drinks in any week.
- They avoid drinking to cope with problems of daily life (i.e., drinking to blunt emotions or facilitate some action such as asserting oneself).
- They do not use alcohol frequently in association with recreational activities and free-time activities.

We stress that the pattern of drinking that is established should fit with the person's lifestyle, while avoiding adverse consequences of drinking. *We also stress that the limits that clients set should be what they judge to be their upper limit of sensible drinking. The goal is not a target that the client is aiming to achieve on each day drinking or in each week, but is the upper limit of what they consider prudent for themselves.*

SETTING THE GOAL

The initial goal

In discussing with clients their approach to their longer-term goal (whether abstinence or moderation), we present three possible routes:

1) to taper down from the present high level of alcohol use until the level of the longer-term goal is reached (be it abstinence, or a specified level of moderate use). This route is seldom selected; those who select it usually have rather high levels of daily consumption (usually 10 or more drinks) and fear the effects of abrupt withdrawal of alcohol.

2) to abstain or start drinking at a moderate level immediately, and continue with the selected pattern.

3) to start with an initial period of abstinence, before deciding on the longer-term goal. This allows more time to carefully weigh the pros and cons of each option. It is the route we generally recommend to clients.

Our program thus distinguishes between the initial goal of treatment and the longer-term goal. If the client believes that he or she can accomplish it, we recommend an initial goal of a short period of abstinence – usually two or three weeks. (The research that supports this recommendation is presented and reviewed in: Sanchez-Craig & Lei, 1987; and Sanchez-Craig, Wilkinson & Walker, 1987.) The client is presented with the following rationale for an initial period of abstinence:

- We have found that clients who manage to abstain for the first three weeks of the program are more successful at achieving long-term moderation outcomes.
- An initial period of abstinence will cause a significant reduction of tolerance for alcohol, so that returning to previous levels of consumption would cause unpleasant effects of intoxication. In addition, marked loss of tolerance is a gratifying objective indication of physical benefits of the change in drinking.

- Cognitive abilities dulled by long-term heavy use of alcohol are likely to improve significantly in two to three weeks of abstinence, but not with mere reduction of use, even if it's quite substantial.
- Clients will discover how they cope spontaneously with temptations to drink, and with social pressures to drink. Discovery of such existing coping skills can significantly facilitate the achievement of the longer-term goal, whatever that goal might be.

SPECIFYING THE GOAL

The goal of abstinence need not be specified beyond being identified. Abstinence means not drinking alcoholic beverages under any circumstances. If a client selects a goal of abstinence we usually make an agreement about a date on which that goal's suitability will be reviewed. Moderate use can range from rare ritual or ceremonial use through to specified levels of regular drinking. When clients specify their goal we ask them to specify seven conditions of moderation as follows:

- **Maximum daily quantity:** the maximum number of drinks that will be consumed in any one day.
- **Maximum frequency:** the maximum number of drinking days in any one week.
- **Maximum weekly quantity:** the maximum number of drinks to be consumed in any one week. (Note: This is often less than the product of maximum daily quantity times maximum frequency.)
- **Types of beverage:** the varieties of alcoholic beverage which the client plans to avoid completely. Most frequently mentioned in this category are straight liquor or cocktails. These more concentrated beverages can more readily lead to intoxication.
- **Contexts for abstinence:** situations of high risk for drinking excessively, in which the client resolves not to drink at all.
- **Contexts for drinking:** environmental, social, cognitive or emotional contexts in which the client has identified low risk of excessive drinking and good coping skills, and in which moderate consumption may occur.
- **Assessment period:** the number of weeks or months over which the client will assess the goal's suitability.

Clients are always urged to attempt realistic goals. By this we mean goals that may initially be challenging, but which the client believes he or she can attain. We encourage clients not to set goals that they are unlikely to achieve. It is preferable to approach the ultimate goal gradually than to set oneself up for disappointment by selecting unrealistic goals.

We also review with clients the most constructive way of interpreting failure to achieve one's goal, i.e., as an opportunity for learning how to be more successful in the future, rather than as failure and an indication of personal inadequacy.

Clients are instructed to remember that the goal is not "carved in stone." It can be adjusted from time to time until it suits the client's lifestyle, while causing no alcohol-related problems. From time to time (e.g., holidays), clients may relax the criteria for a brief period. However, we stress that changes to the goal should be very deliberate, and should not be undertaken while the client is under the influence. Changing the goal on such occasions can serve as a rationalization for drinking too much.

As part of the treatment plan we routinely structure a set of follow-up appointments to review the client's success in achieving the goals of the intervention. At these sessions there can be further adjustments made to the specified goal. Structuring the follow-up emphasizes that the client should continue to abide by the treatment plan in order to succeed over the long term.

A FINAL WORD

Whether the therapist likes it or not, the client ultimately chooses his or her goal. The approach and considerations laid out in this chapter can serve as the basis for making that choice rational and collaborative. In our experience, dogmatic assertions by therapists about what clients can and cannot do tend to undermine the establishment of a collaborative therapeutic relationship.

REFERENCES

Chaudron, C.D. & Wilkinson, D.A., (eds.). (1988). Theories on Alcoholism. Toronto: Addiction Research Foundation.

Cox, W.M., (ed.). (1987). Treatment and prevention of alcohol problems: A resource manual. Orlando, Fl.: Academic.

Duckert, F., Koski-Jannes, A. & Ronnberg, S., (eds.). (1989). Perspectives on controlled drinking. Helsinki: Hakapaino Oy.

Fingarette, H. (1988). Heavy drinking: The myth of alcoholism as a disease. Berkeley: University of California Press.

Heather, N. (1989). Controlled drinking treatment: Where do we stand today? In T. Loberg, W.R. Miller, P.E. Nathan & G.A. Marlatt (eds.), Addictive behaviors: Prevention and early intervention. (pp. 31-50). Amsterdam: Swets & Zeitlinger.

Heather, N. & Robertson, I. (1983) Controlled Drinking (rev. ed.). London: Methuen.

Hill, S.Y. (1986). Physiological effects of alcohol in women. In Women and alcohol: Health-related issues. NIAAA Research Monograph No. 16 (pp. 199-214). Washington, D.C.: U.S. Government Printing Office.

Kissin, B. (1983). The disease concept of alcoholism. In R.G. Smart, F.B. Glaser, Y. Israel, H. Kalant, R.E. Popham & W. Schmidt, (eds.), Research advances in alcohol and drug problems, (vol. 7). (pp. 93-126). New York: Plenum.

MacAndrew, C. & Edgerton, R.B. (1969). Drunken comportment: A social explanation. Chicago: Aldine.

Miller, W.R. (1983). Motivational interviewing with problem drinkers. Behavioral Psychotherapy, 11, 147-172.

Miller, W.R. (1985). Motivation for treatment: A review with special emphasis on alcoholism. Psychological Bulletin, 98, 84-107.

Miller, W.R. (1986). Haunted by the Zeitgeist: Reflections on contrasting treatment goals in Europe and the United States. In T. Babor (ed.), Alcohol and culture: Comparative perspectives from Europe and America. (pp. 110-129). New York: Annals of the New York Academy of Sciences.

Miller, W.R. (1987). Motivation and treatment goals. Drugs and Society, 1, 133-151.

Miller, W.R. & Caddy, G.R. (1977). Abstinence and controlled drinking in the treatment of problem drinkers. Journal of Studies on Alcohol, 38, 986-1003.

Miller, W.R. & Heather, N., (eds.). (1986). Treating addictive behaviors: Processes of change. New York: Plenum.

Miller, W.R. & Joyce, M.A. (1979). Prediction of abstinence, controlled drinking and heavy drinking outcomes following behavioral self-control training. Journal of Clinical and Consulting Psychology, 47, 773-775.

Miller, W.R. & Sovereign, R.G. (1989). The check-up: A model for early intervention in addictive behaviors. In T. Loberg, W.R. Miller, P.E. Nathan & G.A. Marlatt (eds.), Addictive behaviors: Prevention and early intervention. (pp. 31-50). Amsterdam: Swets & Zeitlinger.

Nordström, G. & Berglund, M. (1987). Aging and recovery from alcoholism. British Journal of Psychiatry, 151, 389-392.

Orford, J. & Keddie, A. (1986). Abstinence or controlled drinking in clinical practice: A test of the dependence and persuasion hypotheses. British Journal of Addiction, 81, 495-504.

Orford, J., Oppenheimer, E. & Edwards, G. (1976). Abstinence or control: The outcome of excessive drinking two years after consultation. Behavior Research and Therapy, 14, 409-418.

Parsons, O.A., Butters, N. & Nathan, P.E., (eds.). (1987). Neuropsychology of alcoholism: Implications for diagnosis and treatment. New York: Guilford.

Patterson, G.R. & Forgatch, M.S. (1984). Therapist behavior as a determinant for client noncompliance: A paradox for the behavior modifier. Journal of Consulting and Clinical Psychology, 53, 846-851.

Peele, S. (1984). The cultural context of psychological approaches to alcoholism. American Psychologist, 39, 1337-1351.

Peele, S. (1987). Why do controlled drinking outcomes vary by investigator, by country and by era? Drug & Alcohol Dependence, 20, 173-201.

Sanchez-Craig, M. (1986). How much is too much? Estimates of hazardous drinking based on clients' self-reports. British Journal of Addiction, 81, 251-256.

Sanchez-Craig, M. (1990). Brief didactic treatment for alcohol and drug-related problems: An approach based on client choice. British Journal of Addiction, 85, 169-177

Sanchez-Craig, M., Annis, H.M., Bornet, A.R. & MacDonald, K.R. (1984). Random assignment to abstinence and controlled drinking: Evaluation of a cognitive-behavioral program for problem drinkers. Journal of Consulting and Clinical Psychology, 52, 390-403.

Sanchez-Craig, M. & Israel, Y. (1985). Pattern of alcohol use associated with self-identified problem drinking. American Journal of Public Health, 75, 178-180.

Sanchez-Craig, M. & Lei, H. (1987). Disadvantages to imposing the goal of abstinence on problem drinkers: An empirical study. British Journal Of Addiction, 81, 505-512.

Sanchez-Craig, M., Leigh, G., Spivak, K. & Lei, H. (1989). Superior outcome of females over males after brief treatment for the reduction of heavy drinking. British Journal of Addiction, 84, 395-404.

Sanchez-Craig, M., Spivak, K. & Davila, R. (1991). Superior outcome of females over males after brief treatment for the reduction of heavy drinking: Replication and report of therapist effects. British Journal of Addiction, 86, 867-876.

Sanchez-Craig, M. & Wilkinson, D.A. (1986/87). Treating problem drinkers who are not severely dependent on alcohol. Drugs and Society, 1, 39-67.

Sanchez-Craig, M., Wilkinson, D.A. & Walker, K. (1987). Theory and methods for secondary prevention of alcohol problems: A cognitively based approach. In W.M. Cox (ed.), Treatment and prevention of alcohol problems: A resource manual. (pp. 287-332). New York: Academic Press.

Sobell, M.B. & Sobell, L. (1976). Second-year treatment outcome of alcoholics treated by individualized behavior therapy. Behavior Research and Therapy, 14, 195-215.

Sobell, M.B. & Sobell, L., (eds.). (1986/87). Moderation as a goal or outcome of treatment for alcohol problems: A dialogue. Drugs and Society, 1, 1-171.

Wallace, J. (1987a). Waging the war for wellness. Part I: The attack of the "antitraditionalist lobby." Professional Counsellor, January/February, 21-39.

Wallace, J. (1987b). Waging the war for wellness. Part II: The attack upon the disease model. Professional Counsellor, March/April, 21-27.

Use of Community Resources in Treatment Planning

SUSAN CROSS

Substance abusers presenting for treatment are typically multi-problem clients: they tend to have significant problems in life areas other than substance abuse. For example, a client may have lost a job, have recently separated from the family or have major financial problems.

Treating the addiction problem on its own isolates it from the complexity of a person's life and assumes that treating it will have a positive effect on other life areas. In fact, problems in other life areas may be exacerbated as the substance abuse problem comes under control. The control of substance abuse involves far more than simply deciding not to use drugs. It involves making changes in many life areas. For example, a client who only has friends who drink heavily and who only engages in social activities which involve alcohol will have to work hard to cultivate relationships with friends who do not drink or who support the client's abstinence, and to explore leisure activities that do not involve heavy drinking.

In addition, the client may present with significant problems in other life areas that need to be addressed along with the addiction problem. Unless they are dealt with, such problems will impede the client's work on the addiction problem.

A single resource may not be able to respond effectively to the unique combination of individual client needs identified at intake. The question then becomes how these needs can be met in a community with limited resources.

REFERRAL NETWORK

Each community has a limited number of treatment resources that interact in definable ways to establish referral patterns. Within a community, a number of definable referral patterns may operate concurrently. These constitute the referral network.

When examining the referral network in your community, it is helpful to think of it as a dynamic entity rather than a static permanent feature of the treatment system. In fact, it is affected by a number of factors.

The number of services within a community, and their availability, may limit referral options. Services with long waiting lists or those that require a physician referral are more difficult to access.

Knowledge of the services by personnel in the helping professions also affects referral patterns. A service may historically have limited referral patterns because it is not widely advertised.

The specialization of an agency is another factor to consider. The focus of treatment or service, the actual programs offered, admission criteria and the usual type of clientele affect referral patterns. Any changes in treatment focus or treatment personnel over time also act to modify referral patterns.

Lastly, the success in making previous referrals, both in terms of the client's and the referral agent's satisfaction, has a major impact on whether referrals to that service will continue.

WORKING WITH THE COMMUNITY

Upon close inspection, communities often have a wealth of resources able to respond to problems in major life areas, but which may not be well used by referral agents. Helping professionals may be knowledgeable about other services providing a similar function to theirs, but not about services available to address other life areas. The first task, then, is to determine what is available in your community. Many communities have a Community Information Service that documents all resources available, from medical services to recreational clubs and facilities. Social Planning Councils and some public libraries can also provide this type of information.

Once you know what is available generally, the next step is to determine exactly what an agency provides. This would include goals and objectives of the service, actual services provided, modality (group or individual), hours of service, contact person, eligibility criteria, waiting list, intake procedure, fee schedule (if any), and attitudes towards treating substance abusers. It is also important to communicate precisely what you want the service to provide to your clients. Personal contact is important at this initial stage of constructing links with agencies that are new to your service, or with which you have not had recent contact.

Addictions workers must realize that not all community resources may be receptive to providing service to substance abusers, especially if they have had negative experiences with substance abusers, or have not historically treated this population and have some concerns about doing so. Not all helping professionals have received training in addictions, and some may have some biases against providing service.

When establishing referral patterns, the most important point to make is that you are requesting service only in the area that the agency is mandated to provide. Community resources that do not specifically address addiction problems should know that they are not being asked to provide addiction services, but their particular expertise in another life area that is problematic for the client.

There are many different theories of addictions and expectations of treatment success. Referral resources may have a different belief system than your agency has. It is therefore important to clarify your treatment philosophy. This can be done at a staff in-service or with individual caseworkers on a case-by-case basis. Professionals not knowledgeable about the current literature on stages of change and relapse prevention may have unreasonable expectations of abstinence; that is, they may assume that a client who has participated in addictions treatment and has a relapse is not motivated or is a treatment failure. It is important to specify your role in aftercare or case management with respect to service provided during a relapse. Providing fictional examples of the types of cases the resource might encounter, rather than general theoretical information, will help prepare them, and create a more positive relationship between your agency and the referral source.

Rather than contacting a new resource by making a client referral, offer to attend a staff meeting or meet with an individual caseworker to explain fully the nature of your service, expectations of what their service can provide and how the two can best work together. It is better to negotiate the relationship right from the beginning, rather than wait until a problem occurs.

BASIC COMPONENTS OF AN EFFECTIVE REFERRAL

1. ASSESSMENT

A thorough assessment of problems associated with substance abuse gives both the client and the caseworker an overall picture of the role alcohol or other drugs have played in the client's life. There are a number of comprehensive assessment instruments in the field. Assessment and referral centres in Ontario use the ASIST, an instrument developed by the Addiction Research Foundation, to examine 10 life areas: alcohol and psychoactive drug use, accommodation, financial, marital/family, legal, leisure, physical and emotional health, employment, education/training, and social relationships.

2. COMPREHENSIVE KNOWLEDGE OF AVAILABLE RESOURCES

Without a comprehensive knowledge base of community resources, not all available options will be considered when constructing a treatment plan for the client. It is also important to keep this resource base current, as programs and services continually change. There are many ways to update your resource data base.

Sending out letters annually, asking known resources if their program has changed or if they know of any new resources that have opened since you last contacted them, is one way to stay current.

Inviting staff from community resources to your staff meetings on a regular basis not only expands your knowledge base, it also establishes personal links with the resource – you have a chance to meet the voice at the other end of the telephone and to strengthen the link between agencies.

Having a regular "open house" for all your referral resources can make networking easy. Even if only a few people attend, it is a cost-effective way to network with a group of people. Those persons least familiar with your service are also those most likely to attend. You can use this informal networking time to set up more formal links, e.g., offering to attend a staff meeting to present more information on a particular topic or on your agency's services.

Organizing a community resources "grapevine" conference has been shown to be effective, especially to connect front-line workers with each other. If representatives from several resources meet on a regular basis, make it a point to have a "community resource update" regularly on the agenda. Much of this type of information is passed along by word of mouth.

When you are asked to make a presentation about your particular service to another community resource, ensure that there is an exchange of information so that you also come away with new information or at least have met with new associates.

Although keeping your community knowledge base current may sound time-consuming, the benefits are innumerable, both in terms of providing better service to your clients and in terms of building a network of helping professionals truly working together.

3. MATCHING CLIENT NEEDS TO AVAILABLE RESOURCES

An assessment may reveal identification of problems in a variety of life areas other than alcohol or drug abuse. In constructing a treatment plan, problematic life areas can be ranked in terms of severity. Treatment interventions can be specified for each problematic life area, focusing on matching the client's individual needs to available resources.

When referring clients with problems in other life areas, it is important to focus on the nature of each problem. Rather than matching individual clients to particular resources, the client's problems are matched with an agency or resource best able to deal with them. This assumes the necessary sensitivity on the part of the referring counsellor and the receiving agency to the special needs that the client may have. (See the section on Special Needs of Particular Populations.)

It is extremely important to negotiate the treatment plan with the client. Existing community alternatives can be discussed with the client in order to decide which may be most appropriate. The client's previous treatment experiences are worth discussing in order to examine why certain types of treatment were positive while others were not. Positive and negative reactions can be discussed in terms both of objective behavior (did the problem improve?) and of subjective preferences on the part of the client. A client should never be pressured to participate in an unwanted referral. Clients are unlikely to comply with a treatment plan that they feel is imposed or constructed without their direct input.

In addition, the treatment plan must not overwhelm the client. A multiplicity of referrals may immobilize a client, while proceeding methodically through a treatment plan may allow the client gradually to gain control over his or her problems. However, a treatment plan may involve using a number of agencies simultaneously, each agency focusing on the problem with which it can help. For example, a client may be referred simultaneously to:

- a family physician (who can monitor his or her physical condition)
- financial counselling (to consolidate debts and learn how to budget)
- and a self-help group (to develop a support system).

While some agencies may feel that substance abuse treatment is not necessarily within their purview, they may nevertheless be willing to provide these services to substance abusers if they feel the addiction problem is being looked after elsewhere.

In some instances, clients may really want to attend the referral resource, but for many reasons do not keep their appointment. It is helpful to understand what prevents the client from keeping an appointment, including fear of walking in alone. It is important to empower clients to use the health and social service system on their own; however, when they are unable to do so, appropriate supports at the time of referral may help them follow through on the treatment plan. For example, making an appointment for a client rather than just giving out the phone number may be appropriate for some clients. Arranging an escort for the first appointment – either a family member, volunteer, or staff person – may be the deciding factor that leads the client to follow the treatment plan. It is important, however, to provide this extra support only for those clients who cannot do so on their own. The final goal is to empower clients to use the treatment system to meet their needs.

A client does not necessarily need to be referred to a community resource just because he or she has a problem in a particular life area. A referral should match a client with specific needs to a treatment service or resource that can satisfy those needs better than the client could do on his or her own.

ESTABLISHING POSITIVE REFERRAL PATTERNS

When referrals are made to a community resource, it is beneficial to establish a follow-up procedure. With the signed consent of the client, a letter or assessment summary outlining the problem area gives the referral resource a fuller understanding of the problem and the context into which it fits – and the client won't continually have to detail his or her problems. As well, ask clients during case management whether they are satisfied with the referral contacts. If not, discuss the problems involved and either set up a referral with another resource or help the client work out the difficulties encountered. A telephone call to the resource to ask how everything is going can cement the referral relationship and help to work out a co-ordinated treatment plan.

GAPS IN SERVICE

Many communities have gaps in the continuum of appropriate services to meet the needs of clients. Gaps in service may be apparent both in addictions-specific services and in those addressing problems in other life areas. Rural areas have both more gaps in service and greater barriers to obtaining appropriate treatment than do urban areas.

Within a community, it is important to be aware of and keep track of major gaps in service. Most of Ontario, as an example, is divided into areas in which District Health Councils (DHCs) have been established. Their terms of reference include identifying health care needs in their areas and recommending ways of meeting those needs. Each DHC is responsible for preparing planning documents for the district in major health areas. DHCs should be kept abreast of gaps in service in order to assist the community in service planning.

Establishing a support network for a particular problem area in which there are major gaps in service can be an effective way to educate the community about the problem and lobby for better services. Support networks can be composed of both consumers and helping professionals.

In some cases, if enough clients require a specific service unavailable in the community, two or more similar services can share in trying to establish some form of intervention or support for these clients. For example, assertiveness groups, life skills and support groups can be formed at relatively little cost.

It is also prudent to consider the use of volunteers in addressing gaps in service, although there must be commitment from the service to train and supervise them.

When there are gaps in service, using other professionals as consultants may be helpful. For example, obtaining psychiatric consultation for a client with a dual disorder helps to provide better case management.

It is imperative, however, to be aware of service provision limitations, in terms both of agency mandate and of staff qualifications.

Working with the entire community of services presents a challenge. It is important to continually foster the attitude among helping professionals that the community is working together as a team in a broad sense. However, as in any relationship, work and commitment are required to establish an optimally functional treatment network.

Relapse Prevention

HELEN M. ANNIS AND CHRISTINE S. DAVIS

An earlier version of this chapter originally appeared in Handbook of Alcoholism Treatment Approaches: Effective Alternatives, R.K. Hester & W.R. Miller (Eds.), New York: Pergamon Press, 1989.

*T*he chronic, relapsing nature of alcohol problems has long been recognized. However, only in recent years has research attention begun to focus on factors affecting the process of relapse (e.g., Litman, Eiser, Rawson, & Oppenheim, 1977; Litman, Stapleton, Oppenheim, Peleg, & Jackson, 1983; Wilson, 1980), and on the development of "relapse prevention" treatment strategies that may be particularly effective in reducing the probability and severity of relapse (Annis, 1986; Marlatt & Gordon, 1985).

Relapse, by definition, involves a failure to maintain behavior change, rather than a failure to initiate change. Social learning theory approaches, and specifically Bandura's theory of self-efficacy, hold that the most powerful procedures for inducing behavior change may not be the most effective techniques for producing generalization and maintenance of treatment effects (Bandura, 1977, 1978, 1986). That is, a treatment strategy may be highly effective in initiating a change in a client's drinking behavior but ineffective at maintaining that change over time and avoiding relapse. This distinction between initiation and maintenance of behavior change was of central importance in our choice of Bandura's theory of self-efficacy as a framework to guide development of relapse prevention procedures for treatment of alcohol problems. The theoretical derivation of these relapse procedures has been described elsewhere (see Annis, 1986; Annis & Davis, 1988). In this chapter we provide a detailed description of our relapse prevention treatment approach.

OVERVIEW OF THE RELAPSE PREVENTION MODEL

Our model of relapse prevention, based on self-efficacy theory, proposes that when a client enters a high-risk situation for drinking, a process of cognitive appraisal of past experiences is set in motion. This culminates in a judgment, or efficacy expectation, on the part of the client of his or her ability to cope with the situation. That judgment of personal efficacy determines whether or not drinking takes place (see Figure 1). There is now strong empirical evidence of the power of self-efficacy judgments in predicting drinking behavior (e.g., Condra, 1982; Stiemerling, 1983; Risk & Watzl 1983; Annis & Davis, in press).

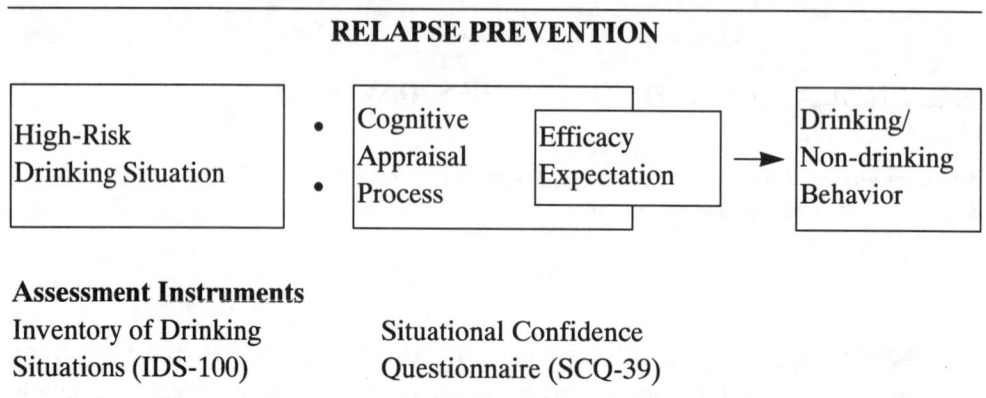

Figure 1 Relapse Prevention Model based on self-efficacy theory.

Therapy begins with an analysis of the client's high-risk situations for drinking, as assessed by the Inventory of Drinking Situations (IDS-100; see below) and the establishment of an individual hierarchy of drinking risk situations, from lowest risk to highest. The purpose of treatment is to effect an increase in the client's self-efficacy or confidence across all drinking situations in the hierarchy. Because behavioral performance has been shown to have the greatest impact on efficacy judgments, treatment focuses on having clients perform homework assignments involving entry into progressively more risky drinking situations in their natural environment and attempting alternative coping responses. Homework assignments are designed to promote maintenance effects that will be reflected in strong gains in the client's confidence or self-efficacy. The Situational Confidence Questionnaire (SCQ-39; see below) is used to monitor progress during treatment in the development of self-efficacy across all drinking-risk situations. Because exposure to real life drinking situations is central to these relapse prevention procedures, treatment must take place while the client is at risk in the community. Typically, treatment is completed in eight outpatient treatment sessions, although further sessions may be necessary for some clients.

Each component of the treatment process is described in greater detail below, beginning with a discussion of the type of client for whom this treatment approach is likely to be most effective.

SCREENING FOR CLIENT SUITABILITY

The model of behavior change on which the relapse prevention strategies described in this chapter are based assumes the existence of adequate motivational incentives;

that is, it is assumed that clients perceive some benefit to working with a therapist toward greater control of their drinking behavior. It is unlikely that the approach would be effective for a homeless alcoholic with few incentives to stop drinking. On the other hand, it should be kept in mind that clients who have a lot to lose in terms of family and work stability, but who are only contemplating change at the time of intake, may be motivated by the early stages of this treatment approach. In terms of Prochaska and DiClemente's (1984) model of change, some relapse prevention procedures can be seen as ways of narrowing the gap between contemplation and action, of demonstrating to the client that change can be gradual and relatively non-threatening and thus motivating the client to attempt to control his or her drinking.

It is also important to consider the belief system of the client. Some feel strongly that their drinking problems reflect deep-seated psychological conflicts, and may insist on an exclusively psychodynamic approach to therapy. In such cases, it would be unproductive to attempt to apply relapse-prevention procedures. More commonly, clients will come to treatment expecting you to take control and solve their drinking problem; such clients must learn that they need to take an active role in the design of homework assignments so that they, in effect, become their own therapist or maintenance agent. Clients who believe in the disease model of alcoholism or have a strong adherence to AA philosophy are still likely to be suitable candidates for relapse prevention training; it is only necessary that they accept the value of learning to prevent relapse by dealing more effectively with high-risk drinking situations. The client's initial belief in abstinence as a treatment goal should also be assessed to ensure that there is no discrepancy between the therapist's and client's outcome expectancy. The question of a treatment goal should be resolved at the outset of treatment. Relapse prevention training may be directed towards a goal of either abstinence or moderation.

Finally, empirical findings on the relapse model to date suggest that clients who have clearly-defined areas of drinking risk, as assessed on the IDS-100, benefit more from brief relapse prevention training than do clients whose drinking is more generalized across situations. Whether clients with generalized (i.e., undifferentiated) profiles on the IDS-100 might show greater gains from more lengthy training is not yet known.

DESCRIPTION OF TREATMENT

ASSESSMENT OF HIGH-RISK DRINKING SITUATIONS

At intake to treatment, the client should complete the Inventory of Drinking Situations, IDS-100 (Annis, 1982; Annis, Graham, & Davis, 1987). The IDS-100 is a 100-item self-report questionnaire designed to assess situations in which the client drank heavily over the past year. You may administer the questionnaire in either paper-and-pencil or software versions. Based on a classification development by Alan Marlatt and his associates (Marlatt & Gordon, 1980, 1985), the client's drinking is assessed in relation to eight categories of drinking situations: unpleasant emotions, physical discomfort, pleasant emotions, testing personal control, urges and temptations, conflict with others, social pressure to drink, and pleasant times with others. You should instruct clients to read each item and indicate the response that most accurately describes their frequency of "heavy drinking" when in that situation during the past year. Clients define "heavy drinking" in the terms of their own comsumption pattern and perception of what constitutes "heavy." Each of the 100 items is answered on a four-point scale where 1 = Never, 2 = Rarely, 3 = Frequently, and 4 = Almost Always.

CONSTRUCTING THE CLIENT PROFILE
OF DRINKING RISK SITUATIONS

From the client's responses on the IDS-100, a "problem index" score, varying from zero to 100, should be calculated for each of the eight categories of drinking situations. By plotting the eight "problem index" scores, you can construct a client profile showing the client's areas of greatest risk for heavy drinking. Client profiles tend to be of two types: generalized or differentiated (Figure 2). A generalized profile is relatively flat with no outstanding high or low categories. A differentiated profile on the other hand, is characterized by peaks and valleys indicating some areas of clearly defined greater drinking risk. The client's profile of risk situations for drinking will serve as the major treatment planning tool.

The client profile, with its graphic portrayal of the client's risk situations for drinking, provides an important framework for focusing and structuring treatment in the early phases of therapy. In the initial therapy session, you should present the profile to the client and ask, in effect, "Is this you?" The client should then be encouraged to discuss how his or her drinking varies across different types of situations and to elaborate on areas of particularly high drinking risk. This discussion serves to provide your clients with feedback on their assessment results, introduces clients to the situational approach to viewing their drinking problems, and begins the process of engaging clients as active collaborators in the treatment process.

WORKING WITH A GENERALIZED CLIENT PROFILE

There are no hard and fast rules for determining whether a client profile on the IDS-100 is generalized or differentiated. However, if the profile is relatively flat across the eight drinking risk categories, you should consider it to be generalized. A generalized profile presents a challenge in that it would seem to indicate that no situation is more or less problematic than any other. The profile may be of either

GENERALIZED PROFILE

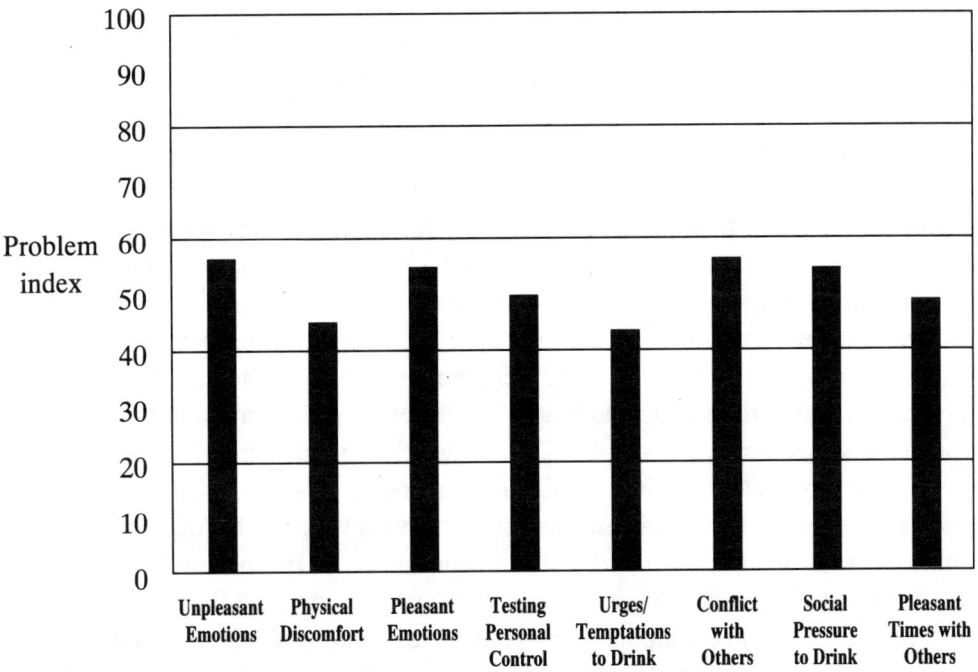

DIFFERENTIATED PROFILE

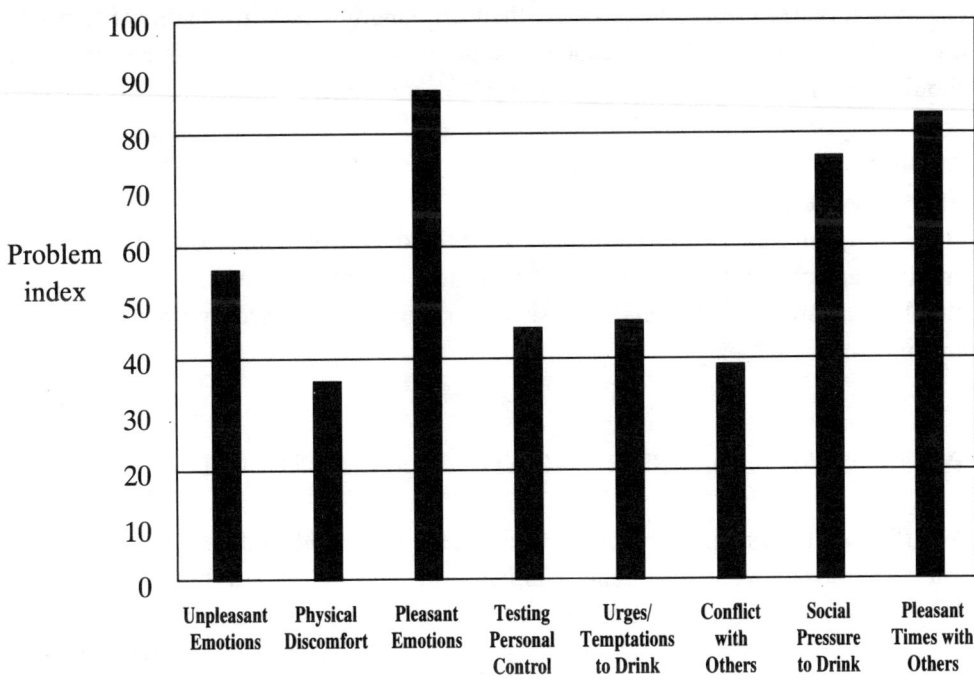

Figure 2 Example of a generalized and a differentiated client profile.

high or low elevation. In a generalized profile of high elevation (e.g., "problem index" scores predominantly greater than 60), the client is reporting frequent heavy drinking across all types of situations; whereas in a generalized profile of low elevation, the client is reporting infrequent heavy drinking across all situations.

Initially, you will want to consider, based on other sources of information, whether the profile is an accurate reflection of the client's drinking behavior. In discussing the profile with the client, you should attempt to determine whether the client may be trying to present a particularly unfavorable view (high elevation profile) or favorable view (low elevation profile) of his or her drinking behavior. Are there environmental demands on or incentives to the client to present in this way? Or is there reason to believe that drinking has become a highly generalized behavior across all categories of risk situations? In our experience, even clients who have been drinking heavily for years are usually able to identify, under supplementary questioning by the therapist, some examples of situations of particularly high risk for them.

A flat profile should also signal you to reconsider whether or not the client is in fact ready to embark on a relapse-prevention treatment approach. Are there adequate motivational incentives for change? Is the client at the precontemplative or contemplative stage only (see Prochaska & DiClemente, 1984) and unwilling to analyze the situational component of his or her drinking problem? Has a decision to change been made? Should motivational counselling (see chapter 3) be offered before attempting to proceed with relapse prevention training?

With other clients, a flat profile may not reflect a lack of commitment to change but rather a reluctance to view their drinking problem in situational terms, or a lack of awareness of the relevance of situational determinants. In either case, you should explore with the client the situational components present in a few recent drinking episodes. In many instances, such a discussion will be sufficient to show the clients the relevance of the approach and help them learn to differentiate risk situations that play a role in their drinking problems. Having the client keep an hourly log, in which both emotional states and interpersonal risk situations for drinking are carefully monitored and recorded, can also be useful in teaching the client to differentiate the relative risk for drinking experienced within commonly encountered situations.

WORKING WITH A DIFFERENTIATED CLIENT PROFILE

A differentiated profile, with clearly defined peaks and valleys across drinking categories, makes your treatment planning more straightforward, because it already suggests areas of high drinking risk for the client. As with generalized profiles, differentiated profiles may be of either relatively high or low elevation. What is important in a differentiated profile is the clear demarcation of peaks indicating areas of increased drinking risk. Differentiated profiles can be of three types: positive, negative or mixed.

Positive Profile

In this type of profile, the client is reporting more frequent heavy drinking in situations that are positive in nature: that is, the peaks occur for one or more of the following: pleasant emotions, testing personal control, social pressure to drink, pleasant times with others; or all of the above. We have found that this type of profile is more common among younger clients and more frequently found in male clients than females (Annis, Graham & Davis, 1987).

Negative Profile

In this type of profile, the client is reporting more frequent heavy drinking in situations that are negative in nature; that is, the peaks occur for: unpleasant emotions, physical discomfort, urges and temptations, and/or conflict with others. Our research indicates that heavy drinking in negative situations is more often reported by female clients, by clients who tend to drink alone, and by clients with more years of heavy drinking (Annis, Graham & Davis, 1987). For these clients, alcohol appears to function as a coping response to negative situations.

Mixed Profile

In this type of profile, the client is reporting more frequent heavy drinking in some specific positive and negative situations; that is, the peaks occur for one or more situations that are positive in nature (pleasant emotions, testing personal control, social pressure to drink, pressure to drink, pleasant times with others) and one or more situations that are negative in nature (unpleasant emotions, physical discomfort, urges and temptations, conflict with others). In our clinical experience, clearly differentiated profiles of a mixed nature are relatively rare.

DEVELOPING A HIERARCHY OF DRINKING RISK SITUATIONS

Following detailed discussion and elaboration of the client's IDS-100 profile, you should then engage the client in the task of developing a hierarchy of very specific drinking risk situations, from lowest risk to highest. The client must understand that this hierarchy will form the basis for the development of homework assignments that will involve entering progressively more risky drinking situations over the course of treatment. Once success is achieved in coping with situations lower in the hierarchy, homework assignments will involve exposure to more difficult situations.

Ideally, in collaboration with the client, you will identify two or more specific types of situations within each of the high-risk categories on the client's IDS-100 profile. (For example, for a client with a peak on the category *Unpleasant emotions*, one problem situation for drinking may involve coping with feelings of loneliness upon returning to an empty apartment after work, while another may involve drinking in response to feeling depressed about a failure to achieve a particular goal.) Once you have elicited specific recent examples of events within each of the client's high-risk categories, a microanalysis of each event should be made. When did the event take place? Where was the client? Who, if anyone other than the client, was present? What exactly happened before and after the drinking occurred? How did the client appraise the event – i.e., what were the client's thoughts and feelings before, during, and after the event? What is the client's current level of self-efficacy or confidence that he or she would now be able to cope successfully in a similar situation? Such detailed analyses of recent problem drinking situations often suggest intervention strategies that may be helpful, while at the same time providing information on how the situation should be ranked in terms of difficulty on the client's hierarchy.

As with any treatment plan, the hierarchy is likely to require frequent review and revision over the course of treatment. Nevertheless, the process of establishing a hierarchy is extremely important in that it clarifies for the client how treatment will proceed, provides a series of benchmarks that will indicate progress in treatment as movement proceeds further up the hierarchy, and establishes a common understanding between you and the client as to what needs to be accomplished. Because the client is engaged in all aspects of decision-making in the formation of the hierarchy, the client will gradually learn to function as his or her own therapist or agent for maintaining change.

IDENTIFYING STRENGTHS AND RESOURCES

The strengths, supports and coping responses already available to a client are invaluable in preventing relapse. They form the groundwork for the development of successful homework assignments. The client must become more aware of the wide variety of strengths he or she possesses and learn to use them effectively. Coping responses that the client may have been using successfully in other areas might be quite effective, with only minor alteration, in addressing problematic drinking situations. Significant others in the client's life, such as a spouse or an employer, may be willing to provide support, encouragement, and even active involvement in helping the client address the drinking problem.

The task, at this point in your treatment planning, is to establish the client's existing repertoire of general coping behaviors, personal strengths and environmental resources. The process of reviewing the client's repertoire should provide you with a better appreciation of the possibilities open to the client, and should afford the client an opportunity to focus on past successes and enduring capabilities rather than on current failures.

Each of the following resource areas should be explored:

Environmental Supports
Are there friends or family members who have provided support in the past or who would be willing to do so now? Are there people at work who could be called upon

when difficulties arise? Are there agencies (such as AA) or individuals (such as a local religious leader) that the client feels comfortable going to?

Behavioral Coping

Has the client ever attempted to solve problems that might have led to drinking, resolved to do something constructive and followed through? Has the client developed any alternative activities or rewards that can take the place of drinking, even if they have not been actively pursued for some time? Has the client ever sought out information or advice from family or friends? Has the client been able to successfully avoid or leave a high-risk situation without drinking?

Cognitive Coping

Is the client able to reason things out, see connections between actions and consequences, and plan alternative ways of dealing with a situation? Is the client able to appreciate the positive benefits of not drinking and believe that he or she would personally benefit from abstinence? When confronted by urges or temptations to drink, is the client able to distract him or herself by thinking of other things or imagining a positive outcome?

Affective Coping

Is the client able to face negative thoughts or emotional turmoil and value feelings of control and self-discipline? Does the client have strong spiritual beliefs that provide comfort? Can the client passively accept things that cannot be changed? Does the client have emotional outlets for releasing tension or anger?

Current strengths of the client in each of the above resource areas should be noted, along with any other ideas that the client would like to try for successful coping. Both you and the client can refer back to this list when discussing the design of homework assignments. The client should be encouraged to use the identified strengths when faced with drinking situations that may not have been anticipated. Because current empirical evidence suggests that reliance on a *wide* range of coping responses, rather than a more restricted repertoire, is related to avoidance of relapse (Litman, Eiser Rawson & Oppenheim, 1979; Litman, Stapleton, Oppenheim, Peleg & Jackson, 1983), the client should be encouraged to draw upon as wide a variety of coping alternatives as possible.

DESIGNING HOMEWORK ASSIGNMENTS

Relapse prevention training focuses on having the client enter formerly problematic drinking situations in his or her natural environment and succeed in coping. Clients are gradually exposed over the course of treatment to progressively more risky drinking situations in their hierarchies until they succeed in coping with all identified areas of drinking risk. Particularly in the early stages of treatment, it is critical that homework assignments be designed so that the client experiences "mastery" and begins to build confidence (self-efficacy) in his or her ability to cope in drinking-related situations. Multiple homework assignments (i.e., three or more) should be agreed to at each therapy appointment, so that the client rapidly accumulates evidence of successful coping across a variety of formerly problematic areas. These homework assignments should draw upon as wide a variety of the client's coping strengths and resources as possible. With the growth of perceived confidence or self-efficacy, movement up the hierarchy to more difficult situations is attempted. At this later stage, a failure experience (i.e., drinking) is unlikely to be the major setback it might have been early in treatment because the client has already initiated a snowball effect in the growth of self-efficacy. Consequently, more "chances" can be taken later in treatment in having the client risk exposure to the most problematic situations in the hierarchy. By the end of the treatment, the client should be assuming major responsibility for the design of all homework assignments.

At the outset of treatment, each client should receive a pocket-sized drinking log and weekly homework assignment booklet. All homework assignments for the coming week that have been agreed upon should be entered in the booklet. Those assignments, together with detailed entries by the client of any drinking that takes place, will be reviewed at the beginning of the next treatment appointment (see Figure 3).

For each problem situation in the client's hierarchy, it is important to have at least a tentative plan of action early in treatment. Discussion thus far has emphasized the highly individual nature of homework assignments that go into relapse prevention training. In our experience, however, there are *five* basic types of homework assignments that are relevant to addressing problems in all categories of drinking risk situations. These basic types are outlined below.

Monitoring specific situations and cognitions

This very basic task is frequently used early in the treatment process, but it can also serve an important function for some clients throughout the course of treatment. When a client indicates that a particular area is problematic (e.g., experiences urges and temptations to drink or feelings of anger or tension leading to drinking) but is unable to describe in detail specific recent examples of this type of event, it can be helpful to have the client monitor on a daily basis all instances in which the situation arises (e.g., all instances in which urges and tempations to drink are experienced, or feelings of anger or tension arise), recording immediate antecedent events, associated thoughts and feelings, and attempted coping responses. The process of monitoring, with its attendant focusing of the client's attention on the problem area, can be useful in revealing important antecedent events and in initiating the client's planning of alternative ways of handling the situation. Future homework assignments in this problem area will thus be more meaningful to the client because they will be based on a clearer perception of the specific drinking antecedents in his or her current life situation.

WEEKLY DRINKING LOG

NAME _____

DAY OF WEEK	DATE (month/day)	NUMBER OF DRINKS (Record "0" if you have abstained)
1.		
2.		
3.		
4.		
5.		
6.		
7.		

ASSIGNMENTS: 1. _____

2. _____

3. _____

DAILY DRINKING LOG – Complete a separate page for each day on which any drinking occurred.

DAY OF WEEK _____ DATE _____ NAME _____

DRINKING OCCASION	TIME			ALCOHOL CONSUMED		SETTING				COMMENT (your thoughts, feelings, etc.)		
	STARTED	STOPPED	TOTAL TIME	TYPE	NO. OF DRINKS	Alone	With others who drank less	With others who drank more	Place (bar, home, etc.)	BEFORE DRINKING	DURING	AFTER DRINKING
1.												
2.												
3.												
4.												

Figure 3 Pocket-sized Client Drinking Log and Weekly Homework Assignment booklet.

Anticipating problem situations

One of the most important skills a client must learn is to anticipate when a difficult situation is likely to arise so that there is time to preplan a coping response before being confronted with the situation. For each major problem area, you should encourage the client to review the likely events of the coming week and note when problematic situations might arise. For example, if social pressure to drink is an identified problem area, the client should try to anticipate when and where he or she might face such pressure on any given day. If the client has difficulty anticipating social pressure situations, concurrent monitoring of when these situations arise (see above) is likely to be helpful in revealing patterns predictive of future occurrences. Forewarning frequently makes the critical difference in whether or not a client can successfully implement an appropriate coping response.

Planning and rehearsing alternative responses

Once the client has identified a specific, high-risk drinking situation and when it is likely to occur, he or she should be asked to plan and rehearse (at least mentally) a number of possible alternative ways of coping with the situation. For example, if being offered a drink when visiting a particular friend is problematic, the client would be asked to generate a number of possible alternative plans of action. For each plan, exactly what would be done or said? What would be the likely consequences? How would the client feel? Is the client confident that she or he will be able to carry out the plan? Of the plans considered, which one would the client like to try first? Such assignments allow the client to consider new ways of coping and to become mentally prepared and comfortable with a plan before attempting to put it into action. To the extent possible, rehearsal of proposed plans with you, in the therapeutic session, should be encouraged (e.g., role playing refusing a drink, ordering a non-alcoholic beverage, declining a social invitation, or suggesting an alternative activity for the evening). Being mentally prepared, with well-rehearsed plans of action, increases the client's feeling of control and confidence in being able to confront high-risk situations and experiment with new ways of coping.

The client should also be prepared with plans of action in the event of a drinking slip. If drinking were to occur, what coping strategies has the client considered to help terminate the drinking and avoid a full-blown relapse? Again, you should encourage the client to consider a range of environmental supports and behavioral, cognitive, and affective coping strategies that could be used (e.g., calling you or a supportive friend, leaving the setting, refusing the next drink, considering the positive benefits of not drinking, taking pride in exercising control). The client must learn to confront the possibility of a drinking slip and to have in place well-developed plans to deal with it constructively. It is important for you to convey to the client the belief that he or she is able to exert control and terminate drinking at any point, and that drinking slips present an opportunity to learn about weakness and to plan more effective ways of coping.

Practising new behaviors in increasingly difficult situations

Having developed and rehearsed coping strategies for dealing with a problematic drinking situation, the client is ready for exposure to such situations, so that "mastery" may be experienced in implementing the new behaviors. Homework assignments of this type, in which the client enters progressively riskier drinking situations, are the essence of relapse prevention training.

Very difficult assignments should be avoided in the early stages of treatment because it is particularly important that the client experience some early success. Using a variety of "external aids" may help ensure that homework assignments can be performed successfully. These may entail your involvement – and/or that of a spouse, boss, or significant other – in accompanying the client on a homework assignment, or the use of an alcohol sensitizing drug (such as Antabuse or Temposil). Having the client avoid certain highly problematic drinking situations is also a useful strategy to initiate a change in drinking behavior early in treatment. While these are excellent methods for quickly bringing the client's drinking behavior under control, they are unlikely to have lasting effects on the development of client confidence and the prevention of future relapse. The development of self-efficacy and strong maintenance effects requires that clients attribute improvement in treatment to an increase in their own ability to cope directly with drinking situations. You therefore need to ensure that such strategies – avoiding common drinking risk situations, use of an alcohol-sensitizing drug, or excessive reliance on others – have faded in prominence before the client is discharged from treatment.

Particularly in the later stages of treatment, homework assignments should be designed to promote strong maintenance effects (reflected in strong gains in self-efficacy – see below) so as to prevent relapse. To have good potential for maintenance or relapse prevention, homework assignments should engender the following self-inferences on the part of the client:

1. The task was challenging (i.e., client perceives that in the past the situation would likely have resulted in heavy drinking).
2. Only a moderate degree of effort was required to cope effectively (i.e., client does not see the degree of effort as highly aversive).
3. Little external aid was involved in being able to cope successfully (i.e., client sees the success as a personal victory and not attributable to the therapist, spouse, significant other, a drug, or other external supports).
4. Success at the task was part of an overall pattern of improved performance (i.e., client sees a pattern of steady improvement in the drinking problem).
5. An increase in personal control was demonstrated (i.e., client attributes the success to a growth in personal capability).
6. The success was highly relevant to the drinking problem (i.e., client sees the success as reflecting improvement in a critical area of his or her drinking problem).

When a client is performing homework assignments successfully but does not appear to be gaining in confidence (see below, Monitoring Outcome and Change in Self-Efficacy), your enquiry along these six dimensions of self-inference should reveal where the problem resides and suggest how further homework assignments should be modified.

Noting improvement competence
Finally, having the client deliberately note examples of improved competence in handling formerly problematic situations can play an important role in consolidating treatment gains. Throughout therapy, clients should be asked to review how their behavior in different risk situations has changed, to reinforce the progress they are making. Clients should be encouraged to take a multidimensional view of their drinking problem, and to note examples of improved competence within each of several different risk areas. Failure to progress in one area, or an actual drinking slip, does not negate the client's real gains in competence in coping with other types of risk situations. Hence the tendency of some clients to catastrophize a drinking episode is discouraged. This multidimensional view places both successes and failures in context. Any single situation or event, whether it is handled successfully or results in a drinking episode, reflects on only one aspect of the drinking problem. By noting specific examples of improved competence, clients learn that improvement involves incremental gain in coping, with occasional setbacks across a range of drinking risk situations.

MONITORING OUTCOME AND CHANGE IN SELF-EFFICACY

At intake, in mid-treatment, and towards discharge, the client should complete the Situational Confidence Questionnaire, SCQ-39 (Annis, 1987; Annis & Graham, 1988), a 39-item self-report questionnaire designed to assess Bandura's concept of self-efficacy for alcohol-related situations. Clients are asked to imagine themselves in a variety of situations, derived from the work of Marlatt and Gordon (1980) and from each situation to indicate on a six-point scale (zero = not at all confident; 20 = 20 per cent confident; 40 = 40 per cent confident; 60 = 60 per cent confident; 80 = 80 per cent confident; 100 = very confident) how confident they are that they will be able to resist the urge to drink heavily in that situation. A client's response on the SCQ-39 will allow you to monitor the development of his or her self-efficacy in relation to coping with specific drinking situations over the course of treatment.

The purpose of treatment is to effect a rise in self-efficacy across all areas of perceived drinking risk. If the client fails to show growth of confidence in coping with a particular type of risk situation, further work in this area should be considered before discharge from treatment. You will need to consider possible reasons for the lack of development of confidence in the identified area. Has the client successfully performed homework assignments involving entry into situations of this type? If so, what self-inferences is the client drawing from those experiences? Are the client's self-inferences consistent with the six dimensions (outlined above) that are known to promote gains in self-efficacy? Your enquiry should suggest the reason for the client's lack of confidence in reaction to the particular risk area and suggest what further work needs to be done before discharge.

EFFECTIVENESS

A variety of empirical findings support the principles of self-efficacy theory on which the relapse prevention procedures described in this chapter are based. A growing body of evidence in the addictions field associates the development of self-efficacy with positive treatment outcome (e.g., Annis & Davis, in press; Coelho, 1984; Colletti, Supnick, & Payne, 1985; Condiotte & Lichtenstein, 1981; DiClemente, 1981; Jeffrey et al., 1984; Marlatt & Gordon, 1985; McIntyre, Lichtenstein & Mermelstein, 1983; Miller, Ross, Emmerson & Todt, 1987; Prochaska, Crimi, Lapanski, Martel & Reid, 1982; and Risk & Watzl, 1983). Moreover, there is evidence that a client is most likely to relapse in an area of low perceived self-efficacy (Annis & Davis, in press; Condiotte & Lichtenstein, 1981). Client attribution of the reasons for drinking to external rather than internal causes and heavy consumption of alcohol have both been shown to be associated with levels of drinking-related self-efficacy (Annis & Graham, 1988; Solomon & Annis, in press). In support of the recommendations of relapse prevention training, patient-generated homework assignments have been found to be somewhat more likely to be completed successfully than therapist-generated tasks (Annis & Davis, in press). There is evidence that client acceptance of the belief of "one drink, a drunk" (i.e., the inevitability of relapse following a single drink and one's inability to exert control) is associated with increased probability of post-treatment relapse (Heather, Rollnick, & Winton, 1983). An inability to deal effectively with high-risk situations involving negative emotional states also has been found to be predictive of relapse (Annis & Davis, in press; Chaney, O'Leary & Marlatt, 1978).

A recently completed study at the Addiction Research Foundation in Toronto (Annis, Davis, Graham, & Levinson, 1987) was designed to provide a controlled evaluation of the effectiveness of relapse prevention procedures derived from self-efficacy theory. Eighty-three employed alcoholic clients who had completed a three-week inpatient program were randomly assigned to receive relapse prevention training, as described in this chapter, or more traditional counselling on an outpatient basis. On the basis of their scores on the Inventory of Drinking Situations (IDS-100), each client was categorized as having either a *"generalized profile"* (i.e., similar drinking across all eight types of drinking risk situations), or a *"differentiated profile"* (i.e., greater drinking risk in some types of situations than in others). All clients received eight treatment sessions over a three-month period. Results for the

68 clients (81%) contacted at six month follow-up showed no differences across the two treatment conditions in typical daily quantity of alcohol consumed for clients with generalized profiles; however, clients with differentiated profiles showed a substantially lower typical daily quantity under relapse prevention treatment than under traditional counselling. This client-treatment matching effect accounted for more than 30 per cent of the outcome variance on this measure of consumption.

SUMMARY

The development of relapse prevention procedures, based on self-efficacy theory, has provided a new and promising direction in the treatment of alcohol problems. The treatment strategies described in this chapter are derived from social psychological research investigating the processes involved in the initiation versus the maintenance of behavior change. Procedures are outlined for determining a client's suitability for relapse prevention training, for assessing a client's high-risk drinking situations, for identifying strengths and resources, for tailoring individual homework assignments, and for monitoring progress over the course of treatment. Cautionary guidelines are provided on commonly used intervention procedures that are likely to have poor maintenance potential. Client self-inferences related to strong gains in self-efficacy are discussed. Initial findings suggest that the focus on homework assignments, aimed at increasing self-efficacy or confidence in identified areas of drinking risk, is a promising approach to the prevention of future relapse.

REFERENCES

CLINICAL GUIDELINES

Annis, H. M. (1982). *Inventory of Drinking Situations (IDS-100)*. Toronto, Canada: Addiction Research Foundation. The IDS is a situation-specific measure of drinking that can be used to identify a client's high-risk situations for alcoholic relapse. The IDS serves as a treatment planning tool, providing a profile of a client's areas of greatest drinking risk. Administration may be by paper-and-pencil questionnaire; computer interactive software also available from Addiction Research Foundation, Marketing Department, 33 Russell St., Toronto, Ontario M5S 2S1.

Annis, H. M. (1987). *Situational Confidence Questionnaire (SCQ-39)*. Toronto, Canada: Addiction Research Foundation. The SCQ-39 is a situation-specific measure of efficacy expectations that is designed to assess Bandura's concept of self-efficacy in relation to a client's perceived ability to cope effectively with alcohol. Administration may be by paper-and-pencil format or computer interactive software available from Addiction Research Foundation, Marketing Department, 33 Russell St., Toronto, Ontario M5S 2S1.

Annis, H. M. & Davis, C. S. (in press). Assessment of expectancies in alcohol-dependent clients. In D. M. Donovan & G. A. Marlatt (Eds.), *Assessment of addictive behaviors*. New York: Guilford. This chapter describes the clinical application of relapse prevention procedures directed toward either abstinence or moderation goals. Clinical examples are presented to illustrate the design of homework assignments in relation to each of the eight categories of drinking risk identified on the Inventory of Drinking Situations.

Annis, H. M. & Graham, J. M (1988). *Situational Confidence Questionnaire (SCQ) User's Guide*. Toronto, Canada: Addiction Research Foundation. The 45-page User's Guide gives a detailed presentation of the development of the SCQ and presents guidelines for clinical and research applications. Reliability and validity data are summarized and normative data are provided. Available from Addiction Research Foundation, Marketing Department, 33 Russell St., Toronto, Ontario M5S 2S1.

Annis, H. M., Graham, J. M. & Davis, C. S. (1987). *Inventory of Drinking Situations (IDS) User's Guide*. Toronto, Canada: Addiction Research Foundation. The 50-page User's Guide describes the development of the IDS and its use in clinical and research settings, presents reliability and validity information plus normative data, and provides guidelines for use in paper-and-pencil or computer interactive format. Available from Addiction Research Foundation, Marketing Department, 33 Russell St., Toronto, Ontario M5S 2S1.

Daley, D. C. (1986). *Relapse prevention workbook for recovering alcoholics and drug-dependent persons.* Holmes Beach, FL: Learning Publications, Inc. This client workbook presents a number of exercises to help the client identify risk situations for drinking and to plan coping responses for those situations. Other topics covered include use of an emergency sobriety card, lifestyle balancing, and what to do if a relapse occurs.

Marlatt, G. A. & Gordon, J. R. (1985). *Relapse prevention: Maintenance strategies in the treatment of addictive behaviors.* New York: Guilford Press. This book presents a model of relapse prevention based on self-management or self-control procedures. Self-control strategies in three main areas are described: skill-training aimed at the acquisition of adaptive coping skills; cognitive procedures designed to foster new attitudes, attributions and expectancies; and lifestyle interventions aimed at developing healthy self-care activities.

RESEARCH

Annis, H. M. (1986). A relapse prevention model for treatment of alcoholics. In W. R. Miller & N. Heather (Eds). *Treating addictive behaviors: Processes of change* (pp. 407-433). New York: Plenum.

Annis, H. M. & Davis, C. S. (1988). Assessment of expectancies in alcohol-dependent clients. In D. M. Donovan & G. A. Marlatt (Eds.), *Assessment of Addictive Behaviors* (pp. 84-111). New York: Guilford Press.

Annis, H. M. & Davis, C. S. (in press). Self-efficacy and the prevention of alcoholic relapse: Initial finding from a treatment trial. In T. B. Baker & D. Cannon (Eds.), *Addictive disorders: Psychological research on assessment and treatment.* New York: Praeger.

Annis, H. M., Davis, C. S., Graham, M. & Levinson, T. (1987). *A controlled trial of relapse prevention procedures based on self-efficacy theory.* Unpublished manuscript.

Bandura, A. (1977). Self-efficacy: Toward a unifying theory of behavioral change. *Psychological Review, 84,* 191-215.

Bandura, A. (1978). Reflections on self-efficacy. *Advances in Behavioral Research and Therapy, 1,* 237-269.

Bandura, A. (1986). *Social foundations of thought and action: A social cognitive theory.* Englewood Cliffs, NJ: Prentice-Hall.

Chaney, E. F., O'Leary, M. R. & Marlatt, G. A. (1978). Skill training with alcoholics. *Journal of Consulting and Clinical Psychology 46,* 1092-1104.

Coelho, R. J. (1984). Self-efficacy and cessation of smoking. *Psychological Reports, 54,* 309-310.

Colletti, G., Supnick, J. A. & Payne, T. J. (1985). The Smoking Self-Efficacy Questionnaire: A preliminary validation. *Behavior Assessment, 7,* 249-254.

Condiotte, M. M. & Lichtenstein, E. (1981). Self-efficacy and relapse in smoking cessation programs. *Journal of Consulting and Clinical Psychology, 49,* 648-658.

Condra, M. St. John (1982). The effectiveness of relapse training in the treatment of alcohol problems. Unpublished doctoral dissertation, Queen's University, Kingston, Canada.

DiClemente, C. C. (1981). Self-efficacy and smoking cessation maintenance: A preliminary report. *Cognitive Research and Therapy, 5,* 175-187.

Heather , N., Rollnick, S. & Winton, M. (1983). A comparison of objective and subjective measures of alcohol dependence as predictors of relapse following treatment. *British Journal of clinical Psychology, 22,* 11-17.

Jeffrey, R. W., Bjornson-Benson, W. M., Rosenthal, B. S., Lindquist, R. A., Kurth, C. L. & Johnson, S. L. (1984). Correlates of weight loss and its maintenance over two years of follow-up among middle-aged men. *Preventive Medicine, 13,* 155-168.

Litman, G. K., Eiser, J. R., Rawson, N. S. B. & Oppenheim, A. N. (1977). Towards a typology of relapse: A preliminary report. *Drug and Alcohol Dependence, 2,* 157-162.

Litman, G. K., Eiser, J. R., Rawson, N. S. B., & Oppenheim, A. N. (1979). Differences in relapse precipitants and coping behaviours between alcohol relapsers and survivors. *Behaviour Research and Therapy, 17,* 89-94.

Litman, G. K., Stapleton, J., Oppenheim, A. N., Peleg, M. & Jackson, P. (1983). The relationship between coping behaviors, their effectiveness and alcoholism relapse and survival. *British Journal of Addiction, 79 (3),* 283-291.

Marlatt, G. A. & Gordon, J. R. (1980). Determinants of relapse: Implications for the maintenance of behavior change. In P. Davidson & S. Davidson (Eds.), *Behavioral Medicine: Changing health lifestyles* (pp. 410-452). New York: Brunner/Mazel.

McIntyre, D. O., Lichtenstein, E. & Mermelstein, R. J. (1983). Self-efficacy and relapse in smoking cessation: A replication and extension. *Journal of Consulting and Clinical Psychology, 51,* 632-633.

Miller, P. J., Ross, S. M., Emmerson, R. Y. & Todt, E. H. (1987). *Self-efficacy in alcoholics: Clinical validation of the Situational Confidence Questionnaire.* Manuscript submitted for publication.

Prochaska, J. O., Crimi, P., Lapanski, D., Martel, L. & Reid, P. (1982). Self-change processes, self-efficacy and self-concept in relapse and maintenance of cessation of smoking. *Psychological Reports, 51,* 983-990.

Prochaska, J. O. & DiClemente, C. C. (1984). *The transtheoretical approach: Crossing traditional boundaries of therapy.* Homewood, IL: Dow Jones-Irwin.

Risk, F. & Watzl, H. (1983). Self assessment of relapse risk and assertiveness in relation to treatment outcome of female alcoholics. *Addictive Behaviours, 8,* 121-127.

Solomon, K. E. & Annis, H. M. (in press). Development of a scale to measure outcome expectancies in alcoholics. *Cognitive Therapy and Research.*

Stiemerling, N. (1983). *Relapse in alcohol abusers: A short-term longitudinal study.* Unpublished doctoral dissertation, Queen's University, Kingston, Canada.

Wilson, G. T. (1980). Cognitive factors in lifestyle changes: A social learning perspective. In P. O. Davidson & S. M. Davidson (Eds.), *Behavioral Medicine: Changing health lifestyles* (pp.3-37). New York: Brunner/Mazel.

Situational Management of Disruptive Behavior

GWEN CARROLL

WHAT IS SITUATIONAL MANAGEMENT?

*T*his chapter is intended to help you manage those events that slow down or block the helping process. Treatment is an ongoing sequence of events designed to help individuals bring about long term lifestyle changes: *the goal of situational management is to defuse potentially disruptive events during counselling sessions so that the treatment process continues.* When applied consistently, counselling strategies in general, especially those based on motivational theory, will lead to a reduction in disruptive behavior. However, it is unrealistic to think that these types of events can be eliminated completely. Our objective is to recognize potentially disruptive situations as they occur and to modify our actions and the environment around us so they don't get out of control.

PRINCIPLES OF SITUATIONAL MANAGEMENT

We have based our management strategies on the following three principles:
- Many individuals learn that disruptive behavior is more effective than cooperation in achieving their immediate objective. This may be to control the session, to end an unpleasant or difficult situation, to have their demands met quickly or simply to gain attention from other people.
- We can contain most disruptions by changing our own behavior and by modifying the environment around the individual.
- Individuals under the influence remain responsive to our actions as well as their environment as long as they remain conscious.

HEAD-TO-TOE SCANNING

All of us have our own way of observing people as we work with them. However, we sometimes wait until an individual shows obvious signs of distress before we look for evidence that a disruption is imminent, or assess the risks involved. As a crisis escalates, the individual often watches us as closely as we watch him or her. Because behavior is often influenced by the actions of the counsellor, a method of observation that does not distract the individual is desirable. The method should also enable the counsellor to establish baseline behavior and recognize changes throughout the session.

One technique that enables us to do this consistently is head-to-toe scanning. This skill develops with practice and provides brief, systematic, objective observations as an individual moves through various topics and situations. It involves simply scanning the individual from head to toe periodically as you proceed through the session. This helps to focus your observations and ensures that they are ongoing, objective and systematic. The following outlines the objectives of head-to-toe scanning:

- Always be aware of the individual's level of central nervous system (CNS) stimulation. This can change several times during an interview or counselling session, especially if the individual is intoxicated. Your observations enable you to distinguish between a stimulated state, a depressed state and distorted perceptions. Your actions and the environment are modified accordingly, adding or removing stimulation as necessary. Distorted perceptions are often accompanied by a state of CNS stimulation – a difficult combination to manage. It is a cue for you to keep distance between you and the client as you reduce stimulation and reassure the individual.

- Assess the individual's physical and emotional state as the session begins and observe for changes throughout the session. Clients may say they are in good health or complain of illness. Your observations help you to assess the meaning of their statements and to validate complaints. For example, perspiration around the eyes and upper lip is often a sign of illness. However, an individual who complains of severe abdominal pain but is not guarding the affected area is unlikely to be suffering from acute appendicitis. Chewed fingernails indicate a high stress level over time while visible pulsations, taut facial muscles, clenched fists or facial flushing indicate increasing tension during the session. Not only are these observations useful in forecasting potential disruptions, they help you to link stress or self-worth statements to other life areas instead of generalizing. For example, instead of saying "He is stressed out," you may report "His stress level increases when he talks about his mother while self-worth statements increase when he talks about his music."

- Finally, you want to know what you are up against at all times, even when the session appears to be going smoothly. This is a basic rule of self-defence. Your scan should include observations for weapons and other dangerous items. Is there an unexpected bulge in the clothing? This could be a weapon or, if you are collecting urine for drug screening, a hidden, drug-free sample. Does the individual repeatedly pick up heavy objects from your desk; is he or she wearing steel-toed boots? You need not necessarily confront the individual about your observations. The objective is to be prepared in the event of a disruption.

These are just some things you may want to build into your head-to-toe scanning routine. When working in teams, work together to develop your list. This way, staff observations become consistent and more meaningful over time.

FUNCTIONAL ANALYSIS

The better we understand human behavior in a variety of situations, and our effect on it, the easier it is to diffuse disruptions. Functional analysis is one way to further develop your understanding. It involves describing disruptions according to a sequence of events. The first step is to describe what the individual is doing that leads you to label him or her disruptive. While we are all concerned with self harm, violence, threats and assault, actions such as swearing, yelling, refusing to talk, flirting or walking out are much more common and can slow down the treatment process. Managing these behaviors can prevent escalation to more serious types of disruptions. In addition to describing the specific disruptive behavior, you monitor its frequency.

The next step is to identify the antecedents to the disruptive behavior. These are cues, triggers and events that lead the individual to be disruptive. These can be environmental, physical, emotional, social, situational or cognitive – even your own actions. This may be as simple as your physical presence or something you said or did. Everything that immediately precedes a disruption is examined as a possible antecedent.

The functional analysis is completed by identifying the reinforcing consequence of the disruptive behavior. The payoffs help the individual achieve something pleasant or avoid something unpleasant. While disruptions are often followed by consequences that should punish the behavior, it is the payoffs, no matter how short-lived, that increase the likelihood that the disruptive behavior will be repeated.

Antecedents and reinforcing consequences may be real or perceived. For example, imagined pain often prompts analgesic use; over time, an individual may start to take the medication to prevent pain, before actually experiencing it. The same learned patterns exist in disruptive behavior. When an individual expects you to create an unpleasant situation, he or she may become disruptive to stop you from proceeding. The following functional analysis demonstrates some of the more common antecedents and reinforcing consequences of disruptive behaviors.

ANTECEDENTS	BEHAVIORS	CONSEQUENCES
• Hostility or aggression on the part of others	• Action by an individual that...	• Get desired results faster than co-operation
• Failure (real or imagined)	- slows down or blocks the treatment process	• Escape from a dull and unrewarding situation
• Unrealistic expectations	- takes the counsellor's attention away from the task at hand	• Release of tension
• Others in control or attempting to control		• Avoid unpleasant thoughts, feelings and activity
• Dull and unrewarding situations	- threatens the safety of the individual or other people	• Stop hostile or aggressive action on the part of others
• Unmet needs	- threatens the physical environment	
• Being told what to do		• Maintain control of situation
• Putdowns	• Throwing things, swearing, yelling, threatening, kicking, clamming up, flirting, destroying property and running away	• Feel powerful
• Fear of exploring painful issues		
• Craving, using, or withdrawing from substances		

MANAGING DISRUPTIVE BEHAVIOR

It is not our intention, nor is it possible, to provide a specific strategy for every type of disruptive event you might encounter in clinical practice. When undesirable behavior is increasing, the idea is to stop what you are doing and to try a different approach. The more strategies you have in your repertoire, the greater your chances of diffusing a disruption. The only measurement of the effectiveness of the applied strategy is whether it results in a reduction of disruptive behavior and an increase in cooperation. Once the disruption is diffused, you continue with the purpose of the session. Don't let the disruptive behavior become the focus of your interaction with an individual; management of these events should be as brief as possible. Initially, you may encounter an increased rate of disruption before the individual settles into a pattern of more co-operative behavior. This is sometimes referred to as testing the counsellor and is more likely to occur when the individual has a long history of maladaptive behavior or tends to be manipulative. Individuals with a long history of involvement with helping agencies or institutions sometimes develop disruptive behavior patterns that repeatedly block treatment efforts. A consistent approach on your part is essential in breaking these behavioral patterns.

Knowing an individual's readiness for change, modifying your approach according to that readiness and consistent application of motivational counselling strategies eliminate many potential antecedents to disruptive behavior. It is important to remain calm and nonjudgmental, to word all your responses positively and to use the individual's name as often as possible. Tell the client what you would like to see him or her do instead of talking about behaviors you don't like. The stress associated with a disruption tends to be contagious. When a disruption continues to escalate, other people should be removed from the area not only to ensure their safety, but also to prevent them from joining in. The more people involved in a disruptive situation, the more difficult it is to manage.

APPLIED FUNCTIONAL ANALYSIS

Whenever possible, avoid putting the individual in antecedent conditions while you help him or her to achieve the desired outcome by behaving in different, more adaptive ways. Often there is nothing wrong with the payoffs of disruptive behavior. It is the way the individual is acting to achieve his or her expectations that causes problems. For example, we all seek attention from other people, but most of us go about it in acceptable ways. The disruptive individual has not found acceptable ways of getting what he or she wants but learns that disruptive behavior is an equally effective alternative. Thus, another step in the application of functional analysis is to translate the disruptive behavior into what you want to see instead. Your interaction then focuses on what you want to see instead of what you do not like or find disruptive. The behaviors we pay the most attention to in our counselling sessions are the ones we are going to see the most of. Selecting what you pay attention to can make the session pleasant for the individual and you. Managing disruptive behavior is a team responsibility in an agency or treatment setting. Functional analysis provides an effective way to report disruptive events. By studying these reports over time, the team establishes a framework for developing guidelines for managing disruptive behavior. In this way guidelines become specific to the agency and allow all team members to participate in their formation.

In treatment, functional analysis is applied a step further. As it is not realistic to continue to protect clients from the antecedents to disruptive or other problematic behaviors, in treatment you help them learn different ways of responding. You help them learn and experiment with different ways of achieving the identified reinforcing consequences, while reducing their need to escape unpleasant situations or events. The more confident an individual is in his or her ability to deal with difficult situations and unpleasantness, the weaker the desire to avoid or escape such events. Skill development in the areas of problem solving, stress management, assertion, anger management and self-control are typical components of such treatment interventions.

SELECTIVE ATTENTION

When attention is withheld from specific behaviors, the rate of the behavior decreases, while the behaviors we pay attention to tend to increase. In selective attention, you pay attention to the behaviors that help clients meet their goals, and ignore the rest. Attention may include your physical presence, head nods, smiles, praise, continued interaction with the individual and a variety of privileges. Too often we focus on problem identification, and when this is what we look for, this is what we are likely to reinforce. You will want to recognize and reinforce adaptive behavior and strengths consistently. The same applies to signs of progress that can be very small steps toward a goal. To apply selective attention successfully, you must first develop a clear vision of how you want your clients to behave, and what constitutes progress towards their treatment goals. Without such a vision, reinforcement tends to be sporadic and ad hoc instead of planned, selective and consistent. When applied consistently, selective attention is a proven way to shape co-operation and discourage disruptive behavior.

CONTINGENCY CONTRACTING

Contingency contracting can be applied when selective attention does not achieve the desired results in a reasonable length of time; it could also be the basis of a treatment relationship. It tells an individual formally what you expect him or her to do and outlines what will happen when expectations are met. The contract can also define behaviors that you will not tolerate and the sanctions that will follow. You are encouraged to limit your use of the latter type of contract, though it is relatively common to identify consequences for drug use or assault on an agency's premises. Privilege systems are examples of reward contracts for desired behavior, while rules tend to outline punishment contingencies. Reward contracts that identify the behaviors we want to see tend to be more pleasant to work with and are congruent with the principles of motivational counselling. The most important aspects of contingency contracting are to ensure that the identified contingency is within your scope to deliver, and to be consistent in applying it. Once a contract is in place, there should be no exceptions when interpreting behaviors or applying the contingencies. However, this is where the consistency is weakest in the use of contracting. For example, a receptionist, faced with an individual who is demanding to see his or her worker immediately, cannot guarantee that the worker will see the individual. All the receptionist can do is contact the worker on the individual's behalf. That becomes the contingency for an identified desired behavior. The receptionist does not say, "When you sit down, I will get your worker to see you." Instead, he or she says "When you have a seat, I will go and see if your worker will see you." The receptionist takes no further action until the individual sits down, and then carries out his or her part of the bargain as quickly as possible. Inherent in this contract is the need to stay in an area where the individual's behavior can be observed and the desired behavior reinforced. Other disruptive behaviors, such as derogatory statements while the receptionist waits for the individual to take a seat, are ignored. Effective contracts are specific, relevant, reasonable and fair. In situational management, it is not always possible to negotiate the contract with the individual ahead of time, but whenever possible this is the desired approach. Negotiation is a priority in the development of treatment contracts specific to the individual's goals.

SUBSTANCE-INDUCED BEHAVIOR

Substances in the body do not cause anger or violence. However, many clients carry a wide range of unpleasant emotions. These are more likely to be acted upon when an individual is under the influence of substances. Aggressive behavior is usually more intense when the individual is in a state of CNS stimulation. Remember: the level of CNS stimulation is a better guide to selecting management strategies than trying to predict how a particular substance will or should influence an individual's behavior. When an individual is stimulated, take actions to reduce external stimulation. Lower your voice, turn down bright lights, reduce noise levels and refrain from offering coffee. Conversely, if the individual is in a state of CNS depression, you will want to add stimulation to the environment. Turn up the lights, raise your voice tone, turn on a radio and offer coffee. The state in which perceptions are distorted is often accompanied by CNS stimulation and is the most risky. You need to be very cautious about touching people in this state. They need to be repeatedly reassured that they are in a safe environment, that what they are experiencing is being intensified by the substances they took and the feeling will pass. If you choose to continue a session with an individual in this state, the pace must be kept quiet and relaxed. When the individual is distressed or panicky about what he or she is experiencing, emergency treatment – preferably in a specially designed quiet room – may be necessary. An individual who is intoxicated should be prevented from driving a vehicle.

The strategies described for the management of disruptive behavior are all effective with someone under the influence of substances as long as they remain conscious. However, it is important to distinguish social conduct from the physiological effects of the substance on the body. Social behaviors such as yelling, swearing, flirting, threatening and loudness will respond to environmental and interactional strategies as well as selective attention. Contracting is sometimes more difficult but should be attempted as necessary. Social behaviors such as those mentioned should never be excused because the individual is under the influence of substances. Neither should they be entertained as comical even though they sometimes are. On the other hand, only time will help the physiological effects of substances such as slurred speech, staggering, blurred vision, headache complaints, nausea or vomiting. Remember that the states of craving and withdrawal carry as much risk for disruptive behavior as being under the influence.

VIOLENT BEHAVIOR

Anyone who uses or threatens to use physical force to damage property, injure themselves or other people is exhibiting violent behavior: these actions must always be taken seriously. Treatment planning for these individuals is complex and not the focus of this section. However, all agency staff need to know that these behaviors can occur, and it is useful to have guidelines that provide a framework for decision making when violence is observed or reported. An agency must ensure that all staff are aware of individuals with a history of violent behavior when they are being seen in the facility. One way is to explore the frequency of such events in each individual's lifetime, and to assess the probability of their occurring during the current treatment phase. This is best done during the initial assessment. It may be useful to consult the individual's family physician, a psychiatrist or a psychologist in these cases. One question to address is whether your agency is appropriate for the individual. In these cases, substance abuse treatment is often an adjunct to other longer-term care.

PROPERTY DAMAGE

This can be as simple as throwing things and punching walls or as severe as arson. The first two are examples of maladaptive stress responses while the latter is symptomatic of more complex problems. Few agencies are prepared to tolerate property damage and a contingency contract should be negotiated with the individual as soon as the potential for such behavior is identified. Any threat to destroy the agency should be reported immediately to a senior administrator who in turn is advised to inform police. These threats should never be minimized.

Generally speaking, the younger the individuals seeking help at your agency, the more damage you can expect in the form of graffiti, scratching symbols on inanimate objects and burning things in ashtrays. It helps to repair or remove this type of damage as soon as possible, as the sight of such destruction may prompt others to engage in the same kind of activity. Property damage cannot be excused because the individuals are young, but most youth workers will tell you that it is difficult to control.

SELF-HARM BEHAVIOR

Hitting oneself, arm cutting, burning oneself and some drug overdoses are deliberate, self-harm behaviors that seldom have anything to do with a wish to die. While individuals who engage in such behaviors are clearly sending the message that something is wrong, they are unable or unwilling to communicate their needs directly. Feeling overwhelmed with one's life situation is a common antecedent to self-harm, and many individuals who harm themselves have problems with impulse control. It is not uncommon for them to have a long history of neglect, deprivation or abuse. Those who engage in acts such as arm cutting often identify an immediate release of stress or pressure as the payoff; a brief escape from life's problems can be the reinforcing consequence of a drug overdose. Self-harm is typically followed by a sympathetic response from other people, while other problems take a back seat to the "crisis," providing a temporary escape. All of these payoffs increase the likelihood that the behavior will be repeated again and again. Over time, the individual must engage in more severe types of self-harm to elicit the same response, and the situation becomes increasingly risky. As involvement in the health care system increases, these individuals look to their workers to fulfil unmet needs. But given the complexity of the factors at work in these cases, it is unlikely that their needs will be met. They then feel rejected by their workers. These cases are difficult and frustrating to work with, and clients pick up on their workers' feelings of hopelessness. This too is perceived as rejection. These feelings, whether real or imagined, may trigger more self-harm. Some individuals who harm themsleves do eventually commit suicide.

Specially trained mental health care workers are in the best position to co-ordinate services for these individuals. Contingency contracting has been effective in controlling self-harm during substance abuse treatment, and abstinence can be instrumental in reducing the rate of self-harm. It is important that a psychiatrist or psychologist concur with the use of contracts in these cases. As with other problems, your objective is to help clients accept that they ultimately control their actions. Maintain contact with the mental health worker and refer new threats of self-harm to that worker. Follow the recommendations of the mental health professionals as you provide counselling specific to substance abuse.

ATTEMPTED OR THREATENED SUICIDE

Anyone who thinks or talks about taking his or her life – who expresses or acts upon a wish to die – is suicidal. It is estimated that as many as nine of 10 people who commit suicide tell someone of their intent shortly beforehand. All verbalizations of intent must be taken seriously.

There are many factors that suggest that someone may be vulnerable to suicide. A family history of psychiatric illness, substance abuse or suicide, a violent death in the family and ongoing family conflict are common among individuals who kill themselves. An early history of severe or chronic illness, physical abuse, sexual abuse, neglect, deprivation, parental separation and the loss of a parent can increase the risk of suicide. Unemployment, poverty, stormy relationships, separation from loved ones, a series of stressful life events or repeated self-harm further increase the risk. Painful or debilitating illness such as rheumatoid arthritis, renal failure or organic brain syndrome increase an individual's vulnerability to suicide, as can some psychiatric illnesses such as depression, mania and schizophrenia. Not surprisingly, many individuals suffering from the above conditions also abuse alcohol and other drugs, and criminal activity is not uncommon. The elderly in our society are also at risk for suicide, and in recent years suicide rates among 15- to 24-year-olds have increased substantially. Middle age is a difficult time for some individuals. It is not known why some people with histories such as those described become suicidal while others go on to lead fairly stable lives. Women are more likely to harm themselves repeatedly while men tend to be more successful at killing themselves. Religion, strong social networks and marriage, except for those aged 15 to 19, seem to provide some protection against suicide, while living alone tends to increase the risk.

While suicide attempts often appear compulsive, people tend to think about it over a period of time. They feel sad, hopeless, helpless, lonely and apathetic. Dying is one way of ending their despair and they keep this option open. Often they withdraw from activities with other people, which robs them of the opportunity for social reinforcement. They become locked into a cycle of despondence and complain of low energy, insomnia, eating disorders, decreased interest in sex and other things that once gave them pleasure, and increased substance abuse. A loss, real or imagined, or the anniversary of the loss of a loved one can trigger the actual suicide attempt. Access to a means of carrying out the act is another factor. Generally speaking, men tend to choose a more violent means of death such as jumping from high places, throwing themselves in front of moving vehicles, hanging or shooting themselves. Perhaps this is why they are more likely to succeed. Women tend to use pills or poisons, or to cut themselves; the presence of medications and weapons in the home provides the means to act out suicidal ideation. Similarly, driving a motor vehicle provides many opportunities to kill oneself and it is unknown how many accidents are actually suicide attempts.

As in the case of self-harm behavior, these individuals should be under the care of a mental health practitioner who can advise you on management of suicidal ideation and treat crisis situations as they occur. When working with these individuals, it is important to continually assess the immediacy of suicide threats. The further developed the plans to carry out the act, the greater the risk. Has the individual selected a method? Does he or she have the means? Ask directly when and where the individual plans to act. The attempt is more likely to succeed if carried out where the individual is unlikely to be interrupted. Those who plan to act in such a location may be close to making a serious suicide attempt. Once the individual has made up his or her mind to act, he or she suddenly becomes calmer, more content and may even appear happy. Too often this appears to be improvement. Giving away personal possessions may be a sure sign that a person is ready to act. Some individuals even plan their funerals and ensure their wills are in order.

A priority when working with these individuals is to increase their involvement in pleasant activities, especially those that increase opportunities for social reinforcement. This helps disrupt the locked-in cycle of despair. Self-help groups such as Alcoholics Anonymous can be helpful, and contingency contracting can motivate the individual to get started. This is a gradual process that often identifies a wide range of social deficits that may impede progress.

Another focus is to encourage the individual to strengthen connections with important people in his or her life. It may be useful to involve others in treatment when the individual is willing and ready. Abstinence can reduce the risk of these individuals acting out their suicidal ideation, and your role as an addiction counsellor can make a difference.

However, we need to accept our limitations when working with such situations. Some of your clients may kill themselves despite your best efforts. There is no proven method to prevent suicide and you cannot protect them 24 hours a day, seven days a week. The best approach is to acknowledge your clients' distress and provide empathetic support as you help them use their own resources to start the change process. Your overt acceptance of the risk of suicide, and your awareness that you cannot meet your clients' needs for them, can move them towards greater self-responsibility and independence.

ASSAULTIVE BEHAVIOR

There is a basic rule in the case of imminent violence. Get out of the way! When leaving the area, be sure to take others who are under your care with you. Do not hesitate to call police for assistance.

While fear of assault is increasingly a concern in many agencies, it is not a frequent event. Conflicts can usually be diffused before they escalate to assault. However, every agency should have emergency procedures in place to summon other staff and police when things get out of control. The arrival of others is often enough to prevent an assault; if not, you will want several people present to contain the individual. When the individual is armed, however, think twice about having other people rush to the scene. This could cause the individual to panic and use the weapon. Instead, you need to calmly get a message to another person to call police for advice and assistance. Many agencies use codes for this purpose. A weapon is any instrument that can be used to injure another person. It could be scissors, broken glass, a chair leg, chains, a stick, gun or knife. Thus it is good practice to keep any potential weapon out of sight when not in use. Anything can happen when you are working with clients. When someone feels trapped, angry or frustrated, the sight of a pair of scissors lying on a desk could provide the antecedent and the means for assault. It should be made clear to all clients that weapons are prohibited in the agency and that the staff will call police at the first sign of violence.

Much can be done to improve the safety of your offices. It is very risky to have one person working alone. Objects that can trigger cravings for drugs or alcohol should be kept out of sight, as should all potential weapons. Staff should sit nearest the door so that they cannot be trapped in an office with a potentially disruptive individual. Those with a history of violence need to be flagged so that all staff know the risks. When counselling someone who has previously threatened violence, you may want to have another person present. You may prefer to leave your door open or station another person just outside. Silent alarms can be installed under desks or tables to summon help in a dangerous situation. It is useful to have a prearranged method of alerting others for help without further upsetting a potentially violent individual.

Physical restraint is discouraged except when staff have specific training in these techniques. Some feel that staff who have had such training tend to carry themselves more confidently and this can deter an assault. Self-defence training may provide the same confidence. Some argue that staff trained in physical restraint tend to act too quickly and might escalate a potentially dangerous situation. Each agency needs to develop its own policies about restraint. Two training films provide more information about physical restraint: "Nonviolent Crisis Intervention Series" from the National Crisis Prevention Institute, Brookfield, WI; and "Prevention and Management of Disturbed Behavior" from the St. Thomas Psychiatric Hospital in Ontario.

CONCLUSION

The situational management techniques described in this section diffuse disruptive behavior and keep potentially dangerous situations from escalating. After implementing development programs on managing intoxicated and disruptive clients, we demonstrated an 80 per cent reduction in the time staff spent managing disruptive behavior – time that can be devoted to treating our clients. When all staff are trained in the same methods and the techniques are applied consistently, the number of disruptive events in an agency will be reduced.

REFERENCES

Addiction Research Foundation of Ontario, Clinical Research and Treatment Institute. (1985). General guidelines for the management of disruptive behavior. Toronto.

Cox, Ann E. (1981). Training guidelines and workbook for the behavioral management of intoxicated and disruptive clients. Toronto: Addiction Research Foundation of Ontario.

Ennis, Jon, M.D. (1983). Self-harm: 1. Suicide. Canadian Mental Association Journal, Vol. 129, 21-27.

Ennis, Jon, M.D. (1983). Self-harm: 2. Deliberate nonfatal self-harm. Canadian Medical Association Journal, Vol. 129, 121-125.

Ennis, Jon, M.D., Barnes, Rosemary, Ph.D. & Spencer, Helen, MSW. (1985). Management of the repeatedly suicidal patient. Canadian Journal of Psychiatry, Vol. 30, No. 7, 535-538.

Monahan, John. (1981). Predicting violent behavior: An assessment of clinical techniques. Beverly Hills, California: Sage Publications Inc.

Perry, Philip E. The beyond content model of crisis intervention. Calgary, Alberta: The Canadian Crisis Intervention Institute.

Ending with Clients: Systematic Termination in Counselling with Individuals, Families and Groups

CARL KENT

INTRODUCTION

*T*he last stage of the helping process is the termination of the helping relationship. Although this stage has received little attention in the literature, when compared to the beginning or middle stages, it is nonetheless critically important. The way in which the helping relationship and process are concluded greatly influences whether clients can maintain the progress they have made and continue to make further gains. For this reason it is important that practitioners plan and handle this stage with sensitivity and skill. This chapter will focus on the termination process and identify relevant tasks, for both practitioners and clients, which are essential to managing termination effectively. No distinctions will be made between terminating the counselling relationship with an individual, a family, or a group. The essential dynamics are the same for all modes of intervention, with minimal adaptation required for each treatment context.

CONCEPTUALIZING TERMINATION

To most counsellors it is obvious that the "beginning" of any treatment contact represents a distinctive and identifiable phase. It makes sense that "starting on the right foot" has implications for the rest of the therapeutic contact.

In treatment, "endings" are as important as "beginnings," though this phase of the treatment contact is not nearly as clearly or frequently written about. Ward (1984) has suggested that this neglect arises out of several sources, including:

(1) normal human tendencies to avoid separation and loss issues;

(2) counsellors' inclination to focus on relationship building rather than on activities aimed at discontinuing relationships;

(3) counsellor training overemphasizes skill building to the exclusion of case-management issues.

Effective termination counselling must begin with the premise that termination is a process or phase, rather than one point in time representing an abrupt cessation of an activity (Cavanaugh, 1982; Corey, Corey, Callanan & Russell, 1982; Shulman, 1979). Yalom (1975) underlined the importance of termination when he wrote: "Termination is more than an act signifying the end of therapy and, if properly understood and managed, may be an important factor in the instigation of change" (p. 365). Hansen, Warner, & Smith, (1980) suggest that if termination is dealt with inappropriately it "may not only conclude this experience without effective change... but also so adversely affect individuals that they may not seek further help when necessary" (p. 539).

There appears to be wide agreement that three main functions are involved in this phase of treatment:

    (1) assessing client readiness for ending the counselling process and for consolidating whatever has been learned;

    (2) resolving remaining affective issues and constructively closing the significant and often intense relationship between the client and the counsellor;

    (3) maximizing transfer of learning (from the counselling situation and specific problem issues to life in general and other problems) and increasing the client's confidence in his or her ability to maintain change after the counselling contact has ended.

Nelson (1983) has noted that successful termination of a therapeutic relationship parallels the stages people experience when dealing with death. Obviously the parallel referred to here is the death/ending of the counselling relationship. If treatment ends too abruptly it might be perceived as rejection, which is a difficult issue for clients and practitioners alike. The client who feels rejected might be tempted in turn to reject the whole therapeutic contact and with it all gains and plans for positive action and referral.

Shulman (1984) proposed, as a rule, that termination constitute one-sixth of the time of the therapeutic process. In fact, there is general agreement that treatment should not be terminated during the session in which termination is first mentioned. Not only will this prevent impulsive and premature termination; it allows a clear review of the counselling process to date, an evaluation of the progress made, and planning for future goals.

PROBLEM AND GOAL DEFINITION: HOW TO DETERMINE WHEN TO END

A clear focus of the helping process is a necessary precondition to successful termination. Being specific about client problems and agreeing on goals helps determine how long treatment will continue and how counselling activities will be structured. When goals have been established in the beginning and included in the terms of the treatment contract, their review at the time of termination will allow for a precise measurement of progress and any work yet to be accomplished.

It must be said here that many effective practitioners insist on explicit, specific and *written* contracts that spell out not only mutual expectations and responsibilities, but also goals, sub-goals and the detailed, operationalized steps and time required to meet them. This obviously leads to frequent revisions, with the advantage of client and practitioner always knowing where they stand. Progress and success will be readily apparent, as will stagnation and poor use of therapeutic time.

It is probably best to comment here about the common problem of the chronically relapsing substance abuser who regularly misses appointments. When does the counsellor say "That's enough, I am terminating my involvement with this client?" What does the counsellor do about the chronic alcoholic who, over an extended period of time, does not get better? What about the person who is unlikely ever to improve? Is this issue related to termination alone or to contracting and goal-setting as well? It would seem that as long as specific, if modest, goals are *agreed upon*, and as long as there is discernible movement towards those goals, the counselling contact is useful and worthwhile. Remember that a practitioner can only facilitate change with those clients with whom he or she has contact. Even if there are no observable positive changes in the client, the focus might be more on realistic contracting than on termination. Intermittent supportive follow-up contact might be agreed on to maintain the therapeutic contact, so as to be ready for action when the situation or client allows it. How much change is enough to justify ongoing counselling contact? That is ultimately a question of staff resources and agency policy.

If the client's problems are developmental in nature (i.e. an adolescent who has difficulties with leaving home, or an adult dealing with the pressures of parenting), the termination might well be designed to allow for extensive follow-up as the transitional aspect of the problem continues to unfold. A specific example might be the teenager, Bill T., who resents parental interference with his choice of friends and his excessive and irresponsible drinking. In this instance, he wants the adult's freedom of decision-making without honoring the other side of the same coin, namely respect for duties and commitments.

On the other hand, if the client's problems are related to specific and concrete issues, a definable end of the treatment contact might suggest itself. In fact, when the expectations of the outcome are shared and based on a thorough assessment, the time of termination will fall into place readily. An example might be to help Jane S. deal with her marital breakdown in a more constructive manner than excessive drinking. When she has learned to stop drinking and grieve the end of her marital relationship, she might be able pick up the pieces of her life on her own and end the therapeutic contact.

What a client expects to gain from the helping process is maintained both by hopes for specific change and the personal validation he or she receives from the helping relationship. As the counselling work progresses, the practitioner must monitor and maintain an appropriate balance between goal achievement and relationship gratification both for himself or herself and the client.

Certainly it is unrealistic to aim for a complete cure of all the client's problems, although helpers are susceptible to accepting such a global goal. It might be much more practical to focus on some major concerns the client identifies rather than to include all the problems the practitioner can pinpoint. After all most people (including counsellors) have some problems they either learn to live with or are content to struggle with on their own.

Concepts such as "clinical judgment" about a client's readiness for termination and "working through" such variables as the ending of the client-counsellor relationship and feelings of grief and sadness are important but hard to operationalize and next to impossible to measure. It seems a lot more realistic to choose specific and behavioral goals against which progress in counselling can be measured. Maholick and Turner (1979, p. 588) identified seven areas helpful for evaluating client readiness to terminate the counselling process:

(1) examining whether initial problems or symptoms have been reduced or eliminated
(2) determining whether the stress that motivated the client to seek counselling has dissipated
(3) assessing increased coping ability
(4) assessing increased understanding and valuing of self and others
(5) determining increased levels of relating to others and of loving and being loved
(6) examining increased abilities to plan and work productively
(7) evaluating increases in the capacity to play and enjoy life.

Practitioners should also evaluate how confident the client has begun to feel about continuing to live competently without the help of counselling.

Further, a number of client behaviors – other than direct and explicit statements – may signal the onset of the termination stage. Among those mentioned in the literature are a decrease in the intensity of the work of counselling, lateness, joking, and intellectualizing (Corey et al., 1982). Also mentioned are missed appointments, apathy, acting out, regression to earlier and less mature behavior patterns, withdrawal, denial, expression of anger and mourning (Shulman, 1984). The client might also express feelings of impotence, dependence, inadequacy, and abandonment. If the client increasingly displays some of these behaviors or feelings but does not talk about a desire for termination, the counsellor may have to initiate the process.

In any case, the counsellor must initiate and help the client come to terms with both task and relationship issues of termination. A detailed review of the counselling process, an evaluation of the progress made so far, and a subsequent plan for future goals is recommended.

One way to guide the client through the termination process successfully is to point out predictable reactions to loss (including anticipated loss) and to help the client to identify those reactions when they are either directly or indirectly expressed. For example, Peter T.'s counselling contact had evidently been coming to a close. He displayed a variety of reactions, including lateness, cancellations, increased digressions into story-telling, and shifting the focus of the session onto the counsellor. When termination was mentioned, however, he would rapidly identify a minor crisis to legitimately prolong the counselling contact. An open discussion of these dynamics allowed the client to face his anxieties about "being on his own." In addition to exploring the issue of confidence and independent functioning, an extended follow-up agreement seemed to be an acceptable compromise solution.

Various authors have written about the predictable stages of the grieving process: denial, anger, sadness, acceptance, and disengagement (Germain & Gitterman, 1980; Kubler-Ross, 1969). However, we cannot assume that all clients uniformly pass through all these stages without variation, though it is generally recognized that both clients and counsellors are likely to experience denial. The expression of this denial may take many forms, ranging from general detachment to premature discontinuation of counselling sessions. Regular clinical supervision can help counsellors identify, face, and finally resolve their own denial. Focusing on the client's denial may be instrumental in overcoming it and allows open exchange about the pain and distress associated with loss and separation.

Clients might be encouraged to summarize their personal reactions to the counsellor and the counselling process. They should give feedback about what they found to be helpful or distracting during the treatment process. It is important that the counsellor face this opportunity to receive feedback (including the occasional criticism) non-defensively. It might help to view this situation as an opportunity for learning; the information received should be taken seriously.

Counsellors may feel uncertain about their own capacity to deal with the termination and may encourage clients to remain in denial as a form of self-protection. It is the counsellor's responsibility to guide the ending process through appropriate timing of interventions and use of self-disclosure. The honest expression of the counsellor's own reaction during termination validates the client's feelings triggered by the termination. (Of course, the counsellor's self-disclosure must never be detrimental to the client and his or her feedback must always be tempered by clinical judgment concerning the best interests of the client.) Through this mutual exchange or sharing of reactions, the reality of the ending is verified.

At this stage the counsellor-client relationship moves from an unbalanced power relationship towards a position of greater equity and balance. The focus may be allowed to shift away from the client towards neutral ground or towards the counsellor. This in turn enhances the client's level of independent functioning, which is appropriate and desirable for the termination stage of counselling.

One major task of the ending experience is to connect treatment to the client's subsequent problem-solving efforts. This may be partly accomplished by a termination review, evaluation of goal accomplishment, and by planning activities and setting goals for the future.

The client needs to be encouraged through the termination process to set out on a self-directed course of action. Of course, the development of new goals or the restating of old, unaccomplished goals must be based on a realistic evaluation of the client's problem-solving capacity.

A constructive use of these termination issues supports client self-esteem and reinforces the client's hope that progress can be achieved. Effective ending also frees up the client to make new efforts at important life tasks and relationships, which in turn enhances his or her problem-solving abilities.

REASONS FOR TERMINATION

When the decision to end treatment is mutual, working through the termination stage helps clients to consolidate and transfer learning, enhance their level of independent functioning, and bring the client-counsellor relationship to a closer level of balance.

Frequently, however, the client decides to terminate with little or no prior consultation with the counsellor. The practitioner may be abruptly informed of the client's decision, or more frequently may find out through a series of missed appointments. Mostly the counsellor learns of the decision and not of the reasons behind it.

If the client initiates termination at the beginning of the counselling process, it could mean that he or she doesn't appreciate the techniques or procedures of counselling. Or the client may disagree with the counsellor's theoretical orientation or plainly just dislike the counsellor. The client may feel that he or she will not get the desired help in this context – or may have returned to the use of substances. Active follow-up contact is encouraged to offer alternative counselling arrangements that more closely fit the client's expectations (possibly through referral to another counsellor or treatment setting) or to make renewed efforts to engage the client in treatment.

To avoid attrition at this stage Zweben and Li (1981) tried to provide new patients with "role induction" information designed to reduce the discrepancy between their expectations of the counselling experience and reality. They speculated that clients with unrealistic expectations of counselling likely need immediate help with their concrete problems as well as "actively engaging 'significant other(s)' or providing them with a 'buddy' at the point of entry, in order to forestall premature termination." (p.172)

During the middle stage of counselling, some clients will terminate prematurely if they feel that the counselling process is creating more problems than it is able to resolve. Termination at this stage is often due to the unsettling feeling that the client experiences as a result of changing behaviors. Frequently the client's life and relationships become destabilized and the perceived cost of continued counselling and changing is seen to be higher than maintaining the previously recognized problem. This kind of reaction is often conveniently explained by the practitioner as a "lack of motivation" on the client's part. Here too, early focus on desensitizing the client against the temporary unsettling effects of change may help to prevent early terminations. In spite of this, clients will still discontinue treatment without specifying the cause.

It is important to examine critically the characteristics, length and type of counselling contact of clients who discontinue treatment prematurely, to identify any commonalities such as family responsibilities, unstable accommodation or length of time on the waiting list. Such analysis may allow the counsellor and/or agency to reach out to clients at risk for early termination and provide support in dealing with such issues. This might include helping the client to better understand the reasons behind the termination and also to offer renewed contact or help with referral.

When a client terminates, or expresses the wish to do so, and significant problems are still unresolved, the counsellor must try to help the client deal with negative reactions and feelings. If the client is willing to engage in an "exit interview," Ward (1984) identifies at least four positive outcomes that may result:

(a) reduction of as many negative influences as possible before the client resumes life without counselling

(b) resolution of critical issues to the extent that the client is able to continue counselling with the same counsellor

(c) preparation of the client for gaining maximum benefit from referral to another "helper"

(d) increased likelihood that the client will re-enter counselling or some other personal growth experience at some future date.

When the practitioner decides to terminate the counselling process it should be presented as a logical and inevitable step in the change process in which the client is engaged. This minimizes the client's feelings of rejection by the counsellor.

The ending of treatment really begins with the first session following assessment. Termination should be treated like any other treatment goal and should regularly be included in treatment planning and goal-setting. This means that the length of the planned counselling contact is constantly reviewed and revised in view of outstanding treatment goals and the rate of progress.

TRANSFER OF THE CLIENT TO ANOTHER COUNSELLOR

The case transfer is a special type of termination that might be called for in a variety of circumstances. Examples are: a counsellor leaving his or her agency, a student concluding a field placement at the end of the school term; ill health or changing responsibilities of the practitioner; or sometimes, when carefully considered, the mutually beneficial transfer of a long-term client to a different counsellor. The same rules of ending that were already discussed apply here. Ideally, case transfers work well when the client and the departing practitioner engage in a cognitive and affective review of the previously shared contacts. Included in this are an agreement of the progress accomplished towards explicitly stated therapeutic goals, an acknowledgment of the work yet to be done, and a mutual processing of the counsellor's and client's feelings about the intimate process that has occurred.

In addition, a positive working relationship must be established between the client and the new therapist so that rapport and trust can develop, the client's feelings of loss can be reviewed and the new goals can be confirmed. All of this must be done without loss of the momentum towards change. To achieve these objectives, clearly and openly discuss with the client – during the course of several interviews – the need for and the implications of ending.

The new counsellor must be well informed about the essentials of the case. At least one transfer interview with the client and both counsellors is suggested, during which the departing therapist and client can share with the new counsellor some of the highlights of their past work together as well as the goals they feel still need to be achieved.

It is common for the new counsellor to feel a bit apprehensive at this time since he or she will feel a lot of explicit and implicit expectations to be as (or more) helpful, warm, friendly, and sensitive as the departing practitioner. If the transfer was well prepared, the comparisons will soon cease and the new relationship will be appreciated by the client in its own right.

Difficulties may arise when the client and departing practitioner did not have enough time to prepare for the case transfer. A client may then feel rejected, sad, hopeless, guilty, worthless or angry. A lot of time, effort and forward momentum will be lost in dealing with these unresolved feelings. It is then left up to the new counsellor to help the client come to terms with these feelings before progress can be made towards identified goals.

CONCLUSION

Thanks to the pioneering work of Kubler-Ross on death, dying, and the grieving process, it is possible today to deal more effectively with the termination of counselling. Specific steps have been identified to evaluate a client's readiness for termination. The importance of identifying and consolidating gains made in counselling has been pointed out, as well as the need to resolve affective issues in order to end the relationship appropriately. Also specific steps to handle clients' attempts to leave counselling prematurely have been highlighted.

Effective closure of the counselling process can help reinforce clients' learning and maximize their continued self-efficacy and success after counselling.

Whether short or long term, the intent of the helping process is to make a difference in the life of the client. It is through the process of termination that this difference can be understood, evaluated and maintained.

REFERENCES

Cavanaugh, M.E. (1982). The counselling experience: A theoretical and practical approach. Monterey, CA: Brooks/Cole.

Compton, B. & Galaway, B. (1984). Social Work Processes (3rd ed.). Homewood, Il: The Dorsey Press.

Corey, G., Corey, M.S., Callanan, P.J. & Russell, J.M. (1982). Group techniques. Monterey, CA: Brooks/Cole.

Germain, C. & Gitterman, A. (1980). The life model of social work practice. New York: Columbia University Press.

Hansen, J.C., Warner, R. W. & Smith, E.J. (1980). Group counselling: Theory and process (2nd ed.). Chicago: Rand McNally.

Hepworth, D.H. & Larsen, J.A. (1982). Direct Social Work Practice, Theory and Skills. Homewood, Il: The Dorsey Press.

Kubler-Ross, E. (1969). On death and dying. New York: Macmillan.

Lackey, M.B. (1982). The termination phase in social work with groups. University of Southern California: Dissertation Abstracts International, Sept. Vol. 43.

London, M. (1982). How do you say good-bye after you've said hello? Southeastern Counselling Association, New Bedford, MA: Personnel and Guidance Journal, March Vol. 60.

Maholick, L.T. & Turner, D.W. (1979). Termination: That difficult farewell. American Journal of Psychotherapy, Vol. 33, pp. 583-591.

Marx, J.A. (1984). An exploratory study of the termination of individual counselling in a university counselling centre. University of Maryland: Dissertation Abstracts International, June, Vol. 44.

Nelson, J.C. (1983). Family Treatment: An Integrative Approach. Englewood Cliffs, NJ: Prentice-Hall.

Shulman, L. (1979), (1984). The skills of helping individuals and groups. Itasca, Il: Peacock.

Ward, D.E. (1984). Termination of individual counselling: Concepts and strategies. Journal of Counselling and Development, Vol. 63, pp. 21 - 25.

Yalom, I.D. (1975). The theory and practice of group psychotherapy (2nd. ed.). New York: Basic Books.

Zweben, A., & Li, S. (1981). The Efficacy of Role Induction in Preventing Early Dropout from Outpatient Treatment of Drug Dependency. American Journal of Drug and Alcohol Abuse, Vol. 8(2), pp. 171-183

Special Needs of Particular Populations

Working with Women

The Physically Disabled Substance Abuser

Substance Abuse and the Older Person

Lesbians and Gay Men

Clinical Issues in the Assessment and Treatment of Adolescent Substance Abuse

Cultural Considerations for the Native Client

Addictions Counselling for Culturally and Racially Diverse Communities: Some Strategies and Tactics

Addiction and the Family

Working with Women

SUSAN HARRISON

INTRODUCTION

Bruised, battered, belittled, beleaguered and bewildered, buffeted by societal attitudes and stereotypes are the women who end up in the offices of addictions counsellors. If we, as counsellors, are to help these women recover and develop their potential, we must understand and empathize with each one individually; we must know the treatment issues that pertain specifically to women; and, as much as is possible with our current state of knowledge, match each client to the types of treatment or interventions that meet her needs.

This chapter compiles what I have learned over the years in my work with women who are struggling with problems related to substance use.[1] This includes work with women in co-ed treatment facilities, in detox, in residential and day treatment programs, in outpatient and aftercare counselling; with women individually, or with their partners, families and children; and with women in groups, both co-ed and gender-specific. Most of what I have learned has come from listening to and working in partnership with my clients – only very recently have research studies started to substantiate many of the things that clinicians working with women with substance abuse problems have come to know from their experience.

Most women with drug-related problems do not present themselves for treatment; those who do have often experienced a range of problems, from physical and psychological health consequences to family, job-related, financial, legal and other problems. Although we are just beginning to see women coming for help earlier – as health promotion, prevention, and early intervention efforts take hold in communities – we can safely anticipate that for some time we will continue to work with women who have been severely damaged by their substance use and abuse (although I will mention Martha Sanchez-Craig's early intervention work for women earlier on the continuum).

This chapter will discuss how attitudes affect women's development of substance use problems, as well as their recovery. Societal attitudes to women in general, to chemically dependent women in particular, attitudes in research and counsellor attitudes will all be explored. Several barriers that women face will also be highlighted. These include: socio-economic status; isolation; unrecognized needs; fear of losing children; and the health and mental health care systems. Some attention will be given to special considerations in female chemical dependency, including physical effects of both alcohol and other drug use, sexual dysfunction and various psychological factors including reasons for use, self-esteem issues, suicide risk, and physical and sexual abuse. The last section will address some major issues in recovery, among them the core components of a treatment program for women, necessary related services, treatment modalities and counsellor characteristics.

ATTITUDES AFFECTING WOMEN'S DEVELOPMENT OF SUBSTANCE USE PROBLEMS AND THEIR RECOVERY

The importance of attitudes in working with chemically dependent women cannot be overemphasized. Attitudes within our society toward women in general, and toward chemically dependent women in particular, have an impact on many levels. Attitudes of significant others in these women's worlds – life partner, other family members, employer, friends, counsellor – and of the client herself may determine when and if a woman decides to seek help and whether she finds supports or obstacles in her road to recovery.

SOCIETAL ATTITUDES TO WOMEN IN GENERAL

As I stated earlier, to help our women clients we must understand and empathize with each of them individually. To empathize with them as women is even more basic and important than to understand and empathize with their chemical dependency. Because, as Beth Glover Reed (1985) stated so simply and powerfully, "women are women long before they become involved in chemical misuse or dependency." Women's reality is much different from men's reality. We must truly appreciate the fabric woven from the various threads in women's lives. Are women the movers and shakers, in positions of real power? Do women yet receive comparable pay to men? Are women's responsibilities for child care and home/family maintenance well-recognized, supported and compensated?

Women still hold secondary status in our society, and minority women even more so if they are of a race, ethnic group, language, or sexual orientation other than the white anglophone heterosexual majority. Women devalued this way become victims of violence; have lower self-esteem and lower aspirations than men. A few statistics, part of a list compiled by Janet Marshall in a 1989 report for Mann House, P.E.I., on women's social conditions, illustrate women's secondary status:

Women's Work

In Canada, in 1986, approximately 44 per cent of women with children under six years of age were full-time homemakers, working an average of 50 hours per week, accounting for 37 per cent of the total working hours of all Canadians (Lowe, 1989, Canadian Advisory Council on the Status of Women, 1987).

Nationally, in 1986, the average work week (includes domestic work and employment) for a mother working full-time outside the home was 68 hours, while for a mother working part-time outside the home it was 56 hours (Canadian Advisory Council on the Status of Women, 1987).

Pink Collar Ghetto

In 1987, 56 per cent of the female adult population in Canada worked outside the home in a paid job. Of these, 57 per cent worked in the clerical, sales, and service sectors, often in part-time employment at low pay, with few benefits, no job security and little opportunity for advancement (Lowe, 1989, Canadian Advisory Council on the Status of Women, 1987).

Income Inequities

Women are still earning, on the average, 66 cents for each dollar earned by men.

Income Levels

In 1986, there were over 700,000 mother-led families in Canada. Over half of these families were living below the Low Income Cut Off Lines (Lowe, 1989, Moore, 1987).

Sexual Abuse

In Canada, a women is raped every 17 minutes (Guberman and Wolfe, 1985). One of three females is sexually assaulted before the age of 18, yet only 10 per cent of sexual assault cases are ever reported (Brehaut, 1989, vis-à-vis 1984). One of eight women is battered every year in Canada (MacLeod, 1987).

Recent studies have documented the detrimental effects of these social conditions on the mental and physical health of women (Lowe, 1989; Thomas, 1988; MacLeod, 1987). Researchers in the fields of women's health and women with addictions have found that stress resulting from social conditions such as violence and poverty may lead to drug and alcohol abuse as a coping mechanism (Groeneveld, 1989).

ATTITUDES TOWARD CHEMICALLY DEPENDENT WOMEN

Women's use of alcohol has always been judged more harshly than that of men. In ancient Rome drinking by a woman was punishable by death. In modern times, although there appears to be a veneer of acceptance of women with substance abuse problems, less tolerant attitudes linger just below the surface. It was well known that Winston Churchill "enjoyed a drink" and no one at the time seemed to question his judgment or his ability to run the government of the day. Had Margaret Thatcher "enjoyed a drink" during her years as British Prime Minister, would she have been judged as dispassionately?

I hope I am wrong but the pendulum appears to be swinging back again in the direction of harsher public opinion toward chemically dependent individuals, whether male or female; media coverage, both print and electronic, has shown less tolerance in the last few years. Because women have always been more stigmatized in this regard than men, we might expect the situation to go from bad to worse, i.e., that chemically dependent women may be judged even more harshly in the future than they are now.

The greater stigma that surrounds women with substance abuse problems delays or prevents their seeking assistance – they actually integrate society's negative attitudes and feel extremely guilty and responsible for their situation. Mothers with drug problems are terrified of losing their children if anyone discovers their problem. Because of alcohol's greater physiological effects on women than men, any delay in seeking help because of negative attitudes puts women at higher risk than men. These physiological effects will be discussed later in this chapter.

ATTITUDES IN RESEARCH

Clinicians working with women should keep in mind that what we read is rarely free of attitudinal bias. Except for a few beginning theoretical formulations about female psychological development (Miller, 1976; Belenky, Clinchy, Goldberger & Tarule, 1986) and the development of women's moral reasoning (Gilligan, 1982), theories of human development, therapeutic models and techniques, and even what are considered acceptable research models, were developed predominantly by and for men. These may be valid for male populations but they are usually generalized to apply to female populations. Women have always been measured with a male yardstick and been found lacking. Women are not lacking; they are just different.

Jellinek knew that alcoholic women were different from men. As a pattern began to emerge from all the data he was collecting (mostly from men), he noticed that the women were not fitting the pattern (Jellinek, 1946 and 1952). He therefore set aside the women's data – he never pretended it applied to women. So what became the famous "phases chart" had some accuracy for the development of male alcoholism, but did not apply to women. But as his chart became more and more widely disseminated, the assumption that it applied to both genders went with it.

This was not unusual. The same thing happened and still happens with other addiction research and research in any other field. When reading studies, be skeptical and question whether they apply to women. Be aware of whether research studies include both males and females. If both sexes are included, are the data for women analyzed separately to see if there are any gender differences?

COUNSELLOR ATTITUDES

Addiction workers have widely held several stereotypes of chemically dependent women, none of which I have found to be true. It was felt that women were sicker and less motivated than men and therefore harder to treat. It is a lot easier for program administrators to come to this conclusion than it is to wonder whether their program might not be designed to meet women's needs. If you find that women are dropping out, try to find out which women and why – maybe they all have family responsibilities or share other concerns that your program could address. It has been my experience, particularly with regard to motivation, that there is generally less denial among women than men. If anything, women carry an exaggerated sense of guilt and responsibility. This can be a two-edged sword: it may produce the anxiety and discomfort necessary to motivate them toward change (although it may also serve as a barrier to the woman's seeking help initially); but at times it can overwhelm the client, whose level of despair then makes her more vulnerable to self-destructive behaviors, including suicide. Psychological denial is evident more often in people who are in a position to help than in the women themselves: helpers often "deny" that the women in their lives may be experiencing drug-related problems.

Counsellors, clinicians, therapists – anyone who works in a helping capacity with women with substance problems – must take a good look at her or his own attitudes. We are not unaffected by the society in which we live or the biases that were part of our own professional training. Those of us who work in the addictions field are not immune from stigmatizing women. We need to begin by asking ourselves the most basic question: "Do I even like women, let alone value and respect them?" In other words, do I have a "positive regard" for women or have I internalized societal attitudes toward them? Did it matter to me, for example, whether my first-born child was a boy or a girl? If, after a soul-searching examination of whether we value and respect women, we answer in the affirmative, we may be able to work effectively with women.

Then we need to ask ourselves more specific questions related to situations we will definitely face if working with chemically dependent women. Could you work effectively with a woman who:
- told you she had abused her children either physically or verbally
- was neglecting her children
- had given up her children or was expressing disinterest or hostility towards them

- revealed heavy drinking and/or drug use during pregnancy
- you felt had totally inadequate parenting skills
- wishes to end a marriage where there are school-age children, where she is well taken care of
- has been married several times
- insists on staying in an abusive relationship
- talks about the difficulties in the relationship with her female lover
- tells you she has had or is contemplating an abortion
- spends most of her time with you in tears
- makes a pass at you
- is grieving the death of a child/spouse/parent
- has killed someone or assaulted someone
- is just starting to acknowledge being a lesbian
- earns a living through prostitution
- has begun to have memories of childhood incest
- has divulged plans to commit suicide
- is totally contented being a housewife
- is often angry in interviews
- is obese
- is HIV-positive or has AIDS?

Visualize yourself working with a client in one of these situations – how do you feel toward her? Could you be supportive, and create a therapeutic environment conducive to client growth? Or do you recognize in yourself personal values or biases that would affect your feelings toward her?

I will return to further discussion of counsellor attributes at the end of the chapter, examining one's ability to empathize with the woman as the primary ingredient in helping her recover. Attitudes and empathy are two key ingredients – the parentheses within which all other knowledge and skills are held.

BARRIERS THAT WOMEN FACE

We have already discussed attititudes – often the greatest barrier a woman faces in recovering from drug problems. In fact, many of the barriers that will be highlighted here are the result of attitudes and women's status in our society.

SOCIO-ECONOMIC STATUS

Women do not generally have the same economic resources as their male counterparts. Some of the statistics cited earlier point to the differences. It is generally understood that a range of social, psychological, and physical consequences arise out of being poor or having a low income. Most important for our purposes here is the inverse relationship between income levels and symptoms of psychological distress (Turner & Beiser, 1987; D'Arcy, 1982). Women are poor; women become depressed.

Although in the work force in increasing numbers, women still do not have equal financial resources or status as a result; more often than men, they work in jobs in which they have little control over their work environment. They also likely have less of a paid-work-related sense of self, which can be a major contributor to self-esteem (Reed & Leibson, 1981).

It is among society's most disadvantaged groups that the highest use of mood-altering prescription drugs occurs. Health & Welfare Canada (Health Promotion Survey's Technical Report, 1988) indicates low income as a common variable among the high use groups: older Canadians, women, low-income Canadians, the retired and those keeping house. The 1989 National Alcohol & Drug Survey findings showed much the same patterns of use. And in all of these categories, women predominate. A lot of women are poor – undereducated, unemployed or underemployed, underpaid, retired and widowed. The chronic stress of attempting to live on a low income often leads to depression – as does the loneliness and isolation so characteristic of many subgroupings of women, such as elderly widows and single women with children.

ISOLATION

The loneliness and isolation so common to these groups of women point out the lack of a support system (which is the reality for most of the clients with whom I have worked, whether poor or not). The catalysts that often connect a man to the help he needs to recover commonly do not exist for a woman. Women less frequently have a life partner; and if they do, he or she often does not support the chemically dependent woman's recovery efforts. Some partners may even sabotage these efforts if they feel the woman will be more compliant, less angry, etc., if numbed by substance use. Or the lack of support may be due to her partner's fear of losing a "drinking buddy."

The isolation that chemically dependent women experience can be seen not only as a barrier, but as a major health risk. In his classic work on suicide, Durkheim pinpointed several common elements among those who take their own lives: alienation, no sense of belonging, not feeling valued or useful, and low self-esteem. A more recent review of several studies involving 37,000 people in the United States, Finland and Sweden has found that individuals cut off from others, either close friends or family, are much more likely to die prematurely than those with a strong social network (House, Landis & Umberson, 1988).

Ironically, as we become more aware of the importance of relationships, they seem to be more and more elusive in our fast-paced society. So much of what goes on in the late 20th century emphasizes and reinforces distance between people, and pits one individual against another. The concepts of extended family and community in their broadest interpretation are barely recognizable as the support systems they used to be. A sense of belonging, of being valuable, respected, cared for and caring of, of relying on and being relied on is crucial to the health of human beings. We are social animals. People who feel good about themselves, who feel connected to other people, valuable and whole, have much less need to seek these feelings – or numb the lack of them – through chemicals.

UNRECOGNIZED NEEDS

Although still the primary nurturers, women rarely benefit from the reciprocal aspects of this role – they do not feel valuable, respected, and cared for. How does the nurturer get nurtured? She is socialized and skilled in attending to the needs of others but not good at identifying her own needs. In fact, the chemically dependent woman rarely feels that she has legitimate needs. She will delay or avoid seeking help because it might temporarily inconvenience or disrupt her family and she believes that their needs come first – even (in some cases) when her survival may be at stake.

She is not alone in her belief. Her family, spouse, children, friends, employer and doctor may explicitly or implicitly convey the same message. I have worked with many women who were emphatic in their need to schedule appointments around hockey practices, spouse wanting to bring someone home from work, children needing help with a project etc. Even as they became stronger in their recovery and more able to acknowledge their right to have their own needs met, they still felt very guilty over the one evening a week they came for their support group (said guilt often reinforced by a spouse or children who felt inconvenienced and wanted things the way they were). A woman's connection with her treatment program may always remain somewhat tentative because of this dynamic – guilt is one of the last destructive (in this case) emotions to go.

CHILD CARE RESPONSIBILITIES AND CONCERNS

Some elaboration on women's child care responsibilities and concerns as a barrier would be useful at this point. Consider a widely quoted idea from a 1970 article by Curlee: "No one likes to think that the hand that rocks the cradle is a shaky one." It encapsulates the essence of the difficulty faced by mothers who might need help for drug problems (although a more basic and practical reality may be that her own financial limitations may prevent her getting appropriate treatment unless the program provides child care). Because of the greater stigma attached to chemically dependent women, it is easy to leapfrog from one idea to another: she is chemically dependent – she has children – she is an unfit mother! There is no denying that some children experience, in varying degrees, the consequences of their mothers' substance use. But there is a world of difference between that and the concept of "unfit mother."

Their fear of having their children taken from them keeps many women from seeking help. The guilt a woman feels because of real and perceived effects of her substance use on her children, her perception of the quality or lack of her parenting skills, often make her reluctant to make child care arrangements even if she admits that she needs help. She fears that the substitute caregiver may take better care of her children; they may not want to come back to her; she is terrified of the separation she may face if she seeks help. Many treatment program staff, in my experience, have not acknowledged these genuine concerns on the part of their women clients. Instead they have accused them of "defocusing," of not taking their recovery seriously, of being in denial, etc. To say this is not helpful to female clients is an understatement!

HEALTH AND MENTAL HEALTH CARE SYSTEMS

Although at first glance it seems bizarre, the health care and mental health care systems often prevent women from getting appropriate help for substance abuse problems. Far too many of the women I assessed had spent years seeing one mental health professional after another, getting one psychiatric diagnosis on top of another before she, on her own – from reading or seeing something that "clicked," or from having a family member or friend suggest she might have a drinking problem – would come in for assessment.

The mental health system's negative consequences for a woman include: sexual exploitation by therapists, drug side-effects, and victim-blaming treatments, according to Susan Penfold, a feminist psychiatrist in British Columbia (Penfold & Walker, 1983). My own clinical experience confirms that much extra therapeutic work is often necessary to undo the damage produced by mental health professionals. Some psychiatrists and psychologists still attribute any mental health problems a client is experiencing to her individual deficiencies. Little, if any, attention is paid to interpersonal, social or environmental factors. Few psychologists and psychiatrists have learned that long-term psychoanalysis can do little to help a client recover from chemical dependency. The impact on self-esteem, the increased guilt and internalizing of a feeling of personal responsibility for the problems she is experiencing cannot be overstated.

This may be a good point to say something about antidepressants, in particular the tricyclics. Prescribing of these medications to women may be increasing. Any minimal levelling off of prescribing of benzodiazepines to women seems to have been offset by antidepressants. I would estimate that at least 25 per cent of the women I have worked with over the last three to four years had been taking antidepressants, usually prescribed by their family doctor. An Australian article hints that this may be a trend there. The article quotes a *Medical Journal of Australia* (October, 1989) article in which general practitioners claim that "they were either prescribing fewer psychotropic drugs overall or were prescribing more antidepressant agents in place of minor tranquilliser agents" (quoted in Butt, 1991, p. 16).

Women were not included in early tests on antidepressants that looked at therapeutic benefits and side effects. So is it any surprise that, even though women receive more prescriptions for antidepressants than men, men seem to respond more to this type of medication and women suffer more side effects (Rodin & Ickovics, 1990)? And among these side effects are symptoms that may lead to a diagnosis of depression, which prompts some doctors to prescribe even more medication (Penfold, 1987). So even though addictions counsellors rarely consider antidepressants a problem because they do not produce physical dependence, they are a serious concern. I am not saying they are never appropriate. I have, on occasion liaised with and referred suicidal women to trusted psychiatric colleagues when I felt antidepressants might be the only alternative to impending need for hospitalization or high potential for suicide.

SPECIAL CONSIDERATIONS IN FEMALE CHEMICAL DEPENDENCY

Another chapter of this book goes into detail about the physical consequences of substance abuse ("Physical Effects of Alcohol and Other Drugs"). For our purposes here I will highlight a few things that are important to know in working with women.

PHYSICAL EFFECTS

Drug Use

Most women who come to you will have been using multiple substances – usually alcohol in combination with benzodiazepines and/or narcotic painkillers (usually codeine) and perhaps a tricyclic antidepressant. Some combinations may also include illicit substances, predominantly cannabis and cocaine. It is also likely that your clients will have been taking the prescribed drugs legally, their prescriptions filled repeatedly by a family doctor; only a small percentage would have been "double-doctoring." In fact, the same family doctor may prescribe two benzodiazepines for a woman, one for anxiety and one to help her sleep. Patients have no idea of the potential risk of becoming dependenct on these medications; they know about the dangers of Valium (diazepam) but they do not know that taking Xanax (alprazolam) for anxiety and Halcion (triazolam) to sleep over an extended period of time is as dangerous. Neither are women routinely told of the dangers of abrupt cessation of these drugs after taking them over a long time period.

Alcohol Use

Although women's use of alcohol and drugs in general has been lower than that of men (the exception being prescribed medications where they are still prescribed at twice the rate of men), it appears to me that young women (18- to 29-year-olds) are drinking more – and more like men. A recent Ontario study bears this out. Adlaf and Smart reported in the Ontario Adult Alcohol and Other Drug Use Survey 1989 that not only was binge drinking increased among this group (women 18-29), but so was their use of stimulants, sleeping pills, tranquillizers and cannabis; use increased regardless of factors such as marital or employment status or occupation.

If this is in fact a trend, it should alarm us. Women are more vulnerable to the effects of alcohol. Given the same amount of alcohol, women get drunker, get drunk faster, and stay drunk longer than their male counterparts. These effects are due to a number of factors such as percentage of body fat (women have a higher percentage and therefore have less body water to dilute the alcohol's effects); metabolism (including diminished activity of the stomach enzyme that breaks down alcohol, as reported by Frezza, Di Padova, Pozzato, Terpin, Baraona, & Lieber, 1990); and hormones (alcohol generally has more effect on women premenstrually). A woman who drinks two-thirds as much as a man probably gets the same effect. So if you have been assessing all clients' quantity and frequency of use of alcohol according to what is hazardous for males, you need to know the facts about females. Women who drink two to three drinks a day have significant risk for developing cirrhosis.

Women also develop other types of alcoholic liver disease at a faster rate than men (Saunders, Davis, & Williams, 1981); prevalence of autoimmune diseases and of autoantibodies is more common in women (Hill, 1984); they are more susceptible to alcohol-related brain damage than men (Jacobson, 1986). Women are also particularly vulnerable to cancer of the lips, tongue, pharynx, and esophagus. They are, however, less prone to peptic ulcers and pancreatitis. It is also important to note whether your female clients have been taking a birth control pill. This medication slows the metabolism of CNS depressants so that drugs (particularly lipid soluble drugs) accumulate more rapidly with continued use (Jones & Jones, 1984).

Studies have also been finding a connection between alcohol consumption and breast cancer, i.e. that there is a significantly elevated risk of developing breast cancer at even moderate levels of consumption (Schatzkin, Jones, Hoover, Taylor, Brinton, Ziegler, Harvey, Carter Licitra, Dufour & Larson, 1987). A few studies question these findings. More research is needed but there appears to be some level of risk.

Sexual Dysfunction

Stephanie Covington, an expert in the area of women, sexuality and addictions, reported at a conference in Winnipeg in 1990 that she had found 74 per cent of women in recovery to be sexually dysfunctional and, interestingly, that they often reported having these problems before becoming chemically dependent. The types of sexual dysfunction reported included: infertility, miscarriages, lack of interest in sex, lack of lubrication, preorgasmia, vaginismus, anorgasmia, and dyspareunia. This becomes a recovery issue that will be mentioned again later in this chapter and is covered in detail in Chapter 20.

I am not going to discuss risk to the fetus of a pregnant woman from her use of substances. Ample information is easily accessible elsewhere and there has been an unfortunate tendency to focus more on the potential damage to the fetus than on the welfare of the woman in her own right (health promotion messages are frequently examples of this).

PSYCHOLOGICAL FACTORS

Women seek nurturance and support from alcohol and drugs where there is often none from other people. The combination of causal and contributing factors – biological, psychological, social and environmental – vary with each individual. However, there are several factors I have seen in all the women I have worked with.

Reasons for Use

Whether they are taking alcohol, prescription or illegal drugs (and they are usually smoking as well), women use mood-altering substances to cope, to deal with stress, to nurture themselves, to escape from and numb the pain of past events in their lives or of their current status, or to allow them to continue functioning in their social roles. This applies to young women and elderly women, financially secure women and women living on limited incomes.

Self-Esteem

It has now been widely documented that women alcoholics have lower self-esteem than their male counterparts (Beckman & Amaro, 1986). But not only do they have very low self-esteem: many have little or no sense of self and no sense of purpose in life (Schlesinger, Susman, & Koenigsberg, 1990). They feel powerless, with no control over their lives, and yet they take total responsibility and blame for anything that is wrong in their lives. Their problem (as Covington so succinctly put it at the Winnipeg conference "Women and Substance Abuse: Strategies for the 90s") is not grandiosity, but invisibility.

Suicide Risk

Considering the social factors affecting women's lives and the attitudes toward chemically dependent women, it is not surprising that they experience an affective disorder (depression) more often than their male counterparts. Although a combination of abstinence and non-pharmacological interventions are usually sufficient for these problems to improve, some women remain depressed for several months despite maintaining abstinence (Goldman & Bander, 1990). Alcoholic women are at greater risk of suicide than nonchemically dependent females – as much as five times so (Gomberg, 1989). At least half the female clients I have worked with attempted suicide and 30 per cent had tried more than once.

You will come across other forms of self-destructive or self-injurious behavior, such as head-banging, hair pulling, slashing, burning, etc. (see Chapter 10), as well as a variety of eating disorders; bulimia more often than anorexia (see Chapter 21 for more details). Although the dynamics of these behaviors are complex, they share the common element of a woman's desperate attempt to have control over something, often to bury memories, particularly of childhood sexual abuse.

Physical and Sexual Abuse

Physical or sexual violence, experienced as a child or an adult, is common among women entering addictions treatment. In fact, if you assume your clients have been abused, you will be right much more often than wrong. A conservative estimate based on my clinical experience would be that two-thirds of these clients have experienced some combination of childhood incest and/or other sexual abuse, physical abuse as a child, physical and/or sexual abuse as an adult. Anyone working with chemically dependent women in recovery must have a reasonable level of expertise in this area.

Although history of abuse should form part of every assessment, working on the abuse issue in depth should not, in my opinion, be initiated by the therapist too early in recovery. It is a different situation if the client initiates exploration of the abuse. If she, for example, in the absence of her mind-numbing drugs, is starting to have memories of abuse, they cannot be ignored. They will cause her to relapse and may place her at higher risk of suicide. I will never forget the director of a 28-day residential treatment program who asked: "How do you keep your clients from defocusing onto their incest issues? They're here for addiction treatment; we can't help them with all their other issues!" He was displaying not only insensitivity to the recovery needs of his clients, but also incompetence, in my opinion, in understanding the lives of his female clients. How much more helpful it would be if he were to understand that recovery issues involve a person's life experiences, not just the standard traditional treatment program components of drug and alcohol education, relapse prevention, etc. where non-traditional issues are considered "defocusing."

I have met very few addiction counsellors who feel they have the knowledge and experience needed to work effectively with women around the trauma of early childhood sexual abuse. Regression is common, often to preverbal stages of their childhood. Clients' memories can terrify them. If you do not have the expertise to help your clients work through these issues, refer them to someone who does – or develop the expertise but do not rationalize that your only job is to help your client stay sober! In the meantime, while you gain expertise and competence, you can help by using the basic steps one uses when a child discloses sexual abuse. Communicate the messages: "I hear you; I believe you; you are not to blame for what happened to you; I will support you while we get you the help you need."

Multiple Personality Disorder

Multiple personality disorder (MPD), although rare, occurs quite frequently among those who have experienced sexual abuse in childhood (Wilbur, 1984). I have known four, a very high number given the frequency of this disorder across a population. In all cases, these women were treated by a therapist who had particular expertise in this area. However, the sequencing of the treatments can probably vary: regression therapy for the MPD followed by addiction treatment; the reverse; or the two overlapping for part of the course of therapy/treatment – it will vary depending on the situation of the individual client (and, sometimes, the length of time it takes to get to see a qualified therapist).

SOME MAJOR ISSUES IN RECOVERY

TASKS IN RECOVERY

The first task for a counsellor is to help his or her client stay sober and avoid other compulsive behaviors, such as bingeing. The client also needs to learn to feel better about herself – this in itself is a journey that usually begins with confronting her self-hate, moving through despair to hope, to beginning to develop a sense of self, upon which self-esteem will be built slowly over the rest of her life. At the same time, she must begin to identify her own needs, not just the needs of others, finding a new balance. Even the basic needs of health – nutrition, sleep, and exercise – can be difficult when she is so accustomed to attending to others' needs. She needs, too, to learn how to seek nurturance from other people and not chemicals. Because this involves elements like relationships, sexuality, and spirituality, it cannot be rushed. She needs some sense of self and how to relate to that new self before she focuses on significant relationships in her life. Finally, she needs to learn to express anger. Healthy anger in women in our society is barely tolerated, let alone encouraged. But the client must learn ways to express it if she is to develop strength, self-esteem, some sense of control over her life, and perhaps, most of all, to avoid depression.

Accomplishing these tasks is not easy in the best of circumstances; the attitudes already discussed compound the difficulty, as do the lack of services needed by women in recovery and the rigidity of many traditional treatment programs that offer standard components through which a client flows, no matter what his or her individual circumstances.

CORE COMPONENTS/SERVICES OF A TREATMENT PROGRAM FOR WOMEN

My suggestions here will focus on those services most likely needed by women whose problems have taken them beyond the point where they could consider moderation: women whose goal is abstinence. As community prevention and health promotion efforts improve, some women may prefer to discuss and ultimately alter their use of substances before they have resulted in serious problems; the early intervention techniques developed by Martha Sanchez-Craig are being found to be particularly effective with women (Sanchez-Craig, 1990).

Assessment

An effective treatment plan or program must begin with a comprehensive assessment. Any instruments should be checked for their reliability, validity and appropriateness for use with women. In order to know what services a client will need, the assessor should ask more than the standard questions about substance use. He or she should also explore:

- any consequences she may experience after even low amounts
- circumstances under which she uses
- whether she uses and shares needles
- whether she smokes
- medical problems (remember to ask specifically about gynecological problems and any previous psychiatric diagnosis, even though it may prove to be wrong – the symptoms of a drinking problem are often misdiagnosed as depression)
- history of violence/abuse
- suicide attempts
- other kinds of self-destructive or injurious behavior, including eating disorders
- partner's substance use
- what, if any, social supports she already has in place
- whether the client has children or other dependents for whom she will need care arrangements
- financial resources – does she even have enough for public transit (do not assume this applies only to low-income women; I have worked with wealthy women who had no access to money without going through their husbands)
- educational/vocational background (might there be a need for upgrading or retraining).

Environment

The environment in which the assessment and core services take place is rarely thought to have any bearing on whether the client enters or stays in treatment. It has been my experience, however, that surroundings play some part in whether a client feels comfortable enough to come back a second time (obviously a less important part than the person doing the assessment). Women, I think, are more field-dependent than men – more attuned to and affected by details in their environments. Because of the violence issues for this population of women, an immediate sense of safety in and around the environment is crucial. Consider the following factors:

- Is public transit very close by?
- Are streets well-lit
- Is her privacy assured – are meetings with her counsellor structured to protect the confidentiality of their discussions?
- Are her personal belongings accessible only to her?
- Is there (in the case of co-ed programs) adequate physical separation from male participants? One client told me why she left a co-ed residential program prematurely: she had been placed initially in a co-ed stabilization unit in which she was the only woman, with only a fabric screen separating her bed from the men. She was terrified of falling asleep and left after three days.

Essential Services

In addition to a comprehensive assessment and attention to the physical and emotional environment, the following are essential ingredients in any treatment program, whether out-patient or day treatment, or short- to long-term residential:

- chemical dependency education following a biopsychosocial model (Donovan & Marlatt ed. 1988), including discussion of possible contributing factors, consequences and effects
- relapse prevention (Annis & Davis, 1989)
- skill training to develop self-esteem and coping (Reed's 1987 list seems complete to me in this regard): assertiveness training, financial management education, instruction in personal goal setting, education in stress and crisis management, assistance in developing communication skills and a support system, discussion of gender and socialization issues, and instruction in basic survival skills.

Also essential are: education on nutrition, exercise and other leisure activities; family (in its broadest sense); and discussions on sexuality including attention to sexual abuse issues, body image, eating disorders, performance expectations.

I should clarify what I mean here: there should not be any performance expectations. With the high incidence of sexual dysfunction, many sex acts, such as intercourse and other forms of two-person sexual activity, need to be delayed or postponed for some time while clients work on other issues. If there is a life partner in the picture, he or she may expect their sex life to resume or improve immediately. It is quite possible, however, that the client has never engaged in any sexual activity without being under the influence of a mood-altering substance. Or she may be retrieving memories of sexual abuse that need attention, etc. In other words, it is not only her right, but a necessary part of recovery in some cases, to proceed slowly in resuming or exploring her sex life with a partner.

Related Services

Other necessary services could be offered as part of the treatment program itself or through referral elsewhere in the community. These include:

- medical services
- vocational services
- services for eating disorders
- appropriately sensitive psychiatric consultation and/or treatment
- services for the children of clients, including child care, prevention/ education and treatment programs
- other types of family (again in its broadest sense) programming, including educational and support groups for partners, parenting education, family therapy and couples' groups (these should not occur too early in recovery – women usually need at least several months of self-focused recovery elements first)
- legal services
- and probably most important, services for recovery from the trauma of sexual abuse.

TREATMENT MODALITIES

Because of the constellation of factors usually found among chemically dependent women seeking treatment – low self-esteem, guilt, social isolation, and history of physical and sexual abuse – I have a strong bias toward gender-specific group treatment, at least in early recovery. Let me begin by describing some of the problems women face in mixed-gender groups. I have built this list over the last 10 years, adding from my own group experience and every study I have found that looked at the issues: interaction in mixed groups reinforces traditional role stereotypes; women speak less often and for less time than men; women are often interrupted; women do not defend their ideas vigorously; issues of body image and sexuality are not discussed; women compete and do not develop closeness with each other; women are passive, talk softly and tend to withdraw; women overtly and covertly defer to men and encourage male participation and interactions; men's language patterns predominate.[2]

If the ultimate goal of a treatment plan is that a woman develop her potential – that she achieve and maintain abstinence, discover a sense of self, build self-esteem, develop social supports and recover from the trauma of abuse – common sense alone should lead us to conclude that these objectives can best be met with the help of other women. All-women groups facilitated by female leaders allow clients to: develop a sense of self through validation of one's experiences and perceptions; attempt personal, behavioral and attitudinal changes; express difficult feelings like anger and shame; share the social determinants of problems special to women; please themselves instead of others; learn to trust and value women. And for almost all women (the exception sometimes being those who have been abused by mothers or lesbian partners), these groups provide the safety necessary to take risks. Some women may be reluctant to engage in an all-women group because they dislike other women. Despite the potential benefits of a woman's participation, you may have to accept that she may reject your advice in this regard: in other words, keep your options open. Women can now access all-women Alcoholics Anonymous and Women for Sobriety groups as well as within some treatment programs and services.

Except for women whose particular combination and quantity of substances would likely result in withdrawal requiring close monitoring (for example, to watch for seizures), or those who need to remove themselves from their living situation or the influence of their significant others, day treatment or outpatient treatment is just as effective and much less costly and disruptive than residential treatment. Although there has not been a lot of good outcome research in general, there has been enough to demonstrate that non-residential treatment is usually preferable. And for women, with all of the other responsibilities in their lives, this is probably even more true.

I realize that my bias for all-women groups, though based on clinical experience, perpetuates what Vanicelli (1984) describes as the "unsubstantiated, but dearly held, beliefs of care providers." I stand by it, however, awaiting more research in the area of treatment outcome and matching clients to treatment modalities[3] before I will consider that I might be wrong. The most ground I will give on this point is that, at the very least, women be given a choice of treatment modalities and sex of therapist.

COUNSELLOR CHARACTERISTICS

In discussing gender of therapist, I have almost come full circle. I began this chapter by stating that if we are to help women recover and develop their potential, we must understand and empathize with each one individually. I truly believe that many components of a treatment program could vary and not greatly affect outcome, as long as there is the essential relational bond between the client and her therapist. Put another way, I hope treatment outcome research in the substance abuse field eventually confirms what psychotherapy research has – that one of the key prognostic variables in treatment is the empathic qualities of the therapist. Empathy means profoundly valuing and understanding the client's reality. It also involves knowing yourself intimately so you can be with your client every step of the way and not lose yourself in the process. I offer the following list of questions, based on those used by the authors of *Women's Ways of Knowing*, for some self-exploration from a perspective you may not have considered:
- How do you express your anger?
- What are your deepest fears? How do you deal with them?
- Do you seek nurturance for yourself? How, in what ways, from whom?
- Have you experienced intimate group sharing with other women/men?
- Have you been through your own therapy?

- Do you know who you are – could you describe yourself to someone?
- In your own family, how are roles assigned; how are finances handled; who makes money decisions? How are household duties handled?
- If you have children, how are they growing up vis-à-vis traditional male/female roles, ways of interacting, etc.?
- What would you (or did you) look for in a helping person?
- What stands out for you in your life over the last few years?
- What kinds of things have been important?
- What is your life like right now? What do you care about, think about?
- Is the way you see yourself now different from the way you saw yourself in the past? What led to the changes? How do you see yourself changing in the future?
- What does being a woman/man mean to you?
- Do you think there are any important differences between women and men?
- How has your sense of yourself as a woman/man been changing?
- What relationships have been really important to you in your life? Why? How would you describe those relationships? How would the other person describe them?
- Have you had a relationship with someone who helped you shape the person you have become?
- Have you had a really important relationship where you were responsible for taking care of another person? How would you describe this? How important was that in your life?

I hope you can see some connection between your own answers to these questions and your ability to walk in step with your women clients.

Again it seems common sense to me that women therapists would generally be more likely than male counterparts to empathize with women clients. Men and women have very different realities, very different experiences of the world. They develop differently, think differently, develop different kinds of moral reasoning, have different experiences of intimacy and sexuality and on and on. The odds are that a woman therapist will understand the world her female client describes better than a male therapist. This is not to say that a male therapist can never empathize with the experiences of his female clients. A study reported by Kaplan (1985) found that very experienced males could achieve the same rate of therapy outcome as moderately experienced or experienced female therapists. I have selectively referred clients to male therapists but never for sexual abuse or other abuse issues, and not in early recovery while a woman is just beginning to develop a sense of self and a support network.

CLOSING NOTES

In preparing for a workshop a few years ago, I wanted to describe to participants the essence of the relationship between a woman recovering from chemical dependency and her counsellor. I used the following analogy, thinking I had developed it, only later discovering that it been used years before in relation to teaching, probably by Paulo Freire. Rather than being disappointed by my lack of originality, I was reassured by the fact that others had conceptualized it in a similar way.

Accompanying an addicted woman on the long journey to recovery – through self-loathing, guilt and despair to self-understanding, self-acceptance, self-respect, and control over her own life – is like being a midwife. The client is in the driver's seat, and you move forward with her when she has the strength; sit quietly beside her while she catches her breath, encouraging her, guiding her to push again, telling her the pain won't last, that the destination is worth it, that you've seen many other women go through this, that you know she has the strength to push again. And ultimately, she has given birth to herself, to the beginning of her potential finally becoming reality.

ACKNOWLEDGEMENTS

1. I would like to express my gratitude to current colleagues within the Addiction Resarch Foundation for their feedback on this chapter, but especially to former clients and colleagues at Amethyst Women's Addiction Centre for giving me their input on the first draft – thank you Lynn, Ellen, Pierrette and Jane.

FOOTNOTES

2. It was a delight to read a sociolinguist's analysis and validation of what had been my own observations of mixed and gender-specific groups. Deborah Tannen (1991) describes many of the above conversational dynamics between men and women, as well as others, as "cross-cultural communication, prey to a clash of conversational styles" (p. 42).

3. Copeland and Hall's 1992 study found that a specialist women's service, in comparison with traditional mixed-sex services, attracted significantly more women with dependent children, or who were lesbian, or who had a maternal history for drug or alcohol problems, or who had suffered sexual abuse in childhood.

REFERENCES

Adlaf, Edward M. & Smart, Reginald G. (1989). Ontario adult alcohol and other drug use survey 1977-1989. Toronto: Addiction Research Foundation.

Annis, Helen & Davis, Christine. (1989). Relapse prevention. In R.K. Hester & W.R. Miller (Eds.), Handbook of alcoholism treatment approaches (pp. 170-182). New York: Pergamon Press, 1989.

Beckman, L.J. & Amaro H. (1986). Personal and social difficulties faced by women and men entering treatment. Journal of Studies on Alcohol, 47, pp. 135-145.

Belenky, Mary Field, Clinchy, Blythe McVicker, Goldberger, Nancy Rule & Tarule, Jill Mattuck. (1986). Women's ways of knowing. New York: Basic Books, 1986.

Brehaut, L. (1989). Believe her! A Report on Sexual Assault and Sexual Abuse of Women and Children. P.E.I. Advisory Council on the Status of Women.

Brody, Claire, M.Ed. (1987). Women's therapy groups. New York: Springer Publishing Co., 1987.

Butt, Louise (1991). Antidepressants: Beyond Benzodiazepines. Connexions, March/April pp.14-18.

Canadian Advisory Council on the Status of Women. (1987). Integration and participation: women's work in the home and in the labour force, Ottawa.

Copeland, Jan & Hall, Wayne. (1992). A comparison of women seeking drug and alcohol treatment in a specialist women's and two traditional mixed-sex treatment services. British Journal of Addiction, 87, pp. 1293-1302.

Curlee, J. (1970). A comparison of male and female patients at an alcoholism treatment centre. Journal of Psychology, 74, pp. 239-247.

D'Arcy, C. (1982). Prevalence and correlates of nonpsychotic psychiatric symptoms in the general population. Canadian Journal of Psychiatry, 27, pp. 316-324.

Donovan, Dennis M. & Marlatt, G. Alan (Eds.). (1988). Assessment of addictive behaviors. New York: The Guilford Press, 1988.

Durkheim, E. (1951). Suicide. New York: Free Press, 1951.

Frezza, M., Di Padova, C., Pozzato, G., Terpin, M., Baraona, E. & Lieber, C.S. (1990). High blood alcohol levels in women: The role of decreased gastric alcohol dehydrogenase activity and first-pass metabolism. New England Journal of Medicine, 322(2), pp. 95-99.

Gilligan, Carol. (1982). In a different voice. Cambridge, Mass.: Howard University Press.

Goldman, Deborah S. & Bander, Karen W. (1990). Six-Month Course of Depression in Female Alcoholics. Journal of Substance Abuse, 2, pp. 375-380.

Gomberg, E.S. (1989). Suicide risk among women with alcohol problems. American Journal of Public Health, 79, pp. 1363-1365.

Groeneveld, Judith & Shain, Martin. (1989). Drug use among victims of sexual abuse. Toronto: Addiction Research Foundation.

Guberman, C. & Wolfe, M. (Eds.) (1985). No Safe Place: Violence Against Women and Children. Toronto: The Women's Press.

Health and Welfare Canada. (1988). Canada's Health Promotion Survey: Technical Report. Irving Rootman, Reg Warren, Thomas Stephens & Larry Peters (Eds.). Ottawa: Minister of Supply and Services Canada.

Health and Welfare Canada. (1990). National Alcohol and Other Drugs Survey (1989): Highlights Report. Marc Eliany, Dr. Norman, Giesbrecht, Dr. Mike Nelson, Dr. Barry Wellman & Scot Wortley (Eds.). Ottawa: Minister of Supply and Services Canada.

Hill, Shirley Y. (1984). Vulnerability to the biomedical consequences of alcoholism and alcohol-related problems among women. In Sharon C. Wilsnack & Linda J. Beckman (Eds.), Alcohol problems in women (pp. 121-154). New York: The Guilford Press, 1984.

House, J., Landis, K. & Umberson, D. (1988). Social relationships and health. Science, Vol. 241, pp. 540-545.

Jacobson, R. (1986). The contribution of sex and drinking history to the CT brain scan changes in alcoholics. Psychological Medicine, 16, pp. 547-559.

Jacobson, R. (1986). Female alcoholics: a controlled CT brain scan and clinical study. British Journal of Addiction, 81, pp. 661-669.

Jellinek, E.M. (1946). Phases in the drinking history of alcoholics. Quarterly Journal of Studies on Alcohol, 7, pp. 1-88.

Jellinek, E.M. (1952). Phases of alcohol addiction. <u>Quarterly Journal of Studies on Alcohol</u>, <u>13</u>, pp. 673-684.

Jones, Marilyn K. & Jones, Ben Morgan. (1984). Ethanol Metabolism in Women Taking Oral Contraceptives. <u>Alcoholism: Clinical and Experimental Research</u>, <u>8</u>, pp. 24-28.

Kaplan, Alexandra G. (1985). Female or male therapists for women patients: New formulations. <u>Psychiatry</u>, <u>Vol. 48</u>, May 1985.

Lowe, G.S. (1989). <u>Women, paid/unpaid work, and stress: new directions for research</u>. Background Paper. Ottawa: Canadian Advisory Council on the Status of Women.

MacLeod, L. (1987). <u>Battered but not beaten: preventing wife battering in Canada</u>. Ottawa: Canadian Advisory Council on the Status of Women.

Marshall, Janet. (1989). <u>Where do the children go?</u> Women, Addictions, and Childcare. A Research Report for Mann House Corporation, May, 1989.

Miller, Jean Baker, M.D. (1976). <u>Toward a new psychology of women</u>. Boston: Beacon Press, 1976.

Moore, M. (1987). Women parenting alone. <u>Canadian Social Trends</u>, Winter, pp. 31-36.

Penfold, P.S. & Walker, G.A. (1983). <u>Women and the psychiatric paradox</u>. Montreal: Eden Press, 1983.

Penfold, Susan (1987). Antidepressants. <u>Proceedings of a National Consultation on Women and Drugs</u> (pp.14-15). Ottawa: Minister of Supply and Services.

Reed, B.G. & Leibson, E. (1981). Women clients in special women's demonstration programs compared with women entering co-sex programs. <u>The International Journal of the Addictions</u>, <u>16</u>, pp. 1425-1466.

Reed, Beth Glover. (1985). Drug misuse and dependency in women: the meaning and implications of being considered a special population or minority group. <u>The International Journal of the Addictions</u>, <u>20(1)</u>, pp. 13-62.

Reed, Beth Glover. (1987). Developing women-sensitive drug dependence treatment services: why so difficult? <u>Journal of Psychoactive Drugs</u>, <u>19(2)</u>, pp. 151-164.

Rodin, Judith & Ickovics, Jeannette R. (1990, September). Women's health review and research agenda as we approach the 21st century. <u>American Psychologist</u>, pp. 1018-1034.

Sanchez-Craig, Martha (1990). Brief didactic treatment for alcohol and drug-related problems: an approach based on client choice. British Journal of Addiction, 85, pp. 169-177.

Saunders, J.B., Davis, M. & Williams, R. (1981). Do women develop alcoholic liver disease more readily than men?, British Medical Journal, 282, pp. 1140-1143.

Schatzkin, A., Jones, D.Y., Hoover, R.N., Taylor, P.R., Brinton, L.A., Ziegler, R.G., Harvey, E.B., Carter, C.L., Licitra, L.M., DuFour, M.C. & Larson, D.B. (1987). Alcohol consumption and breast cancer in the epidemiologic follow-up study of the first national health and nutrition examination survey. The New England Journal of Medicine, 316, pp. 1169-1173.

Schlesinger, S., Susman, M. & Koenigsberg. (1990). Self-esteem and purpose in life: a comparative study of women alcoholics. Journal of Alcohol and Drug Education, Vol. 36(i), 1990 Fall, pp. 127-141.

Stoppard, Janet M. (1988). Women and the mental health system: mental health policy as though women mattered. Paper presented at the Symposium on Women and Mental Health, Section on Women and Psychology, Canadian Psychological Association Annual Convention, Montreal, June, 1988.

Tannen, Deborah, Ph.D. (1991). You Just Don't Understand. New York: Ballantine Books, 1991.

Thomas, E. (1988). Issues and priorities for women's health in Canada. Health Promotion Directorate, Health and Welfare Canada, Ottawa.

Turner, R.J. & Beiser, M. (1987, October). Major depression and depressive symptomatology among the physically disabled: assessing the role of chronic stress. Paper presented at the meeting of the American Public Health Association, New Orleans.

Vannicelli, Marsha (1984). Treatment outcome of alcoholic women: the state of the art in relation to sex bias and expectancy effects. In Sharon C. Wilsnack & Linda J. Beckman (Eds.), Alcohol Problems in Women, (pp. 369-412). New York: The Guilford Press, 1984.

Wilbur, Cornelia B., M.D. (1984). Multiple Personality and Child Abuse. Psychiatric Clinics of North America, Vol. 7(1), pp. 3-7.

The Physically Disabled Substance Abuser

DOUG BULLOCK

INTRODUCTION

*O*nly since the early 1980s have attention and resources been directed to understanding and helping persons with addiction problems and disability issues (Boros, 1989). Increased attention to these issues has come mostly through a concerted lobbying effort on the part of individuals with disabilities, and passage in the U.S. of the Disabilities Rights Legislation (De Miranda & Cherry, 1989). As with many groups who find themselves outside the mainstream of North American cultural reality, they have gained addiction services only through hard-fought efforts. Those gains, especially in Canada, are small indeed at this time. Research on addiction and disability issues is scant, and what little exists has been done in isolation. There are as yet few common definitions or a solid base of knowledge on which to build a consensus for developing therapeutic guidelines or training opportunities.

This situation presents a clear challenge for the clinician working with a person with a disability. You will need to spend more time building the therapeutic relationship and advocating on behalf of the client. This chapter explores these issues and suggests some therapeutic approaches to meet the challenge.[1]

DISABILITY: DEFINITION AND MEANING

Defining disability is a complex issue and very much depends on who does the defining. Various studies of disability issues focus the definition to include only a particular type of disability and generally examine a selected sample, often within an institutional setting. Statistics Canada (1992) completed the second Canada-wide survey of disability. The Health and Activity Limitation Survey used the following definition of disability:

"Disability was assessed through an internationally standardized set of questions known as 'Activities of Daily Living.' This is a practical series of questions designed to identify any difficulties people have in performing their daily routines. For example, respondents were asked if they had difficulties in moving from room to room, carrying objects 10 metres, dressing themselves, reading a newspaper, following a conversation, or being understood while speaking.... Six types of disabilities were identified, namely, disabilities relating to mobility, agility, hearing, seeing and speaking, and mental disabilities."

Using this definition, the Canadian survey estimated that approximately 4.2 million Canadians (15.5 per cent of the population) reported some form of disability.

For planning and lobbying purposes, it is important to have a broad sense of the types and numbers of persons with disabilities. However, without more complete research, formal survey definitions of disability have limited therapeutic use. Little is known about the personal meanings of disability, and this information must be sought from clients directly. According to Hart & Trotter (1977), how the individual defines and views his or her disability is most important to recognize. It is often not the fact of disability (as formally defined) that concerns the individual but the "handicaps" it creates for them. Robert Christie (1992) summed this notion up perfectly in a letter to the Ottawa *Citizen:*

"Many disabled people, especially those born with their disability, don't see themselves as being disabled, although everyone else does. Rather they think of them selves as being 'normal.' They have always been the way they are and they are used to being that way."

These thoughts are important. Self-acceptance in the face of society's negative attitude towards disability is often a major issue to be resolved as part of recovery from addiction.

DRUG USE: PREVALENCE, PATTERNS AND TREATMENT UTILIZATION

Many studies, especially in the U.S., have tried to determine the rate of drug use and abuse among persons with a disability (Moore & Polsgrove, 1989). I will not attempt an exhaustive review of these studies but point to a few patterns that emerge on review. Individuals with spinal cord and head injuries seem consistently to record higher levels of pre-injury drug/alcohol use than the general population; many were actually injured while under the influence of drugs or alcohol (Heinemann, Doll & Schnoll, 1989). Adlaf, Smart & Walsh (1990), in examining the connection between alcohol/drug use in those with work limitations due to disability, found problems with alcohol were highest among those with moderate work-role limitations and that the use of prescribed psychoactive medication rose with increased disability.

U.S. studies have found higher rates of alcohol and street drug use than Canadian studies. Canadian studies, however, find higher rates of prescription drug use among persons with a disability, possibly reflecting the lower cost to users for medically prescribed drugs.

Tyas & Rush (1990), reporting on the use of addiction treatment services in Ontario by persons with disabilities, found that 3.7 per cent of clients were considered to have a mobility impairment, 2.3 per cent a developmental handicap, 1.5 per cent has impaired vision, and 1.4 per cent impaired hearing, with an overall total of approximately 16 per cent of clients in treatment having a disability. According to Statistics Canada (1992), of the general population in Ontario between the ages of 15 and 64, seven per cent report a mobility impairment, one per cent a vision impairment, and three per cent a hearing impairment. Except for the comparative rates for those with seeing disabilities, it is consistent with care giver observations that persons with disabilities are underrepresented in the treatment population if we assume that the prevalence rate for substance abuse problems among them is the same as in the general population. Since these surveys did not use exactly equivalent methods or definitions of disability this analysis should be seen as suggestive only.

Tyas & Rush (1990) also report that six per cent of addiction services have specially tailored services for those with physical or sensory disabilities. Respondents, however, indicated a wide variation in what constituted a specially tailored service. Most services reported physical accessibility modifications within their program or access to sign language interpreters, but very little in the way of specialized training for staff. Only half the respondents felt that specialized training was even necessary for their staff to respond to the needs of persons with disabilities.

Moore & Polsgrove (1989), in analyzing a series of U.S. studies, conclude that:
> "Existing research has frequently been compromised by sample or design problems which are associated with limited resources. There needs to be a closer factoring of the nature of the disabilities being studied, whether the disabilities were congenital or traumatic in origin. Also the need to look at drug use pattern evolution, age of onset, etc. ...to assist in mounting effective prevention, intervention or treatment efforts." (page 82)

In conclusion, a review of drug use and treatment program utilization studies gives us little clinical guidance. The main lessons are that drug use among persons with disabilities probably parallels that of the general Canadian population; the most notable exception is a higher rate of prescribed drug use among those with severe work-role limitations and alcohol use among those with disabilities resulting from trauma. Given that drug use rates are generally similar, why do we find proportionally only half as many persons with physical and hearing limitations participating in treatment? The only conclusion is that existing treatment programs and methodologies are not meeting the needs of this community.

RISK FACTORS

To succeed at intervention, we must understand the unique risk factors for drug abuse identified for persons with a disability. They face many of the same risk factors as others, including relief from anxiety and frustration, low self-esteem, sensation seeking, drug and alcohol availability, poverty, genetic influences, etc. However, these influences can take on unique meanings. They are often magnified in significance because of general social attitudes to disability.

Several authors have described and corroborate unique risk factors influencing persons with disability (Boros, 1989; Kelly, 1991; Schaschl et al, 1989). They are listed below:

- more sensitivity to alcohol and other non-prescribed drugs because of drug interactions and medical conditions resulting from the disability
- chronic pain, spasticity, etc. can lead to self-medication
- lower self-esteem related to the disability and to architectural or physical barriers preventing participation in activities that provide social contact and development of social skills
- vicarious excitement and sensation-seeking when normal activity and mobility is limited
- people with disabilities, especially those with a disability from a young age, are taught to comply with medical and professional advice, institutional rules, etc. This can result in low self-esteem
- unemployment leads to low economic status, increases isolation and removes people from situations where drug and alcohol problems might be identified and help offered
- negative attitudes by society at large give messages that people with disabilities are incapable and dependent and lead to low self-esteem
- care givers, family members and health care professionals may feel that the person with a disability has enough to cope with without having to address a drug or alcohol related problem
- physical and attitudinal barriers prevent access to community programs and services that could provide early intervention for substance abuse problems
- heightened vulnerability to physical abuse and consequent emotional issues that increase risk of drug abuse.

These factors demonstrate the complexity of issues to consider when helping a person with a disability. The list highlights the fact that many of the unique risk factors are not intrinsic to the individual, but imposed by cultural and social values.

These risk factors could apply to all persons with a disability. However, other unique risk factors associated with particular disabilities should be noted. Sinclair (1992) in describing his experience with deaf culture states:

"...many deaf people do not consider themselves to be an 'impaired' population (since they communicate perfectly well with signs) but rather an ethnic population... and includes a strong moral opposition to addiction, as well as a strong enabling (us against the world) attitude."

Traumatic head injury is often associated with alcohol abuse (Parkinson, Stephensen & Phillips, 1985) and the consequences of brain injury for alcohol or drug abuse treatment can be complex. As with developmental handicaps, cognitive deficits may require slowing the pace of treatment and more reliance on supportive interventions and short term goal-oriented approaches. Burganowski (1992) describes a risk factor particular to persons with traumatic brain injury. Common symptoms of this type of injury include slowed speech or unsteady gait. These behaviors are often accepted in bars and taverns but not in everyday society. People with brain injuries may feel much less anxiety and negative judgment in such environments. Once again, this risk factor is not intrinsic, but precipitated by cultural values and expectations.

These factors must be carefully assessed in treatment planning. Often, the therapeutic role will have to include a strong element of advocacy and systems work. These issues are explored in more detail in the next section.

TREATMENT AND RECOVERY ISSUES

As noted earlier, there is no standard model of treatment for persons with disabilities. A few programs exist in the U.S., but to date there is no formal body of research to guide us on what works best and for whom. Most information is anecdotal, and your own intervention work must be guided by your own instincts, and most importantly, by your client's experience. Knowing the risk factors and the treatment issues discussed in the next section should help you understand your client's needs and factors involved in developing and following a treatment plan.

One area of clinical concern that can be highly relevant for a person with a disability are the conditions enabling or supporting drug abuse. Enabling conditions go far beyond the immediate family situation: friends, the legal system, health care providers, etc., all inadvertently work together to maintain an addiction. Two attitudes on the part of care givers contribute to this situation. One is sympathy and "hero" biases, where those around the abuser feel the struggles and difficulties caused by the disability justify the use of drugs or alcohol – he or she has enough to cope with without worrying about the drug use. This attitude may reflect the feeling that "the drug use is the only pleasure in the person's life and it would be wrong to take that away."

Society's negative attitudes towards both disability and addiction also enhance enabling. "Physically impaired" persons often are perceived as hopeless, helpless, fragile and sick (Schaschl & Straw, 1989). Attach a further label of "alcoholic" or "drug addict" and we can see why those around the individual will go to great lengths to deny a drug problem, preferring instead to attribute consequences of drug abuse to the disability itself. Thus typical signs of drug abuse – lack of motivation, low energy levels, increased physical problems, etc. – are easily seen as a consequence of the disability, not of drug abuse.

Both these attitudes work closely but tragically in tandem: thus the individual may have easy access to drugs from sympathetic friends and care givers, while the inevitable consequences of abuse are attributed to the disability. A person with a disability and growing addiction will often understand these forces at a sophisticated level, making effective intervention a real challenge for the inexperienced.

PRACTICAL INTERVENTIONS IN A SERVICE VACUUM

Working with people having a disability requires a unique type of creativity, especially for therapists without prior experience in this area. You will need an accessible location for meetings; flexibility around scheduling because of less predictable access to public transportation; and possibly technical aids or interpreters for communication purposes. Although Tyas & Rush (1990) found that six per cent of Ontario's addiction treatment services reported specially tailored services for the physically disabled, anecdotal evidence suggests that these provisions are often partial, requiring a greatly modified treatment protocol for the client. This can make it difficult for him or her to identify and bond with other clients. Programs that require complete abstinence from all psychoactive drugs may deny access to a person with a disability who legitimately uses a prescribed psychoactive drug to control spasms or epilepsy. Finally, most staff in existing treatment programs have not been trained to understand the particular cultural and psycho-social factors that accompany disability – few training opportunities exist.

Since little formal research has been done to clarify these unique treatment issues and give guidance on what works best (Moore & Polsgrove, 1989), we are exploring new territory when first counselling the client with a disability. Treatment programs for the physically disabled – both inpatient and outpatient – exist in the U.S. (Schaschl et al., 1989; Boros, 1992). A poll of the provincial addiction agencies in Canada, completed with the cooperation of the Canadian Centre on Substance Abuse (Hawley, 1993), indicates that no provincially funded programs are specifically tailored to the needs of persons with a disability. Private counselling or counsellor services may exist, but would need to be determined at a local level.

For most counselling situations, outpatient treatment is probably the most practical choice, involving a combination of professional and peer support interventions. Those requiring inpatient care would have to go to the U.S., at least until suitable programs are developed in Canada. Outpatient models, however, provide a number of advantages for treating all but the most severely addicted individual, with or without a disability. The advantages include:
- flexibile location – anywhere from a traditional office setting to the client's home (this allows the client a greater sense of anonymity and allows the

service to exist in smaller communities without formal addiction services)
- flexibile scheduling (the pace and duration of treatment can be tailored to suit the client)
- tend to work with the unique goals of the client, not necessarily enforcing abstinence as a criterion for providing assistance; the client is very much in charge of the treatment direction and resources employed
- may not require the client to accept the label of "alcoholic" or "addict," which deters many persons concerned about their substance abuse from contacting traditional services
- draw on a variety of social service resources to meet the unique needs of a client; not restricted to providing a standard set of interventions to all clients, regardless of their utility
- treatment progress is constantly tested against the backdrop of the client's day-to-day life, thus real life difficulties are continually being addressed and incorporated into the treatment plan.

A central feature in outpatient treatment approaches is the comprehensive and ongoing assessment of client needs and progress during treatment. Modifications are made as new information is gathered while the client progresses through self-discovery and a series of behavior changes. This feature is a real advantage when working with a person with a disability. Without clear directions from previous experience, we must constantly listen to our clients to understand the issues, and try a variety of creative approaches to understanding and solving problems. Many existing resources now support the use of outpatient approaches. Training in outpatient and early identification approaches is available through organizations like the Addiction Research Foundation, and publications detailing these methods are available, e.g., Hester & Miller (1989). Many communities have excellent resources to help a person with a disability with practical issues, such as housing, transportation, technical devices, advocacy, and social and psychological support. With outpatient approaches, these can be used as required to address problems contributing to drug use. These resources can be discovered through local organizations serving persons with a disability.

Of particular relevance to addiction issues is the independent living movement, a relatively new development in Canada. Sixteen centres that base their programs on this philosophy are now funded in Canada and several others are in developmental stages. These centres are guided by the following mission statement:

"To promote and enable the progressive process of citizens with disabilities taking responsibility for the development and management of personal and community resources" (CAILC, 1985).

As this statement implies, Independent Living Centres (ILCs) are consumer controlled and encourage the development of independent living both in terms of accessing services and in the development of self-esteem. Many ILCs have concerns about addictions, as they severely hamper the development of personal responsibility and independence. The Canadian Association of Independent Living Centres

(CAILC) has published a pamphlet on addiction warning signs for persons with disabilities, and presented a brief to the Canadian Centre on Substance Abuse (CAILC, 1992) recommending ways to provide addiction treatment to this population.

The ILC philosophy and programming approach link closely with the outpatient approaches described earlier. The Ottawa, Ontario, ILC, for example, trained their peer support workers to recognize addiction issues and talk with an individual about addiction concerns. This material is being compiled as part of a training manual for new volunteers to the centre and will eventually be available to all ILCs. Clinicians are urged to develop a working relationship with the nearest ILC, to learn about the various resources available to aid their work with clients and to develop a link for ongoing support and aftercare.

Ultimately, the work of organizations such as ILCs – which encourage the development of self-esteem and appropriate service response – will pressure necessary prevention and treatment resources to deal adequately with the avoided issue: drugs and disability.

ACKNOWLEDGEMENT

1. I wish to express my appreciation to Nancy Kelly and Sue McKay, staff of the Ottawa Carleton Independent Living Centre, for their review and helpful critique of this manuscript.

REFERENCES

Adlaf, E.M., Smart, R.G. & Walsh, G.W. (1990). Substance Use and Work Disabilities. Toronto: Addiction Research Foundation.

Boros, A (1989). Facing the Challenge. Alcohol Health and Research World, 13(2), 101-103.

Boros, A. (1992). Editor, AID Bulletin. Sociology Department, Kent State University. Ohio, U.S.

Burganowski, D. (1992). Conference Presentation. Disabilities and Drug Abuse: The Avoided Issue. Rehabilitation Centre. Ottawa, Canada. June 1992.

Canadian Association of Independent Living Centres, (1992). Brief on Substance Misuse and Persons with Disabilities. Ottawa. March 1992.

CAILC, (1985). First National Independent Living Centre Meeting. Kitchener, Ontario.

Christie, R. (1992). as quoted in Contacts. The Newsletter of the Ottawa-Carleton Independent Living Centre. Vol. 4, No. 3. December 1992.

De Miranda, J. & Cherry, L. (1989). California Responds: Changing Treatment Systems Through Advocacy for the Disabled. Alcohol Health and Research World, 13(2), 154-157.

Frieden, A. L. (1990). Substance Abuse and Disability: The Role of the Independent Living Centre. Journal of Applied Rehabilitation Counselling, Vol. 21(3), Fall, 1990. 33-36.

Hart, L. & Trotter, A. (1977). Alcoholism – disability versus handicap: An important distinction. Journal of Studies on Alcohol, 38(7), 1443-1446.

Hawley, M. (1993). Poll of Canadian Provincial Addiction Organizations. Canadian Centre on Substance Abuse.

Heinemann, A.W., Doll, M. & Schnoll, S. (1989). Treatment of Alcohol Abuse in Persons with Recent Spinal Cord Injuries. Alcohol Health and Research World, 13(2), 110-117.

Hester, R.K. & Miller, W.R. (1989). Handbook of Alcoholism Treatment Approaches: Effective Alternatives. New York. Pergamon Press. ISBN 0-08-036428-4.

Kelly, N. (1991). Personal Communication. Ottawa-Carleton Independent Living Centre. Ottawa, Canada.

Moore D. & Polsgrove L. (1989). Disabilities, developmental handicaps and substance misuse: a review. Social Pharmacology, 3(4), 375-408.

Parkinson, D., Stephensen, S. & Phillips, S. (1985). Head Injuries: A prospective, computerized study. Canadian Journal of Surgery, 28(1), 79-83.

Schaschl, S. & Straw, D. (1989). Results of a Model Intervention Program for Physically Impaired Persons. Alcohol Health & Research World, 13(2), 150-153.

Sinclair, J.R. (1992). Counselling the Hearing-Impaired. Paper prepared for presentation to the Community Addiction Network. Ottawa, Ontario.

Statistics Canada (1992). 1991 Health and Activity Limitation Survey – Highlights. In "The Daily" Ottawa: Tuesday, October 13, 1992.

Taking Control (1992). Pamphlet prepared by the Canadian Association of Independent Living Centres. Ottawa, Canada.

Tyas, S.L. & Rush, B.R. (1990). Treatment Issues for Disabled Clients: Results of a Survey of Alcohol and Other Drug Services in Ontario. Toronto: Addiction Research Foundation.

Substance Abuse and the Older Person

JANE BARON AND VIRGINIA CARVER

Evidence suggests that alcohol is the foremost substance of abuse by the elderly, followed by drugs obtained legally through prescriptions or over the counter (NIAAA, 1982).

INTRODUCTION

C an you imagine someone close to you – a parent or grandparent, an elderly friend or neighbor – having an alcohol or drug problem? If we think at all about the older person with such a problem, it is usually the older skid row alcoholic.

However, in recent years the chemically dependent older person has been receiving increasing attention in the literature. A recent National Library of Medicine Literature Search of publications between 1980 and 1985 produced nearly 50 citations concerned with substance misuse or abuse among older people (Kenton, 1985). Provincial governments have also identified the misuse or abuse of pharmaceuticals by seniors as a concern, (for example, Baker, 1992; Health and Community Services, New Brunswick, 1991; Lankin, 1992).

There are a number of reasons for this interest in chemical dependency among older people. One may be our increasing lifespan and aging population. By the year 2036, approximately one-quarter of Canadians will be aged 65 or over (Health and Welfare, 1989a). Also, since the 1960s, many new psychoactive medications have come on the market, particularly the benzodiazepines (Valium, Xanax, Halcion, etc.). It has taken some time to recognize that they may be a mixed blessing, particularly for the older person. Finally, there is increasing understanding of the effects of various substances on the body and how certain groups such as the elderly or women may be more vulnerable to these effects.

EXTENT OF SUBSTANCE USE AMONG OLDER CANADIANS

Generally, as people get older, they are less likely to drink but more likely to use prescribed medication.

National surveys (Andrews, 1988; Health & Welfare Canada, 1989b, Health and Welfare, Canada, 1990) indicate that between 66 and 72 per cent of men and between 45 and 52 per cent of women aged 65 years and older are current drinkers. This compares with 84 per cent of males and 72 per cent of females in the general population.

Average weekly consumption for older men is approximately five drinks a week, whereas younger men average six to eight drinks a week. For older women, the average weekly consumption is between two and three drinks, not much different from younger age groups.

Also, older people are far less likely to be in the heaviest drinking categories of 15 or more drinks a week.

To some extent, the drinking patterns of older Canadians may reflect the drinking mores with which they grew up. As younger people with more exposure to alcohol grow older, there may be an increasing number of older heavy drinkers.

In contrast, use of psychoactive prescribed drugs such as tranquillizers and sleeping pills increases with age. Among those 65 and over, 11.1 per cent use sleeping pills and 5.4 per cent tranquillizers. This contrasts with 3.6 per cent of the general adult population who report using sleeping pills and 3.1 per cent who report using tranquillizers. In all age categories, women are more likely to use sleeping pills and tranquillizers than men (Health and Welfare Canada, 1990). Older people may also use a number of prescribed psychoactive drugs simultaneously (Lamarche & Rootman, 1988).

Community surveys that have examined rates of heavy or problem drinking among older people invariably find higher rates in men than in women (for example Blazer and Pennybacker, 1984; Adlaf, Smart and Jansen, 1989; Adlaf and Smart, 1988; Holzer et al., 1983; Warheit and Auth, 1983). These rates range from one to two per cent for women to four to 24 per cent for men.

Older problem drinkers are more likely than younger drinkers to drink daily and to consume smaller amounts. However, levels of alcohol or other drug use that may be safe in a younger person can be problematic in someone older because of physiological changes.

These changes have been well described by a number of authors, (for example, Baker, 1985; Lamy, 1985; McKim and Mishara, 1987; and Sellers, Frecker and Romach, 1983) and can be summarized as follows

DISTRIBUTION

A. Changes in body composition – reduced body water and lean body mass and increased body fat – mean that water-soluble drugs such as alcohol will reach higher concentrations in older people.

B. Reduction in the extent to which drugs bind to protein plasma may mean that highly protein-bound drugs are more freely available at the site of action.

ELIMINATION

A. Decline in kidney function with slowed excretion of some drugs will lead to higher blood concentrations and longer duration of action of those drugs eliminated via the kidneys.

B. Decline in liver function due to changes in blood flow and liver size will affect the rate of elimination of drugs metabolized by the liver.

Though some heavy drinkers may reduce their intake as they get older, they may still experience problems due to these changes. Older people using prescribed drugs may require different dosages to compensate for the physiological changes.

TYPOLOGIES

Chemically dependent older persons are not a homogeneous group. They cover a wide range from 55 years and older, come from all educational and socio-economic backgrounds, and present in all stages of dependence. These stages can be described as follows:

Early: beginning to move from light or moderate social drinking to using alcohol to cope with the stresses of life; may experience increased alcohol consumption or mild adverse effects; may increase or extend use of other mood altering drugs.

Acute: experiencing acute symptoms directly associated to present alcohol or other drug consumption, i.e., symptoms of alcohol or other drug intoxication, withdrawal, severe depression, suicidal ideation or problematic behavior changes.

Chronic: experiencing ongoing physical (e.g., cardiovascular, gastrointestinal, or neurological symptoms), psychological (e.g., memory loss, low self-esteem, lack of coping skills) or social (e.g., loneliness, isolation) symptoms associated with alcohol or other drugs.

Recovering: abstinent or decreasing alcohol or other drug consumption to a non-hazardous level and attending to other adverse symptoms associated with use.

Observations of this broad range of older chemically dependent persons over the past 20 years has led many workers and authors to develop sub-groups or types based on age of onset, patterns of use, or other problems present. Most of these studies have been done with problem drinkers.

One of the earliest and simplest alcohol dependence typologies was done by Rosin and Glatt (1971). Two different groups were identified based on patterns of use and age of onset:

1. Early onset – long-term alcohol use associated with personality or mental health difficulties
2. Late onset – the development of problems associated with use later in life and usually in reaction to stresses associated with aging.

Carruth (1973) described three sub-groups of older alcoholics:

1. The person with no history of a drinking problem before retirement or the loss of a significant person (reactive drinking pattern).
2. The person who has intermittently experienced problems with alcohol but did not develop regular patterns of abuse until late middle age or old age (late-onset alcoholic).
3. The person typically defined as "alcoholic" who has had significant problems with alcohol for a long period of time (early-onset alcoholic).

Dunham (1981) conducted a study on *drinking patterns* with 310 persons 60 years of age and older. He developed four categories:

1. The "rise and sustained" pattern, where the heavy drinker continues drinking into old age
2. The "light and late riser," where drinking is very light throughout one's life but rises when one reaches old age
3. The late starter, who is abstinent or drinks irregularly early in life, then starts to drink moderately or heavily later in life
4. The highly variable, where the second rise in drinking is later in life.

More recently, Graham (1989) conducted a study to identify particular types using case studies of clients in a Toronto program for chemically dependent older persons (COPA). Throughout the process of this study, a number of sub-groups were identified:

(1) reactive drinking in response to grief

(2) dissociated problem drinker (cognitive impairment)

(3) chronic heavy drinker

(4) dual problem – alcohol abuse and victim of spouse abuse

(5) dual problem – alcohol abuse and a major psychiatric disorder.

However, in the conclusion of this study, it appears that in particular, the essential/reactive distinction made in previous reports proved to be conceptually valid. Essential comprises the group where heavy, long-term chronic drinking is the primary problem (could be termed early onset). Reactive describes the person who abuses in response to stress; this could be the intermittent or late onset drinker.

For the purposes of this discussion, we use two categories: *early onset*, meaning persons who developed alcohol or drug problems early in life and have survived to older age, and *late onset*, who develop dependencies later in life, often in reaction to stresses associated with aging, mainly losses or illness.

Intermittent problem drinkers could belong to either category, depending on the perspective: i.e., intermittent problem drinking can be one pattern (perhaps reactive) of long-term alcohol abuse (early onset), but not become consistent, manifest or out of control until later years (late onset). In our clinical experience, the social and health problems of the long-term (early-onset) chemically dependent person differ from those of the late-onset or less severe intermittent user. Following this, methods of identification and treatment strategies also differ.

IDENTIFICATION

Whether a substance use problem is early onset or late onset, it is often difficult to identify and easily confused with other problems generally attributed to aging.

Because of physiological changes mentioned earlier, smaller amounts of mood-altering substances can cause problems for the older person. As well as the normal changes that occur with aging, the older person may have damage to organs such as the liver or kidneys from drinking or some other health problems, which further reduces the body's ability to handle chemical substances.

Health care professionals need to know that even quite low levels of alcohol use or use of medication at the prescribed dosage may in fact cause problems. For instance, two to three drinks a day for women, or three to four for men over a number of years may result in serious health consequences, including liver or neurological damage. Similarly, therapeutic dosages of prescribed medications such as sleeping pills or tranquillizers that are appropriate for a younger person may cause a toxic reaction in someone older. This may present as difficulties in motor functions, confusion, forgetfulness, etc.

The variety of prescribed and over-the-counter medications used by an older person may have a synergistic or interactive effect with each other. For instance, a person may simultaneously use several drugs that depress the central nervous system. These could include alcohol, a prescribed sleeping medication, and an over-the-counter painkiller containing codeine, such as 222s. Also, there may be problems in managing multiple medications because of difficulty in reading the instructions, forgetfulness, etc. This can result in double dosing or missed doses. Thus it is very important to take a careful history of prescribed and over-the-counter medications being taken (how much and when) as well as quantity and frequency of alcohol use. The following example illustrates this.

Example

A 70-year-old, 100-lb woman is being treated by her physician for high blood pressure. The physician has prescribed two medications, a minor tranquillizer (a benzodiazepine) as a mild sedative and an antihypertensive medication. In addition, she is taking over-the-counter pain medication containing codeine for her arthritis. She uses the maximum recommended daily dosage and occasionally exceeds it. She has not told her doctor about taking this over-the-counter medication. Several times a week she consumes two to four standard drinks in the course of an afternoon bridge game. The minor tranquillizer, codeine and alcohol have a synergistic effect because they are all central nervous system depressants. She experiences occasional dizziness, confusion, and recent memory loss. She has also had several unexplained falls, the most recent of which fractured her wrist.

Family members or health care professionals are sometimes reluctant to confront the older person's alcohol or drug use. They may believe that the older person has only a few more years to live – why not leave her or him to drink in peace? This is misleading since reducing or stopping use of problem substances improves the quality of life in a number of areas: more interest in socializing, less confusion or memory problems, less depression or anxiety, and improved physical health. It is often hard for family members, particularly adult children, to talk to a parent about his or her behavior. Parent effectiveness training teaches parents to confront their children, but seldom the other way round!

It may be difficult to distinguish a substance misuse or abuse problem from other signs of aging. The health care professional should be alert to the extent of alcohol or other psychoactive drug use when the client is confused, depressed, has memory or other neurological problems, frequent falls and fractures or is neglecting him- or herself and the environment.

Standardized diagnostic measures of substance abuse such as the Michigan Alcoholism Screening Test (MAST) and Drug Abuse Screening Test (DAST) may not be suitable for the elderly because indicators of problem use such as work, family, and legal difficulties are often not relevant to the older person's life. They are usually not working, are often isolated from family and friends and may not drive. Also, because of their own attitudes to heavy drinking and sometimes poor memory for events, older people may not report problems when asked about their drinking or other drug use (Graham, 1989).

ASSESSMENT

As mentioned earlier, it is important to take a careful history of all substances used by the older client, even though this may not be the focus of the initial contact. When assessing an older client, consider the following issues:

- The assessment may require a number of contacts, rather than a structured, time-limited interview. This is because the initial presenting problem, or in some cases a crisis, may have to be dealt with first. Also, an older person may have a shorter attention span, or tire easily.
- The initial focus is on the client's presenting problem – which is rarely alcohol or drug use or abuse. It is important to attend to the client's concern in order to engage the person in a process of change. The substance use is best introduced when the client is most receptive – when the initial concern is attended to and a therapeutic and caring relationship has been developed.
- Older clients need time to tell their story and may not be willing or able to complete forms or other structured tests.
- The assessment may focus on different areas than would an assessment of a younger person. In older people it is important to assess such areas as sensory functioning, mobility, living environment and lifestyle, losses, diet,

mental condition, physical health, social support, literacy and speech. If information on some of these areas is already available from other involved health professionals, don't repeat a questioning process that may feel invasive or tiring for an older person.

• The level of functioning in the above areas determines the older person's ability to make changes in their lives. Someone who is in poor health, cannot get around, is living in unhealthy circumstances or is confused will not be able to deal with alcohol and drug use until these immediate problems are addressed. In contrast, the younger person who presents for treatment, once he or she has stopped drinking or using drugs, is more likely to be in good health and have the energy and motivation to develop a healthy lifestyle.

The following section details the areas that may be addressed in a comprehensive assessment of an older person:

Sensory Function: How well does the person hear or see (e.g., read labels on medication containers, books, newspapers)? Has sense of taste been lost?

Mobility: Can the person move about inside and outside, walk without aids, bathe/dress independently, shop for him- or herself?

Living Environment & Lifestyle: Is the person happy in her or his living situation? Have there been housing problems because of substance use? Can the person maintain his or her living environment? Are there fire hazards or sanitation problems? Is it close enough to stores, buses, etc.? Does the person go out? How often does he or she see other people?

Losses: Has she or he lost family, friends, physical health (hearing, sight), a job or home?

Diet: What are the person's eating habits (i.e., does he or she eat alone)? Does the person have a good appetite/enjoy food? How is food prepared and stored?

Mental Condition: Is the person experiencing confusion, memory problems or psychiatric problems?

Physical Health: Ask about sleeping patterns, weight change, disabilities and illnesses, medical supervision, dizziness, vision, hearing, senses, footcare, digestion/elimination and dental problems.

Social Support: Is there contact with family and friends? How much contact with other people? Does the person have close support vs. acquaintances?

Literacy and Speech: Are there reading or writing problems?

Alcohol and Other Drug Use: How often and how much does she or he drink? Has the pattern of drinking changed (increase, decrease, periods of abstinence)? Has drinking affected other areas of functioning? What medications (prescribed and over-the-counter) are being used? How often, for how long, and why?

REFERRAL

Because many older people do not consider their alcohol or other drug use a problem, they may not always be accepted by addictions treatment programs that require them to be motivated to stop using substances upon entry. For a number of other reasons, traditional addictions programs do not fit the special needs of the older person:

> • most programs require the person to travel to and/or be in residence to participate
> • many older persons are not ready or able to leave their homes because of physical or emotional problems such as depression
> • the kinds of issues discussed in many programs may not be relevant to the life of an older person; they may be uncomfortable participating in a group that requires them to talk about themselves
> • they may have difficulty in following group interaction because of hearing or sight problems.

Thus older people need interventions geared to their special needs and life circumstances. These needs and circumstances are related to the physical, emotional, mental, social and spiritual effects of substance use and society's attitude to older people, particularly those with a chemical dependency.

INTERVENTION

In order to understand these needs more clearly and develop an effective intervention, the needs of the early-onset and late-onset substance abuser will be looked at separately.

1. EARLY ONSET

The *early-onset* chemically dependent senior most often presents in the chronic stage. Those who still use addictive substances often use less and fewer times per week than younger people, or than they did when they were younger. This can mislead both the user and others to believe that the severity of the problem has decreased, while in fact, they are still using at hazardous levels for their age and physical condition.

Some older people may be abstinent for one reason or another when they enter treatment, often in response to some acute injury or illness associated with their substance use. However, many of the physical, psychological and social problems associated with long-term use are still acute. These range from physical illnesses such as diabetes, arthritis, digestive disorders and heart disease to the social and psychological problems of depression, isolation, loneliness and low self-esteem.

The early-onset person may enter treatment in his or her fifties but present with problems usually associated with the elderly, i.e., chronic illness, isolation and multiple losses. Housing, financial constraints and inadequate social support are often problems. Thus, these people often require a specialized intervention, one that responds to needs associated with the person's physical, psychological, emotional and spiritual needs.

A. Physical: Alcohol affects every system of the body. It adversely affects the appetite and digestion of food, sleep patterns, and nerve, muscle and joint functioning. Thus, poor nutrition, inadequate sleep and lack of exercise over many years weaken the person's physical condition and predispose him/her to chronic illnesses. Some of the major effects of chronic alcoholism are diseases such as hypertension, diabetes, arthritis, and disorders of the digestive system. Other psychoactive substances can also harm the physical system and it is important to treat the chronic physical condition while also focusing on withdrawal from the drug. The older person may have to withdraw under the supervision of a physician rather than in a non-medical detox setting.

B. Psychological: The early-onset substance abuser may present with a particular psychological picture. Often the earlier tasks of development have been interfered with or have not been completed because of substance use. Such tasks include: becoming an individual with adequate ego strength; developing one's life work and becoming productive in a job; developing intimacy with a partner and learning to be interdependent; becoming responsible to others in a family or similar situation and finding one's place in society.

The older person with inadequate ego strength may have poor coping skills and lack of assertiveness accompanied by feelings of anger, frustration, helplessness and inadequacy. Empathetic understanding and acceptance of the person's feelings, seeking out and supporting her or his strengths, as well as new training in coping and assertiveness skills will help the individual develop a higher level of ego strength.

Failure to fully develop one's potential, and the loss of many jobs as a result of substance use, also adds to psychological problems associated with failure, insecurity, and condemnation from family, friends and society. Poorly developed work habits and skills are accompanied by feelings of low self-esteem and inadequacy. In most cases the older person will not be returning to the workforce; treatment should focus more on leisure activities and helping the person rediscover earlier skills and interests or develop new ones.

Throughout the years, as alcohol or drug dependence became the main focus of life, these clients may have failed to do the work necessary to develop intimate relationships. Problems associated with developing relational skills were solved by the use of chemicals. The result is poor social skills, inability to relate to others at a deep-feeling level and loss of family and friends due to behavior associated with alcohol and drug use.

Treatment that includes an opportunity to socialize, and helps a person become comfortable expressing his or her feelings, will help to alleviate loneliness. Though many older people will initially prefer individual counselling, a goal of the intervention should be to help them feel comfortable joining a group. This can often be a key to developing new friendships and a stepping stone to assisting the person to move out into the wider community.

The ability to be interdependent, to be responsible to and for others and have others responsible to and for oneself, has usually been inadequately developed in the person with a long-term drug problem. This may present in various ways: not showing up for appointments, demanding behavior, or over-dependence on the care giver. The client may fluctuate between angry feelings of "I don't need anyone, leave me alone," to clinging to the care giver. It is often necessary to allow a person the opportunity to depend on the care giver for a period of time. The goal, of course, is to broaden the base of support gradually and help the person interact with others in a give-and-take relationship.

C. Social: Social isolation is a major problem for the early-onset client and the physical and psychological limitations mentioned above affect the person's ability to form and maintain friendships. Compounding this is the loss of family and friends because of addictive behavior.

Social isolation can be a problem for many older people as they lose the company of work colleagues, children leaving home, and partners or other close friends who have died. For the early-onset person, these changes often occur earlier in life and are more extensive than for others of a similar age. Friends and family have been replaced with "drinking friends" and places. The long term effects of drug use may have decreased the ability to actively participate in relationships – communications are blurred, energy for social activities is decreased, and even though drugs may have reduced the anxiety associated with difficult social interactions, the problems of interaction often persist.

Social isolation promotes the feelings of loneliness and fear, as well as anxiety when with people. It must be attended to gradually in treatment. As mentioned above, a relationship with one caring person is often a good place to start, before encouraging the client to extend the circle of contacts gradually.

D. Spiritual: The spiritual issues attendant on long-term alcohol and other drug use usually revolve around the meaning of life and feelings of guilt and remorse. Freedom to talk about these issues is a necessary part of treatment. Recent understanding about and more acceptance of the process of addiction can help a person relieve the guilt and accept the personal strengths that have allowed him or her to survive the ravages of abuse.

Finally, it is important to consider the effect of society's attitude toward the chronically-dependent older person.

Frequently this attitude is pessimistic. Family and care givers have observed many years of substance abuse, promises made and broken, efforts to stop using followed by even greater use. Many attempts at control are brief and then the cycle begins again. The family reaches the end of its coping ability and moves away in an effort to reclaim its own health. Eventually friends and colleagues look on from a distance and it is left to the professional care giver to offer support and to try once again.

Without a good understanding and acceptance of the chronic relapsing nature of the problem, even the health care professional may give up. If this happens, the client's feelings of hopelessness and helplessness are reflected by all those around him or her. This impasse must be broken by using creative interventions to engage the chronically dependent person in a process of change. It is essential to find areas of change that are important to the client and in which he or she feels some confidence for success. Often this is not initially in the area of substance use. However, as people become stronger both physically and emotionally, and with support, they can change their use of alcohol and other drugs.

The best approaches (Kola, 1980; Zimberg, 1978; Olsen-Noll, 1989; Kinney, 1983; Hogstel, 1990; Graham, 1989) to intervening with early-onset substance abusers include:

- an individual approach focusing on areas for change that the client sees as both important and achievable. For example, a relationship with a counsellor can be the first step toward alleviating loneliness, to be followed later by other social activities; basic needs such as food and shelter can be addressed as well.
- a supportive one-to-one relationship, which is non-confrontational and nurturing, recognizing the possible initial need for dependence.
- outreach – working with the client in his or her own home, allowing for physical and emotional comfort. Reach out to offer help instead of waiting for the person to seek help.
- group activities that offer support and social interaction with peers. This may take the form of a supportive counselling group, as well as recreational activities undertaken by the group.
- a thorough knowledge and use of available health and social services in the community.

2. LATE ONSET

As mentioned earlier, late-onset chemical dependency develops later in life, often in reaction to stresses associated with aging or stage in life. The person usually enters treatment at a later age, commonly 65 to 75 or older, with fewer years of substance abuse and fewer losses associated with it. Thus the late-onset person presents quite a different picture than the early-onset person. Often they have lived a full life, having successfully managed a career and family. Skills and interests have been developed during the adult years and family ties are more likely to be intact.

Chemical dependency can develop through two routes. Some people may have been social drinkers all their lives. After retirement, with more leisure time and drinking-related social activities and fewer work-related constraints, drinking may escalate. Combined with increased physical sensitivity to the effects of alcohol as people age, this is sufficient to initiate major health and possibly other problems related to substance use.

The second route occurs when an older person self-medicates with alcohol or other psychoactive drugs, or is prescribed psychoactive drugs to alleviate stress caused by physical ill-health or loss of someone close to them.

As with early onset, late-onset people's problems may occur in many dimensions of their lives, physical, psychological, social and spiritual. However, their problems may present somewhat differently.

In some ways, the late-onset person resembles the younger substance abuser. Recognition and acceptance of crossing the line from social to harmful use is difficult. As well, symptoms or problems associated with heavy alcohol or drug use – confusion, disorientation, recent memory loss, tremors, inflammation of joints, gastritis, hypertension, depression, heart disease and sleep disturbances – are often erroneously accepted as normal signs of aging. Thus, the client, the family and care givers may fail to identify the problem in its early stages.

The late-onset person is often dealing with a crisis, and it is important to identify this stressor and attend to it along with the substance abuse. Crises in later years most often pertain to loss. As one client aptly described it, after reading about the stages of grief in a popular magazine, "I am perpetually in several stages of grief at the same time. I never get out of it." Caregivers must be aware of the impact of multiple losses on the older person. These losses and the resulting grief are best responded to by interpersonal rather than chemical means (Harrison, 1987).

Understanding the normal grief reaction and facilitating its appropriate response is a key element in addiction treatment for the elderly. Grief is the personal response to loss, real or symbolic. This response often affects the person both physically and emotionally. In the older person, grief may occur in response to losses associated with role change, physical and mental illness, death or separation from meaningful persons in one's life, financial changes, and changes in living arrangements. Grief can be understood through an adaptation-to-loss model as described by Harrison (1987) which includes four tasks:

Accepting the reality of the loss
To accept a loss, a person must experience it. To experience it often means allowing painful physical and emotional responses to occur. Physical responses may include shortness of breath, a physical feeling of emptiness, changing in bowel and bladder habits, changes in appetite and sleep patterns.

Feelings of acute fear, anger, sadness and anxiety often accompany the recognition of loss. Cognitively, the person may fluctuate between preoccupation with the object of loss and denial of it. Careful listening with empathetic responses will allow the person to feel and express their grief safely.

Emancipation emotionally from ties with the person or object

Freeing oneself emotionally from the loss occurs gradually as one feels and expresses one's emotions. It is important to have these feelings validated by recognition and caring from another person, who can provide a touchstone to reality for someone who is still experiencing overwhelming feelings of loss. People experiencing acute grief often say that they feel they are losing their minds. Tranquillizers, sedatives and alcohol only serve to mask, repress and delay these normal feelings of grief, which resurface when the chemical is withdrawn. A careful history with attention to life's losses will help the care giver understand and respond to a client's emotional and physical needs.

Adjusting to the environment without the person or thing that has been lost

This means making active choices that emphasize other parts of one's life, establish new roles or relationships, or rearrange one's life pattern to deal with the loss. For example, an older person whose eyesight begins to fail might have to adjust to not being able to drive, fill out forms, read directions or see price tags, or to enjoy a good book. Support is needed at this time when change is necessary but the desire and emotional fortitude is low. Groups can sometimes help at this stage by offering support, new ideas for adaption and opportunities to meet new people.

Reinvestment in a new relationship or activity

This fourth task occurs when one redirects one's time, energy, activity and emotions into a different person or area. It means developing new relationships as important as the old; putting time and energy into new activities to replace the ones that have been lost; and enjoying and developing new roles. The care giver in this stage can encourage and validate the person's efforts toward reinvestment. For example, a person reinvesting in a new relationship may feel guilt over betraying the person he or she has lost. The care giver can validate these as natural feelings, while supporting the person in the new relationship.

In helping older persons deal with life changes, it is important to understand how their responses differ from those of younger people:

- The tasks of grief generally take longer to complete. This may be related to diminished energy to perform the grief work.
- Responses appear to be less emotional than in younger persons, but there are more physical symptoms.
- There is a greater tendency to idealize the lost person, object or physical or mental ability.
- Significant losses lead to greater social isolation than would occur in a younger person. Older people have less physical and emotional energy to

reinvest in a new lifestyle.

- There appears to be greater hostility to living persons, often specific family members. This hostility is common in many grieving persons. Its increased intensity in the elderly is not clearly understood.
- There is some evidence that the elderly person "gives up" or "withdraws" from completing the adaptation process. For some, the task appears overwhelming; for others, the internalization of emotions leads to a decrease in the energy needed to complete the grief work.

Two further factors must be considered in working with both the early-onset and late-onset older person. These are: (1) the high incidence of dual disorders – substance abuse and mental illness, and (2) the developmental tasks of aging.

Though there are no estimates of the prevalence of dual disorders in the elderly, professionals working with them know that the combination of mental illness and alcohol or other drug dependence is a major treatment challenge. Depression is particularly common, though it is often unclear whether the depression preceded or was the result of substance use. Also the extent of the depression may be unclear until the person is fully detoxified. Both need to be investigated and treated.

Finally, anyone working with the elderly should know the normal developmental tasks of aging. The major tasks are: to resolve one's life's conflicts successfully; to review and integrate one's past events with a personal value system that reflects the achievement of life satisfaction; the emergence of a developed life philosophy; and the acquisition of wisdom (Birren & Renner, 1981). Older people need to both face their mortality and accept, understand and value their life as it has been lived. Success in achieving this personal integration is highly influenced by the successful completion of earlier developmental tasks (as discussed previously). For the older client, attention to developmental tasks is a necessary part of treatment and recovery. It is particularly important to either resolve or accept one's life conflicts that were related to alcohol or drug use. This can be positively influenced through an understanding of the addiction process. Thus, education is an element of treatment. Reminiscing is another way an older person sorts through the events and meaning of his or her life in order to understand and achieve self-acceptance. This process often involves the expression of feelings and some problem solving. The care giver can facilitate this process of integration by: recognizing its importance; lending support and validation through careful listening and affirmation of the person's life achievements; helping clients understand traumatic issues, including those associated with the addiction; and helping them solve, where possible, remaining conflictual issues.

In conclusion, the older person in treatment covers a wide age range and presents at all stages of chemical dependency. The early- and late-onset substance users form two fairly distinct groups. They share some similarities in terms of the developmental tasks of aging, but also have different needs and require different treatment approaches.

Early-onset clients suffer more widespread physical, psychological, social and spiritual losses. As a result, they present for treatment with major problems such as chronic illness, loneliness, poor self-esteem, poor coping mechanisms, isolation, depression and loss of meaning in life. These problems often create a sense of helplessness and hopelessness. A treatment approach which attends to these problems, as well as to the drinking or drug use, is most effective for this group.

On the other hand, the late-onset client usually suffers fewer overall losses. He or she may develop a dependence on alcohol or other drugs through two different routes: (1) social drinking becomes hazardous to the person because of increased amounts, decreased ability to metabolize the substance, or interactions with other medications or (2) a person experiences a crisis or severe stress associated with later years, often loss, and alleviates the symptoms through chemical means. Education about chemical use, attention to the crisis, fostering healthy ways of dealing with distress and support are important treatment approaches for this group.

For both the early- and late-onset person, attention to tasks of aging and a knowledge and use of community resources is essential for successful treatment.

REFERENCES

Adlaf, E.M., Smart, R.G. & Jansen, A. (1989). Alcohol Use, Drug Use and Well-Being Among a Sample of Older Adults in Toronto: Preliminary Report, Toronto: Addiction Research Foundation.

Adlaf, E.M. & Smart, R.G. (1988). Alcohol and Drug Use Among the Elderly: Trends in Use and Characteristics of Users. Canadian Journal of Public Health, 79, July/August, 236-242.

Andrews, Florence (1988). Alcohol Use. In Irving Rootman, Reg Warren, Thomas Stephens and Larry Peters (Eds.) Canada's Health Promotion Survey; Technical Report, Health and Welfare Canada.

Baker, M.J. (1992). Saskatchewan's Patient Profile Release Program: A Province-Wide Drug Monitoring Program. Paper presented at the Canadian Association on Gerontology Pre-Conference Workshop on Medications and the Elderly, October 2, 1992, Alberta.

Baker, W.W. (1985). Psychopharmacology of Aging: Use, Misuse, and Abuse of Psychotropic Drugs, in Ed. E. Gottheil, K.A. Druley, T.E. Skolada and H.M. Waxman, The Combined Problems of Alcoholism, Drug Addiction and Aging. Charles C. Thomas, Springfield.

Birren, J.E. & Renner, V.J. (1981). Concepts and Criteria of Mental Health and Aging. American Journal of Orthopsychiatry, April, 1981. p. 51.

Blazer, G.G. & Pennybacker, M.R. (1984). Epidemiology of Alcoholism in the Elderly. In Ed. J.T. Hartford and T. Samorajski, Alcoholism in the Elderly, Rower Press, New York, Rockville, Maryland, pp. 25-33.

Carruth, B. et al. (1973). Alcoholism and Problem Drinking among Older Persons: Community Care Providers and the Older Problem Drinker. Paper presented at the Alcohol and Drug Problems Association of North America, New Brunswick, N.J. Sept. 28, 1973.

Dunham, Roger G., Ph.D. (1981). Aging and Changing Patterns of Use. Journal of Psychoactive Drugs. 18(2), 40-41.

Graham, Kathryn; Saunders, Sarah; Flaver, Margaret C.; Birchmore Timney, Carol; White-Campbell, Marilyn & Zeidman, Anne (1989). Evaluation of the COPA Project: A Description of Client Charateristics, Interventions & Outcomes. Unpublished Draft Report. Toronto: Addiction Research Foundation.

Graham, Kathryn (1986). Identifying and Measuring Alcohol Abuse Among the Elderly: Serious Problems with Existing Instrumentation. Journal of Alcohol Studies, 47(4), 322-326.

Harrison, Mary K. (1987). Loss, Grief and Adaption. In ed. Donald Wasylenki Psychogeriatrics: A Practical Handbook, Gage Educational Publishing Co., Toronto, pp. 17-28.

Health and Community Services, New Brunswick (1991). Study of the Application of a Drug Utilization Review Model to Benzodiazipine Use in the Senior Citizen and Income Assistance Population in New Brunswick, New Brunswick Health and Community Services, June, 1991.

Health and Welfare Canada (1989a). Charting Canada's Future, Minister of Supply and Services.

Health and Welfare Canada (1989b). Alcohol in Canada, Minister of Supply and Services.

Health and Welfare Canada (1990). National Alcohol and Other Drug Survey 1989: Highlights Report. (Eds.) Marc Eliany, Norman Giesbrecht, Mike Nelson, Barry Wellman, Scot Wortley. Minister of Supply and Services Canada.

Hogstel, Mildred O. (1990). Geropsychiatric Nursing. Toronto: The C.V. Mosby Company. pp. 232-233.

Kenton, Charlotte. Drugs and the Elderly. November, 1980 through March, 1985, National Library of Medicine Literature Search, No. 85-2.

Kinney, Jean & Leaton, Gwen (1983). The Elderly. Loosening the Grip. Toronto: The C.V. Mosby Company. pp. 282-294.

Kola, Lenore A., Kosberg, Jordan I. & Wegner-Burch, Karen (1980). Perceptions of the Treatment Responsibilities for the Alcoholic Elderly Client. Social Work in Health Care. 6 (2), 69-76.

Lamarche, Pierre & Rootman, Irving (1988). Drug Use. In Irving Rootman, Reg Warren, Thomas Stephens and Larry Peters (Eds.) Canada's Health Promotion Survey: Technical Report, Health and Welfare Canada.

Lamy, P. (1985). The Aging: Drug Use and Misuse. In Ed. E. Gottheil, K.A. Druley, T.E. Skolada and H.M. Waxman, The Combined Problems of Alcoholism, Drug Addiction and Aging. Charles C. Thomas, Springfield.

Lankin, Frances, the Honourable Minister of Health, Speaking Notes at the ADRAO Annual Conference and General Meeting, "Looking Towards the Future," June 7, 1992.

McKim, W.A. & Mishara, B.L. (1987). Drugs and Aging. Toronto, Butterworths.

National Institute on Alcohol Abuse and Alcoholism. Alcohol and the Elderly. In Brief 1/82.

Olsen-Noll, Cynthia & Bosworth, Michael (1989). Alcohol Abuse in the Elderly. American Family Physician. 39, 173-179.

Rosin, A. & Glatt, M.M. (1971). Alcohol Excess in the Elderly. Quarterly Journal of Studies on Alcoholism. 32, 53-59.

Sellers, E.M., Frecker, R.C. & Romach, M.K. (1983). Drug Metabolism in the Elderly: Confounding of Age, Smoking and Ethanol Effects, Drug Metabolism Reviews, 14(2) 225-250.

Warheit, G.J. & Auth, J.B. (1984). The Mental Health & Social Correlates of Alcohol Use Among Differing Lifecycle Groups. In Ed. George Maddox, Lee N. Robins and Nathan Rosenberg, Nature and Extent of Alcohol Problems Among the Elderly Research Monograph No. 14, NIAAA, pp. 29-82.

Zimberg, Sheldon (1978). Treatment of the Elderly Alcoholic in the Community and in an Institutional Setting. Addictive Diseases: An International Journal. 3(3), 417-425.

RECOMMENDED READINGS

Alcohol and the Elderly (1984). Alcohol Health and Resource World. Vol. 8, Number 3, Spring 1984 (the whole edition is on Alcohol & Elderly).

Atkinson, R.M. (1988). Alcoholism in the Elderly Population. Rochester, Minnesota: Mayo Clinic Proceedings. 63, 825-828.

Cramlich, Edwin P. (1968). Reognition and Management of Grief in Elderly Patients. Geriatrics. July 1968.

Daley, Dennis et al. (1987). Dual Disorder. Minneapolis: Hazelden Foundation, Library of Congress, Catalogue Card Number 87-80363.

Hutchens, Anne & Miederholl, Patrick (1988). Sleeping Medications Cause Dependence in the Elderly, The Addiction Letter. Dec. 1988.

Kenney, Jean (1983). Loosening the Grip. Toronto: The C.V. Mosby Company. 283-295.

Kofoed, Lial et al. (1986). Treatment Compliance of Older Alcoholics: An Elder Specific Approach is Superior to "Mainstreaming," Journal of Studies on Alcohol. 48 (1), 47-50.

McKim, William A. & Mishara, Brian L. (1987). Grief, Drugs and Aging. Toronto: Butterworths.

Mishara, Brian L. & Kaslenbaum, Robert (1980). Alcohol and Old Age. Toronto: Grune and Stratton.

Nayer, Nath (1985). Alcoholism and the Elderly. Geriatric Medicine, 1 (3), 135-137.

Olsen-Noll, Cynthia G. (1989). Alcohol Abuse in the Elderly, American Family Physician. 39 (4), 173-179.

Roberts, Anne (1988). Alcohol and Elderly People, Nursing Times. 24 (8), 49-52.

Wasylenki, Donald A. et al. (1987). Psychogeriatrics: A practical handbook. Toronto: GAGE Educational Publishing Company. (Chapters 2. Loss, Grief and Adaptation; 4. Depression; 8. Substance Abuse; 11. Medication; 12. Elder Abuse.)

RESOURCES

1. LESA: A Program of Lifestyle Enrichment for Senior Adults with Alcohol and Other Psychoactive Drug Prblems. This manual is available from the Centretown Community Health Centre, 340 MacLaren Street, Ottawa, Ontario K2P OM6. It provides a comprehensive description of the components of the treatment program as well as addressing administrative issues.

2. Alternatives: An educational package including print materials and a video developed by LESA, the Addiction Research Foundation of Ontario (ARF) and the Community Older Persons Program, Toronto (COPA). It includes a presentation for persons working with seniors on how to identify and intervene with seniors with substance abuse problems, as well as a presentation for seniors on common stresses of aging, ways seniors may cope by using alcohol or other drugs and alternatives to using drugs to cope with these stresses. Available in English or French from the ARF Marketing Department, 33 Russell Street, Toronto, Ontario M5S 2S1 or by calling 1-800-661-1111 (in Toronto, call 416-595-6059).

Two brochures – Alcohol and the Older Adult, and Sleeping Pills, Tranquillizers and Pain Medication and the Older Adult are also available from the ARF.

3. *Drug Wise: A Book for Older Women about Safe Drug Use* and *Drug Wise: A Book about Safe Drug Use for Older Women Who are Caregivers.* Both published by Action on Women's Research and Education, Aware Press, Kingston, Ontario.

Lesbians and Gay Men

BETTY-ANNE M. HOWARD AND BLAIR EDWARD COLLINS

INTRODUCTION

Very little is presently known about how, and indeed whether, lesbians and gay men differ in their substance use compared to the general population, since most research studies rarely ask people about their sexual orientation. Consequently, their data would be assimilated into the results of whatever particular target group was being focused on. However, self-identifying lesbians and gay men are found in about 10 percent of any and every population, whether ethnic, cultural, socio-economic or religious. Working with lesbians and gay men may prove to be particularly challenging for counsellors, as many of the issues pertaining to this group require a close examination of commonly held attitudes, beliefs and assumptions that go very deep inside all of us. This chapter will offer assistance with a process of self-examination; provide a better understanding of the factors involved in dealing with lesbian and gay alcohol/drug problems; and offer suggestions on how to serve this population better. In order to do this, we will discuss various definitions, examine myths and misconceptions, address addiction-related issues pertaining to both the community service organization and the counsellor, and review some of the limited research that has been conducted to date on the needs of lesbians and gay men with alcohol or drug problems. We also contend that, by taking what one already knows about substance abuse and combining this with the wealth of contemporary lesbian and gay resource material that is available, the counsellor will be empowered to deal with lesbians and gay men in a sensitive and understanding way.

We will begin by providing information on the definitions of sexual continuum/ sexual orientation, lesbians, gay men, coming out, and heterosexism/homophobia/ homo-hatred. This section will lay the groundwork for understanding the issues presented in the subsequent parts of this chapter.

DEFINITIONS

Sexual Continuum/Sexual Orientation

It is very easy to separate ourselves from the plight of others when we draw a dividing line between us and them. It's much easier not to identify with the struggles and challenges that a particular group of people must face. It is much safer to rest easy with the illusion that we are in no way like those other people. This also touches on the belief that in some way whatever misfortune befalls a particular group, they got what they deserved for being different or "other than" the predominant group. When counsellors look at sexual orientation from a dichotomous perspective, they fall into the trap of drawing a very rigid dividing line. This is not to say that being identified as heterosexual is the same as being identified as gay or lesbian; there are big differences.

It is widely believed and accepted that sexual orientation falls on a continuum with exclusively heterosexual at one end and exclusively homosexual at the other (Kinsey, 1948). Kinsey's sexuality continuum is a seven-point scale with the middle point representing a sexuality that includes the same amount of sexual thoughts, feelings and behaviors towards both men and women. As Lewis and Jordan (1989) point out in their review of the literature on sexuality and sexual orientation, there are multiple components of sexual orientation including sexual activity, primary affectional relationships and fantasy, and sexual feelings can be expressed in many different ways, not exclusively through genital sex. When all these factors are considered, most people's sexuality falls somewhere around the middle of the continuum, with relatively few existing exclusively at either end. In addition, this less rigid and more accurate concept of sexuality recognizes that most individuals will, throughout their lives, exist at various points on the continuum. On the other hand, our society operates exclusively on the basis of the two opposite ends of this spectrum, insisting that most individuals identify as either gay (homosexual) or straight (heterosexual). As a result, one end is socially acceptable and the other is not; one is good and the other is bad.

Many myths and misconceptions regarding lesbians and gay men have been perpetuated in order to maintain intense hatred, fear, and mistrust and to justify discriminatory practices. In order to dispel many of the myths, it is important to look at who lesbians and gay men really are and their experience of being put in the "bad" category.

It is important to keep in mind that lesbians and gay men are a remarkably heterogeneous group. They can be found in all ethnic groups and all occupations (Lewis & Jordan, 1989).

Recognizing that homosexuality exists along a continuum, definitions are difficult to create (Israelstam & Lambert, 1986). However, in order to begin to understand what it means to be a lesbian or gay man in our society and to begin addressing the needs of this special population, one must understand who lesbians and gay men are.

Lesbian

Lesbians define themselves in many different ways and live their lives in ways that fit their own definitions. For example, there are lesbian separatists who prefer to separate themselves from all men and male influence; lesbian feminists who are committed to achieving the goals of the women's movement; and gay women who don't identify as different from other women beyond the fact that their sexual partners are women.

The following definition embraces the multi-dimensional nature of lesbianism: "A lesbian is a woman who *prefers* other women on many levels: sexually, emotionally, intellectually, psychically – and who defines herself as a lesbian" (our emphasis), (Hughes et al., 1984). Part of our society's way of defining a woman is through her relationship to men, i.e., Miss or Mrs., an engagement ring to indicate that she is "taken" but none to so designate him, fathers "giving away" their daughters to future husbands, etc. Women whose primary sexual, emotional, and intellectual relationships are not with men do not fit society's definition of women. Here we begin to see the basis for many of the myths about lesbians. Lesbians, in varying degrees, defy the standards set out for proper/normal female behavior. As a result, lesbians are severely punished and oppressed. One thing that all lesbians have in common is their love for women. This, by itself, is a threat to many people in our society.

Oppression is a frequently-used term, so it is important to establish exactly what is meant by the oppression of lesbians.

> "The oppression of lesbians shows itself in many different ways. We are invisible and invalidated. History books make no mention of us and we rarely appear in fiction. When we are mentioned in psychology or sociology we are seen as deviant or ill. The media rarely gives us images of ourselves, and never positive images. A young woman growing up has no chance of receiving the information and support she needs in order to see lesbianism as a valid life choice.

> "Images of lesbianism in both popular myth and 'objective' scholarly writings portray us as evil, sick, shameful, corrupting and exclusively sexual. We are presented to ourselves – even from the more 'enlightened' viewpoints – as tragically doomed to promiscuity, alcohol, drugs, violence, despair and suicide.

> "These stereotypical images reinforce negative attitudes about lesbianism and sanction more overt forms of oppression. Lesbians are ridiculed, harassed, verbally abused, shunned. As lesbians we are disowned by our families, evicted from our homes, fired from our jobs. Our children are taken from us. We are sexually assaulted, beaten, raped. We are incarcerated in mental hospitals and psychiatric institutions" (Hughes et al., 1984, p. 17).

No matter how much a lesbian may try to "pass" as heterosexual (and it certainly must be tempting under the circumstances!), and no matter how privileged she may be in this society (economically, educationally, racially, etc.), every lesbian lives with this oppressive environment. Any counsellor working with lesbians must be aware of this oppression and respect the strength it takes to function under these conditions.

Gay Men

Just as there are many different kinds of lesbians, so are there many different kinds of gay men who live a variety of lifestyles appropriate to the personal sense they have made of their gay identity. For example, some gay men have chosen roles contrary to the socially-limited and stereotypic masculine roles as defined in contemporary society with its patriarchal privilege. They are willing to explore fully the gamut of those emotional feelings and practical ways of relating and functioning in our society that have traditionally been limited to the arena of the "feminine" or "female role." Still others are more hesitant to challenge and renounce the masculine social privilege they enjoy as males in our society, and prefer to limit the meaning of their gayness to the emotional and sexual/genital aspects of their lives; and, in some instances, solely to the genital expression of their sexuality.

As a result, an adequate, all-encompassing definition of a gay man is extremely difficult to offer, but for the purposes of this discussion let us borrow from Hughes et al.'s (1984) definition of "lesbians" cited earlier and apply it to the gay male: "A gay man is a man who *prefers* other men on a number of levels: sexually, emotionally, intellectually, psychically – and who defines himself as a gay man."

This definition must, however, be further qualified with caution. Here one already encounters one of the ramifications of living in a homophobic, and in many instances, homo-hating society:

> "Many researchers no longer believe that people can be clearly divided into groups of homosexual (lesbians, gay men), heterosexual, and bisexual by simply asking about the sex of past or present sexual partners. When it comes to labeling one's sexual orientation identity (not sexual behavior), the best judge is the individual himself or herself. And often you cannot predict behavior accurately from the label a person has selected" (Reinsch & Beasley, 1991, p. 144).

Consequently, it is well worth considering that even in terms of self-definition, there are many men who, while engaging almost exclusively in same-sex genital activity and/or emotional relationships, would still hesitate to define themselves as "gay" because of the contemporary social climate of homophobia and/or homo-hatred. Thus, even the process of self-definition is affected by such discrimination.

Because of the social privilege traditionally enjoyed by men, gay males have endured still other forms of oppression that are both similar to and different from the oppression of lesbians.

As with lesbians, gay men are invisible and invalidated. Their historical achievements or contributions have often been recorded, but what *has* been consistently overlooked, or even blatantly denied (especially regarding those historical male figures whose contributions have been valued as "outstanding"), is their gay sexual orientation. It is as if recognizing their gay sexuality would somehow lessen their contributions. Thus, the myth is maintained and perpetuated: "gay men are misfits who have nothing to contribute to society." And the world continues to believe that there are no positive gay role models.

Contemporary media images of gay men (if they are presented at all) continue to perpetuate the stereotype of the overtly effeminate male who is emotionally "weak" and laughably comic in appearance and demeanor. In fact, only a small minority of gay men can be identified as such by this stereotype. Other men who are wrestling with homosexual feelings, but who do not fit the stereotypic definition, will continue to feel confused – one explanation for the discrepancy between an individual's self-determined label and sexual/emotional activity.

Both the gay man and the lesbian pay the same emotional price for living in such an oppressive environment. Both must live with socially sanctioned acts of violence and discrimination, ridicule, harassment, verbal and emotional abuse and ostracism. The act of declaring one's sexual identity or having it discovered carries with it a number of possible penalties: loss of family, employment, friends, children, social status and religion.

The result: many gay men prefer to "pass" themselves off as heterosexual in this heterosexual male-privileged society, and pay a heavy emotional price: the destruction of self-image, a sense of alienation, and incredible stresses and burdens on any attempts at intimacy and committed relationships. A counsellor must be aware of both the psychic energy it takes to stay closeted, and the emotional cost of trying to live openly and authentically as a gay male or lesbian in our society – a "catch-22" situation.

"Coming Out"

The phrase "coming out" has its origins in the term "coming out of the closet." This comes from the idea that homosexuality is one of those "skeletons in the closet," i.e., something to be ashamed of and kept hidden. "Coming out" can take two forms: acknowledging to yourself that you are lesbian or gay, and telling someone else. Both are ongoing processes that can be problematic. Even individuals who have felt since birth that they were lesbian or gay have to deal with family expectations that they be heterosexual (Rothblum, 1989). "Many gays are in a state of stress caused by stigmatization and the fact that their upbringing by no means prepares them for what they have to cope with from the time they first realize they are homosexual on" (Israelstam, 1986, p. 27). No matter how many times a lesbian or a gay man comes out, they must daily combat both society's assumption that they are heterosexual and the many negative responses when this assumption is addressed. As Sarah Pearlman so aptly put it in *Invisible Lives* (1990), "Throughout life there is a decision of whether to come out or not to come out, and that always is either a major or a minor crisis" (p. 47).

The healthy "coming out" process for an individual involves the removal of the negative attitude/belief about homosexuality implanted by a homophobic society and the development of a positive gay/lesbian identity in its place.

Heterosexism/Homophobia/Homo-hatred

Heterosexism is the belief that everyone is, or should be, heterosexual:

> Just as a *sexist* perspective is one that uses male behavior and experience as the norm, a *heterosexist* perspective uses heterosexual behavior and experience as the norm by which to measure all human social and sexual activtity [and]...can shape an individual's language, concepts, values and fundamental ways of thinking about human relations and society. Heterosexist viewpoints can bias research on lesbians and gay men, in the way research questions are formulated, in the methodology and in the interpretation of results. Another serious outcome of a heterosexist viewpoint is the invisibility of lesbians and gay men: the language, meanings and concepts in popular usage often fail to recognize gay and lesbian existence. (Toronto Board of Education, *Sexual Orientation: A Resource Guide for Teachers of Health Education in Secondary Schools*. February, 1992.)

According to Pearlman (1989) "A primary demand of the dominant heterosexual culture is that lesbians [and gay men] participate in their own invisibility through 'passing'" (p. 84). Because of this, many positive role models that could be found in all areas of society are missing because many lesbians and gay men are in hiding (Israelstam, 1986). This passing/hiding represents another form of oppression for lesbians and gay men who fear that discovery could lead to job loss, denial of housing, and loss of friends and family support (Schwartz, 1980).

As stated earlier, other stressors include a society that sees lesbians and gay men as inferior (Lewis & Jordan, 1989), unable to cope with heterosexual responsibilities of marriage and family – as deviants who need help (Schwartz, 1980).

In their work *After The Ball* (1989), Kirk and Madsen contend that much of what is defined as "homophobia" is not based on individual and group fear of gays but rather on

> "...hating. Fear need have nothing to do with it.... Clearly when we call our enemies "homophobes," we run the risk of underestimating them, which is a big mistake. Worse, the specious "diagnosis" suggests an equally specious "cure:" that if straights just got to know us, they'd necessarily get over their fear – which, as with fear of tarantulas, is simply not true (p. xxii).

Furthermore, this underestimation of heterosexual discrimination suggests that lesbians and gay men are in a position of power in that they evoke fear from many heterosexuals. Fear doesn't kill gay men and lesbians or put them at risk of physical violence and bashing – hatred does. For Kirk and Madsen (1989), it is essential that we call hatred by its real name if society is to come to grips with the seriousness of this issue.

MYTHS/MISCONCEPTIONS

LESBIANS AND GAY MEN

A number of myths and misconceptions – stemming from a lack of awareness, and from homophobia and homo-hatred – impinge upon our attitudes and practices pertaining to lesbians and gay men. It is imperative for counsellors working with lesbians and gay men to examine and dispel these myths embedded in their own belief system, and often in their clients' as well.

The first set of myths or assumptions revolve around sexual issues. These are illustrated in comments like "It's only what you do in bed," or "Your whole life is nothing but sex." To address the first, lesbians and gay men do not leave their identity and their lives in their bedrooms! If you are a lesbian or gay man, you are that 24 hours a day, seven days a week. It is not something that miraculously happens to you upon entering a bedroom. The second comment implicitly denies the public aspects of heterosexuality: it is present in sex scenes in movies, television programs, books and magazines, in advertisements, displayed by heterosexual couples holding hands, hugging and kissing in public, and in family photos in the workplace, implied by invitations to "naughty nighties" lingerie parties, discussions about or displays of pregnancy, and anything public having to do with weddings and marriage, to name just a few.

These myths reflect a very narrow view of lesbians and gay men and sexuality itself. They also serve to negate the day-to-day reality of lesbians' and gay men's lives, as partially discussed in the definitions section of this chapter. Counsellors who believe they can work comfortably with a lesbian or a gay man by limiting their understanding of lesbian and gay sexual identity to the arena of the bedroom run the risk of trying to "heterosexualize" the client. To judge, on the other hand, a lesbian or gay client's need to process sexual issues denies her or him the same heterosexual need, which is taken for granted as a more "acceptable" or "normal" enterprise.

The next myth, which is perhaps the most insulting, is that lesbians and gay men are child molesters. This myth serves to further isolate and degrade lesbians and gay men and is simply not true. "More than 85 per cent of all child molestation in schools involves heterosexual males and is directed at females" (Thayer, 1993). In fact, many lesbians have been the "vanguard of social change" (Rothblum, 1989) addressing issues of sexual abuse/sexual violence, helping establish rape crisis services and lobbying for changes at all levels of government and society to make the world a safer and more respectful place to live.

Another commonly held belief is that there is something unnatural about lesbians and gay men, that somehow heterosexuality is the natural way to be, and that anything different is by definition unnatural. Many authors have disputed this assumption in a variety of ways. Lewis and Jordan (1989) cite literature that establishes homosexual behavior as part of the natural order within other species in the animal kingdom, and considered quite normal and acceptable in many other cultures, present and past. These authors also place friendships on the continuum of sexuality, pointing out that the many forms of caring and affection expressed within these relationships is entirely acceptable to our society. Since friendships can naturally lead to romantic relationships, this should, in turn, lead to the acceptability of homosexuality. Lewis and Jordan (1989) further report that studies examining lifestyles and functioning find that lesbians and gay men can be fully functioning, well adjusted, healthy human beings. Other authors cite literature that asserts that lesbians are more self-confident than female heterosexuals and gay men are less defensive than male heterosexuals (Rothblum, 1989).

A belief that comes up particularly among religious people is that homosexuality, especially the inter-male sex act, is immoral. Biblical scholars addressing this issue have examined the original references and have repeatedly corrected this assertion, which has arisen from misconceptions and misrepresentations of ancient words and phrases (Lewis and Jordan, 1989; Bullough, 1979). They conclude that the genital act of homosexuality is not in and of itself immoral.

Another commonly held misconception is that homosexuality is a psychological disorder; not until 1987 was it finally removed as a diagnostic category by the American Psychiatric Association. Unfortunately this categorization has led to the belief that homosexuals are pathological, less happy than heterosexuals, less responsible, and less capable of mature and loving relationships (Rothblum, 1989). Historically this has meant that when a lesbian or gay man sought treatment of any kind, the approach was to treat or eradicate the homosexuality and not the presenting problem (Israelstam, 1985).

Although, as stated earlier, we do know that many lesbians and gay men lead happy, fulfilling lives despite the heavy doses of homophobia levied each and every day, we won't know exactly how healthy (or unhealthy) lesbians and gay men really are until more research is conducted in this area. Homophobia has been cited as the reason why more research has not been done with this population and why gays are left out by most writers (Israelstam, 1985).

LESBIANS

Some beliefs pertaining specifically to lesbians range from ridiculous to outrageously absurd. For example: "Lesbians are not real women.... lesbians want to be men... lesbians hate children," etc. Lesbians are not perceived to be "real women" because they often do not perform traditional female roles. Because lesbians are sexual with other women they are *ipso facto* considered to be "man haters" and because some lesbians defy what is considered to be appropriate female behavior they are believed to be men or at least wanting to be men. Hughes et al. (1984) examine in close detail the whole range of myths as they pertain to lesbians, refuting them in a both factual and humorous way. They suggest there are four groups of myths in circulation: male/female roles, causes and explanations (of lesbianism), sex and sexual functioning, and myths within the women's movement. What stands out about all of these myths is that lesbians are depicted as "different" or "other" or "not women;" they also establish a belief that "unacceptable female behavior constitutes lesbian behavior" (p. 20) and that with these myths we are also being taught what constitutes *acceptable* female behavior.

GAY MEN

Perhaps the most insulting and ridiculous belief about gay men is that they are "inferior" and emotionally weak men made so by domineering mothers who, if still alive, will always control their sons' lives. There are no data to support this belief, nor any data to suggest that any one particular kind of family situation results in the formation of gay male children (or lesbians for that matter).

Another equally disdainful myth is the belief that gay men are interested in, and intent on, having sex with every other man they encounter. Again, there is no research whatsoever to suggest that gay men in general are any more promiscuous than their heterosexual counterparts. This commonly-held belief has been suggested as one explanation for the high levels of discomfort so many heterosexual men feel around self-proclaimed gay males. This heterosexual male discomfort is worth considering because it surfaces a very interesting phenomenon. Heterosexual males have traditionally enjoyed the privilege of being able to pursue or discourage sexual interaction without much personal fear or discomfort, whereas women in our society have experienced much less freedom and comfort in this same pursuit; they have always had to live with the fear of continued aggressive male sexual advances even when they have made their lack of interest very clear, and too often the result is sexual assault or even rape. A heterosexual male being pursued by a gay male, on the other hand, has much less privilege in this kind of interaction, and possibly for the first time experiences a lack of safety as it relates to his own sexual choices: the power balance is completely different, and although he may not experience the same vulnerability as women, he suddenly experiences an interaction which is, perhaps for the first time, more equal in terms of power and safety.

Another commonly held belief is that "most gay men really want to be women." Some men do feel that they are "females trapped inside male bodies," and seek sex-change operations to correct their internal struggle. Such men are defined as transsexual, and have nothing to do with homosexuality. Many gay men rejoice in and celebrate the experience of their masculinity, and the masculinity of the other gay men they may find themselves attracted to. They have no desire to be women, and feel happy and comfortable relating to other men both genitally and emotionally in the context of their own "maleness." As mentioned earlier, only a small percentage of the gay male population may be readily identified by the stereotype of the "effeminate male." While some gay men have chosen to explore living alternative roles to those traditionally assigned to men in our society, it must be stressed that there is no limit to the ways in which gay men choose to live out their sexual identities.

Another commonly held belief is that men choose to be gay: "If that's what he's chosen, it's okay for him, but I don't want him flaunting it around me!" While lesbians and gay men can and do choose to identify themselves as homosexual, individuals do not make the personal internal choice of who they are or are not sexually, emotionally, physically and psychically attracted to. Individuals can only decide what to do with the feelings they have discovered. For the gay male, then, sexual identity has nothing to do with choice, and everything to do with acceptance or denial of the identity one discovers. For those men who struggle to deny their same-sex attractions, counsellors should recognize that most often this is a direct result of homophobia: who, after all, would choose to be something frowned upon (to say the least) by society. There is also a marked difference between the notion of choice between the lesbian and gay male: for lesbians, the concept and notion of choice to self-identify can be empowering. It can be a step towards gender equality in a patriarchal society that has always tried to impose definitions and positions on females. But for the gay male, the concept of choosing to self-identify also involves giving up some of the gender-privilege they have enjoyed simply by being male in our society.

Another common but ridiculous belief is that if only the gay male "met the right woman, he would be okay; namely, he would become heterosexual." The success or failure of any individual's sexual or relational history with a member or members of the opposite sex has nothing to do with one's sexual identity. Indeed, continued failure to develop sexual or emotional heterosexual intimacy can be attributed to the fact that such a male is desperately trying to live something that he is fundamentally incapable of, because it does not reflect his true self.

All of these myths point to similar themes running through the false beliefs associated with lesbians; namely, that such men are less than their heterosexual counterparts; that they are strange, inferior and different.

These myths are perpetuated by the fact that the media are always quick to identify the criminal, the psychopath or any other individual in any kind of negative media coverage as being "gay." The "heroes" of our world who also happen to be gay get little of the same kind of recognition regarding their gay self-identification.

ADDICTION ISSUES

INCIDENCE/PREVALENCE

In most of the literature that looks at alcohol and drug problems among lesbians and gay men, a frequently cited statistic is a 30 per cent rate of alcoholism or a significant drinking problem among homosexuals: a rate three times that of the general population (Zigrang, 1980; Glaus, 1989; Schwartz, 1980; Lewis & Jordan, 1989; Israelstam & Lambert, 1986). Unfortunately there is no consistency regarding the definition of alcoholism or even drinking problems in either this or the mainstream literature. In light of this, and given that the estimates for alcohol-dependent males in North America are five to seven per cent, and the estimates for non-dependent alcohol abuse (problem drinking) are between 15 and 35 per cent (Skinner & Horn, 1984), it would be safer to assume that the extent of the alcohol problem in the lesbian and gay population is the same as in the general population. Also, heterosexist bias in research methods and fear of oppression keeps most "ordinary" lesbians and gay men hidden from researchers. Until more broadly based lesbian and gay male populations are studied, and until the criteria for alcoholism and alcohol problems are agreed upon and used consistently, we cannot yet truly argue that lesbians and gay men have significantly greater alcohol problems than the general population. It is important, however, to acknowledge the significance of whatever research has been done on the incidence/prevalence of alcohol problems in the lesbian/gay population; until recently, this particular population was largely ignored.

Factors contributing to alcohol and drug problems among lesbian and gay populations may differ from those of the general population. The reason most often cited for the high rate of alcoholism among lesbians and gay men is homophobia and the emotional difficulties that result from experiencing it (Zigrang, 1980; Schwartz, 1980; Lewis & Jordan, 1989).

The second most frequently cited factor contributing to alcohol and drug problems among the lesbian/gay population is the "gay bar scene," with suggestions that gay people spend most of their time in bars and have few alternatives for "out" socializing (Zigrang, 1980). However, other researchers such as Ziebold (1978) refute this assertion, reporting that gays do not spend any more time in bars than do single heterosexual Americans. This particular factor may only be relevant in urban communities where gay bars are able to operate. Lesbians and gay men who live in rural communities and don't have access to gay bars are probably underrepresented in these studies and are likely to present some different factors contributing to their drinking behavior.

CURRENT TREATMENT CLIMATE

What treatment options now exist for lesbians and gay men with an alcohol/drug problem? How are lesbians and gay men treated if and when they "come out" to their counsellors? Are the needs of lesbians and gay men being addressed in treatment agencies? These are but a few of the questions we now intend to address. The picture is rather bleak in many ways.

First of all, Israelstam (1986) acknowledges that research on lesbians and gay men and related interventions is only now being done and is rather sparse. At the same time, he points out that there is little to no work on this in Canada; most has taken place in the United States. There are indeed many reports that discuss needs of "special populations" (blacks, youth, women, the elderly) and yet rarely are lesbians and gay men mentioned (Israelstam, 1985; Westermeyer, 1990; Zigrang, 1980), a glaring omission that speaks to the invisibility of this group. One could reasonably argue then that the needs of lesbians and gay men are not being effectively met. Israelstam (1985) noted that therapists, counsellors and researchers looking into the alcohol and drug problems of lesbians and gay men report that there has been both inappropriate treatment delivered and a lack of facilities to meet the needs of this group. Service providers largely ignore the needs of lesbians and gay men, with some clinicians seeing little if any relevance of a person's sexual orientation to their drinking (Zigrang, 1980). This attitude is probably an "over-correction" of the old belief that homosexuality itself needed to be cured. Schwartz (1980) recognizes that little has been done in the way of treatment for lesbians and gay men and that some of the professionals in treatment facilities are not facing their own homophobia, their own fears about being homosexual, or their own unresolved sexuality issues. In a more recent study conducted by the Addiction Research Foundation in Ontario, Israelstam (1986) found that staff at ARF who intervene in alcohol and drug problems felt that sexual orientation should be taken into account, but also recognized that the current climate does not encourage lesbians and gay men to come forward for treatment. Israelstam clearly considers identifying the special problems of this group an important aspect of intervention, along with reducing hostility and homophobia in society, taking into account the special problems of lesbians who are even more overlooked, educating the gay community about alcohol issues, the intervention community about gay issues, and beginning to forge links between the two communities.

WHAT IS BEING DONE?

There has been some significant effort put forward by particular groups in an attempt to address the special needs of lesbians and gay men. It is beyond the scope of this chapter to cover all that has been done in both the United States and Canada. We will highlight four particular initiatives.

Alcoholics Anonymous
AA has been acknowledged as the first and by far largest organization to intervene into gay alcohol problems (Israelstam, 1985; Kus, 1987; Zehner & Lewis, 1984 and Zigrang, 1980). Literature, special groups for lesbians and gay men, and workshops at annual conferences of AA are examples of the types of efforts made by this group. However, it is also acknowledged that homophobia still exists within the brotherhood of AA, which poses a problem for lesbians and gay men seeking help for an alcohol problem.

The National Association of Lesbian and Gay Alcoholism Professionals (NALGAP)
This group was formed in the United States to help alcoholism agencies and professionals better serve the needs of alcoholic lesbians and gay men. According to Schwartz (1980), the goals of NALGAP are to:

> "encourage everyone in the alcoholism field to create a safe and supportive atmosphere for both gay staff members and gay clients and to ensure that every workshop, seminar, conference, newsletter and journal that deals with alcoholics and their families addresses the needs and problems special to gay alcoholics and their families" (p. 11).

It would be most encouraging if all addiction agencies shared these goals. Perhaps many of the barriers to lesbians and gay men receiving appropriate treatment would then begin to be addressed.

The Donwood
A treatment service in Ontario is beginning to address the needs of lesbians within the framework of sensitizing its services to the needs of women. This is truly an encouraging effort.

In response to a Key Informant Survey on Issues and Priorities for Women's Health in Canada (Thomas, 1986) conducted by the Health Promotion Directorate of Health & Welfare Canada, the Donwood established a focus group on women with the purpose of recommending a program that would better meet the needs of women. Their recommendations included providing training and education for all staff regarding gay sexuality issues, resources in the community, and homophobia, and offering therapy groups for lesbians and their partners.

Training materials have been developed by the Women's Alcoholism Program of CASPAR – the Cambridge and Somerville Program of Alcoholism Rehabilitation (Finkelstein, Duncan, Derman & Smeltz, 1990) – to address the issue of lesbians with alcohol problems.

WHAT CAN AGENCIES AND COUNSELLORS DO?

An important question to consider is whether existing treatment programs can also serve the special needs of particular groups. Should separate facilities be established to address the needs of lesbians and gay men? Many authors suggest that despite the homophobia among some treatment service providers, education and training can begin changing the services now offered (Schwartz, 1980; Zigrang, 1980).

INTERNAL

Within organizations, it is important to educate staff to create a safe environment where lesbians and gay men can acknowledge the reality of their lives and be treated respectfully. This will begin to make existing services more available and accessible (Westermeyer, 1990) to this often neglected "special population."

Homophobia on the part of the counsellor will have to be addressed. What Glaus (1989) so aptly expressed in reference to working with lesbians can be applied to working with gay men as well:

> "It is unfortunate but true that persons reared in this culture cannot escape the inculcation of at least some homophobia attitudes and beliefs and the therapist is no exception. A readiness to deal with the client's lesbianism requires that the therapist surface and deal with her own homophobia" (p. 141).

This homophobia acts as a barrier to lesbians and gay men receiving appropriate treatment (Finkelstein et al., 1990).

Homophobia is also evident in agencies where lesbian and gay staff members are not "out" in their own work setting. The fear that they will be avoided by homophobic colleagues, and by clients who are not lesbian or gay, contributes to their reluctance to "come out" (Rothblum, 1989). Clearly an environment where it is safe for counsellors to "come out" would make for a safer environment for lesbian and gay clients. Zigrang (1980) and Israelstam (1986) indicate that many lesbians and gay men do not reveal their sexual orientation in treatment. This leads to silencing and hiding parts of oneself, which inhibits and interferes with recovery, while disclosure may result in rejection, isolation, derision and humiliation.

Israelstam (1985) offers the Gay Client's Bill of Rights (Department of Public Health in San Francisco, 1983) when discussing working towards prejudice-free treatment and intervention. This bill of rights clearly establishes the responsibility of providers to offer services that promote the dignity and respect of lesbians and gay men and the opportunity to request a counsellor who is either gay-identified or at least sensitive to and knowledgeable about gay lifestyles.

One way of exploring many of the long-held stereotypes about lesbians and gay men is by asking non-gay counsellors to answer these questions as though they themselves were in the minority (Schwartz, 1980): "Why are you heterosexual? Isn't it out of fear of rejection? We have read heterosexuals like you have histories of failures in gay relationships; isn't it possible that you are just going through a phase and that sooner or later you'll get over it and be gay like the rest of us? Why would anyone want to hire a heterosexual? Why do you feel like you have to tell everyone you are heterosexual? Can't you just keep quiet?"

These questions, along with additional training and education regarding lesbian and gay issues and ongoing supervision, will help counsellors meet the needs of this population. However, the bottom line still remains that:

"if the counsellor's morals, values, or belief system places him or her in conflict with those of the client, it will be extremely difficult if not impossible to intervene effectively in the addictive process" (Lewis & Jordan, 1989, p. 175).

Israelstam (1986) suggests that agencies dealing with alcohol problems need to decide if their programs benefit or are relevant to the lesbian and gay community. (The CASPAR training manual offers a tool for evaluating organizational attitudes and practices for homophobia [Finkelstein et al., 1990]). If not, then these agencies need to decide if this is the situation they want. Clearly there is room for improvement on many fronts, including increasing workers' knowledge of gay issues and addressing homophobia as it affects the staff, their services and the agency.

EXTERNAL/OUTREACH

In order to begin providing effective and appropriate services to the lesbian and gay community, outreach is required and will serve several functions. First, becoming aware of the lesbian and gay organizations and services in your community will enable you to recommend ways in which clients can overcome their isolation and become a part of this network/community (Rothblum, 1989). Second, outreach opens your service to the lesbian/gay community by sending a message that you are making an effort to meet its needs. Third, it gives you an opportunity to become more familiar with and knowledgeable about gay/lesbian lifestyles, which is imperative to your work with this client group.

One final suggestion offered by Israelstam (1985) in the area of prevention involves alleviating homophobia among gays themselves, and in society at large. He proposes that any health professional who agrees that homophobia is dysfunctional should be involved in initiating "public health campaigns aimed at changing the social, psychological and ultimately the physical environment to a more honest and safe one as regards homosexual-homophobic issues" (p. 25).

TREATMENT

LESBIANS AND GAY MEN (ISSUES PERTAINING TO BOTH)

Clearly, some of the reasons lesbians and gay men have for excessive drinking or drug taking are different from those of the general population (Israelstam, 1986). In addition, certain factors need to be considered with this population.

Assessment
It is important to ensure that assessment instruments incorporate value-free

questions. For instance, when conducting an assessment, instead of assuming (as most people do) that the client is heterosexual, you can ask questions that leave the door open to either possibility. For example, you can ask, "Do you have a current partner/significant relationship with a woman or man?" (Finkelstein et al., 1990). Even if the client is a lesbian or gay man and is not yet comfortable disclosing this to you, you have left the door open to discuss the issue later on.

The CASPAR training manual (Finkelstein et al., 1990) offers the following advice. If a client "comes out" to you, it is important *not* to reassure him or her that "That's not an issue for you" and/or "We are only dealing with your drinking/drug problem and not your sex life." These comments will only serve to silence the client, sending the message that you are really uncomfortable with this issue. Instead, a more appropriate response would be to ask how it feels for him/her and what fears or concerns he or she may have regarding "coming out" to you. It is also extremely important to treat this information respectfully – always allow the client to judge when and to whom he/she comes out.

Another phrase we have often encountered among counsellors is: "If you are comfortable with your sexuality and it's not a problem, then I don't/won't address it." No matter how "out" a person (client or otherwise) may be, there is no escaping the homophobia in our society. As such, experiencing "problems" that result from identifying as lesbian or gay is inevitable so long as we live in a homophobic/heterosexist world. A recent publication, *Invisible Lives: The Truth About Millions of Women-Loving Women,* by Martha Barron Barrett (1990) looks at what it is like to be a lesbian in today's world. Based on her interviews with "invisible lesbians" she came to understand that "even the benign attitude (in our society) of 'live and let live' is in fact discriminatory. That toleration, even acceptance, is a far cry from genuine empathy..." (p. 17). Her understanding came from gaining a deeper level of understanding of lesbian life based on hearing the stories of the women she interviewed.

If your client has decided to acknowledge the reality of his or her life and is "out" to you, it is important to determine where he or she is in the coming out process. Is he or she "out" at work, school, with parents, friends? If he or she has a partner/lover, how "out" is that person? A great deal of stress in relationships can come from one person being severely closeted and the other being very "out." It is very difficult to maintain this balance because the more closeted person may fear being discovered by being associated with his or her partner.

The client may also be uncertain about his or her sexual orientation. In this case, it is important for the counsellor to remain as neutral as possible (Finkelstein et al., 1990), supporting the client by providing information on community services that could help the client better understand her or his sexual feelings.

It is not uncommon for a person who is beginning to address an alcohol/drug problem to start feeling the conflicts and homophobia that were once masked by the alcohol/drugs (Finkelstein et al., 1990). These feelings may correspond with a "desire" not to be lesbian or gay in order to escape having to deal with issues that arise from being a member of a despised and degraded group. Helping clients by trying to cure or dissuade them from their sexual orientation is unhelpful and unethical (CASPAR Manual). Becoming familiar with the resources in your community for lesbians and gay men and linking your client up with these resources is helpful.

When acknowledging the existence and role of a partner or extended family (friends and/or members of the lesbian/gay community), it is important to ensure they are acknowledged and treated as would a heterosexual client's partner/spouse and family members, and that they are educated about alcoholism and chemical dependency (Glaus, 1989).

Treatment Considerations

When individuals have been rejected by their family or friends because of their sexual orientation, the focus needs to be on finding alternative support systems. In addition, discussing the advantages and disadvantages of "coming out" to friends, family, employers, etc. needs to be considered (Zigrang, 1980).

Making a referral to self-help groups such as Alcoholics Anonymous or Narcotics Anonymous can pose particular problems for the lesbian or gay man. Schwartz (1980) suggests that the total honesty required as part of the AA program may present a conflict because lesbians and gay men may be forced either to be open and therefore possibly face ostracism, or to hide behind a "false heterosexual front," which can create a great deal of stress. Fear of encountering homophobia – and the presence of so many men – may lead some gays and lesbians to resist attending AA meetings. Glaus (1989) recommends that the counsellor be aware of alternatives, such as gay-positive AA groups or lesbian/lesbian-positive Women For Sobriety Groups.

Individuals who come from a highly religious background that emphasizes that homosexuality is immoral and unnatural have to deal with particular issues (Zigrang, 1980). One solution might be to acquaint the client with various lesbian/gay-positive church-related groups, such as DIGNITY, the Roman Catholic organization of lesbians and gays; AFFIRM, the Anglican organization of lesbians and gays, etc.; or the Metropolitan Community Church, a lesbian/gay-positive church with communities in most major (and not so major) cities in Canada and the United States. Yet such a referral assumes that the solutions to the client's religious or spiritual issues lie in some form of organized religion, which isn't always the case. Fortunately, there are also a number of good references dealing with the spiritual dilemmas of lesbians and gay men from various perspectives. It would be a good idea to acquaint yourself with the resource list of books and publications dealing with spiritual issues at the end of this chapter.

The CASPAR training manual proposes a treatment strategy for lesbians (which can be applied to gay men as well). It takes a positive view toward lesbians and lesbianism, which in turn can prove to be greatly beneficial to the well-being of your clients:

"The most helpful treatment strategy will be founded on the perspective that sees a lesbian as a whole person, and her lifestyle as one which fits within the definition of a healthy and viable option. The main goal of treatment in this perspective is to help a woman live to her fullest potential, and have healthy and affirming relationships with the people in her life" (Finkelstein et al., 1990, p. 473).

Lesbians and Addiction-related Issues

Lesbians who have an alcohol or drug problem experience a triple oppression (Lewis & Jordan, 1989; Glaus, 1989; Swallow, 1983): that of being an alcoholic/drug addict, a woman and a lesbian. Very little has been written regarding lesbians and addictions as lesbians continue to remain a fairly invisible group (Barrett, 1990; Israelstam, 1986), and addiction workers tend to be unaware of any differences that may exist when it comes to the treatment needs of lesbians versus gay men (Israelstam, 1985).

According to Lewis and Jordan (1989), and their review of the literature regarding the needs of lesbians who have an addiction problem, several factors need to be considered. Recognizing society's expectations for appropriate female behavior, these authors forewarn counsellors to be aware of the possible prejudice against women who display independent and autonomous ideas and behaviors. The temptation may be to counsel the client to become less assertive, and to behave in a manner that is more in line with the roles expected for women.

Anthony (1985) has also reported that the most common presenting problem of lesbians seeking counselling is difficulty with a lover relationship; some of these difficulties stem from a lack of social and personal support systems available to lesbians, who often remain closeted to varying degrees because of societal oppression. A clear understanding of this oppression, as discussed earlier, is needed to work effectively with lesbians.

According to Glaus (1989), who refers to the literature on women and addictions, women are more likely than men to be depressed and have low self-esteem; this factor needs to be addressed with lesbians. The counsellor also needs to acknowledge that for lesbians who are severely closeted and isolated from the lesbian community, and are therefore missing out on positive role models, these negative affective states may be more pronounced.

One final factor to consider, which is addressed by Loulan (1984), is sexual functioning. Many of the women in her study experienced significant difficulties in their sex lives, especially in early sobriety, with a general trend for sexual satisfaction to improve over the course of recovery. Included in her book, Lesbian Sex (Loulan, 1984) is a chapter on Sex and Sobriety, which contains helpful procedures a woman can follow to regain full and satisfying sexual experiences.

Keep in mind when working with lesbians that "emotional bonding, social and friendship networks, and a lifestyle with a strongly woman-identified emphasis is also part of a lesbian's existence" (Finkelstein et al., 1990, p. 468). And, that "the strength of a lesbian relationship is often cited to be the level of intimacy, uniqueness, and equality that can be achieved by two women" (Rothblum, 1989, p. 8).

Gay Men And Addiction-related Issues

Gay men who have an alcohol or drug problem also deal with a number of oppressions: that of being an alcoholic or drug addict, and a gay male, and of being considered inferior in a male-dominated society that tolerates little or no diversity in terms of the roles assigned males and females. This adds another complication absent from the lesbian experience. Many gay men who have tried to assume traditional societal male roles have paid the price of repressing many "sensitive feelings," and may lack the ability to process and self-reflect and thus have great difficulty dealing with internal feelings and emotions – traits more acceptable to traditional feminine social roles. As a result, it might take the gay male considerably longer to come to terms with his inner feelings and emotions. Indeed, it is common knowledge that far more women take advantage of the various levels of psychiatric services than men. This is not to suggest that women have more problems than men, but rather that women generally have a better understanding of themselves, and are more willing to engage in the process of personal growth and self-reflection. A gay male who has attempted to identify with the traditional male model has yet to learn this.

As with lesbians, there are also possible prejudices against gay men that counsellors must watch out for. An important starting point is for the counsellor to take a courageous personal inventory of his or her own areas of homophobia and homo-hatred. This self-awareness will enable the counsellor to guard against trying to direct the gay male to assume roles and traits according to the former's personal definition and/or level of comfort of what might be considered appropriate or acceptable. For example, the heterosexual male counsellor may have difficulty relating to the gay male who is comfortable exhibiting many qualities traditionally defined as "feminine," or have trouble accepting the self-definition of a gay male who exhibits extremely masculine and virile qualities.

As with lesbians, counsellors must have a clear understanding of the emotional and psychological burden of being a gay male in a homophobic world. They must be conscious of the fact that heterosexual men have – and take for granted – many "free choices" that are not available to the gay male because of consequences of oppression, lost job security, family relationships and other factors discussed earlier. In short, a counsellor must understand the institutionalized and socialized discrimination that compromises the freedom of the gay male client. In his book *Growing up Gay in a Dysfunctional Family* (1991), Rik Isensee discusses those elements of institutionalized homophobia that limit freedom of choice, and thus may prevent the gay male from successfully completing some levels of healthy emotional and psycho-sexual development.

It is extremely important that the therapeutic community at large begin to understand that many of the emotional issues brought to them by the gay male are a direct result of the ramifications of oppression in a homophobic culture and society, and not a result of any particular individual's inability to cope with various issues.

Otherwise, there is the danger of "blaming the victim" for experiencing the results of such oppression.

CONCLUSION

This chapter has attempted to introduce the counsellor to many of the issues pertaining to this group by close examination of commonly-held attitudes, beliefs and assumptions that go very deep inside all of us. It is imperative that the counsellor engage in such a process of self-examination and be honest about his or her own attitudes, misconceptions about and prejudices towards lesbians and gays. It is by far the better option for a counsellor to recognize his or her own limitations of prejudice or discomfort and responsibly choose not to engage in a therapeutic relationship with a lesbian or gay male than to pretend that these issues simply do not exist or affect treatment protocol: they do. And they will manifest themselves in countless ways that the client will pick up and interpret as disapproval, judgment, etc.

For the counsellor who is genuinely interested in pursuing a better understanding of the issues involved, it is not only acceptable but also helpful to ask your clients about their own experience; to invite your clients to help you better understand them. This will assure clients that you care, and are genuinely interested in understanding and validating their personal experiences as influenced by their lesbian or gay sexual orientation. You need not be an "expert" in this area: the most important thing you can offer is a genuine caring and acceptance of your clients just as they are – including (not in spite of) their homosexuality. Take what you know about treatment protocol for any individual and contextualize these with the issues raised in this chapter, and you will be moving in the right direction.

REFERENCES

Anthony, B. (1985). Lesbian client-Lesbian therapist: Opportunities and challenges in working together. In J. Gonslorek, (Ed.), A quide to psychotherapy with gay & lesbian clients, New York: Harrington Press, 1985.

Barrett, Martha Barron (1990). Invisible Lives: The Truth About Million of Women-Loving Women. New York: Harper & Row Publishers, 1990.

Bullough, Vern L. (1979). Homosexuality: A History. Scarborough, Ont.: The New American Library of Canada Ltd., 1979.

Clunis, D.M. & Green, G.D. (1988). Lesbian Couples. Seattle, Washington: Seal Press, 1988.

Department of Public Health, City & County of San Francisco (1985). Gay Bill of Rights, Division of Alcohol Programs, Alcoholism Evaluation & Treatment Centre, San Francisco.

The Donwood Institute (1989). The Focus Group on Women's Issues: The Emerging Self. Toronto, Ont.: The Donwood Institute, 1989.

Finkelstein, N., Duncan, S.A., Derman, L. & Smeltz, J. (1990). Getting Sober, Getting Well: A Treatment Guide for Caregivers Who Work With Women. Cambridge, Mass.: Women's Alcoholism Program of Caspar, Inc., 1990.

Glaus, Kathleen O'Halleran (1989). Alcoholism, Chemical Dependency and the Lesbian Client. In E.D. Rothblum & E. Cole (Eds.), Loving Boldly: Issues Facing Lesbians, New York: Harrington Park Press, 1989.

Hughes, Nym; Johnson, Yvonne & Perreault, Yvette (1984). Stepping Out of Line: Workbook on Lesbianism and Feminism. Vancouver, B.C.: Press Gay Publishers, 1984.

Isensee, Rik (1991). Growing Up Gay in a Dysfunctional Family. New York: Prentice Hall Press, 1991.

Israelstam, S. (1985). Alcohol and drug problems of Gay males and Lesbians: therapy, counselling and prevention issues. Internal Document No. 48. Toronto, Ont: Alcoholism and Drug Addiction Research Foundation, 1985.

Israelstam, S. (1986). Knowledge and Opinion of alcohol workers at the Addiction Research Foundation of Ontario regarding issues affecting Gay males and Lesbians.

Internal Document No. 75. Toronto, Ont: Alcoholism and Drug Addiction Research Foundation, 1986.

Israelstam, S. & Lambert, S. (1986). Homosexuality and alcohol: observations and research after the psychoanalytic era. The International Journal of Addictions, 21 (4 & 5), 509-537, 1986.

Kent, Debra (editor) (1990). The Kinsey Institute New Report on Sex. New York: St. Martin's Press, 1990.

Kinsey, Alfred C., Pomeroy, W.B. & Martin, C. (1948). Sexual Behavior in the Human Male. Philadelphia: W.B. Saunders, 1948.

Kinsey, Alfred C., Pomeroy, W.B. & Martin, C. (1953). Sexual Behavior in the Human Female. Philadelphia: W.B. Saunders, 1953.

Kirk, Marshall & Madsen, Hunter (1989). After The Ball: How America Will Conquer Its Fear and Hatred of Gays in the 1990s. New York: Doubleday, 1989.

Kus, Robert J. (1987). Chapter 5: special problems. Alcoholics Anonymous and Gay American Men. Haworth Press Inc., 1987.

Lewis, Gary R. & Jordan, Susann M. (1989). Treatment of the Gay and Lesbian alcoholic. Alcoholism and Substance Abuse in Special Populations. In G.W. Lawson & A.W. Lawson (Eds.), Maryland: Aspen Publishers Inc., 1989.

Loulan, JoAnn (1984). Lesbian Sex. San Francisco: Spinsters/Aunt Lute Book Company, 1984.

Loulan, JoAnn (1987). Lesbian Passion: Loving Ourselves and Each Other. San Francisco: Spinsters/Aunt Lute Book Company, 1987.

National Association of Lesbian & Gay Alcoholism Professionals. P.O. Box 376, Oakland, New Jersey 07436. Phone (201) 666-0600.

Pearlman, Sarah F. (1989). Distancing and Connectedness: Impact on Couple Formation in Lesbian Relationships. In Rothblum & Cole (Editors) (1989)

Pearlman, Sarah F. (1990). Quoted in The Truth About Millions of Women-Loving Women: Invisible Lives, by Martha Barron Barrett, New York: Harper & Row, 1990.

Reinsch, J. & Beasley, R. (1991). The Kinsey Institute New Report on Sex, New York: St. Martin's Press, 1991

Rothblum, E.D. (1989). Introduction: Lesbianism as a Model of a Positive Lifestyle for Women. In E.D. Rothblum & E. Cole (Eds.), <u>Loving Boldly: Issues Facing Lesbians</u>, New York: Harrington Park Press, 1989.

Rothblum, Esther D. & Cole, Ellen (Eds.) (1989). <u>Loving Boldly: Issues Facing Lesbians</u>. New York: Harrington Park Press, 1989.

Schwartz, Linda R. (1980). <u>Alcoholism Among Lesbians and Gay men: A Critical Problem in Critical Proportions</u>. Phoenix, Arizona: Do It Now Foundation, Box 5115, 1980.

Skinner, Harvey & Horn, John L. (1984). <u>Alcohol Dependence Scale (ADS) User's Guide</u>. Toronto: Addiction Research Foundation, 1984.

Swallow, Jean (Ed.) (1983). <u>Out From Under: Sober Dykes & Friends</u>. San Francisco: Spinster's Inc., 1983.

Thayer, P.A. "Attitude Quiz: Empirical Data & Relevant Facts Associated with Homosexuality," in Toronto Board of Education, <u>Sexual Orientation: A Resource Guide for Teachers of Health Education in Secondary Schools</u>, February, 1993, pp 90-92.

Thomas, E. (1986). Issues and priorities for women's health in Canada, 1984. Health Promotion Directorate, Health & Welfare Canada.

Toronto Board of Education. <u>Sexual Orientation: A Resource Guide for Teachers of Health Education in Secondary Schools</u>, February, 1993.

Westermeyer, Joseph (1990). Treatment for psychoactive substance use in special populations: issues in strategic planning. <u>Advances in Alcohol and Substance Abuse</u>. Vol. 8 (3/4). Haworth Press Inc., 1990.

Zehner, Marta Ann & Lewis, Joyce (1984). Homosexuality and Alcoholism: Social and developmental perspectives. <u>Homosexuality and Social Work</u>. Haworth Press Inc., 1984.

Ziebold, T.O. (1978). Alcoholism and the gay community. A publication of Blade Communications Inc., April 12-13, Washington, D.C., Whitman-Walker Clinic.

Zigrang, T.A. (1980). "Who Should Be Doing What About the Gay Alcoholic?" Paper presented at: <u>National Alcoholism Forum. National Council on Alcoholism Inc.</u>, in Seattle, Washington, May 4, 1980.

RESOURCES

There are hundreds of lesbian/gay publications, organizations, bookstores, and groups across Canada and the United States. In order to find them you might try looking in the telephone book under "Lesbian," "Gay," or "Women." Most larger communities also have lesbian/gay-sponsored information telephone services, usually listed under "Lesbian and/or Gay Information." Your local women's bookstore may also have information on local groups and activities.

SUGGESTED READINGS

Many of the books listed in the references section of this chapter might be of interest to you. Here are some additional readings, and/or ones we believe that will be especially helpful to you.

Becker, Carol S. (1988). <u>Unbroken Ties: Lesbian Ex-Lovers</u>. Boston: Alpon Publications Inc., 1988.
> This book covers the gamut when it comes to lesbian break-up. It explores what it feels like to go through separation and how to cope with the loss.

Clunis, D. Merilee & Green, G. Dorsey (1988). <u>Lesbian Couples</u>. Seattle: Seal Press, 1988.
> A guide for lesbians dealing with the pleasures and challenges of being a couple. Written by two experienced lesbian therapists, who pay attention to issues of race, class, age, physical ability, and the problems when one or both partners are recovering from substance and/or sexual abuse.

Finkelstein, N., Duncan, S.A., Derman, L. & Smeltz, J. (1990). <u>Getting Sober, Getting Well: A Treatment Guide for Caregivers Who Work With Women</u>. Cambridge, Mass.: Women's Alcoholism Program of CASPAR, Inc., 1990.
> An excellent hands-on treatment guide for caregivers who work with alcohol- and drug-abusing women. To order, write: The Women's Alcoholism Program of CASPAR, Inc., 6 Camelia Ave., Cambridge MA 02139, or phone (617)661-1316. The cost: $77.00 (US).

Isensee, Rik (1991). <u>Growing Up Gay in a Dysfunctional Family: A Guide for Gay Men Reclaiming their Lives</u>. New York: Prentice Hall, 1991.
> This books describes the chaotic and traumatic family histories of millions of gay men, and provides an excellent guide for healing and recovery from the effects of growing up in a homophobic world. It is

written sensitively in the spirit of a 12-step recovery program, and can provide extremely useful information for any gay male struggling with his sexual identity, and/or counsellor working with such a client.

Loulan, JoAnn (1984). Lesbian Sex. San Francisco: Spinster Inc., 1984.
Written by a lesbian counsellor who has pioneered work in the area of female child sexual abuse, this book about lesbian sex includes a chapter on sex and sobriety.

Money, John (1988). Gay, Straight, And In-Between: The Sexology of Erotic Orientation. New York: Oxford University Press, 1988.
In this book, John Money explores the continuum of human sexuality dealing with such topics as the evolution of the term "homosexuality," and the issue of gender-identity and bisexuality. He explores the diverse historical, cultural and psychological influences that affect sexual orientation.

Sang, Barbara, Warshow, Joyce & Smith, Adrienne J. (Eds.) (1991). Lesbians and Midlife. San Francisco: Spinster Book Co., 1991.
This book is an anthology by and about lesbians from 40 to 60, with personal stories, poems and insights, covering such diverse topics as sex after menopause, changing body image, re-emerging creativity, being single at midlife, retirement and more.

Schneider, Margaret S. (1988), Often Invisible: Counselling Gay & Lesbian Youth. Toronto: Central Toronto Youth Services, 27 Carlton Street, 3rd Floor, Toronto, Ontario, M5B 1L2, 1988. (Copies may be ordered directly from their address as listed)
This textbook is written specifically for counsellors dealing with lesbian/gay youth.

Sexual Orientation: Homosexuality, Lesbian and Homophobia, A Resource Guide for Teachers of Health Education In Secondary Schools. Toronto Board of Education, February, 1993.
In this ground-breaking manual for teachers, a specific program of education and sensitization is set up for the understanding of lesbian and gay sexual orientation, and challenges homophobia and intolerance. It also contains a chapter with a complete list of the lesbian/gay resources in the greater Toronto area. An excellent resource guide for any counsellor or agency!!

SPIRITUAL ISSUES

Boyd, Malcolm (1984). <u>Gay Priest</u>. New York: St. Martin's Press, 1984.
>Malcolm Boyd, an Anglican priest, explores his own journey of coming to terms with his sexual identity and commitment to Christian ministry, and offers sound advice for lesbian or gay Christians in understanding their spiritual commitment.

Edwards, George R. (1984). <u>Gay/Lesbian Liberation: A Biblical Perspective</u>. New York: Pilgrim Press, 1984.
>Written in the context of Roman Catholic liberation theology, this books explores lesbian and gay spirituality from the biblical perspective. A good rebuttal to the fundamentalist abuse of scripture to condemn homosexuality.

Guindon, André (1986). Chapter Seven: Gay Fecundity or Liberating Sexuality. <u>The Sexual Creators: An Ethical Proposal for Concerned Christians.</u> New York: University Press of America, 1986.
>Rev. André Guindon, a Roman Catholic priest and theologian from Ottawa, Ontario, explores not only the validity of lesbian and gay sexuality, but also the contribution lesbians and gay men can make to the understanding and meaning of human sexuality in the Christian context.

Fortunato, John E. (1983). <u>Embracing the Exile: Healing Journeys of Gay Christians</u>. New York: Seabury Press, 1983.
>John Fortunato, a gay psychotherapist, explores the faith dimensions of lesbian and gay Christians seeking hope and encouragement as they struggle to make sense of their spirituality in the context of their sexual orientation.

MacNeil, John J. (1985). <u>The Church and the Homosexual</u>. New York: Next Year Publications, 1985.
>This is a key Christian theological treatise on homosexuality written in the Jesuit tradition of Roman Catholic theology. Rev. John J. MacNeil is co-founder of the New York chapter DIGNITY, the Roman Catholic organization for lesbians and gay men.

Clinical Issues in the Assessment and Treatment of Adolescent Substance Abuse

DARRYL UPFOLD

INTRODUCTION

*M*uch of our empirically derived knowledge about the treatment of addictions is based on research with adults – more specifically, male adults – with relatively serious problems with one substance: alcohol. This includes the development of assessment instruments and methods, selection of treatment goals and treatment approaches. With adolescents, the counsellor is challenged to modify these methods for a population that is not only younger, but also experiencing rapid and often confusing developmental changes. And, unlike many adults, adolescents presenting for treatment have often been abusing more than one substance.

Assessment strategies, treatment methods and goals must be relevant to the age and stage of development (early, middle and late adolescence) of the client. The youth counsellor needs to have in-depth knowledge of the physical, emotional and cognitive changes of adolescence, as well as the psychological tasks that the adolescent must achieve in order to make a successful transition into adulthood.

Some research suggests that "peer pressure" is the most consistently important influence on substance use among adolescents (Newcomb & Bentler, 1989). Yet the peer group is a necessary and important dimension of the adolescent experience, and its influence cannot be avoided. The peer group provides a safe and supportive context within which the adolescent develops social skills and learns to work through the challenges of adolescence to achieve independence.

It is therefore not realistic to expect the young client to separate easily from his or her friends even though they may also be involved with alcohol or drugs. This can be a problem for the adolescent client. However, many youth counsellors have a modified concept of "peer pressure" and the role it plays in initiating and maintaining substance abuse. The modified position suggests that peers do not always demand that others conform to certain behaviors (like drinking) in order to belong to the group. Often it is the young person who wrongly believes he or she must use alcohol or drugs in order to belong to the peer group. The issue of peer influence will be discussed in relation to developing "refusal skills" (page 286).

Several models of addiction treatment are practised with adolescents. The approach described in this chapter is a behavior model. The model is derived from social learning theory (Bandura, 1977), which suggests that much human behavior is learned, can be unlearned and can be replaced with more adaptive behavioral responses.

This chapter will review the assessment and treatment of adolescent substance abuse from a behavioral perspective. The section on treatment is most readily applied to individual counselling. The section on assessment is relevant to all adolescent clients, assessment being a necessary precursor to treatment of any kind. A review of group and family approaches exceeds the expectations of this chapter.

ASSESSMENT

Assessment is conducted to determine:
- problem severity
- the client's personal strengths and resources
- the appropriate "match" for treatment.

Issues related to conducting an assessment include:
- client preference
- identifying the real client
- client self-monitoring.

An assessment can be conducted in one session with a willing client. In other cases it may take many sessions of motivational counselling to prepare the client to participate in the assessment. In all cases, assessment is an ongoing process of gathering data, reviewing problem severity and modifying treatment decisions accordingly.

PROBLEM SEVERITY

Problem severity is determined by considering:
- quantity-frequency data (how much and how often)
- the behavioral consequences of substance use
- the extent of control the client has over the use
- age of the client
- the presence of predisposing factors.

There is no single, agreed-upon method to determine problem severity, and no universally accepted scale or language to describe problem severity with adolescents. Many youth counsellors use a three-point scale of "low-level severity," "moderately severe," and "very severe" to describe problems.

Quantity-Frequency and Behavioral Consequences Data

Typical models of determining problem severity with adults focus on: (1) gathering quantity-frequency data (i.e., quantity used and frequency of use), and (2) quantifying other behavioral consequences of the client's use (for example, the presence of withdrawal symptoms, missing school or work). Quantity-frequency data are then compared to the appropriate database, which objectively determines problem severity. Unfortunately, a quantity-frequency database for adolescents has not been developed as it has for adults (e.g., a mean number of eight standard drinks per day – a quantity-frequency measure – is commonly considered to indicate a severe dependence on alcohol for adults. This amount is probably too high for women).

With adults, data related to the negative behavioral consequences of alcohol or drug use are typically determined by administering psychometrically tested questionnaires. These measure the extent to which substance use has affected various life areas (e.g., physical health, mental health, legal status, school or employment performance, family and social relationships, financial status). There are, however, few readily available and accepted assessment instruments for use with adolescents. In their review of adolescent assessment instruments, George and Skinner (1991) note that only recently have attempts been made to develop instruments exclusively for adolescents. They review several instruments now available, including the Personal Experience Screening Questionnaire (PESQ), the Personal Experience Inventory (PEI), and the Adolescent Diagnostic Interview (ADI). Although many of the instruments have undergone or are undergoing psychometric testing to determine their validity and reliability, George and Skinner do not recommend the use of one instrument over the others. Rather, they call for a five-year trial of a comprehensive assessment model for adolescents. The reader is referred to George and Skinner (1991) for a thorough review of the adolescent instruments now available to assess problem severity.

An alternative to the use of questionnaires in assessment is the interview, structured to gather the same data as the questionnaires just discussed. Some counsellors (and clients) prefer using interviews to gather quantity-frequency and behavioral consequences data, because they can begin to develop the therapeutic relationship, and can also explore in more depth the important issues that may emerge during an interview.

In using the interview method, however, the counsellor needs to have a clear idea of the information that he or she needs to assess the problem, and to ensure that he or she guides the interview accordingly. Many youth clinics have developed their own structured interview schedule for this purpose. The limitation of the interview method is that it leaves the counsellor with the responsibility to make a clinical judgment regarding problem severity, whereas standardized questionnaires are designed and tested to yield an objective determination.

The remainder of this section reviews the variables that should be explored in an assessment interview, and the problems that contribute to the challenge of assessing problem severity in adolescents.

First, developing an accurate quantity-frequency index is difficult with many adolescent clients. Adults' patterns of use are often relatively constant and predictable, and therefore easily quantified. A quantity-frequency analysis of one month is likely to be similar to the next. This may not necessarily be true with adolescents, whose patterns of consumption often vary over time. Their shifting patterns of use are likely somewhat dependent on variables over which they do not have total control, such as *availability* of money or the substance itself, the *opportunity* to use, and the day-to-day *influence of peer activities*. During assessment, a frequently heard statement is: "I drink whenever I'm at a party and if it's offered to me;" or "I drink when I'm with my friends." It can be difficult to determine a quantity-frequency measure accurately when the behavior appears to be situationally driven.

A second problem in accurately assessing problem severity is that, unlike many adults, adolescents are frequently using more than one substance. A common pattern of adolescent substance use includes alcohol and cannabis (which is often easier for the adolescent to obtain than alcohol), and perhaps hallucinogens or cocaine. Is the occasional use of two substances equal to the moderate use of one? Is the moderate use of two substances equal to a serious problem with one? The counsellor must use clinical judgment to answer these questions in assessment.

A third issue related to assessing problem severity is the research finding that in many cases there is spontaneous remission from heavy alcohol use in young adulthood or adulthood, without treatment. In their review of this research, George and Skinner (1991) conclude that: (1) a majority of adolescent alcohol abusers will "mature" out of their excessive use without treatment; and (2) a smaller number are likely to progress to chronic alcohol dependence. Although this research focused on adolescent alcohol abusers, George and Skinner offer the opinion that a similar pattern likely exists for other drug use.

Although these factors can be problematic in accurately assessing problem severity, it still is helpful to conceptualize adolescent substance abuse as a continuum from *experimental* use to *recreational* or *irregular* use, *regular* use and *dependent* use.

The following chart can guide the counsellor's determination regarding which stage on the continuum the client may be at.

STAGE	CHARACTERISTICS
Experimental	• has tried a substance once or twice • motivated by curiosity
Recreational or Irregular	• use is infrequent, usually restricted to recreational activities, like birthdays, holidays, or when opportunities present themselves • usually with friends • thoughts not preoccupied with getting and using substances

Regular	• predictable pattern to use, no longer restricted to recreational activities and weekends
	• thoughts and behavior preoccupied with getting and using substances
	• negative consequences in one or more life areas evident
Dependent	• regular, predictable, and frequent use
	• physical addiction possible
	• psychological dependence present (feels a need to have the substance)
	• knows there is a problem, but continues to use.

(Source: Modified from *Youth & Drugs*, Tupker [Ed.] [1991], p. 3-46.)

Quantity-frequency and behavioral-consequences data can be used to place the client on this continuum. This is one factor in determining problem severity.

Experimental and recreational users will be more dependent on external variables like availability and opportunity to use. Regular and dependent users may go to great lengths to obtain the substance (like stealing money or selling drugs) and to create the opportunity to use (by ignoring curfews or moving out of the house).

Assessing Control

An important factor in assessing problem severity and treatment planning is the extent to which the young client has control over the use of substances when in potential drug-using situations. Abstinence may reflect the lack of availability or opportunity rather than the client's ability to refuse the substance. The counsellor should consider whether the adolescent has had episodes of:

• resisting a substance when it is offered
• using moderate amounts.

This will help to differentiate adolescents who appear to choose to use substances from those who simply appear to be unable to resist when they are available. In planning for treatment, the former might benefit from counselling that focuses on increasing awareness regarding the significant role that alcohol or drugs has in his or her life. In the latter case, skills training is required to teach the client behavior control mechanisms.

Age

The age of the young client must be considered in assessing problem severity and planning treatment. Developmental theorists hypothesize that substance use during adolescence may impede psychosocial maturation and successful resolution of the psychological challenges of adolescence. Some research evidence suggests that the later the onset of regular use, the less the involvement will be, at least with tobacco, alcohol, and cannabis (Jessor, 1982).

Although most developmental theories relating to substance abuse have not been tested empirically (Newcomb & Bentler, 1988), clinical experience supports the proposition that the younger user (for example, age 12) is at greater risk of developing a serious problem than, for example, a 17-year-old, even if each has a similar quantity-frequency index. Early-stage adolescents (up to approximately age 14) and middle-stage adolescents (approximately 15-17) should be assessed as having a "serious" problem if they are using recreationally/irregularly or regularly. With late-stage adolescents (approximately 18 and up), age may not be as critical a determinant of problem severity.

Predisposing Factors

During assessment the counsellor should identify the presence of predisposing "risk" factors. Some research suggests that, statistically, certain adolescents may be at higher risk of developing a problem with alcohol or other drugs due to the presence of such factors (e.g., Hawkins, Lishner, Catalano & Howard, 1986; Jessor, 1984).

These researchers have identified numerous hereditary, environmental and developmental variables that may increase an adolescent's vulnerability to alcohol or drug abuse. Perhaps the most commonly cited predisposing factor is a family history of substance abuse: adolescents who have a parent with an alcohol or drug problem may be at greater risk (statistically) of developing a similar problem (Goodwin, 1981).

There is no clear convergence on a limited, specific list of predisposing factors, but the following are reported in *Youth & Drugs* (Tupker [Ed.], 1991, pp. 1-42) as "primary risk factors:"

- developmental lags
- learning difficulties and disabilities
- deficiencies in interpersonal and social competence
- a history of behavioral difficulties
- family circumstance, including substance abuse.

To this list of "risk factors," Forney, Forney & Ripley (1989) add the important role of alcohol- or drug-using peers as a "predictive factor" for initiating substance use among adolescents.

This aspect of assessment differs from adult assessment. With adults, predisposing factors have already resulted in whatever influence they are likely to exert on use. With adolescents, the influence of predisposing factors may not yet be clear. Researchers rightly caution that predisposing factors relate *correlationally* to substance abuse and cannot be interpreted *causally*. Keeping this distinction in mind, it is important to note in assessment that the presence of predisposing factors may put an adolescent at greater risk of developing a problem even if the present quantity-frequency data are not excessive. For example, a recreational/irregular user with one or more predisposing factors in his or her background may be at risk of developing a more serious problem. Limited availability and opportunity may temporarily prevent the problem from being more serious.

In this case the counsellor might develop a treatment plan that includes ongoing but not necessarily frequent contact over a lengthy period of time in order to intervene should the problem become more serious. An adolescent of any age with several predisposing factors who is using regularly should be assessed as having a serious problem. Counsellors should familiarize themselves with the literature relating to predisposing factors in order to explore fully the potential impact that these factors may have on the development of an alcohol or drug problem.

PERSONAL STRENGTHS AND RESOURCES

Frequently, assessment emphasizes the problem and its various manifestations, usually described in terms of how the young person has violated expectations at home, school and in the community. The counsellor often neglects to identify and assess the young person's strengths and resources.

It is relevant to note that when any person attempts to change a behavior, he or she will do so based on personal strengths and resources, which in turn determine one's preferred change strategies. For example, adults who engage in a program of weight loss have several approaches from which they can select one that is consistent with their preferred change strategy. One person might choose to cut back on the quantity of food consumed at each meal but continue to eat three meals a day. Another might choose to eliminate one meal, perhaps lunch, and continue to have a hearty breakfast and supper. The result in both cases is the same – a decrease in caloric intake and a corresponding weight loss. However, one approach may work for one person but not another. The success of the change process depends on identifying and using the strengths and preferred change strategies that the client brings to the counselling experience, and having several strategies, from which the client can select one that most closely matches his or her strengths. The reader might try to identify the personal strengths and change strategies that would be required to be successful in the two weight loss examples.

Young clients may need guidance in identifying their personal strengths. They may not be aware of how they typically go about solving problems. The counsellor and client will benefit from identifying "what works" by reviewing previous problem situations that were successfully resolved. A second technique is to review recent problem situations and ask the client "What could you have done in order to have a different outcome?" As clients discuss how they could have changed the situation, the counsellor can frame the discussion in terms of strengths and strategies.

deShazer (1985) notes that no problematic behavior occurs all the time – there are always exceptions. Helping young clients identify when they have not consumed alcohol or other drugs is a third technique that can lead to the identification of particular strengths and preferred change strategies they may have used in the past, sometimes without being consciously aware of it.

Counsellors should use the reflective counselling skills of paraphrasing, probing and summarizing to explore and identify client strengths and preferred change strategies.

SUMMARY OF PROBLEM SEVERITY

Clinical experience suggests the variables that have been reviewed here merit consideration in determining problem severity:

- quantity-frequency data – to place the client on the continuum from experimental (less severe) to dependent (most severe)
- behavioral consequences – the more life areas affected (e.g., school, health, financial, legal, family), the more serious the problem
- control – the less control demonstrated by the client, the more serious the problem
- age – the younger the age of regular use, the more severe the problem potential
- predisposing factors – the presence of one or more suggests increased risk
- personal strengths – the fewer the skills, the more serious the problem potential
- personal resources – the fewer the supports (e.g., non-using peers, family members, guidance counsellors, special interests and activities), the more serious the problem potential.

These factors interact to determine the current problem severity, and the potential severity.

In general, the more serious the problem and the fewer the personal skills and resources, the greater the structure (e.g., residential or day treatment) and intensity (e.g., types of interventions) of treatment should be.

ISSUES RELATED TO ASSESSMENT

The ideal assessment and referral to treatment involves gathering assessment data to determine problem severity and objectively selecting the appropriate structure and intensity of treatment required (matching). In practice however, other issues can frequently affect the ideal assessment process.

CLIENT PREFERENCE

As the literature on adult assessment indicates, the counsellor should consider the client's preference for the structure and intensity of treatment (e.g., Miller & Hester, 1986). Client preference, however, can sometimes be at odds with treatment approaches and treatment goals suggested by assessment data. For example, the data may indicate that the client has a severe dependence on alcohol and that a short-term residential program and a goal of abstinence is recommended, but the client may prefer outpatient counselling with a goal of reduced use. This is a common situation faced by youth counsellors. Many young clients have not yet experienced the full negative impact of alcohol or other drug use, and may not be willing to consider the somewhat daunting goal of life-long abstinence.

There is no easy solution to this problem, and little research to help the counsellor assess the risks associated with supporting client preferences that may seem unwise. This problem emphasizes the necessity of constantly re-assessing and evaluating the initial assessment findings, evaluating progress and outcome, and processing these observations with the client. Accurate and honest feedback regarding progress can lead to renegotiating treatment decisions that were based on client preference rather than assessment data.

Identifying the Real Client

The question of "who the client really is" should be considered early in assessment. The majority of adolescents do not refer themselves (although this seems to be changing as schools develop policies and programs that encourage self-referral). Most are referred by adults (teachers, parents, probation officers, family counsellors) who have identified substance abuse as a problem for the young person. This frequently occurs as the result of a formal rule violation (such as drinking at a school dance or while on probation), or an informal rule violation (such as drinking that contravenes parental expectations). The young client, though, may believe that there is no problem, and that no change is required. In this case, we should consider who has the "problem" and who wants help to solve it. Is the young person actually a "client" if he or she does not think there is a problem and does not want any help to change? A useful discussion of client "types" appears in deShazer (1985).

If the young person clearly resists assessment and counselling, an option might be to engage the adult referral agent as the "client." The goal for counselling would be to explore how the referral agent could develop a supportive relationship where motivational counselling (see page 291, Stages of Change) could lead to a successful referral.

In other cases, the counsellor may decide to engage the young person in motivational counselling. (A detailed motivational model of counselling is described in Chapter 3, and a brief discussion of this model as it pertains to adolescents is included later in this chapter.)

Self-Monitoring

Self-monitoring is a useful technique in any program of behavior change. This technique can be used to increase motivation, gather assessment data, make treatment planning decisions, and monitor progress. It involves developing a method for the client to keep a record of his or her substance use on a daily basis. Often the counsellor will need to individualize a method that is appropriate to the client's level of cognitive development, personal circumstances and preferences. This can range from a journal to a wallet-sized card to the back of a cigarette package. Problem-solving around how and when to record self-monitoring data will probably be required.

Quantity-frequency data gathered by self-monitoring can be used to determine problem severity in terms of the continuum of use described earlier.

SUMMARY OF ASSESSMENT

During assessment the counsellor has determined how serious the problem is, identified the client's strengths and resources, and is prepared to recommend a treatment plan of appropriate intensity and structure. Substance use goals may or may not yet be set. In some cases, especially when the client acknowledges a serious problem, he or she may be willing to set goals during the first assessment session. With others, motivational counselling may be required to help the client reach the decision and action stage.

Assessment is not a discrete event, but a process that takes place throughout the treatment process. The counsellor must continue to assess the problem and evaluate the suitability and effectiveness of the treatment strategy. More with adolescents than adults, assessment and treatment blend into one fluid process, where the counsellor may need to conduct re-assessment during treatment, or motivational counselling during assessment.

TREATMENT

The treatment approach presented here is a behavioral approach derived originally from Bandura's social learning theory (1977) which posits that much human behavior is learned, based on responses to stimuli and reinforcement contingencies. The behavioral approach to treating addictions has been modified in recent years to include cognitive factors to blend into what Bandura (1986) calls cognitive social learning theory. This approach emphasizes the cognitive (the client's "self-talk" – what the client says to him or herself) and environmental determinants of drug use. Understanding and modifying these determinants helps the client gain control over the addictive behavior.

It may be tempting to ask, "Why doesn't this client just stop using?" – especially when the client recognizes a problem. Some individuals do just that – they recognize a problem and take the necessary steps to change the behavior behind it. These steps may range anywhere from using "will power" (stopping use without making significant modifications to the determinants) to engaging in a self-directed program of altering determinants. These individuals are often referred to as "self-changers," people who have the necessary motivation and skills to change.

Clients who seek help from counsellors may not be self-changers. A treatment plan is developed to provide the client with the necessary motivation, skills and interventions to gain control over his or her behavior by modifying the cognitive and environmental determinants that trigger episodes of use.

This section will review:
- conducting a functional analysis of behavior
- developing an individual treatment plan
- setting abstinence or non-abstinence treatment goals
- structure and focus in treatment
- case management.

FUNCTIONAL ANALYSIS OF BEHAVIOR

Functional analysis of behavior is the core concept in developing an individualized treatment plan during the decision and action stages of change. Functional analysis is described in most texts on cognitive-behavioral therapy (e.g., Robin & Foster, 1989; Tupker [Ed.], 1991). Based on social learning theory (Bandura, 1977), functional analysis has been widely applied in behavior therapy. It is based on the premise that *antecedent conditions* trigger a *behavioral response* of alcohol or drug use, and that the immediate positive consequences (*consequent conditions*) reinforce the drug-using response.

These are the three dimensions of functional analysis: (1) antecedent conditions; (2) the behavioral response to them; and (3) consequent conditions. To conduct a functional analysis, the counsellor reviews the client's recent episodes of alcohol or drug use to identify specific antecedent and consequent conditions.

This produces a list of antecedent conditions; shows how the client reacted to each antecedent; and identifies the positive reinforcements that were provided by the substance. The next step is to develop a treatment plan that can include interventions in one or all three dimensions of the functional analysis.

DEVELOPING AN INDIVIDUAL TREATMENT PLAN

The treatment plan includes interventions to: (1) avoid, modify, eliminate or tolerate antecedent conditions so they no longer trigger an episode of alcohol or drug use; (2) develop alternative behavioral responses through refusal training; (3) acquire positive feedback similar to that provided by the substance use.

In the following discussion there are several examples of interventions for antecedent conditions, refusal-skill training and consequent conditions. These are typical examples that often emerge during a functional analysis with adolescents. It is not an exhaustive list of effective interventions. Interventions are limited only by the counsellor's creativity.

Antecedent Conditions

Some reviews of functional analysis identify five categories of antecedents (thoughts, feelings, situations, behaviors and physiological states). Our work with adolescents suggests that the majority of antecedent conditions that young clients identify can be captured within three categories:

- thoughts or "self-talk" (e.g., "I'll have more fun if I drink")
- feelings (e.g., to cope with anger, anxiety, boredom)
- situations (e.g., being at a party where drug use is encouraged, a fight with a boyfriend or girlfriend).

Interventions are developed to avoid, modify, eliminate or tolerate antecedent conditions that can trigger an episode of alcohol or drug use.

ANTECEDENT	EXAMPLE	INTERVENTION
Thought	I'll have more fun if I get drunk	• Cognitive therapy to re-appraise thinking
Feeling	I was so angry I just wanted to get drunk	• Anger management • Avoid situation
Situations	Fight with boyfriend or girlfriend Fight with parents	• Communication skills • Problem solving skills
	Parties where drug use is encouraged	• Avoidant strategies • Peer intervention

Behavioral Response to Antecedent Conditions

This refers to interventions to help the client develop "refusal skills" when he or she does not want to use an avoidant strategy (e.g., a client may choose to attend a party rather than avoid it, but learn verbal and behavioral skills to turn down alcohol).

Refusal skills will often be applied in the context of peer interaction – that is, learning how to "say no" to friends who are offering alcohol or drugs.

The following interventions can be helpful in developing refusal skills in relation to peers.

(1) Role-playing with the counsellor acting as the friend who is most influential, or inviting the friend(s) to a session where the client can address directly the issue of stopping his or her use.

(2) Introduce the client to a trained "peer counsellor" who can discuss the client's fears around changing in a personal, meaningful way. Young adults who have recovered from a substance abuse problem themselves often make the best peer counsellors and role models for clients who are ambivalent about change, or are

struggling with using refusal skills.

(3) Group therapy or self-help groups. Group therapy can be used to create and deal with typical situations where drug use is influenced by peers. At our clinic, at least one group session takes place in a restaurant selected by group members. Clients have supper and spend the evening socializing drug-free in an environment (including peers, music, and other cues) that may trigger an urge to use. Using refusal skills (e.g., "Can I get you something from the bar?") to manage the urge successfully gives the client confidence that he or she is capable of being with peers without using alcohol or other drugs. This creates a good opportunity to frame drug use as a *choice* over which they have control, and can refuse, rather than being an automatic event that "just happens."

(4) Discrimination training. Some clients may choose to make changes regarding how often or under what circumstances they will see certain friends – "I'd like to be with you, even if you're drinking, but I can't be around you if you're going to do coke – it's too much of a temptation for me."

While exclusion from the peer group might occur if the client uses refusal skills to eliminate or reduce drug use, it has been our experience that the client's friends will support his or her behavior change. Young adults often recognize the healthy nature of eliminating drug use, and frequently provide appropriate verbal reinforcement to the client. It has been more common for peer group members to say they believe that the client actually does have a problem with drugs, than to be non-supportive. In some cases we have heard a client's friend say, "I've been telling you that you have a problem for a long time now, but you wouldn't listen." Verbal support for change coming from peer group members is often a surprise to the young client, and is a powerful reinforcer. These interventions can turn "peer pressure" into "peer support."

Consequent Conditions

This refers to interventions to help the client obtain positive reinforcement similar to what he or she receives from substance use.

CONSEQUENT CONDITION	INTERVENTION
Increased sense of belonging when smoking cannabis with friends	• Assertiveness skills • Self-esteem approaches
Becomes more outgoing	• Social skills training to overcome shyness
Overcomes boredom	• Leisure counselling • Tolerating low activity levels

Clients may choose different dimensions of the functional analysis as the focus for their interventions. One young client decided that he wanted to stop drinking but emphasized that he did not want to make any changes in his lifestyle, which involved considerable amounts of time in social and recreational activities with peers, all of whom used alcohol regularly. With this client, no interventions were developed to avoid, eliminate or tolerate antecedent conditions (i.e., peer-related situations). The treatment plan focused on developing refusal skills for various friends under various conditions.

SETTING ALCOHOL AND DRUG TREATMENT GOALS

The setting of substance abuse goals can be discussed during the initial assessment, or during the development of the individual treatment plan. In most cases the client can begin to consider goals in the contemplation stage, but the counsellor should not expect a commitment to a goal, or a willingness to pursue it, until the client is in the decision and action stage.

Setting substance abuse goals involves:
- deciding on a goal of abstinence or reduced use with each substance used
- deciding on a time frame for each (e.g., short-term, long-term).

Many young clients often shift goals from abstinence to reduced use, and even to allowing the occasional episode of intoxication to mark adolescent rituals like the end of the school year, birthdays, and long weekends.

Adults more easily support setting long-term goals partly because they have a longer history of substance use, which validates the necessity of adhering to goals, and partly because adults understand life in the long term.

Adolescents often have a weekend-to-weekend time frame that makes long-term goals difficult to conceptualize. The counsellor will probably get greater compliance if short-term goals are set. Often goal setting will relate to a particular event, like a party, a long weekend or a birthday. Goal setting may become a weekly activity in counselling.

Adolescents who are assessed as having a serious substance abuse problem may be more willing to set longer-term goals, and to endorse a goal of abstinence. However, for the majority of young clients we have found that treatment goals are constantly under revision and negotiation.

Abstinence and Non-abstinence Goals

Abstinence from the problem substance has been accepted historically as the traditional goal of treatment with adults. An abstinence goal was usually imposed on the client by the counsellor as a condition of treatment, rather than being identified as necessary by the client. Recent reviews of the literature (e.g., Miller, 1983; Marlatt, 1983; and Peele, 1992) and clinical experience have suggested that, for less severe cases, non-abstinence goals may be appropriate and achievable. Non-abstinence goals are also described as "reduced" or "controlled" use.

This controversial issue is a dilemma for youth counsellors whose clients are frequently unwilling to accept a goal of abstinence. This is controversial enough in a case of alcohol use, but an even greater problem with cannabis use, which is illegal but believed by many adolescents to be no worse than alcohol, and is often easier to get.

The position presented here is but one way of attempting to deal with it. Other clinics and counsellors may take a theoretical, philosophical or legal position that supports only abstinence goals.

From a legal perspective, the use of all illicit substances needs to be discouraged. From a clinical perspective, the reality seems to be that many young clients will not initially endorse a goal of abstinence from alcohol and often from other substances as well, most usually cannabis.

A compromise that is often acceptable to young clients who will not endorse a goal of abstinence is to suggest a goal of "reduced use working towards abstinence." This approach serves several functions. First, it encourages the young client who does not wish to abstain to engage in a counselling process that is acceptable at that point in time. Second, it may ease the counsellor's dilemma by including abstinence as a longer-term treatment goal.

We believe that many adolescents are unwilling to accept abstinence goals because they do not believe they could successfully avoid alcohol and other drug use completely. They may also fear the loss of friends, identity or "fun." These concerns (antecedents, "thought" category) prevent the young client from engaging in the change process if abstinence is required.

The young person who engages in a process to reduce use will learn new behavioral skills, interventions and reinforcement contingencies. As the young person becomes more skilled and confident, he or she may become more open to discussing additional goals. We have seen many cases where the young client, having achieved the goal of reduced use, becomes amenable to, or may even suggest, a goal of abstinence. This approach, which is often referred to as "rate reduction," is commonly used with other behaviors, including smoking cessation.

Most adolescents in treatment are using more than one substance. If an adolescent is unwilling to endorse a treatment goal of complete abstinence from all substances, the rate reduction approach can be used to eliminate one substance at a time.

In summary, it seems more sensible to help clients work towards goals that they themselves identify and are willing to set than it does to insist on goals that the counsellor identifies. Clients are not likely to commit seriously to treatment goals that are simply not important to them. On the other hand even minimal change in rate reduction can create confidence and therapeutic momentum which can be used to work toward more significant behavior change.

STRUCTURE AND FOCUS

Many adolescents who present for treatment have little structure in their day-to-day lives. For example, they may not attend school full time or be employed, may have little contact with family members and family rituals, and little community involvement (such as sports or church). The number of single-parent and double-income families has increased. There has also been a significant change in the relationship between the nuclear family and the extended family, with less contact between the two in this generation than the last.

These changes result in decreased structure and supervision for the adolescent. Many youth counsellors believe that providing structure for adolescent clients is a requisite element of an effective treatment plan.

Structure comes in many forms. Some examples are:
* planning free time
* scheduling homework or job hunting at the same time every day
* having regular meals
* setting times to get up in the morning and go to bed at night.

Counsellors can also increase structure by making several appointments at a time, calling to remind the client of the appointments, not easily accepting cancellations and rescheduled appointments, and assigning behavioral "homework" between appointments.

The counsellor must maintain a focus on the treatment goals. This will ensure that counselling is not crisis oriented, which can easily happen since there are many events in most teenagers' lives that they could easily see as a "crisis." It is difficult to maintain a focus on treatment goals when the counselling deals one week with parental conflict, the next with a problem with a boyfriend or girlfriend, and with a school problem the following week.

Although crises, transient or otherwise, may emerge from time to time, it is important that the counsellor maintain a focus during each session to review and confirm treatment goals, progress toward them, barriers that prevent achieving them, and preferred strategies to initiate and maintain changes. This brings predictability and positive expectation to counselling.

CASE MANAGEMENT

Structure and focus can be more easily maintained through effective case management and the use of community resources. Adolescents who present for substance abuse treatment frequently have other psychosocial problems as well, particularly school or employment, family, legal, leisure and accommodation problems. Treatment for substance abuse will be more effective if a comprehensive treatment plan that addresses all of the young client's needs is developed and co-ordinated among all the service providers. Each service provider needs to have a clear idea of what is expected of him or her – and of the client. Although it can be time-consuming to co-ordinate, we have found that with multi-problem adolescents it is most effective to have all service providers meet occasionally with the client to review treatment goals, progress towards achieving them, any barriers that the client has experienced and what could be done to overcome them. In this way the client will receive positive reinforcement and encouragement from the service providers and at the same time solve or avoid problems by having key people present.

Effective case management and community reinforcement is a method of creating a predictable and supportive environment in which the client's needs are more likely to be met. In this way the counselling relationship is perceived to be helpful and supportive, and the client will experience more success than failure.

STAGES OF CHANGE

Adolescent clients are frequently referred by adults due to value or rule violation. It is important to recognize that these are precontemplative clients who will not be prepared to set behavioral goals to reduce or eliminate substance use.

We have found that the stages of change as described by Prochaska and DiClemente (1984) are as apparent in adolescents as they are in adults, the target group with which the model was initially developed.

PRECONTEMPLATION

Precontemplation can be expressed in two ways: (1) clients who deny using alcohol or other drugs, and (2) clients who acknowledge using but do not believe their use to be a problem. Experimental and recreational/irregular users may appear to be precontemplative because their use may not yet involve significant negative consequences. Both of the above positions are intended to help the client avoid being in counselling.

The following techniques have been helpful in promoting progress from precontemplation toward contemplation:

(1) Acknowledge Feeling State

Identify, acknowledge and support the young client's feelings about being referred (Miller & Rollick, 1991). He or she will probably have a negative feeling about it, like anger, worry or resentment. Supporting their feelings help clients to understand that the counsellor is interested in them, not just in the referral agent's opinion.

(2) Acknowledge Positive Reinforcement Provided by Substance Use

Allow clients to talk about what they like about drinking or using drugs. This creates the opportunity for them to understand that the counsellor is nonjudgmental.

(3) Ask What Not To Say Or Do

Ask clients what they do not want the counsellor to say or do during the session; ask also what the counsellor could say or do that might be helpful. This will help the client understand that the counsellor is prepared to listen to, and attempt to provide "help" in a way that is meaningful.

(4) Identify Smallest Change

Ask the client to identify the smallest change possible that would result in his or her not having to see the counsellor again. This creates the opportunity to identify the easiest way to initiate change successfully.

(5) Challenge Self-concept

Ask clients if they see themselves as "drinkers" or "drug users," and if they wants others to see them that way. This may produce conflict between their emerging self-concept and their substance use.

(6) Bibliotherapy

This involves the client reading about some aspect of alcohol or drug use. We have found that some clients have begun to question their use after reading about rock musicians who have died as a result of drug use.

(7) Self-Monitoring

Precontemplative clients can often be persuaded to self-monitor if it is made clear that there is no requirement to change their substance use, just to keep track of it.

> EXAMPLE: "Perhaps you're right – maybe you don't have a problem. I don't know enough about your situation to help you make any decisions. Maybe it's OK that you don't want to make any changes right now, it would give us a chance to find out a bit more about your situation."

The motivational value of self-monitoring is that it makes implicit behavior more explicit, bringing it more clearly into awareness. Anyone who has ever self-monitored calories as part of a weight loss strategy will likely confirm that a new level of awareness results. As awareness increases regarding quantity, frequency and consequences, the counsellor can look for opportunities to discuss the role alcohol or drugs play in the client's life.

The counsellor must maintain a nonjudgmental position with self-monitoring. Without this, the client will self-monitor defensively, if at all. This will block the process of increasing awareness.

These techniques are intended to assist in developing a relationship with the precontemplative client; or to increase awareness about the significant role alcohol or drugs have in his or her life, and consequently to create discomfort regarding continued use. These are two objectives with precontemplative clients.

CONTEMPLATION

In contemplation, clients experience ambivalence between their fear of change and their willingness to change, due to the discomfort that emerged in precontemplation. The following techniques have been successful in moving the client closer to the decision stage by overcoming the fear of change.

(1) Personal Experiments

The counsellor can suggest that the client set a goal to abstain or reduce on one occasion, on an "experimental" basis. The client is asked to be a "scientist" by noticing how friends are acting, how the client was acting and feeling, how the client felt about him- or herself the next day, and so on. Many questions can be developed for the "scientist" to observe and answer. The personal experiment does not involve commitment, so the client is often willing to try it. The client often experiences positive reinforcement as a result of the experiment: physically, because he or she avoided a hangover or withdrawal, and psychologically, because it will contribute to his or her self-esteem. The positive reinforcement increases the likelihood that the young client will set another treatment goal. The client has no doubt avoided using substances on occasion in the past, but it is the deliberate effort to change that is reinforcing.

(2) Self-Administered Reinforcement

The client rewards him- or herself (e.g., with a new audiotape) on achieving a short-term goal, even one episode of abstaining or reducing. Parents can be included in this technique. This creates the opportunity to reward a positive behavior.

(3) Reinforce Internal Locus of Control

The counsellor takes the position that the client – not the counsellor – is responsible for making decisions about him- or herself (Miller & Rollick, 1991). This increases the client's sense of personal responsibility to manage his or her life effectively.

In contemplation, clients may be persuaded to set initial, modest goals that begin to give them control over their use.

Youth counsellors need to be aware of their own skills, preferred treatment approaches and limitations to determine if they can work with precontemplation- and contemplation-stage clients and the significant clinical challenges that they present. Not all counsellors are well matched to clients who need to process information and experience before being ready to set initial treatment goals.

In motivational counselling the counsellor must evaluate whether the client is moving from precontemplation to contemplation, and closer to setting goals. If counselling sessions are merely giving the client an opportunity to recount the events of the week without taking responsibility for them, or reducing guilt associated with substance use without setting goals to change it, then counselling has become counter-productive, or "enabling." There is a thin but sharp edge between a non-judgmental relationship and an "enabling" relationship.

The counsellor must be able to move the client in the direction of setting and working toward goals (decision and action stages) in order to be therapeutic. If this is not happening, the counsellor might consider terminating counselling.

DECISION AND ACTION

This is the stage of change that was generally considered to be "treatment" before concepts like assessment, motivation and relapse prevention were developed.

As mentioned, some clients with adequate personal skills and resources are capable of achieving their goals rather quickly when they are in this stage. For others, though, "action" is a gradual process that begins with learning techniques to gain control of their behavior. For these clients, the change process may appear to be "hit or miss," with some successful experiences sprinkled in with some unsuccessful ones.

The following techniques are effective in helping clients gain control of their behavior by initiating change in small, manageable steps.

(1) Verbal Rehearsal

When the client has decided on a goal and is ready to change, it is effective to have the client repeat the goal for the day/weekend/week, and the interventions and refusal skills he or she needs to use to achieve it. This increases the commitment to the goal.

(2) Mental Imagery

This is a similar technique that can be used in conjunction with verbal rehearsal. The client is asked to develop a mental picture of achieving the goal for a particular occasion. This can also be presented as a "movie," with the client as "director," ensuring that the "plot" (i.e., a successful drug-free occasion) develops as planned. Envisioning the desired outcome also increases commitment to the goal, and increases the likelihood that the client will attempt to achieve it.

(3) Delay techniques

If the client has selected a non-abstinence goal, the following delay techniques can be effective in helping the client learn how to reduce:

• delay the first drink by one hour
• agree to having no more than two drinks during the first two hours of the occasion
• agree to drink a certain number of non-alcoholic drinks during the night.

(4) Written "Prescriptions"

Write on a small pad of paper the client's goal and interventions. Develop prompts to indicate when it should be reviewed (e.g., once an hour, after a drink, etc.). The ongoing reminder may increase the client's resolve to implement the interventions.

(5) Self-control Training

Have the client consume a small amount of a substance that is considered hard to resist, like chocolate or peanuts, while "refusing" the remainder. This may create an urge to continue consuming, which the client can practice managing. This can be done in the counsellor's office. Clients can identify their own hard-to-resist substance with which to practice.

(6) Change Behavior Sequences

Have the client try to change anything to give him or her the experience of deliberate change. Examples are: change the sequence of getting dressed in the morning, or take a different route to school or work. This will help the client understand that deliberate change usually involves some effort, and perhaps initial unease, but also that he or she is capable of it.

Many of these techniques can help clients in contemplation.

EVALUATING PROGRESS

Even treatment that ultimately "succeeds" is not likely to follow a linear, unobstructed pathway. Research shows that even clients who do achieve their stated treatment goals will frequently have one or more lapses during which they will use a substance, and that reduced use seems to be a more common outcome of treatment than abstinence (Wilkinson & Martin, 1991).

It is often helpful to ask the client to evaluate his or her own satisfaction level with the progress being made. One way to do this is to ask the client how satisfied he or she is on a 10-point scale. The counsellor can both reinforce the client's progress and also ask what the client could do to "move up" on the scale. This can lead to additional goal setting.

This will add to the client's sense of self-efficacy by reinforcing that it is important for the client – and not just the counsellor –to evaluate how well he or she is doing.

The client is usually honest in his or her assessment of progress when the treatment plan is a shared responsibility. In these cases, it has been common for the client to be critical of the progress, which sets the stage for additional goal setting. When clients report being satisfied with their progress even though it is minimal, they may need to be more comfortable at that level of use and with the techniques they have used to get it there, before being confident enough in their skills to set additional goals.

However, it is also important for the counsellor to observe whether the client is actually making progress. If little or no behavior change regarding substance use has taken place over a period of time – for example, four weeks – then the counsellor must consider the reasons for this. For example, the client may not be at the decision stage when behavioral goals can be set; the client may not have the requisite skills to initiate change; or the specific interventions may not be consistent with the client's strengths and preferred change strategies.

With clients who are reluctant to set goals, it is tempting, though a mistake, for the counsellor to gradually assume full responsibility for developing and directing treatment. Because the unwilling client is not likely to bring this clinical mistake to the counsellor's attention, the counsellor must ensure he or she is not taking too much responsibility for initiating change.

In summary, evaluating progress should consider the following factors:

- satisfaction level with progress should be assessed by the client and used to renegotiate treatment goals
- barriers should be identified when progress is not made (motivation, skill

deficit, or inappropriate change strategies)
- the relative benefits and liabilities of maintaining a counselling relationship when little or no behavior change is made should be considered.

SUMMARY

The assessment and treatment approach presented in this chapter includes concepts of developmental and adolescent psychology, cognitive-behavioral therapy, and motivational counselling. There is much research to be done before a model that articulates the role of predisposing factors, non-abstinence goals, the maturational process and sociological factors such as changes in family structure – just to name a few – could be confidently supported as the most effective approach to assessing and treating adolescent substance abuse.

Wherever possible, discussion has been based on empirically derived findings. In other cases, the observations and clinical experiences of the staff of the Young Adult Substance Abuse Clinic have guided the discussion.

The model presented here has been clinically relevant to our experience in working with adolescents and young adults with substance abuse problems. However, our experience has also been that very few cases follow a linear pathway to successful termination. Frequently, clients will shift gears motivationally, have other issues emerge that are considered more important, or miss several consecutive appointments, all of which affect the focus and continuity of the treatment process.

It has been our experience that many clients who leave treatment prematurely return to counselling voluntarily at a later date. This suggests that the approach described in this chapter is perceived to be relevant and helpful to adolescents and young adults with alcohol or drug abuse problems.

REFERENCES

Bandura, A. (1977). Social learning theory. Englewood Cliffs, NJ: Prentice-Hall.

Bandura, A. (1986). Social foundations of thought and action: A social cognitive theory. Englewood Cliffs, NJ: Prentice-Hall.

deShazer, S. (1985). Keys to solutions in brief therapy. New York: Norton.

Forney, M.A., Forney, P.D. & Ripley, W.K. (1989). Predictor variables of adolescent drinking. Advances in Alcohol and Substance Abuse, 8(2), 97-113.

George, G.S. & Skinner, H.A. (1991). Assessment. In H.M. Annis, & C.S. Davis (Eds.), Drug use by adolescents: Identification, assessment and intervention (pp. 85-108). Toronto: Addiction Research Foundation, 1991.

Goodwin, D.W. (1981). Adoption studies of alcoholism. Progress in Clinical and Biological Research, 69(C), 71-76.

Hawkins, J.D., Lishner, D.M., Catalano, R.F. & Howard, M. (1986). Childhood predictors of adolescent substance abuse: Toward an empirically grounded theory. In S. Griswold-Ezekoye, K.L. Kumpfer, & W.J. Bukoski (Eds.), Childhood and Chemical Abuse: Prevention and Intervention (pp. 11-48). New York: Haworth Press, 1986.

Jessor, R. (1982). Critical issues in research on adolescent health promotion. In T.J. Coates, A.C. Peterson, & C.L. Perry (Eds.), Promoting adolescent health: A dialogue on research and practice. New York: Academic Press, 1982.

Jessor, R. (1984). Adolescent development and behavioral health. In Matarazzo et al. (Eds.), Behavioral Health: A Handbook of Health Enhancement and Disease Prevention (pp. 69-90). New York: J. Wiley.

Marlatt, A.G. (1983). The controlled-drinking controversy. American Psychologist, October, 1097-1110.

Miller, W. (1983). Controlled drinking: A history and critical review. Journal of Studies on Alcohol, 44(1),68-83.

Miller, W.R. & Hester, R.K. (1986). Matching problem drinkers with optimal treatments. In W.R. Miller & N. Heather (Eds.), Treating addictive behaviors: Processes of change. New York: Plenum Press, 1986.

Miller, W.R. & Rollnick, S. (1991). <u>Motivational interviewing: Preparing people to change addictive behavior</u>. New York: The Guilford Press.

Newcomb, M.D. & Bentler, P.M. (1988). Impact of adolescent drug use and social support on problems of young adults: A longitudinal study. <u>Journal of Abnormal Psychology</u>, 97 (1), 64-75.

Newcomb, M.D. & Bentler, P.M. (1989). Substance use and abuse among children and adolescents. <u>American Psychologist</u>, 44, 242-248.

Peele, S. The diseased society. <u>The Journal</u>, October/November 1992, 7-8.

Prochaska, J.O. & DiClemente, C. (1984). <u>The transtheoretical approach: Crossing the traditional boundaries of therapy</u>. Homewood, IL: Dow Jones/Irwin.

Robin, A.L. & Foster, S.L. (1989). <u>Negotiating parent-adolescent conflict</u>. New York: The Guilford Press.

Tupker, E. (Ed.) (1991). <u>Youth & Drugs: An education package for professionals</u>. Toronto: Addiction Research Foundation, 1991.

Wilkinson, D.A., & Martin G.W. (1991). Intervention methods for youth with problems of substance abuse. In H.M. Annis & C.S. Davis (Eds.), <u>Drug use by adolescents: Identification, assessment and intervention</u> (pp. 109-130). Toronto: Addiction Research Foundation, 1991.

Cultural Considerations for the Native Client

AUDREY HILL

The importance of Western acculturational influences on the native client is a critical consideration in addiction counselling, particularly for the assessment and treatment-planning phases. This chapter will illustrate this influence on the native client by examining four native family types that have developed along a continuum of Western acculturation. This will help the addiction counsellor (native and non-native) understand the significance of the native client's family of origin.

The relevance of family systems therapy has been addressed in current literature in the addictions field, but its theories and concepts have rarely been applied to the native family system. Sources cited within this chapter will provide further information for the reader.

Lawson, Peterson and Lawson (1983) provide insight into the significance of family systems theory in the addiction field. Within the family system perspective, the entire family is seen as the client and the development of an addiction is seen as a symptom of a dysfunctional family system. Assessment and treatment planning for the "family-as-client" would be facilitated by understanding the family structure.

The individual client in addiction counselling may or may not have a current family. However, the counsellor must not lose sight of the fact that the client was once a family member and is a product of his or her particular family system. The structure of the family fundamentally influenced the client's personality development, values, perceptions, socialization, behaviors, etc. For the native client, the addiction counsellor requires at least a general understanding of the family as a natural social system that functions according to a set of values, rules, roles, power structure, communication style and problem-solving strategies (Goldenberg & Goldenberg, 1985).

In addition to basic family structure concepts, the addiction counsellor must be aware that the native family is a culturally unique social system with a different historical and developmental frame of reference for the native client (Attneave, 1982). The historical differences have evolved with the influences of acculturation into the Western society.

The impact of Western influence on the development of the native family structure can be viewed along a range, or continuum, of acculturation that provides for four general types of native families (Redhorse, Lewis, Feit & Decker, 1978). These four types are: reserve-based, migratory, transitional and bi-cultural native families.

It is also important to recognize the cultural diversity that exists among these native family types. For example, one reserve-based family type (Iroquois culture of southern Ontario) will differ significantly from another (Ojibwa culture of northern Ontario). Each native family type in this framework must be viewed with an understanding of the particular cultural society of the individual client.

The following will briefly summarize the four native family types along the range of acculturation in light of contemporary Iroquois society and provide a short commentary on its significance in assessment and treatment planning for the native client.

RESERVE-BASED NATIVE FAMILY

In contemporary Iroquois society, these families are generally characterized by a large, extended matriarchal family system. They have been born, raised, educated and continue to reside on the reserve. Traditional language, cultural knowledge and history have been retained, passed on orally by family members. Traditional Iroquois families continue to adhere to the longhouse and observe the traditional teachings of the "Great Law of the Iroquois Confederacy." This source of knowledge is extremely important to the native client: an essential link to the cultural identity of the individual and the family system.

Elder family members retain an integral role in the lives of their extended family members. The primary developmental task of family members is to become an interdependent member of the family system, rather than becoming independent as in a nuclear family system. Individuality is the secondary developmental task, emphasizing the fundamental values of sharing, generosity and equality within the group.

Personal and family experiences of reserve life play an important role in the personality dynamics of the addicted native client. Consideration of these early childhood memories is clinically significant in assessing the psychosocial history and determining role models, exposure to various childhood trauma, major losses, rules, communication patterns and self-image. In the treatment planning phase, the motivation for change is fundamental. It is important for the counsellor to understand what the native client perceives as a healthy, constructive lifestyle. What is a functional native family system? If the client perceives a value for his or her culture, lifestyle must be changed without sacrificing the integrity of cultural identity.

MIGRATORY NATIVE FAMILY

In contemporary Iroquois society, many families frequently migrate from the reserve to nearby urban communities to search for a means of subsistence: employment, housing, health services, educational opportunities, etc. These temporary absences have created a sense of alienation from the traditional family supports of the reserve-based, extended family system. While residing in the urban environment, the native family has been exposed to Western influences and advanced acculturation. These influences and experiences of urban living create psychosocial stress for each individual. The stressors, often termed "culture shock," have tested the family's ability to adapt to frequent changes. Substance abuse often becomes a dysfunctional coping strategy for the multiple stressors of a migratory lifestyle, alienation from traditional family supports, cultural knowledge and identity.

Assessment of the native client should include an understanding of the childhood influences and experiences of a migratory native family that abused substances in an effort to cope with its lifestyle. Urban experiences would also lead to a "differentness" that would be perceived as a loss of cultural identity. Because of these different experiences and alienation from reserve-based family members, the individual internalizes "differentness" as another psychosocial stressor. It is necessary to determine the family influences as well as the significance of cultural identity for the individual. Treatment planning, from this perspective, should address the native client's motivation to adopt a lifestyle that promotes resolution of a cultural identity crisis and the acquisition of healthy, coping skills for dealing with psychosocial stress.

TRANSITIONAL NATIVE FAMILY

In contemporary Iroquois society, this native family has adjusted to an urban community, functions as a nuclear family unit and has become alienated from the traditional, reserve-based native community and extended native family system. The closed social system that characterizes this family structure tends to deny younger family members access to the reserve's community and family experiences, cultural language and knowledge. At the same time, adult family members maintain a low level of acculturation with the dominant society. This family may be second- or third-generation "urban," yet may remain in transition. If a cultural identity remains, it is based on a Western perspective that may range from stereotypical to prejudicial toward the native community.

The addiction counsellor may see a client from this native family structure as an individual who is having an identity crisis. Assessment should address the client's perception of the importance of a cultural identity in addiction counselling. The native client may or may not consider cultural identity as a primary issue surrounding their addiction. The client may openly acknowledge a sense of loss for their cultural "roots" or they may adamantly claim that cultural identity is not important to them. Pervasive Western influences and the lack of cultural ties and knowledge have led family members to adopt Western values that primarily advocate individuality and independence within a nuclear family system. This orientation is diametrically opposed to the traditional Iroquois values of collective rights, community development and interdependence within an extended family system.

The addiction counsellor should be aware that reserve-based native individuals often view their urban counterparts as "apples:" red on the outside but white on the inside. The native client may be aware of – may even have experienced – this stigma. This situation often prevents the native client from reintegrating into the native community, if he or she chooses to do so. Therefore, treatment planning should help the native client obtain cultural information and, if possible, referral to an urban native social service or program that may facilitate his or her return to the native community. Urban native community services are an essential cultural link for the native individual. Some reserves have developed health, social and educational services. It would be helpful for the client and the addiction counsellor to have access to information about the client's reserve community.

BICULTURAL NATIVE FAMILY

This native family type may reside on the reserve, in an urban community or own land and homes in both areas. Generally characterized by higher levels of employment, education and income, family members are able to function as a nuclear family unit but have maintained their ties with the extended native family and community. They have successfully adapted to a Western lifestyle without sacrificing their cultural identity, knowledge and values, although they may no longer speak their traditional language. In other words, they have bridged both the native and Western worlds and can effectively function in both. In contrast to the transitional family, this native family type has successfully acculturated toward a harmonious balance of biculturalism.

CONCLUSION

The reserve-based and bicultural native family types are, in contrast to the migratory and transitional native family types, the most functional family types, both socially and psychologically. Based on the range of acculturation among native family systems and the four family types outlined here, addiction counsellors must also recognize the cultural diversity that exists. Each family type must be viewed with an understanding of the particular culture of the native client. The native family structure becomes an important cultural consideration in terms of assessment and treatment for the native addicted client.

Although this chapter has focused on the Iroquois family types, it can provide a model for the counsellor to explore the family types of other native clients, since many of the acculturational influences impact other tribes in a similar fashion.

REFERENCES

Attneave, C. (1982). Native American families. In M. McGoldrick, J.K. Pearce & J. Giordano (Eds.), Ethnicity and family therapy. New York: Guilford Press.

Goldenberg, I. & Goldenberg, H. (1985). Family therapy: an overview. Monterey, CA: Brooks/Cole Publishing Co.

Hill, A. (1989). Treatment and prevention of alcoholism in the native American family. In G. Lawson & A. Lawson (Eds.), Alcoholism and substance abuse in special populations. Rockville, MD: Aspen Publications.

Lawson, G., Peterson, J. & Lawson, A. (1983). Alcoholism and the family: a guide to treatment and prevention. Rockville, MD: Aspen Publications.

Mohatt, G., McDiarmid, W. & Montoya, V. (1988). Societies, families and change: the Alaskan example. In Behavioral health issues among American Indians and Alaska natives. American Indian and Alaska Native Mental Health Research, Monograph No. 1, pp. 325–365.

Redhorse, J., Lewis, R., Feit, M. & Decker, J. (1978). Family behavior of urban American Indians. Social Casework, No. 59, pp. 67–72.

Addictions Counselling for Culturally and Racially Diverse Communities: Some Strategies and Tactics

BERYL TSANG

WHAT ARE CULTURALLY AND RACIALLY DIVERSE POPULATIONS?

Culturally and racially diverse populations are groups in Canadian society who, because of cultural, ethnic, linguistic, racial, religious or spiritual traditions, are different from those of the Anglo-Celtic, Anglo-Saxon and francophone mainstream. They include: immigrants, those who have chosen to leave their homes and resettle in Canada; refugees, those who have fled to Canada because of a well-founded fear of persecution; ethnic and linguistic minorities, those who have chosen to identify themselves as having ethnic or linguistic heritages distinct from those of the dominant groups; in-settlement populations, those who emigrated several decades ago but have not had the opportunity to fully integrate into the mainstream; racial minorities, those who see themselves as racially different from the dominant racial group; and religious or spiritual minorities, those who view their religious and spiritual beliefs, practices and values as distinct from those of dominant religious or spiritual groups.

The purpose of this chapter is to share strategies and tactics for providing service to clients from culturally and racially diverse populations. Since there has been very little theoretical or clinical research in this area, the content of this chapter is based on the experiences of health and human service providers who have provided addictions counselling to these groups. Guidelines, ideas and practices have been developed from their experiences to help addiction service providers better serve the needs of culturally and racially diverse populations.

UNDERSTANDING OTHERS AND HELPING THEM TO UNDERSTAND YOU

Providing service to culturally and racially diverse populations may seem like a difficult task at first. You may be concerned that you won't be able to fully understand your clients' needs because: you are unaware of their experiences; you fear inadvertently offending them because you may not be familiar with their norms, values and practices; you worry about not being able to provide them with adequate or appropriate services because you are of a different background. Yet the task won't be difficult if the basic rules of cultural and racial sensitivity listed below are observed.

i) Remember that everyone has cultural, ethnic, linguistic, racial, religious and spiritual biases. Be aware of your own and try to "check" them when you are providing service to a client from a different background.

ii) Remember that different people have different ways of expressing themselves. Expect and anticipate different forms of self-expression and self-presentation.

iii) Think about how you express yourself. How do you make others feel comfortable and safe? How may you inadvertently confuse or alienate others?

iv) Learn to actively listen when someone speaks to you. Try to hear exactly what they say. Be sure to check your interpretation of what you think they said with what they really said in a concerned and validating manner. (i.e., "So what you believe you need is..." "Your concern is..." "I understand that..." or "You feel that...").

v) Take all comments and concerns seriously even if they have no apparent relationship to the issue at hand. If possible, validate comments and concerns. Acknowledge that they are real. Once rapport is established, discussing specific issues may be easier.

vi) When communicating any sort of information, ask yourself the following questions:
• Can they hear me properly?
• Am I using words they may not understand (i.e., jargon, technical words)?
• Am I using gestures or body language that may make them uncomfortable?
• How familiar am I with their day-to-day experiences and challenges?
• How well do they understand English or French?
• How familiar are they with the issues we are discussing?
• How much can they remember at once?
• Are they too nervous or shy to ask questions?

vii) If there is a language barrier, do not be afraid of using innovative means of communicating with your clients, e.g., drawing, referring to pictures in magazines, using props, etc.

viii) If you have difficulty communicating, stop the situation or conversation for a few minutes and take a rest.

ix) Remember that providing service to clients from culturally and racially diverse populations will become easier with practice.

x) Remember: you could someday be the one who is "different" and needing services.

HOW TO PROVIDE APPROPRIATE SERVICE TO CULTURALLY AND RACIALLY DIVERSE POPULATIONS

When providing service to culturally and racially diverse populations, it is not only important to follow the above guidelines for sensitivity but also to be aware of the common differences in values, practices and norms that could lead to misunderstandings and prevent the provision of relevant and suitable service. Some differences to watch out for are:

- personal and social boundaries
- body language, personal distance and use of touch
- age, family and gender roles
- use of intonation, humor, language and metaphors
- importance placed on things such as the education, money, relationships and self.

There are also some ways to bridge differences. Acknowledge that there are different ways of doing things and that no one way is right. Ask your clients about their values, practices and norms. Discuss how your values, practices and norms are different in order to help them understand your approach to counselling. You can also look for similarities between your client's experiences and your own. For example, you have a client who expresses a deep reluctance about discussing her alcohol use because of her religious upbringing. To better understand her reluctance, think about how your own religious upbringing might make you reluctant to discuss certain subjects. In conclusion, when you are unsure about how to respond to a client who is behaving in an unfamiliar way, observe how he or she interacts with you and follow his or her lead.

ADDICTION SERVICE NEEDS OF CULTURALLY AND RACIALLY DIVERSE GROUPS

To fully understand the addiction service needs of culturally and racially diverse populations, it is important to understand their general health and human service needs since the three are often related. The following sections illustrate the health and human service needs of immigrants, refugees and in-settlement populations as well as those of ethnic, linguistic, racial and religious or spiritual minorities.

THE IMMIGRANT SETTLEMENT PROCESS

Time Period: 6 months before arrival

Thoughts and Feelings
- anticipation of move
- disengagement from existing life
- enthusiasm and excitement
- assumptions of happiness and
  success in new country.

Issues and Needs
- preparation of logistics
- everything is focused on the move
- inability to think clearly about what will actually
  happen once move is complete.

Resources Required
- information about what to expect in new country: housing,
  transportation, employment, health and human services,
  education, child care, values, norms, practices, weather, etc.

Potential Resources Required
- names of groups or individuals to contact in new county.

Time Period: 0 to 6 months after arrival

Thoughts and Feelings
Range FROM
- holiday spirit
- delight in new things present in new home
- fascination with new things unique to new home
- favorable comparison of new home with old home.
TO
- "culture shock"
- sense of displacement
- no context for understanding new home
- no desire to get to know new home
- criticism of new things
- avoidance of things unique to new home
- unfavorable comparison to old home.

Issues and Needs
- sightseeing phase
- physical orientation to institutions and services in new home
- getting professional or vocation accreditation, learning English or French, looking for work and skills development
- creation of a home or "nesting"
- establishing a peer group
- contacting people of the same cultural, ethnic, linguistic, racial, religious or spiritual background.

Resources Required
- assistance meeting basic physical needs, such as work, shelter, food, clothing, etc.
- information on professional or vocational accreditation
- language training
- "life skills" training
- information on skills development
- orientation to basic health and human services (e.g., hospitals, health centres, senior or youth groups etc.)
- orientation to educational facilities and child care
- recreational opportunities.

Potential Resources Required
- help accessing financial institutions, receiving legal help or setting up a business
- information on cultural- or racial-specific social clubs
- information on heritage programs.

Time Period: 6 months to 3 years

Thoughts and Feelings
Range FROM
- "honeymoon" or "desire for divorce" phase
- happiness over move
- reinforcement of original reasons for move
- positive mechanism for coping with change.
TO
- anxiety over separation with what is familiar
- reasons for move are now unclear
- fear of further change
- anger and depression which is not expressed over inability to cope in a new environment
- sense of loss over old life
- mourning of old life.

Issues and Needs
Range FROM
• desire to achieve something in new home
• desire to contribute to new home
• rising expectations.
TO
• sense of disillusionment at not being able to achieve something or meet expectations
• frustration over inability to contribute in a meaningful way
• desire to bring friends and family to new home.

Resources Required
Range FROM
• connect with achievements in previous life
• information on how to establish ties to former achievements
• new challenges and activities
• assessment of skills, resources and knowledge.
TO
• assistance identifying thoughts and emotions which are unsettling
• learning to express thoughts and emotions
• validation of loss
• information on how to sponsor friends and family members.

Potential Resources Required
• counselling or help to deal with mourning
• help finding or creating mutual aid or support groups
• information on self care.

Time Period: 3 to 5 years

Thoughts and Feelings
Range FROM
• sense of permanent disassociation from old life sets in
• realization that there has been a shift in values, practices and norms
• resolution about move
• identification and familiarity with new home
• desire to "go back" to make sure that leaving was the right thing to do.
TO
• uncertainty about self and future
• reluctant resolution to stay
• perhaps a loss in self-esteem
• ongoing questioning of reasons for leaving.

Issues and Needs
Range FROM
• pursuit of permanent connections to new home
  (e.g., development of long term career plans, plans
  for children, involvement in the community,
  establishment of peer groups, etc.)
• return to old home for a visit.
TO
• negative coping mechanisms developed
  (e.g., withdrawal from friends and family,
  substance use, idealization of former home).

Resources Required
• assistance making connections that bind individuals and
  families to communities
• help establishing goals and objectives to be achieved
• ongoing help establishing ties to former achievements
• ongoing help assessing skills, resources and knowledge
• ongoing help finding new challenges and activities
• ongoing help identifying unsettling thoughts
  and emotions
• learning to express thoughts and emotions.

Potential Resources Required
• ongoing counselling or help to deal with mourning
• ongoing help finding or creating mutual aid or
  support groups
• ongoing provision of information on self care.

Time Period: 5 years onwards

Thoughts and Feelings
• sense of belonging.

Resources Required
• becomes a resource.

Please note that different immigrants settle at different rates and that
these timelines may vary. Also note that if the health and human
service needs of immigrants are not met in the earlier stages of
settlement, the resources required to meet their needs in later stages
will usually be greater.

REFUGEE INTEGRATION PROCESS

Time Period: 0 to 6 months

Thoughts and Feelings
• thoughts and feelings are often contradictory or in conflict
• sense of excitement and happiness
• pre-occupation with safety and well-being
• relief at escaping persecution and torture, fear or
  uncertainty about safety
• disorientation and confusion
• sense of potential or sense of loss.

Issues and Needs
• fulfilment of basic physical needs (e.g., work, shelter, food etc.)
• orientation to new institutions and services in new home
• contact with those who share their culture, ethnicity, language, race, religion,
  spirituality or experiences
• being cared for by someone "who knows."

Resources Required
• assessment of pre-arrival experience (e.g., time spent in refugee camp, if any;
  family and friends left behind; experiences with violence or torture, etc.)
• determination of need for mental health services
• legal assistance if claiming refugee status under the United Nations Convention
• assistance meeting basic physical needs, such as work, shelter, food and clothing
• language training
• "life skills" training
• information on skills development
• orientation to basic health and human services (e.g.,
  hospitals, health centres, senior or youth groups, etc.)
• recreational opportunities.

Time Period: 6 months to 3 years

Thoughts and Feelings
• anxiety over separation with home
• guilt about leaving friends and family behind
• guilt about being "safe"
• ongoing fear for personal safety and well-being
• fear of further change
• unexpressed anger and depression over inability to cope in a new environment.

Issues and Needs
- desire to achieve something in new home
- desire to contribute to new home
- rising expectations
- sense of disillusionment at not being able to achieve something or meet basic expectations
- frustration over inability to contribute in a meaningful way
- desire to bring friends and family to new home – sadness at not being able to do so.

Resources Required
- connect with achievements in previous life
- information on how to establish ties to former achievements
- new challenges and activities
- assessment of skills, resources and knowledge
- introduction of new ideas and opportunities
- assistance identifying thoughts and emotions that are unsettling
- learning to express thoughts and emotions
- validation of anger and depression
- information on how to sponsor friends and family members.

Potential Resources Required
- counselling or help to deal with anger and depression
- help finding or creating mutual aid or support groups to serve as surrogate families
- information on self care.

Time Period: 3 to 5 years

Thoughts and Feelings
- realization that there has been a permanent shift in values, practices and norms
- sense of social dislocation sets in
- stress
- uncertainty about self and future
- withdrawal from friends, family and community
- search for stability, control and new coping mechanisms
- questioning of self and resources
- perhaps a loss in self-esteem
- mourning what was left behind
- desire to return to what is familiar.

Issues and Needs
- physical manifestations of uncertainty, stress and dislocation set in (e.g., colds, flus, aches, pains, difficulty eating and sleeping, etc.)

- negative coping mechanisms developed (e.g., withdrawal from friends and family, substance use, idealization of former home)
- conflict with friends, family and community.

Resources Required
- assistance dealing with symptoms of social dislocation
- help establishing realistic goals and objectives to be achieved
- ongoing help establishing ties to former achievements
- ongoing help finding new challenges and activities
- ongoing help assessing skills, resources and knowledge
- ongoing introduction of new ideas and opportunities
- monitoring of psycho-social status
- referral to appropriate services
- assistance and advocacy accessing services.

Potential Resources Required
- ongoing counselling or help to deal with loss
- ongoing help finding or creating mutual aid or support groups
- ongoing provision of information on self care.

Time Period: 5 years onwards

Thoughts and Feelings
- sense of belonging, happiness
- resolution to new life and new home
- realistic expectations established
- hope.

Issues and Needs
- have friends, interests and structure in life.

Resources Required
- ongoing orientation to services and society .
- becomes a resource.

Potential Resources Required
- orientation to rights and responsibilities as member of a larger society.

Please note that refugees, like immigrants, integrate at different rates. The timelines given here may therefore vary. Also note that if health and human service needs of refugees are not met in the earlier stages of the integration process, the resources required to meet health and their needs in the later part of the integration process will be greater.

IN-SETTLEMENT COMMUNITY PROFILE

General Description

- first generation
- emigrated to Canada between 1920s and 1960s
- integrated economically into mainstream but not politically or socially
- developed own service organizations, recreational clubs and mutual aid groups
- health and human service needs traditionally met within the community
- heavily dependent on professionals (e.g., medical) in the community
- retained or revived values, practices and beliefs from original home
  (e.g., alcohol consumption patterns)
- most have had little access to language training and have limited fluency
  in English or French.

Issues
- aging population
- in some groups and families, status is lost as a result of aging (e.g., opinions are no longer considered valid)
- fears around aging (e.g., does not want to become a burden on the family)
- in other groups and families, status is gained with age (e.g., experiences are finally considered important)
- happiness over aging process (e.g., getting the respect deserved)
- adjustments to changing roles in both cases
- loss of family, friends and peers becomes a reality
- development of coping mechanisms to deal with grief
- as the aging process continues, there may be isolation from family
  or smothering by family
- family responsibilities shift
- illness may set in
- substance use may occur or increase.

Needs
- recognition by family, friends and community of emotional and
  physical changes associated with aging
- recreational and social activities or the expansion of existing recreational
  and social activities
- opportunities to explore and develop skills and interests
- reinforcement of relationships with peers
- connection with past self.

Resources Required
- assistance seeking or developing services

- opportunities to participate in recreational activities, socialize and talk about life
- support in a family or community setting where programs are culturally and linguistically appropriate
- therapy for those suffering from depression, grief and loss of status
- work with medical profession to reach out to those in need.

General Description

- second generation
- children of immigrants who came between the 1920s and 1960s
- may see themselves as belonging to two worlds
- are also integrated economically and, to a certain extent, politically but may choose not to be integrated socially
- may still remain tied to own service organizations, recreational clubs and mutual-aid groups
- dependence on professionals (e.g., medical) in community remains
- active in supporting the development of health and human services in own community so that community needs can be met within traditional structures
- retained many of their parents' values, practices and beliefs but may have also taken on new ones
- most often fluently bilingual.

Issues
- may feel caught between two worlds sometimes, and at other times happy with the duality
- "sandwich generation" involved in taking care of parents as well as children
- stress over this role
- guilt over not being able to care for aging parents or other family members
- grief over loss of parents and other family members
- depression over inability to cope with guilt and grief
- anger and frustration which is not expressed
- development of positive and negative coping mechanisms to deal with stress and lack of service (e.g., spending more time with friends and peers, substance use or increased substance use).

Needs
- community support for those in "sandwich" role
- information on self care
- may need health and human services not traditionally provided within community
- new programs provided by existing community services (e.g., stress reduction, health promotion, etc.)

- opportunities to explore and develop interest and skills outside of
  family and community
- new and different recreational activities
- reinforcement of relationships with peers.

Resources Required
- assistance seeking or developing services
- opportunities to participate in recreational activities, socialize and talk about life
- support in a family or community setting where programs are culturally and
  linguistically appropriate
- therapy for those suffering stress, frustration and anger
- work with medical profession to reach out to those in need.

General Description

- third generation
- grandchildren of those who emigrated between the 1920s and 1960s
- similar to parents but are economically, politically and socially integrated
- may retain strong recreational ties to their communities but also have
  recreational ties in the mainstream.

SYNOPSIS OF ETHNIC, LINGUISTIC, RACIAL, RELIGIOUS AND SPIRITUAL MINORITY EXPERIENCES

Time in Life: Early Childhood (1 to 7 years)

Thoughts and Feelings
- development of sense of self
- identification of ethnicity, language, race, religion or spirituality as an asset or barrier
- understanding of self as unique or different.

Issues and Needs
- positive image of self reinforced
- education about ethnic, linguistic, racial, religious or spiritual background
- recreational and social activities reflective of a variety of values, practices
  and norms.

Resources Required
- role models of same ethnic, linguistic, racial, religious or spiritual background
- opportunities to get to know others who are the same or different
- discussion of the value of difference.

Time in Life: Late Childhood (7 to 13 years)

Thoughts and Feelings
- understanding of how the dominant group views ethnic, linguistic, racial, religious and spiritual minorities develops
- desire to identify with these views, whether they are positive or negative
- need to assert self
- experiences with being the "other" or with discrimination may occur. This may result in the internalization of the experience or an expressed reaction
- lowering (or reinforcement) of self-esteem at being "other" or different.

Issues and Needs
- validation of experiences
- positive reinforcement of self image
- outlets to express anger, frustration, joy, pride, etc.
- help identifying talents, skills, resources and individuality
- assistance learning to assert self in positive way.

Resources Required
- people in authority who understand how it feels to be a minority and can facilitate discussion around it (e.g., teachers, family, friends, counsellors etc.)
- parental love and support
- more exposure to peers who are the same and different
- more education around the value of diversity
- corrective action when "otherness" or discrimination is encountered.

Time Period: Adolescence

Thoughts and Feelings
- systemic discrimination may be encountered
- direct challenge to discrimination or denial of its existence
- desire to identify with – or separate from – own ethnic, linguistic, racial, religious or spiritual group
- unexpressed anger and frustration with self or society
- experimentation with coping mechanisms, both positive and negative (e.g., overachievement, acting out)
- sense of social dislocation at not being able to cope or sense of power at being able to cope.

Issues and Needs
- to take control of life
- be recognized as an individual
- assert self.

Resources Required
- opportunities to change environment
  (e.g., organizing a human rights day)
- reinforcement of positive self image through popular culture
  (e.g., television, music magazines, etc.)
- social activities that increase self-esteem
- validation of individuality
- support or peer groups to discuss experiences
- corrective measures when discrimination is encountered.

Time Period: Adulthood

Thoughts and Feelings
- sense of self develops and matures
- desire to recognize and live with being an ethnic, linguistic,
  racial, religious or spiritual minority
- ability to challenge or accept one's "otherness" or differences
- development of coping mechanisms to deal with the dominant groups'
  view of ethnic, linguistic, racial, religious or spiritual minorities.

Issues and Needs
- coping mechanisms may be negative
  (e.g., withdrawal from society, deviant behavior, etc.)
- may be barriers to self-fulfilment
- may be unexpressed frustration and anger.
OR
- view of self may be positive
- desire to educate others about one's "otherness" or differences
- barriers to self-fulfilment may exist in larger society but
  individual has resources to deal with these barriers.

Resources Required
- help understanding discrimination
- help identifying and changing negative coping mechanisms
- help identifying personal and social resources
- help in assessing personal assets and skills
- empowerment through education, political and
  social action
- counselling
- support groups
- participation in activities where anger, frustration, joy, etc.,
  may be expressed.

SERVICES AVAILABLE TO CULTURALLY AND RACIALLY DIVERSE COMMUNITIES

Services available to culturally and racially diverse communities are listed in the service directories, phone books and information centres in every community. Description of various services offered are provided here for your information.

i) *Social and Recreational Clubs:* These organizations not only offer social and recreational activities to specific ethno-cultural and ethno-racial groups but also act as mutual support groups and community mobilization and action centres for the populations they serve.

ii) *Settlement Services:* These organizations provide support, language training, information, family and individual counselling and assistance to groups and individuals during the settlement process – which usually lasts three to five years.

iii) *Reception Centres:* These organizations serve the immediate social, psychological and physical needs of newcomers to Canada. Many are actual hostels or shelters for newcomers.

iv) *Multicultural Associations:* These organizations are usually umbrella groups active in developing and disseminating information, programs and services that can be used by all of their members.

v) *Ethno-specific Agencies:* These organizations are specifically geared to meet the social service needs of a particular ethno-cultural/ethno-racial community. There is a great deal of variation in ethno-specific agencies. Some serve large populations, and are well resourced with large staffs; others who serve smaller communities are continually fundraising and have limited staff but many volunteers.

vi) *Multi-ethnic Agencies:* These organizations are specifically geared to meet the social service needs of many ethno-cultural/ethno-racial communities. Some may exclusively serve ethno-cultural/ethno-racial groups with common geographic, linguistic or racial origins, while others may try to serve as many populations as they can.

vii) *Ethno-specific or Multi-ethnic Mental Health Services:* These organizations are specifically geared to meet the mental health needs of a particular ethno-cultural/ethno-racial community or set of communities.

viii) *Literacy and English/French As A Second Language Services:* These organizations not only provide literacy and E/FSL services to newcomers, they also act as meeting places where knowledge, information and friendship are exchanged.

ix) *Training and Development Centres:* These organizations provide life skills training and professional upgrading for the unemployed or underemployed, many of whom are newcomers.

x) *Multi-service Legal Clinics:* These organizations not only provide legal services but also help in obtaining workers' compensation, social assistance benefits and housing.

xii) *Community Information Centres:* These organizations serve as clearinghouses of information and experiences about community-based agencies. Some are specifically geared to the information service needs of ethno-cultural/ethno-racial communities.

xiii) *Interfaith Groups and Spiritual Communities:* These organizations provide a variety of social services to members of their faith and others.

xiv) *Cultural Interpreter Programs:* These organizations facilitate cultural understanding and provide linguistic translation between non-English/French speaking service users and English/French speaking service providers.

xv) *Host Programs:* These organizations match "old" and "new" Canadians for friendship and support.

xvi) *Advocacy and education organizations:* These organizations educate society about the social, political and economic issues facing immigrants, refugees, insettlement populations and minority groups. They also advocate social change to create more equity.

USING A CARE MAP

A care map is a tool that can be used to develop a holistic addictions counselling program for culturally and racially diverse populations. It has 12 sections, all of which are intended to help the service provider determine the thoughts and feelings of their clients, identify their specific health and human service needs and match or provide them with the appropriate resources. Service providers may also find care maps useful in managing their case loads for culturally and racially diverse clients.

WHAT A CARE MAP LOOKS LIKE

Name of client: _____

Status: Immigrant, Refugee, In-settlement, Ethnic, Linguistic, Racial, Religious or Spiritual Minority.

Problems
presented: As determined by the client.

Potential underlying causes:	As identified by service provider from his/her interactions with the client. Use the descriptions of the health and human service needs of culturally and racially diverse populations included in this chapter to determine the potential underlying causes.
Significant relationships:	As identified by the client.
Current life situation:	As determined by the client.
Potential services needed:	As identified by the service provider from his/her interactions with the client. Use the descriptions of the health and human service needs of culturally and racially diverse populations included in this chapter to determine the potential services needed.
Type of service contacted:	_____
Role of service provider:	As negotiated between the service provider and the client. i.e., will the service provider function as a facilitator, an expert, an advisor, etc.
Wellness schedule:	This is a time-limited counselling program developed by the service provider in consultation with the client.
Referral to other agencies:	Consult the list of services available to culturally and racially diverse populations included in this chapter.
Follow-up:	_____

Example of a Care Map for an Immigrant Client

Name:	An Li Xing
Status:	Immigrant, from China. In early 30s. Has been in Canada for two years.
Problems presented:	Arguments with husband, children misbehaving at school, inability to sleep. Has seen a doctor about stress. He prescribed sleeping pills for her, which she uses occasionally. She, however, feels that she is becoming psychologically dependent on them.

Potential underlying causes:	Left China just before the Tiananmen Square Massacre. Has some guilt about leaving. Expectations of a new and better life in Canada not met. There is a loss in socio-economic status and an inability to connect with past achievements and positive aspects of former life.
Significant relationships:	Husband and children. Relationships with husband and children have changed significantly since moving to Canada. Relationship with husband no longer equal. Her children no longer regard her as an expert or guide in their lives; they have become dependent on their peers.
Current life situation:	Was a chemistry professor in China. Her PhD is not recognized in Canada. She is currently working as a research assistant in a university lab. She is her family's income provider. Her husband is a post-doctoral fellow working towards a tenure-track job so he does not have much time for his family. She has few recreational opportunities and does not spend as much time as she would like with her family. She speaks academic English well but is unfamiliar with colloquial English. She therefore spends most of her time with other Chinese immigrants. Most of them, like her, live and work in an academic setting.
Type of service contacted:	International student counselling centre.
Potential service needs:	Assessment of her use of sleeping pills. Discussion of intervention and treatment options. Help choosing an option. Help assessing skills, resources and knowledge. Help re-establishing expectations. Help setting new goals and objectives. Language and life skills training for professionals. New contacts in the Chinese and larger community. Recreational opportunities for self and family. Perhaps couple or family therapy to deal with changing roles.
Role of service provider:	Friend and facilitator. Begins helping An Li by listening to her family problems and helping her work through them. Refers her to other services but maintains regular contact through phone calls and scheduled visits.
Wellness schedule:	Six-month program. In months one to three, An Li's service provider finds a play therapy group for her and her children, identifies language training and life skills program for her, helps her plan recreational activities and refers her to social and recreational clubs.

An Li makes a contract with service provider to come in once a month to discuss her life situation, to set aside two weekends a month for social and recreational activities and to sign up for language training and life skills. With the help of her service provider, she learns some behavioral change techniques to reduce her use of sleeping pills.

In months three to six, An Li continues counselling and language and life skills training. Now her service provider refers her to a career counselling centre for immigrant women to discuss her future life and work plans, helps her set goals and objectives for upgrading her education, and encourages her to connect with professional associations. As she begins to develop new expectations and hope, her use of sleeping pills stops.

An Li's relationship with her husband, however, does not improve and her service provider suggests marital therapy, which she rejects. Her service provider lets her know that the option is always open to her.

Referrals: ESL/Life skills classes, social and recreational clubs, ethno-specific agencies, training and development centre.

Follow-up: One phone call a month for the next six months to monitor life situation and psycho-social status.

Example of a Care Map for a Refugee Client

Name: Mohammed Omar-Nur

Status: Refugee claimant from Somalia. In mid-40s. Has been in Canada for 10 months and is still waiting to have his claim heard. Before that, lived in refugee camp in Egypt.

Problems
presented: Complains of not feeling physically well. Depression. Expression of anger and frustration towards service providers. Reports inability to sleep and eat. Use of alcohol while socializing with other Somalis, during meals and before bedtime. Does not use much alcohol, only one to two drinks per day but, prior to coming to Canada, did not drink or believe in drinking. Feels guilty about drinking but considers it his one pleasure. Has gone to Alcoholics Anonymous but is uncomfortable with their approach. Hears that there is a pill to control alcohol use and wants to know how he can get it.

Potential underlying causes:	Refugee claimant living in limbo. Left Somalia hoping to send for family but lost touch with family after reaching Egypt. Lived in refugee camp where he was assaulted and possibly raped. Grief and guilt about leaving family behind. Experience in camp created a loss of dignity. Mourning loss of family and self. Constant fear for safety. Uncertainty about present and about future.
Significant relationships:	Few significant relationships. Has connected up with other middle-aged Somali men who are alone in Canada.
Current life status:	Was a teacher in Somalia, is now driving a taxi. Speaks limited English. Reluctant to socialize but is very lonely. Limited contact with people outside of work and few friends.
Type of service contacted:	Alcohol and drug assessment and referral centre.
Potential service needs:	Accurate information about alcohol use. Determination of whether alcohol use is problematic. Discussion of intervention and treatment option. Identify level of motivation for dealing with problem, if any. Help choosing an option, if help is desired. Legal assistance. Thorough assessment of pre-arrival experience by mental health service provider who understands post-traumatic stress disorder. Referral to appropriate mental health services. Language and life skills training. Assistance identifying thoughts and emotions that are unsettling. Learning to express thoughts and emotions. Validation of anger and depression. Establishment of connection to old life.
Role of service provider:	Advisor and advocate. Begins helping Mohammed by referring him to a legal aid clinic to discuss his refugee status. Finds him a self change program at a treatment centre to control his alcohol use and an ad hoc support group for refugees at a reception centre. Offers to provide him with help and information as needed. Intervenes on his behalf with other service providers.
Wellness schedule:	One-year program. In months one to five, Mohammed's service provider refers him to a mental health agency that has experience dealing with refugees suffering from post-traumatic stress disorder. There is a waiting list to get an assessment and a waiting list for the agency's refugee program. His service provider convinces the agency to do an assessment and then helps him to identify some immediate issues he would like to deal with and refers him to a family counselling service for therapy, which he discontinues.

In months six to eight, Mohammed is still waiting to get into the refugee program. He continues with his self change program and goes to his support group. While he waits, his service provider helps him identify language, life skills and vocational training he would like to undertake. Helps Mohammed register for training programs (i.e., filling out forms). Puts him in touch with an international aid organization that can help him find out about his family. Urges him to participate in the social activities sponsored by his self change program and support group.

By months eight to 12, Mohammed is in the refugee program and attending a job re-training program. He feels his drinking is under control but he still feels isolated. His service provider refers him to a "host program" where he is matched with a family that helps him feel more integrated.

Referral to other agencies:	Legal clinic, addiction service, settlement agency, community counselling centre, mental health service, training and skills development centre, host program.
Follow-up:	Mohammed is encouraged to check in with service provider periodically.

Example of a Care Map for an In-settlement Client

Name:	Dominica Arano
Status:	Homemaker and homeworker. Second-generation Italian-Canadian in early 50s.
Problems presented:	Trouble sleeping. Stressed. Difficulty dealing with mother's recent death and father's increasing frailty and alcohol use. Concerned about losing control over her life. Cannot seem to relax and has anxiety attacks. At the same time, her husband has just retired and her children are leaving home. Has discussed her issues with her priest, siblings and doctor. No one seems very sympathetic. Doctor has prescribed anti-depressants; she has not yet taken any, but is tempted to – just to see what they will do.
Potential underlying causes:	Grief over mother's death, while having to care for father, who is angry, depressed and verbally abusive, especially when he starts drinking. Guilt over not being able to properly care for father. Desire to have someone else care for him. Tired of being her father's cook,

friend, nurse and translator. Confusion about changes in wife and mother role as children leave home. Depression over inability to cope, feels that depression will last forever.

Significant relationships:	Husband and children. Relationship with husband has changed significantly since he sold his butchershop and retired. Places more demands on her attention. Children need her less and less, no longer her helpers or allies in the family. At the same time, her father needs more time. Creates conflicts with husband. Husband deals with conflict by drinking and socializing with friends. She deals with conflict by avoiding it.

Current life status:

Lives in a small community near a larger urban centre. Leads a comfortable life. Was a garment worker before she married, then became a homemaker, is now a homeworker, making wedding and bridesmaid dresses for friends and neighbors when she wants. She enjoys working and does not feel that she has enough time for this. She is fluently bilingual in English and Italian but feels more comfortable living and socializing in the Italian-Canadian community.

Potential service needs:

Information about emotional and physical changes associated with aging. Information about alcohol use and the elderly. Information about anti-depressants. Culturally appropriate therapy to deal with loss and grief. Culturally appropriate senior support care for father. Regular recreational activities with her husband. Contact with other women in a similar situation.

Type of service contacted:

Seniors support service.

Role of service provider:

Expert, mediator and parent. Begins helping Dominica by providing her with information about why she feels the way that she does and why her father and her husband are acting the way that they do. Refers her to a doctor who discusses the proper use of anti-depressants and helps her decide whether to use them. (She decides to use them for a limited period of time, six to eight months.) Sympathizes with her over her difficulties.

Wellness schedule:

Eight-month program. Few programs are specifically geared to the health and human service needs of Italian-Canadians in Dominica's community. In months one to five, Dominica's service provider arranges to have a senior support worker visit her father. This worker has little experience with Italian-Canadian seniors but, from information Dominica provides, is able to give adequate care. Her service provider then finds a family counselling service in the community and helps her become comfortable with the idea of seeking therapy. Dominica's service provider also tries to make her potential therapist more understanding of Dominica's cultural background. Later, her service provider identifies a culturally appropriate service in the nearby urban centre and encourages her to try both services.

In months six to eight, Dominica begins therapy, first with the culturally-appropriate service but later (because of the long drive) switches to the local counselling service. She also starts scheduling time with her husband. Although she still feels out of control, she does not feel she needs to take the anti-depressants anymore and her relationships with both her father and husband improve.

Referral to other agencies: Family counselling services, Italian-Canadian service, seniors support group.

Follow-up: Monthly phone calls to check on father's welfare and Dominica's well-being. Provision of information and advice on how to deal with seniors and substance use.

Example of a Care Map for a Minority Client

Name: Kurpinder "Kirk" Singh

Status: Sikh-Canadian in mid-20s who identifies himself as a person of color.

Problems presented: Seeking help for recreational cannabis use. Motivated to stop. Feels a need to take control of his life and that stopping his cannabis use is one way to do this.

Potential underlying causes: Anger at parents for not understanding that he feels caught between two cultures, the traditional Sikh culture and mainstream Canadian culture. Frustration with friends who seem to either reject their Sikh heritage or embrace it without question. Outrage at mainstream society for not accepting the fact that he can be both a Sikh and a Canadian. Has experienced racial and religious discrimination throughout his life and feels a sense of social dislocation as a result of it.

Significant relationships:	Few significant relationships. Lives with family in the heart of a suburban Sikh community but feels alienated from family and Sikh friends. Spends most of his time watching television, "hanging out" and attending sports events with co-workers who are also minorities.
Current life status:	Graduated from university four years ago with Computer Science degree but was unable to find work with a major company because of his insistence that he be allowed to wear his turban. Instead he found a job in a university computer lab where the work was more stimulating and he seemed to be accepted for himself. It was through his co-workers that he was introduced to recreational cannabis use. While he enjoys the effects of cannabis and does not feel he has a problem, he wants to stop – it is costing him too much, creating suspicions at home and aggravating an asthma condition.
Type of service contacted:	Community health centre.
Potential service needs:	Determination of extent of cannabis use and the interventions or treatment necessary. Forum for expressing anger, frustrations and outrage. Help identifying personal and social resources. Validation of experiences with discrimination.
Role of service provider:	Referral agent.
Wellness schedule:	None created. Because Kirk was motivated, he was referred to an outpatient facility, provided with information about racism and self-esteem and advised to contact a race relations organization to discuss his experiences with discrimination.
Referral to other agencies:	Outpatient facility.
Follow-up:	None.

CONCLUSION

The purpose of this chapter was to outline strategies and tactics for addiction service providers working with culturally and racially diverse populations. Since there is no one way of working with these groups, it is important that service providers understand the basic rules of cultural/racial sensitivity; know about the various services that are available to culturally and racially diverse communities; and be aware of the general health and human service needs of immigrants, refugees, in-settlement populations and minority groups.

FOOTNOTES

Information for the chapter has been compiled from interviews with service providers at:

Abrigo Centre for Victims of Family Violence
Access Alliance Multicultural Community Health Centre
Costi Family Counselling Centre
Canadian Centre for Victims of Torture
Hong Fook Mental Health Centre
Metro Toronto Addiction Assessment and Referral Centre
Multicultural Association of Thunder Bay
Scarborough Cultural Interpreters

REFERENCES

Access Action Council. <u>Aging in a Multicultural Society.</u> Toronto: Social Planning Council of Metropolitan Toronto.

Bhaggityia, Sri & Brand, Dionne. <u>Rivers Have Sources, Trees Have Roots.</u> Toronto: Cross Cultural Communications Centre, 1985.

Galway, Janis. <u>Immigrant Settlement Counselling.</u> Toronto: Ontario Council of Agencies Serving Immigrants, 1991.

James, Carl. <u>Seeing Ourselves: An Exploration of Culture, Ethnicity and Race.</u> Brampton: Sheridan College Press, 1991.

Masi, Ralph. "Multiculturalism Medicine and Health Parts 1–5" in <u>Canadian Family Physician,</u> 1988.

Ontario Ministry of Citizenship. <u>Cultural Interpreter Training Manual.</u> Toronto: Queen's Park Printer, 1989.

Addiction and the Family

RICHARD J. BOUDREAU

WHY INVOLVE THE FAMILY

*T*here is still a widespread view of addiction, even among counsellors, as a problem that primarily afflicts the individual. There may be some recognition that others around the person are affected, but not necessarily in the sense that they may be playing a role in maintaining the addiction or, more importantly, could be a vital asset in its resolution.

Such views persist despite growing evidence that family and other social supports are key factors in addictions intervention. Although the role of other family members will vary in each given situation, it remains true that addiction problems generally develop within a family context. And research findings suggest that involving the family to some extent in treatment contributes to a better outcome.

A basic tenet of family counselling is that whatever happens to one member of the family affects all the other members, and similarly, the response of the other members in turn affects the original member in question. This fundamental principle of family work holds true not only in terms of a family's weaknesses and deficits, but more importantly, in relation to its strengths. And it is an implicit assumption of this brief chapter that any work involving family at any level should, despite the recognition in many cases of notable deficits, address and build upon family strengths.

Clearly then, the family represents a primary setting where issues of addiction are manifested. It is also a context where problems related to addiction are either successfully dealt with or inadvertently reinforced and perpetuated. For this reason, any treatment intervention that neglects this important dimension may, at the very least, miss out on potent treatment strategies, or at worst, work against itself by ignoring factors that often contribute to relapse. Most addictions counsellors can likely recall having successfully intervened with an individual only to have her or him relapse upon return to an unchanged family environment.

WHAT IT MEANS TO INVOLVE FAMILIES

Many mental health and social services, in promoting their work, advertise that they "see families" or "work with families" or "counsel families." What does it mean?

Work with families can involve an array of services ranging from basic orientation to long-term in-depth family therapy. The family might merely be oriented to the program in which an addicted family member is enrolled, or might embark upon a carefully developed regimen of family therapy, or something in between. This would be determined on the basis of the assessed family needs and resources available to meet them. Table 1 below outlines four categories of family involvement with suggested levels of interventions and related objectives. It should be noted that these are broad categories with numerous possible varieties within each.

TABLE 1

TYPES OF FAMILY INVOLVEMENT	LEVEL OF INTERVENTIONS	OBJECTIVES
Family Orientation	Orienting the family to the philosophy and approaches of the service.	To inform the family about the program that the identified patient is embarking upon, and to enlist family support.
Parenting/family education group	Involving parents and/or families in family life education with special reference to substance abuse issues.	To inform family members about family relations issues, and how they may be relevant to substance abuse.
Family counselling	Contracting with the family for interventions aimed at resolving specifically identified problems.	To bring about the resolution of problems identified by family members, and related to the substance abuse.
Family therapy	Contracting with the family for interventions aimed at chronic and systemic family dysfunction.	To bring about change to elusive and intractable areas of systemic family dysfunction related to the substance abuse.

In addition to the services outlined above, which would typically be offered in family and social-service agencies, family issues are also addressed by a growing array of mutual help groups such as AlAnon, Children of Alcoholics Groups (COA), Parents Against Drugs (PAD), etc. Many agencies that work primarily from an individual perspective collaborate with such groups in having family issues addressed during therapy. It would be a mistake to assume that because a service is not set up to do formal family counselling or family therapy, it should therefore not undertake any family work. The evidence would indicate that very important and very effective changes can be brought about through simple but well-developed educational programs, especially with families presenting early-stage addictions problems.

A very important distinction needs to be made in working with families with an addiction problem. This is whether the problem with addiction lies with the parent(s) or in one (or more) of the children. And a growing number of families are presenting with addictions issues in both generations.

Whether the problem is in the parenting or offspring generation will have important bearing on issues such as the following:

- Should the focus of the family work be primarily on marital or parental matters?
- Which family members most significantly need to be involved in the family sessions?
- If there are substance abuse issues in both generations, will they be addressed separately or together?

Decision-making around such important matters will vary greatly from family to family. For example, in the situation referred to above, where there is substance abuse in both generations, important factors to consider would be: the worker's experience and ability to deal with both generations; and the advantages and disadvantages of dealing with each generation conjointly or concurrently; or of each generation being seen by separate workers collaboratively. The unique circumstances of each case will help determine the best approach.

Everything said to this point should make clear the importance of a comprehensive assessment in determining precisely what will be required in terms of family work for a given family. This will vary considerably from situation to situation depending on factors such as the following:

- What is the history and extent of the substance abuse? Is it early-stage or long-standing? Is there evidence that the family, to a great extent, organizes around addiction?
- Does a comprehensive assessment suggest that the substance abuse is inextricably tied in with other marital/family dysfunction? Are other possibly more serious family problems being displaced upon the identified substance abuser?

- If family work is indicated, should it take place concurrently and conjointly? Should the substance abuse be brought under control before marital/family work is initiated? Which family members should make up the sessions?
- Will all the work be done in the one facility, or will the family work be referred to another service?

These are some of the essential questions that need to be addressed in determining the nature and extent of family work that may be required in conjunction with or in addition to specific addictions management interventions.

WHO SHOULD WORK WITH FAMILIES

Once a comprehensive assessment has established that family work will be required, and what the nature and level of that work might be, then it must be determined who will do the work.

A major consideration in determining this is the mandate of the service of initial contact. Does its range of services include family services? Or is its mandate restricted to assessment/referral, primary care, detoxification, individual treatment modalities, etc.?

Given that family work is within the general mandate of the service, another important consideration is the range of skills available within the staff to carry out the level of family involvement that is indicated. And not only do the skills of individual staff need to be clearly assessed; the combined resources of the agency to carry out family work need to be determined. These would include factors such as service hours to accommodate the school and work schedules of family members; agency attitudes and philosophies regarding family influence on addiction; the opportunities for collaborative work among staff, which can be critical in family work; etc. Such factors are important not only in terms of client service, but also in the ongoing assessment of staff and agency development needs in this important area of addictions intervention.

If a referral outside the agency of initial contact is indicated, the referring agency should have a thorough knowledge of family resources available in the community. This represents a key juncture in the treatment process for a number of reasons. It is at this point that some worker or agency must assume primary care responsibilities for the client and her/his family, so that continuity of care and linkages between agencies can be maintained and co-ordinated. At this point, decisions must also be made about division of roles and responsibilities. Will the addictions management and family work be done concurrently or successively? Will it be done within the same or different agencies? By one or more workers? How these co-ordinating and referring (and follow-up) functions are carried out determines to a great extent whether the clients and their families remain and progress in treatment. Without effective co-ordination, usually assumed by a primary care worker, clients can easily become entangled and lost within even a fairly simple treatment system.

It should be noted that there is still a great deal of debate in the addictions field about the optimum timing of family work in the treatment of addiction. Whether it can go on while the substance abuse is being addressed, or whether it can only begin once the substance abuse is well under control continues to be argued. Many important factors enter into this debate, including:

- the extent and duration of the substance abuse
- the level of deterioration in the marital/family relationships due to the substance abuse
- the possible presence of family violence associated with the substance abuse
- the willingness of spouses or other family members to be involved before the substance abuse has been brought under control.

Again, these issues need to be clarified by a comprehensive assessment. Beyond that, and for our purposes here, suffice it to say that it is crucial that there be clarity between collaborating agencies about philosophies and policies regarding this whole area of timing of family work, so that families seeking service are not encumbered by this ongoing debate.

HOW TO WORK WITH THE FAMILY

It is well beyond the scope of this chapter to present in detail all the various schools and approaches to family counselling and family therapy in the treatment of addiction. This information is readily available in many related resources. It is important, however, for addictions counsellors to have some working knowledge of the major approaches broadly identified as structural, strategic, behavioral and multigenerational models of family treatment. Such knowledge allows the worker to make more informed decisions in matching clients and their families, not only in terms of the level of family work required, but also in regard to the model or approach that may be most compatible with a given family. For example (without invoking a hard and fast stance in these matters) one could expect that a family that appears to respond well to concrete contractual assignments would perhaps do better with a behavioral model of family therapy ; or a more multigenerational/Bowenian model might seem a more appropriate choice where substance abuse in a given family has had a clear multigenerational history and influence. Table 2 highlights the four major schools of family treatment, with their underlying theories and major objectives.

TABLE 2

MODEL/APPROACH	UNDERLYING THEORY	FOCUS OF INTERVENTION
Structural	Theory of family relations in terms of proximity/distance and designated boundaries.	Restructuring of interactions between family members.
Strategic	Problem solving theory.	Resolving presenting problem through assignment of therapeutic tasks, directives and prescriptions.
Behavioral	Social learning theory.	Modification of family behavior through contracted changes in behavior of individual members.
Multigenerational/ Bowenian	Intergenerational dynamics theory.	Resolution of individual member's role within the extended family system.

Regardless of what level of family intervention is indicated, or what modality of family work is finally adopted, three fundamental elements have been found to enhance and contribute to the effectiveness of family treatment.

The first would be the importance of identifying and promoting family strengths. Many families present with a diminished sense of their abilities and strengths because of their failure to resolve the identified problem(s) on their own. No individual or family is left devoid of all strengths or skills, no matter how intense or chronic the problem at hand may be. It is incumbent upon the effective family worker to help identify these family resources, no matter how compromised they may be under the circumstances, and develop strategies and interventions that build upon them. For example, a family may retain good problem-solving skills in other areas of life such as money management or the upkeep of the home, but be unable to bring these skills to bear on the problem of substance abuse. An important dimension of family work in such a case might be to reinforce these skills, and enable the family to apply them to the area of substance abuse.

Closely related to the question of building upon family strengths is the importance of mobilizing family members to do their own problem solving. In the final analysis, the most effective family treatment is one where family members hardly recognize that the counsellor had any part in solving their problems.

Finally, almost all the literature on family counselling and family therapy encourages a team approach to this work. Even very basic work with families can become somewhat involved and taxing to an individual working alone. A team approach – which might be as minimal as regular consultation with colleagues, or as elaborate as that provided by observation mirrors and highly technical feedback equipment – provides many assets, including a range of insights into complex family dynamics, support to the worker, rich resources to the family, ongoing monitoring of treatment effectiveness of the individual and the agency, and a continuous atmosphere of learning and development of the team members.

CHECKLIST FOR DECISION-MAKING ABOUT FAMILY INCLUSION

By way of conclusion and summary, the following represents a line of questioning that addictions workers might follow in deciding whether or how to include the family in their approach to addictions management.

- Is the identified client in the parenting or offspring generation? Is there substance abuse in both generations?
- Is the substance abuse of recent origin or long-standing?
- Is there evidence that the family is organized around substance abuse? Are there indications that other family problems or dysfunctions are displaced onto the identified substance abuser?
- What level of family involvement is indicated? Will a strategy of family support and education be adequate, or will a more structured regimen of family treatment be required?
- Given the characteristics of the identified client, and other family members, what model or approach of family treatment (structured, strategic, behavioral or intergenerational) would seem most appropriate?
- Who will undertake the family work? Will it be done by the worker/ agency of initial contact? Or will it be referred to a specialized worker/ agency?
- If referred, who will assume the responsibility for ensuring that the family becomes effectively engaged, and that proper linkages are maintained between involved agencies from assessment through follow-up?
- In terms of specific strategies of family treatment, are they based on identified areas of family strengths? Are strategies planned to clearly empower the family to identify and resolve its own problem(s)? And finally, is the family work organized to make the best use of the competencies, experience and support of the entire treatment team?

GENERAL REFERENCES AND RECOMMENDED READING

The following references are provided to enable further exploration of the subject. The brief notations indicate the technical level and comprehensiveness of the individual items.

Boudreau, R. (1982). Alcohol abuse and the family system. Canada's Mental Health, 30, (17–18). (Brief introduction to the topic.)

Kaufman, E. (1985). Family systems and family therapy of substance abuse: An overview of two decades of research and clinical experience. The International Journal of the Addictions, 20, (897–916). (A readable summary that outlines the research and clinical issues.)

Paolino, T. & McCrady, B. (1977). The alcoholic marriage: alternative perspectives. New York: Grune & Stratton, 1977. (Provides an important comprehensive background to the subject.)

Pearlman, S. (1988). Systems theory and alcoholism. In C.D. Chaudron & D.A. Wilkinson (Eds.), Theories on alcoholism (pp. 289–324). Toronto: Addiction Research Foundation, 1988. (A comprehensive and detailed analysis of the topic.)

Stanton, M.D., Todd, T. et.al. (1982). The family therapy of drug abuse and addiction. New York: The Guilford Press, 1982. (A thorough and well-presented treatment of the subject.)

Steinglass, P. et. al. (1987). The alcoholic family. New York: Basic Books, 1987. (A very detailed analysis of important research questions related to the topic.)

Usher, M., Jeffrey, J. & Glass, D. (1982). Family therapy as a treatment modality for alcoholism. Journal of Studies on Alcohol, 43, (927–938). (Good clinical overview of issues involved in a family approach to alcoholism.)

Weidman, A. (1985). Engaging the families of substance abusing adolescents in family therapy. Journal of Substance Abuse Treatment, 2, (97–105). (A practical and clinically-based approach to the subject.)

Wermuth, L., Scheidt, S. (1986). Enlisting family support in drug treatment. Family Process, 25, (25–33). (Authors describe a practical application of a psycho-educational approach with families.)

Addressing

Related Issues

Sexuality, Sexual Problems, and Sexual and Physical Assault

BETTY-ANNE M. HOWARD AND DEBORAH HUDSON

INTRODUCTION

A holistic approach to addictions assessment includes sexuality. Feeling joy and connection sexually is a right of all. This sensitive and most often private area of our lives is affected physically, emotionally and relationally by substance use. In order to be sexually healthy, we must be able to feel comfortable with our bodies, protect ourselves from unwanted touch, and be able to discern what feels good and okay and what doesn't. An addiction can dull one's awareness of all these aspects of oneself. Being sexual under such circumstances could prove more than unrewarding; it could be psychologically and emotionally damaging, even abusive.

This chapter presents an overview of a wide number of issues related to sexuality. The hope is to give the reader tools to assess problems within the area of sexuality, to determine the need for referral to more specialized care, and to outline the wide range of issues that influence or interfere with one's sexual experience.

ADDRESSING THE ISSUES

ATTITUDES

We have all been affected in a variety of ways by our own personal experience, by the messages we receive through the media, by the lessons we learned from our parents, peers, school, and other people around us. No one is exempt from these influences.

For instance, what are your stereotypes for gays and lesbians? What are your feelings and knowledge about gay and lesbian sex? Do you believe that making love without intercourse is less than the ideal, or not really sex at all? Is it all right to stop lovemaking at any time because you feel uncomfortable? Is it all right for someone to choose celibacy?

It is important to notice our feelings in a counselling situation. Is the tone judgmental? Is there any sense of feeling shocked, scared, angry, grief stricken? These reactions may be clues about our own traumatic sexual experiences that need attention, or our attitudes and beliefs that need examination. For example, if you believe that sexual experience outside of marriage is wrong – even somewhat unacceptable – then when a single 24-year-old woman discusses her sexual experiences with you, you could very well pass judgment on her in many ways. Needless to say this could have a negative impact on your ability to help this client. If you were assaulted at age 17 and have blocked these feelings, a young woman talking about a rape may evoke a lot of your feelings. If you assume a client is sexually active, or knows the facts of life, or is orgasmic, or is heterosexual, you may miss an accurate description of their sexual experience.

It is important to acknowledge male and female differences in sexual needs and experiences, and society's sex-specific pressures, attitudes and judgements. For example, female alcoholics are often viewed as promiscuous. Be aware that you are probably working with a survivor of sexual abuse and that her sexual behavior is closely linked to her history. Also, female alcoholics are very vulnerable to continued sexual abuse, within a culture that still believes women ask for abuse by their behavior, dress, and where they go. There seems to be more cultural tolerance for men being sexual and inebriated. Men, on the other hand, are pressured by expectations to perform. For example, men often believe that if they are unable to obtain and maintain an erection during sex, then they are somehow inadequate. Even the word impotence – which means "lack of power" – reflects the underlying attitude that exists. This definition immediately puts a man on the defensive. His self-image demands he do anything not to seem powerless.

Our sexually-oriented culture puts pressure on relationships. Sex has been elevated to such a level of importance it is often the test of the significance of a relationship. Thus, natural differences and desires may be interpreted as signs of something fundamentally wrong with the relationship. An underlying assumption seems to be that a man, by his nature, needs sex, and a partnership will fail if a woman cannot satisfy his appetite. Relationship difficulties are sometimes labelled as sexual difficulties. As a counsellor it is important to be aware of this possibility. Rather than a "sexual problem," you may be dealing with a communication problem, or a scarcity of any physical contact, or a feeling that one partner does not have enough time for the relationship. It could be a relationship phase where emotional energy is going elsewhere such as to children, to work, or to healing from a sexual abuse history and a related addiction to drugs or alcohol.

Finally, dealing with sexuality issues can cause anxiety. Most of us were taught that sex is not something you discuss in public – that what goes on in the privacy of someone's bedroom is his or her own business. When you consider the discomfort a client may already be experiencing in discussing his or her alcohol/drug problem, and add to that an increased dose of anxiety that both the client and the counsellor may experience when discussing sexual issues, what you get at the very least are some foreseeable difficulties. One way to reduce these difficulties is for the counsellor to begin doing some personal work in this area. Initially, the goal would be to begin getting comfortable discussing and addressing sexual issues. Going to workshops on sexuality, talking to other staff and reading some of the material cited in the Resource section at the end of this chapter would be a good start. Many clinicians who have not been trained in the area of sexuality and sexual functioning tend to gloss over this topic with their clients, hoping that nothing that needs to be addressed will surface. Still others may revel in the thought of delving into someone else's sex life. Neither of these approaches is helpful or respectful towards the client.

CONSULTATION NEEDS

There may be times you need to consult with others to talk over what your client has shared with you, while of course respecting the rules of confidentiality. An exception is child sexual abuse: those who know of or suspect abuse are legally obliged to report it to the appropriate authorities. Issues you may want to discuss with a colleague are your feelings about homosexuality, sado-masochism, bisexuality, celibacy, etc. These are some of the issues you might face. An unwillingness to examine your own attitudes or any resistance to changing them can prove detrimental to the people you are trying to help.

It is not uncommon to become sexually aroused while discussing sexuality issues with clients. What is most important is that you be aware that this is happening and to tell yourself to stop. There are absolutely no situations or circumstances where it is okay to engage in any form of sexual behavior with your client. This is a violation of professional ethics and could do serious damage to your client. It is important to be clear about your own boundaries.

Boundaries serve to protect both you and your client, and enable you to work together. By boundaries we mean the respectful lines you draw between yourself and your client. It is important to acknowledge that you are a counsellor functioning in a professional role. You are not a friend, a potential date, a surrogate parent/protector or rescuer. It is important for you to be a counsellor and stay a counsellor. You are there for the client in a therapeutic role. It is not a friendship with a 50-50 exchange of energy. Acknowledge the power differential and do not abuse it. Given the sensitive and difficult nature of dealing with these types of problems, ensure that appropriate supervision is available – and used.

Action
The first step, after understanding and addressing your own attitudes and

assumptions, is to assess the problem. Given what you will come to know about the types of sexual problems that can occur and how alcohol and other drugs affect sexual response, you can begin to put this information together by asking appropriate questions to determine whether a problem exists, its nature, and the best course of action for the client. Providing a safe, nonjudgmental environment where you are able to display a certain comfort level in discussing these issues can be very effective.

Basic education may be all that is needed to solve a sexual problem. In this society we tend to shy away from teaching our children how to be loving towards their own bodies and towards a partner. As a result the learning process is often trial and error. For instance, children are often discouraged from what is perceived as inappropriate sexual self-exploration and, therefore, as adults may need encouragement to explore their own sexuality. The counsellor can guide this process with written or audiovisual information, discussion, and suggestions.

It is important to stress with clients that they need to say no to unwanted sex. It is all right to begin having sex and to change your mind and stop. To begin healing, your body needs to know you will respect its signals.

SEXUAL RESPONSE

Physiological, cognitive and cultural/social factors affect sexual response. This section will discuss the research on the physical effects of drugs and alcohol on sexual functioning. The cognitive factors include the beliefs that become part of a brain's functioning, which directs sexual response. Cultural and social factors are the sexual expectations placed on an individual because of his or her gender, race, sexual orientation, age and physical disability.

To aid in understanding the effects of alcohol and drug abuse on sexuality issues, these factors will be discussed individually.

ALCOHOL AND DRUG USE AND PHYSIOLOGICAL RESPONSE

Much of the research in this area has been conducted on animals (Wilson, 1977). It is difficult to generalize from these findings to the human population, especially since cognitive and social factors play such an important role in how we respond sexually. However, a small body of literature has examined the impact of specific chemicals on sexual performance. Doweiko (1990) provides a brief summary of this literature according to drug type (i.e. alcohol, narcotics, amphetamines and cocaine, marijuana, hallucinogenics, CNS depressants and other drugs). Doweiko points out that we are dealing in many instances here with a "chicken and egg" situation. It is very difficult to determine whether using drugs created a sexual problem or whether the sexual problem existed first and then led to the use of drugs. There is some evidence that drug use may occur as a way of dealing with a lack of adequate intimacy skills and/or other sexual problems that already exist. These observations are important to consider when working with clients.

You may be counselling on the premise that alcohol has negatively affected your client's sexual performance, but if problems continue following a period of sobriety, more intensive sex therapy may be required.

Alcohol use can lead to a decrease in a man's ability to achieve and maintain an erection (Kolodny, Masters & Johnson, 1979 and Gold, 1988) and a decrease in sexual pleasure for women (Gold, 1988; Kolodny et al., 1979). The probable basis for this is alcohol acting as a depressant on the central nervous system, thus interfering with pathways of reflex transmission of sexual arousal. According to Doweiko (1990), Masters and Johnson (1966) concluded that "the excessive use of alcohol was the most frequently encountered cause of impotence in middle-aged men" (p. 298).

Other CNS depressants (tranquillizers, sedatives, and hypnotics) affect people in a similar fashion, that is by decreasing sexual responsiveness. Kolodny et al. (1979) noted that barbiturate users describe depressed libido, impotence, or loss of orgasmic responsiveness associated with drug use.

The analysis of the effects of marijuana on sexual response and behavior is quite interesting. Cognitive factors seem to play an important role when determining the effects of this drug on sexual functioning. Although it has been reported that some men have been found to be impotent after chronic use of the drug (Kolodny et al., 1979), and that 20 per cent of men using this drug on a daily basis will experience erectile problems (Masters et al., 1966), many users report an increase in sexual desire and pleasure.

With narcotic use, sexual desire, performance and satisfaction are impaired (Gold, 1988). Amphetamines and cocaine may inhibit orgasm, especially in women. (Kaplan, 1979)

In summary, though there is some evidence regarding the impact of alcohol and drugs on sexual functioning, most researchers forewarn the reader that the evidence is inconclusive.

COGNITIVE FACTORS

The circumstances under which alcohol and other drugs are used may be more important than the effects of the drugs themselves on male or female sexual arousal (Wilson, 1977). For example, studies conducted with women have shown that there is an increase in reported sexual arousal with increased alcohol consumption and yet at the same time their physiological response does not correspond with this perception. That is, there is a decrease in vaginal responsiveness (Wilson & Lawson, 1978). In addition, Wilson (1977) notes that the presence of alcohol may create a certain environment where attitudes toward sexual behavior may become more permissive. Another point to consider is that in using alcohol, the initial physiological response mirrors that of sexual arousal (i.e. an increased heart rate, and increased warmth as blood vessels dilate). It is no wonder then that there are many different issues to consider when assessing sexual functioning among people experiencing an alcohol or drug problem.

Kolodny et al. (1979) offer a similar perspective on issues pertaining to women's sexual functioning and heroin use, illustrating the confounding variables that may exist. They suggest that because many women resort to prostitution as a means of supporting their drug habit, they may have negative feelings toward sex that reflect guilt, low self-esteem or hostility towards men. In addition, given that many (60 to 90 per cent) women in treatment programs for chemical-dependence problems are survivors of childhood and adult sexual abuse (Covington, 1983; Benward & Densen-Gerber, 1975; Wachtel & Lawton-Speert, 1983), one can assume that sexual difficulties will be present.

Cognitive factors in marijuana use are also quite evident. Although most users report an increase in sexual responsiveness, Doweiko (1990), notes that research "...has demonstrated that marijuana either has no impact on tactile perception, or that it actually lessens touch perception" (p. 301). However, Kolodny et al. (1979) report that although both men and women report an increased sense of touch, a greater degree of relaxation and being in tune with one's partner, they are also very quick to point out that both people needed to be "high" *at the same time* for the sexual experience to be enhanced.

Finally, for the drugs that lower anxiety (i.e. tranquillizers, sedatives and hypnotics), it is anticipated that a reduction in anxiety means enhanced sexual performance. According to Kolodny et al. (1979, p.331), "Barbiturates may sometimes lower sexual inhibitions and in this sense may enhance sexual function, but more commonly barbiturate users describe depressed libido, impotence, or loss of orgasmic responsiveness associated with drug use." This is usually associated with high dosage levels and infrequently reported.

CULTURAL/SOCIAL FACTORS

Alcohol, within the majority of North American and other cultures, is associated with friends and good times, romance, courtship and special events. These activities often include sexual experiences. As stated earlier, alcohol can sometimes set the wheels in motion for sex to occur by creating a more permissive atmosphere. Indeed, the saying "to wine and dine someone" certainly implies a potential sexual encounter. These types of societal expectations and pressures to perform certainly affect people's attitudes and experiences.

ASSESSING SEXUAL DIFFICULTIES

Asking questions about sex can be uncomfortable at first. Remember that people generally feel very alone in learning about sex and in wondering about their sexual experiences, and rarely talk openly about their concerns, fears, and pleasures. Thus it is important that the counsellor provide an environment in which asking questions about sexual issues is as natural as asking about diet, work habits and recreation.

An opening statement could be "Problems with addictions are often related to sexual problems, so this is part of our assessment today." At this point, the client may indicate that this is okay or definitely not okay. Respect that choice and let the client know that this is a place where he or she can discuss any sexual concerns when ready.

Talking about sex can feel degrading or unsafe to a survivor of sexual abuse, so it is important to be aware of your client's history and to let her or him know that you are aware of the impact it can have. Because substances may have been used to block out memories of assault, the counsellor needs to also be knowledgeable about the effect that recall may have on the client and allow the client to set the pace. "Remembering" is terrifying, so do not push this. As the client reduces or stops substance use, memories often surface rapidly. Be sure that the necessary supports are in place for the client before beginning exploration of this sensitive subject.

In exploring sexual abuse, it may be useful to start with a neutral statement such as: "Using alcohol or drugs can be a way of helping us block out frightening or unpleasant experiences we may have had as children. Do you remember any experiences as a child where you felt afraid or were touched in a way that you didn't like or that felt uncomfortable?"

There are also fears that are common among survivors, for example, being afraid of the dark, of putting their face under water, of falling asleep. Be aware, however, that many other people also have these fears. Many survivors may also repeat their childhood experiences in adult relationships. That is, they may have repeated relationships in which they are physically or sexually abused. For a checklist of possible survivor behaviors, an excellent resource is Secret Survivors (Blume, 1990).

Remember, this is simply a way for you to get a sense of whether a sexual abuse history is an issue and to help your client acknowledge this possibility.

If clients disclose sexual abuse, they need to hear that you believe them, that it was not their fault, and that help with healing can be found. Most communities have sexual assault crisis services that can help survivors. This would be a very good place to find information, crisis support for survivors, support groups, and counselling. It is also important to note the comments of Harrison et al. (1990), who stress the need for agencies to develop policies and procedures to help identify and help victims of abuse. Otherwise, the addictions intervention may prove ineffective, and in the case of adolescents you may be returning the client to an abusive situation that could be extremely harmful.

If disclosure has occurred, it is probably wise not to extend the assessment, but take some time to ensure that the client is not disoriented – that he or she is in the present, able to leave your office and cope with the aftermath of disclosure. If you are inexperienced in sexual assault assessment and counselling, it would be helpful to consult someone on how to proceed before meeting the client again.

As you proceed with an assessment, it is important to acknowledge sexual orientation early on, or you might be asking some irrelevant questions and the lesbian or gay client will feel discounted. A simple question like "Is your sexual preference currently for women, men or both?" will suffice. Use language that will include everyone, for example "Is your partner aware of this?" rather than boyfriend or wife.

You may want to do a very specific assessment of possible sexual difficulties in order to determine the need for referral. The nature of the referral will depend on the type of sexual problem or the phase of the sexual response that is problematic.

SEXUAL RESPONSE

Sexual response has been divided into three phases: the desire phase, the excitement phase, and the orgasm phase. Loulan (1984) adds willingness (to have sex) to the cycle, suggesting this can lead to desire. These phases are interconnected but governed by separate narrow physiological systems – there is therefore the possibility of separate inhibitions of the phases. Certain traumas, if sufficiently intense, disturb the entire system, but often only one component is disturbed. For example, a woman may have no sexual desire but be able to lubricate and have orgasms.

Understanding the nature of sexual response allows a specialized counsellor to intervene at certain points with specific therapeutic tools. However, in an addictions assessment, it would be sufficient to get a definition of the problem, assess whether it is a priority concern at this time, and if so, offer some self-help literature and/or a referral to a sex therapist. The context of a relationship makes working on sexuality far more complex, as sex works best in a healthy relationship. Allow room for self-sexuality and celibacy as healthy choices for some people. Only the client knows what he or she wants and needs.

SEXUAL PROBLEMS IN WOMEN

Desire Phase Problems
Asking simply "Do you feel desire for sex?" is a good start.

Desire-phase problems can be classified as primary or secondary. Primary problems are rare and represent a life-long history of asexuality. Secondary problems represent a loss of sex drive, which may be the result of physical illness, psychological traumas – such as incest, rape, or receiving oppressive sexual messages – and major life changes such as the birth of a child.

Desire-phase problems can be global or situational. With global problems a woman ceases to be interested in sex at all; this is associated with depressive states, severe anxiety and physical causes. With situational problems a woman feels desire in only certain situations and often not with the most appropriate and desirable partner. As noted earlier, it is common for survivors of sexual abuse to find themselves in sexually abusive relationships in adulthood. It generally takes a great deal of personal work for survivors to feel worthy of a respectful relationship, to understand what it may be like, to learn to protect themselves and to feel desire for gentle loving sex. Generally this experience is quite foreign to them. If they did feel some pleasure with the abuse as children, which would be a normal reflexive body response to stimulation, they may feel shame with desire as adults. It is important to validate that the assault should never have happened and their bodies were just responding normally – as their tastebuds would respond to food they liked.

In general, a desire-phase problem is characterized by asexual behavior; it is as if a woman's sexual circuits have been shut down. She will not pursue sexual gratification, and loses interest in sex. She may be able to experience lubrication and orgasm, but in a mechanical manner without much pleasure. Anxiety is evoked early, often when sex is anticipated or as soon as the initial sensations or erotic desire are experienced. These early stirrings are threatening, and the individual defends herself by suppressing desire rapidly and involuntarily, often before it can develop fully and emerge into conscious awareness. This may be accomplished by focusing on negatives – the opposite of conjuring up fantasies to liberate sexual desire. Characteristically the individual has no insight into the mechanism of active suppressions.

The reasons for suppressing desire may be quite realistic: a woman may be reacting to a dangerous situation, or sexual activity may always have disappointed her.

Kaplan (1979) has found that generally a woman's anger toward her partner will inhibit her sexual desire, while men can feel intense desire for a partner even when angry. This is an example of emotional differences between men and women that may impinge upon sexual desire and experience.

Kitzinger (1983) has found from women's experiences that when a couple communicates well about their feelings and all other things happening in their lives, there are likely to be fewer sexual problems. When sex is approached out of context, seen as an isolated activity separate from all else, there are more likely to be obvious differences in desire.

Excitement phase

Asking "Do you experience pain during sex?" and "Do you have trouble lubricating?" defines these problems.

The excitement phase in women is characterized by the vascular engorgement of the genital organs, the swelling and coloration of the vaginal walls, formation of the orgastic platform, and lubrication. Excitement-phase disorders are marked by difficulty with lubricating during lovemaking. Inhibition of lubrication may become more common following menopause because of lower estrogen levels. The painful and uncomfortable experience of intercourse with a dry, undistended vagina can cause a secondary inhibition of desire and/or avoidance of sex. A referral to a sensitive family doctor knowledgeable in this area would be appropriate.

Orgasmic problems

Asking "Do you experience orgasm?" will define this problem.

Problems with orgasm can range on a spectrum of severity from total anorgasmia (inability to experience orgasm) to mild situational difficulties. Orgasm is a genital reflex that can be under the individual's voluntary control. All reflexes subject to voluntary control can be inhibited when conscious attention is focused on the process. For example the knee-jerk reflex cannot be elicited when an individual is staring at his or her knee. Self consciousness makes us awkward, as when we attend to swallowing or dancing. The causes of inorgasmia vary. Studies have revealed fears of losing control of aggressive as well as sexual impulses, fear of urinating, unrealistic fantasies about dangers and pleasures of orgasm, performance anxieties related to fear of failure, taking too long, and so on. The specific inhibition of the orgasmic reflex may be accompanied by secondary inhibition of arousal, but as a general rule women who have problems achieving orgasm are responsive sexually, experience erotic feelings and lubricate.

Often women are not orgasmic because they have never been taught how to do it. Learning to become orgasmic can be a fairly straight-forward process. Self-help groups and self-help books such as Lonnie Barbach's (1975) *For yourself: The fulfilment of female sexuality* are excellent starting places and may be sufficient to solve the problem. It is important for a woman to have the time she needs to learn to become orgasmic herself without being pressured in any way to be sexual with a partner.

FEMALE SEXUAL PROBLEMS NOT RELATED TO A SPECIFIC SEXUAL PHASE

Vaginismus

Asking "Does your vagina sometimes close up tight without your control?" can define vaginismus.

Women with vaginismus often feel a lot of shame and hopelessness and are under a great deal of pressure in their relationships. If the client feels ready a referral to a therapist *knowledgeable in this area* could be offered. Vaginismus is a conditioned reflex spasm of the vaginal entrance that occurs whenever entry is attempted. In milder forms, this genital spasm causes dyspareunia, where entry is possible but intercourse is painful. Otherwise, women with vaginismus tend to be sexually responsive.

Kitzinger (1983) reframes vaginismus, describing it as the natural protection of women against penetration. She suggests: "Why not respect this and look for options?" Kitzinger describes an approach to dealing with vaginismus focusing primarily on the couple's communication, with women in complete control of vaginal penetration, and the understanding that they may (or may not) move to partner penetration. For example, in heterosexual situations she teaches other ways for an erection to be contained, such as between the thighs, under an arm or between breasts. Kitzinger views vaginismus as occurring in women who do not enjoy penetration or like it only occasionally and usually prefer other ways of love making. She questions the focus of our society on penetration as the normal necessary routine and challenges sex therapists to be creative in encouraging their couples to find solutions to their sexual difficulties and to question their own belief systems about the necessity of penetration.

Sexual Phobias

Asking "Do you have some specific fears about sex?" should open this discussion.

Sexual phobias are an avoidance of erotic feelings and/or certain sexual activities. For example, a woman may have a phobic avoidance of penetration, oral sex, anal sex, masturbation, semen, pubic hair, getting undressed in front of a partner. Sexual phobias are common in adult survivors of sexual abuse. Psychotherapy instead of or in addition to sex therapy is called for.

MALE SEXUAL PROBLEMS

Problems with Erection

Asking "Do you have problems getting or keeping an erection?" should open this discussion.

Secondary impotence is the development of impotence in men who have previously not had problems with erection. Men with primary impotence, which is rarer and far less amenable to treatment, have never functioned well in terms of erection. As noted previously, erectile problems can be due to physical, cognitive, or social factors. Although the man may be aroused and want to make love, his penis will not cooperate. The erectile and ejaculate reflexes are dissociable and some men are able to ejaculate despite their flaccid penis.

Generally a man has trouble with his erection the moment he becomes anxious. Some men cannot achieve an erection before intercourse, others attain an erection easily but lose it upon entry or during intercourse. Some men can achieve an erection only if their partner dominates, others lose their erection if a partner tries to assume control.

In talking with men about erectile problems, it is important to take a detailed account of what happens, the first time they remember the situation arising and how they felt. Be aware that the cure may be in the present: it may be a statement about whether he wants to have intercourse. Ironic as it may seem, most men would rather feel they have a medical problem than say very simply to their partner, "I don't want to have sex with you." Of course the possibility of a physiological basis for erectile problems cannot be ignored but generally it is more constructive to begin by looking at other possibilities.

In addressing erectile problems, it is important to remove the expectation to perform, asking the couple to refrain from attempting intercourse, and to take time to explore the total sensuality of each other's bodies. The ban on intercourse can be for an extended time. It is important to know that just because a man gets an erection doesn't mean he has to use it; he will get another. In other words, change the focus of lovemaking to more total sensual experience. Although as an addictions counsellor you are not expected to do sex therapy, this simple advice may suffice.

Premature Ejaculation

This is a condition where a man is unable to control his ejaculatory reflex voluntarily. It is important again to assess feelings: does this problem translate into "I want to get this over with as fast as possible?" It is possible to become increasingly aware of the point of ejaculatory inevitability by stopping stimulation well before ejaculation, letting the excitement subside and then starting again. This way awareness increases and the ability to control improves.

To summarize this section, in looking back on the sexual response cycle, it is important to determine whether a client's problem is one of willingness, desire, excitement or orgasm. In the area of willingness and desire you would need to determine whether clients are really interested in experiencing sex at this point in their lives. Perhaps they are not ready and need to be reassured that their own timing is important. Were they sexually abused as children? This could affect their desire for sex. Are they sexually attracted to the opposite sex? Perhaps they are homosexual and forcing themselves to engage in sexual activity with the opposite sex for fear of being rejected or taunted by peers. These are but a few examples of the types of questions that can be pursued in this situation. From there, in looking at the excitement and orgasm phase, it would be important to isolate a specific problem if possible: i.e., getting and maintaining an erection, lubricating or experiencing an orgasm. Each area may be affected by alcohol and drug use and could be explored in more detail.

SEXUAL AND PHYSICAL ASSAULT

One cannot consider sexuality and addiction without a keen awareness of the part sexual and physical abuse play in the histories of many with alcohol and drug addictions. Given that the pioneering work in the area of sexual assault has been done by the grass roots feminist movement, most of the information has focused on women's experience. Consequently the female pronoun is used in this section of the chapter. With increasing awareness and attention to sexual assault of boys, one can anticipate that the literature will address the male perspective in more detail.

INCIDENCE

General Statistics

A woman is raped every 17 minutes in Canada and sexually assaulted every six minutes. One out of every five Canadian women will be sexually assaulted at some point in their lives. Eighty per cent of the time, women are assaulted in their homes and 67 per cent of the time by someone they know.[1]

Connection between assault and alcohol and drug abuse

The Abusers[2]

Drinking is estimated to be involved in about 50 per cent of spouse abuse cases and up to 38 per cent of child abuse cases (NIAAA, Fifth Special Report). A Minnesota study of nearly 100 abused wives reported 87 per cent of the violent abusers to be alcohol abusers (Carder, 1978, as found in the Double Jeopardy Alcohol and Domestic Violence Fact Sheet). According to Claudia Black (as cited in the Double Jeopardy Fact Sheet), adults who grew up in alcoholic families experienced, or witnessed, a significantly greater amount of violence than individuals from non-alcoholic homes. Sixty-nine per cent of children of alcoholics reported violence on the part of fathers and 26.5 per cent reported violence on the part of mothers, as opposed to 6.8 per cent and 6.7 per cent respectively reported by individuals from non-alcoholic backgrounds.

The Survivors

The estimates of the number of women in chemical-dependency programs who are survivors of some form of either adult or child sexual abuse range from 30 to 70 per cent (Covington, 1983; Benward & Densen-Gerber, 1975; Wachtel & Lawton-Speert, 1983). At a conference of the 45 federally-funded programs in the United States, it was reported that 45 to 70 per cent of their clients had been victims of incest or rape (Hamilton and Volpe, 1983, p. 32). According to the Alcoholism Centre for Women (Los Angeles) in the Double Jeopardy Fact Sheet, the incidence of alcohol problems in families experiencing violence is estimated to be as high as 80 per cent.

Two recent studies conducted in the United States with adolescents in chemical-dependency treatment programs found the following:

Harrison and Hoffman (1989) found that among the adolescent girls, 35.2 per cent identified as being victims of sexual abuse. Victims of abuse reported earlier onset of alcohol and drug use and more use of medication – with use of sedatives, minor tranquillizers, painkillers and opiates higher than among non-victims. In terms of the function of the drugs, all sexual abuse victims were significantly more likely to acknowledge that the substance was being used to "get away from family problems," which one would assume includes the sexual abuse.

Harrison, Edwall, and Worthen (1990) found a small proportion (6.6 per cent) of males in treatment for chemical dependency who disclosed a history of sexual abuse. Certain behaviors distinguished them from the non-victims in treatment. The victims experienced more family violence (they were twice as likely as the other boys to have been physically abused by a family member or by someone outside the family); they reported more substance abuse (i.e., the frequency of use was higher, they were twice as likely to be drinking daily; more likely to report regular use of stimulants, sedatives, tranquillizers, opioids, hallucinogens, inhalants, painkillers and over-the-counter drugs); more agitation (i.e., nervousness, tension, insomnia and sexual problems); more suicidal behavior; and earlier legal troubles. Similar to the findings cited earlier regarding adolescent girls, the boys who were victims started drinking and drug use earlier than non-victims. Half the victims were drinking at age 10, compared with one-third of the non-victims, and one-third of the victims were using drugs other than alcohol or marijuana by age 12 compared with 14 per cent of non-victims. The incidence of sexual abuse in boys is probably grossly under-reported. We are just beginning to focus on this issue and the aftermath of abuse for boys.

A recent series of studies in Ontario by Addiction Research Foundation researchers Groeneveld and Shain (1989) found that women who were sexually assaulted either as adults or as children are at least twice as likely as non-abused women to use medication to calm them down or to help them to sleep. They also noted that women physically abused by their current partners were 74 per cent more likely to use such medication than non-abused women.

This evidence demonstrates the importance of examining the role of alcohol and drug use as a method of coping and surviving. As mentioned earlier, once the drugs are no longer being used, memories of the abuse may well surface. Working on other means of coping with this trauma is an essential component of working with survivors of child or adult sexual or physical abuse who are also chemically dependent.

GENERAL ISSUES RELATED TO ABUSE

We will now provide a brief look at some of the issues present in the sexual abuse literature. Issues pertaining to boundaries, flashbacks, abuse of power, loss of control, multiple personalities and self-injurious behavior will be discussed.

When a person is sexually abused, her boundaries are violated in the most terrifying way. She may have no sense of how far to let people go. Even if she is feeling horrible, she has little or no sense of how to limit what is asked or demanded of her (Utain & Oliver, 1989; Bass & Davis, 1988). In many instances she has no real sense of her own thoughts and feelings apart from what other people think and feel. The ability to know who you are as a separate, fully functioning human being is not something that comes easily for a survivor of childhood sexual abuse. It is extremely important therefore for the counsellor to do everything possible not to violate the boundaries of the client. For example, pushing or forcing clients to discuss sexual abuse experiences when they don't want to is a violation of their right to say no. Learning to say no should be supported and celebrated. The client should be entitled to share this painful experience with you only when he or she feels ready and feels you can be trusted. It is important to reinforce with a client that trust is something to be earned, and to take the time he or she needs to do this. It is important to ask survivors which gender of counsellor they prefer.

Abuse of Power and Loss of Control
Sexual abuse is not sex – it is an act of violence, with one person wanting to exert power and control over someone else less powerful (like a child).

In a *Report on Sexual Assault in Canada* (Kinnon, 1981) the author notes that researchers have suggested that sexual assault is perceived as the most serious violation of the self, short of murder. Kinnon (1981, p. 20) goes on to say that, "the experience of sexual assault is the total loss of power over one's destiny. The victim is totally under the control of the assailant and has no knowledge of the outcome of the attack."

Memories/Remembering
It is possible that a survivor may begin to experience her first memories of abuse once she is no longer using alcohol or other drugs. It is quite common for survivors of childhood sexual abuse to suppress the memories of the abuse as a method of coping with their trauma. Remembering the abuse and the feelings associated with it can be very frightening. It is important that the client receive the counselling she needs to deal with the abuse. You will hear, "I never had any problems with sex until I gave up alcohol." It may be that she didn't really let herself feel before she gave up alcohol, which gave the misconception that sex was easy. Reassure the client that with healing from the abuse, she will be able to be sexual in the way she wants to be, and to feel pleasure.

Because drugs and alcohol were used to cope and suppress memories, the positive effects of remaining abstinent will not be readily and quickly experienced. It is important to be nonjudgmental and to work closely with the sexual abuse counsellor to be able to pace your work and to set realistic expectations.

Flashbacks and Repressed Memories

Flashbacks are images that are reminders of the abuse. Clients may feel, see, hear or smell something in the present that was part of the past abuse experience. This can happen anytime and many women report experiencing flashbacks during sexual activities (Bass et al., 1988). It is important to reassure the survivor that she is not crazy and that flashbacks are quite common. If a client feels comfortable, often the best way to deal with these experiences is to talk about them. However, some women prefer to be alone, to stay with the flashback and open it up to gain information about the past (Bass et al., 1988). If a woman is with a supportive lover, it would be important to discuss what would help if she has a flashback. Perhaps being held and rocked and being told "she is safe now" would reassure her and allow her to release some of her suppressed fear, hurt and anger.

Multiple Personalities

According to Bass and Davis (1988), one result of repressing the memories of abuse is a feeling of being divided into more than one person. In cases of extreme abuse, this kind of splitting can result in the development of multiple personalities. It is important to be alert to the possibility that you may experience this in your clinical practice and be prepared to identify it and make a necessary referral.

Self-Injurious Behavior

Injuring oneself physically, by "slashing" or "cutting" is one way survivors control their experience of the pain associated with remembering and working through the abuse (Bass et al., 1988). It is quite natural that survivors struggle with self-abuse, and again important that you treat the survivor respectfully and help her get the help she needs. These are all methods of coping the woman has created in order to keep surviving – they should be acknowledged as such while helping her find alternative ways to cope that are not self-abusive.

ROLE OF THE COUNSELLOR

Many survivors of physical or sexual abuse also have problems related to substance use. In addressing substance use problems with your client, it is very important that you work closely with those who are addressing the abuse issues so that the client and her counsellors can have a common understanding of her goals and progress towards them. This is particularly important when dealing with issues like relapse prevention, since clients are at increased risk of relapse when processing their abuse issues.

CONCLUSION

Substance abusers often wonder whether their drug use has in any way affected their sexual functioning. It is difficult to answer this conclusively considering the impact that cultural, social and physiological factors have on sexual response. However, you can begin to explore how these factors affect the client's sexual experience.

In this chapter you have been exposed to a fairly detailed description of the sexual response cycle and sexual difficulties. The purpose was to provide you with a broad range of background information from which you can form assessment questions. However, the role of a substance abuse counsellor is not to be a sex therapist, which requires extensive training. If you are interested in more extensive work with clients, seek a training program and the supervision of an experienced sex therapist.

We encourage you to refer to the Resource section at the end of this chapter to broaden your understanding of sexual assault issues, as this is critical in helping clients who have a substance abuse problem and a history of sexual assault.

In conclusion, the connections to be made between addictions and sexuality are many. As the addictions counsellor you will often be the central person defining the problems and forming the team of helpers. Your contribution will be invaluable in this process.

NOTES

1. Canadian Advisory Council on the Status of Women. Sexual Assault, Ottawa: 1985.

2. This information was gathered from the Fact Sheet on Alcohol and Domestic Violence compiled by the Alcoholism Center for Women and Haven House Inc. and is a part of the Double Jeopardy Training Package.

REFERENCES

Alcoholism Centre for Women (1987). Double Jeopardy: Alcohol & Domestic Violence. Cross Training Manual. Los Angeles, CA, 1987.

Barbach, Lonnie (1975). For yourself: The fulfilment of female sexuality. New York: Doubleday, 1975.

Bass, Ellen & Davis, Laura (1988). The courage to heal: A guide for women survivors of child sexual abuse. New York: Harper & Row Publishers, 1988.

Benward, J. & Densen-Gerber, J. (1975). Incest as a causative factor in anti-social behavior: An exploratory study. Contemporary drug problems, (4), (pp. 323–340).

Blume, E. Sue (1990). Secret survivors. New York: John Wylie & Sons, 1990.

Covington, Stephanie, Ph.D. Alcoholism and family violence. Paper presented at the 29th International Institute on the Prevention & Treatment of Alcoholism in Zagreb, 1983.

Doweiko, H. (1990). Concepts of chemical dependency. Pacific Grove, California: Brooks/Cole Publishing Company, 1990.

Findelstein, N., Duncan, S.A., Derman, L. & Smeltz, J. (1990). Getting sober, getting well: A treatment guide for caregivers who work with women. The Women's Alcoholism Program of CASPAR, Inc., Cambridge, Massachusetts, 1990.

Gold, M. (1987). Impotence, infertility, interest loss, sexual dysfunction, challenges today's addiction clinicians. Alcoholism and Addiction. July-August, (Vol.7) (6).

Gold, M. (1988). Decreased desire: alcohol, drugs and sexual dysfunction. Alcoholism and Addiction. December. Vol. 9 (2).

Groeneveld, J. & Shain, M. (1989). Drug Use Among Victims of Physical and Sexual Abuse: A Preliminary Report. Addiction Research Foundation.

Hamilton, G. & Volpe, J. (1982/83). How women recover: Experience & research observations. Alcohol Health and Research World. Winter 1982/83.

Harrison, P.A., Edwall, G.E., Hoffman N.G. & Worthen, M.D. (1990). Correlates of sexual abuse among boys in treatment for chemical dependency. Journal of Adolescent Chemical Dependency. Vol. 1 (1).

Harrison, P.A. & Hoffman, N. (1989). Differential drug use patterns among sexually abused adolescent girls in treatment for chemical dependency. The International Journal of the Addictions. 24 (6), (499–514).

Kaplan, H.S. (1979). Disorders of sexual desire. New York: Brunner/Mazel, 1979.

Kaplan, H.S. (1974). The new sex therapy. New York: Brunner/Mazel, 1974.

Kinnon, D. (1981). Report on Sexual Assault in Canada. Canadian Advisory Council on the Status of Women, 1981.

Kitzinger, Sheila (1983). Women's experience of sex. New York: G.P. Putnam's Sons, 1983.

Kolodny, R.C., Masters, W.H. & Johnson, V.E. (1979). Textbook of sexual medicine. Boston: Brown & Co., 1979.

Loulan, JoAnn (1984). Lesbian sex. San Francisco: Spinsters/Aunt Lute Book Company, 1984.

Masters, W.H., Johnson, V.G. & Kolodny, R.C. (1966). Sex and human loving. Boston: Little, Brown & Co., 1966.

Murphy, W.D., Coleman, E., Hoon, E. & Scott, C. (1980). Sexual dysfunction and treatment in alcoholic women. Sexuality and Disability. Vol. 3 (4), Winter.

Utain, M. & Oliver, B. (1989). Scream louder: Through hell and healing with an incest survivor and her therapist. Dearfield Beach, Florida: Health Communications Inc., 1989.

Wachtel, Andy & Lawton-Speert, Sarah (1983). Incest and Childhood Sexual Abuse Program. Child sexual abuse: Descriptions of nine program approaches to treatment. Child Sexual Abuse Project. Working Paper 3, Vancouver, B.C. Social Planning & Research, 1983.

Wilsnack, Sharon (1983). Drinking, sexuality and sexual dysfunctions in women in: Alcohol problems in women (eds.). New York: Sharon Wilsnack & Linda Beckman, Guilford Press, 1983.

Wilson, G.T. & Lawson, D.M. (1978). Expectancies, alcohol and sexual arousal in women. Journal of Abnormal Psychology. Vol. 37 (3), (pp. 358–367).

Wilson, G.T. (1977). Alcohol and human sexual behavior. Behaviour, Research and Therapy. Vol. 15, (pp. 239–252).

RESOURCES

SEXUAL ASSAULT

Services

Most communities have services in place to provide assistance, support and counselling to sexual assault survivors. Try looking in your phone book under Rape Crisis Centre or Sexual Assault Crisis Centre.

Books

Blume, E. Sue (1990). Secret survivors. New York: John Wylie & Sons, 1990.

This is an excellent resource book on the after-effects of childhood sexual abuse and the healing process.

Bass, Ellen & Davis, Laura (1988). The courage to heal: A guide for women survivors of child sexual abuse. New York: Harper & Row Publishers, 1988.

This "ground-breaking" book provides a comprehensive guide that offers hope and encouragement to every woman who was sexually abused as a child, and those that care about her. The authors provide clear explanations, practical suggestions, a map of the healing journey and many moving first-person examples of the recovery process drawn from their interviews with hundreds of survivors.

SEXUALITY

Books

Barbach, Lonnie (1975). For yourself: The fulfilment of female sexuality. New York: Doubleday, 1975.

This book is a concise self-help manual for women on becoming orgasmic.

Kitzinger, Sheila (1983). Women's experience of sex. New York: G.P. Putnam's Sons, 1983.

This book places techniques and methods of lovemaking in the context of who women are as people, their values, their relationships with others and the emotions that their experiences arouse in them. Sexuality in the midst of the crises some women face, including childbirth, menopause, mastectomy and hysterectomy is also addressed.

Eating Disorders and Substance Abuse

FRED J. BOLAND

*T*he eating disorders of concern to addiction counsellors are anorexia nervosa and bulimia nervosa. This chapter is largely devoted to a consideration of bulimia nervosa as it is much more likely to be encountered by addiction counsellors. Nevertheless, a great deal of the material on bulimia is directly relevant to both disorders.

ANOREXIA NERVOSA

According to DSM III-R (1987), the essential diagnostic criteria for anorexia nervosa are (a) refusal to maintain body weight above 85 per cent of normal for age and height; (b) intense fear of gaining weight or becoming fat; (c) disturbances in the experience of body shape, weight and/or size; (d) in females, absence of at least three consecutive menstrual cycles. The incidence of the disorder among substance abusers is unknown, but among women under 30 generally is about one in 100 and about one in 1,000 for males.

An enquiry relevant to the diagnostic criteria, together with the person's emaciated appearance, give a good indication of the presence of anorexia nervosa. Often, a family member or friend will directly express concern about the person's weight or eating behavior. Be aware, however, that the disorder is associated with denial and resistance. To the anorectic, treatment threatens weight gain and lack of control. These are her most central fears.

The disorder is definitely life-threatening, with many associated medical complications. Hospitalization is commonly needed to raise weight to a safer level. Treatment tends to be a long and difficult process. The addiction counsellor is strongly advised to refer any suspected cases of anorexia nervosa to professionals who are familiar with the disorder. The counsellor can work concurrently to resolve the substance abuse problem. However, consultation between the addiction counsellor and the therapist treating the eating disorder is highly recommended, as a decision may be made to treat the disorders sequentially. Patients with full blown anorexia nervosa may be so wrapped up in their disorder that it is extremely difficult to involve them in treatment for substance abuse, or vice versa.

BULIMIA NERVOSA

The DSM-III-R essential criteria for bulimia nervosa are: (a) recurrent episodes of binge eating, defined as eating a large amount of food in a relatively short, discrete period of time; (b) feeling of lack of control over eating behavior during a binge; (c) regular engagement in some form of purging (vomiting, laxatives, diuretics, strict dieting, fasting or compulsive exercise) in order to prevent weight gain; (d) minimum average of two binge-eating episodes a week for at least three months; (e) persistent overconcern with body shape and weight.

DSM-III-R gives rates in the general population of 4.5 per cent for women, and 0.4 per cent for males. However, many people seek help who do not completely satisfy these criteria. The majority of bulimics are in the normal weight range, with a minority being overweight, or underweight (Fairburn, 1984). At least a third of anorexia nervosa patients are also bulimic.

THE CONNECTION TO SUBSTANCE ABUSE

An association between substance abuse and bulimia is not hard to document. Surveys of bulimics suggest that 30 per cent or more have a history of alcohol abuse (e.g., Mitchell, Hatsukami, Eckert & Pyle, 1985). A survey of female alcoholics found three times as many bulimics as in a matched sample of non-alcoholic women (Boland & Butt, 1989). A recent survey of patients in treatment for chemical dependency also reported that up to three per cent of the males satisfied DSM-III criteria for bulimia (Perlman & McKenna, 1988).

Both alcoholic and bulimic women share an increased association with depression (e.g., Hatsukami, Eckert, Mitchell & Pyle, 1984), and similar MMPI profiles with elevations on depression, impulsiveness, anxiety, and social withdrawal (Hatsukami, Owen, Pyle & Mitchell, 1982). Increased incidence of disturbed childhoods and sexual abuse are also associated with both populations (Walker, Bonner & Kaufman, 1988). Clinical experience suggests that both groups tend to be poor at coping with stress, and to have very low self-esteem.

Patients with dual problems are likely to present with more depression, anxiety, obsessiveness, and somatic concerns than their non-bulimic, substance-abusing counterparts (Boland & Butt, 1989). The Hazelden survey reports that they are more likely to be polydrug abusers, have experienced more adolescent antisocial behavior problems, more self-reported suicidal thoughts and attempts, and more previous treatment for mental health problems (Perlman & McKenna, 1988). They are more likely to have been hospitalized for psychiatric problems, to have a history of stealing, abuse of diuretics and social impairment (Hatsukami, Mitchell, Eckert & Pyle, 1986). Women who have both disorders report great overlap in the emotions and situations prompting both abuses (Rand, Lawlor & Duldau, 1986).

We could find no association between the severity of dependence on alcohol and the severity of the bulimic problem, nor was there any relationship between the frequency of bulimic episodes and whether the person was drinking or abstinent (Boland & Butt, 1989). Some were worst when drinking; some after they stopped. One exception to this may be women who abused cocaine or amphetamines. It would appear that the voracious appetite experienced coming off stimulant abuse can trigger severe bingeing with associated purging.

REFER, CONSULT OR TREAT

If bulimia nervosa is suspected or confirmed, it is wise, if possible, to refer the person to a therapist familiar with eating disorders as well as substance abuse. If that is not possible, some liaison should be maintained between the therapist responsible for the assessment and treatment of the eating disorder and the therapist responsible for the treatment of the alcohol or drug-abuse problem. At the Hazelden inpatient program, psychologists assess patients for eating disorders and make a judgement as to whether they can be managed in a chemical dependency unit. If patients are so preoccupied with bingeing, purging, and related behaviors that they miss groups and are otherwise not available to treatment efforts aimed at their substance abuse, they are referred to more suitable treatment for their eating disorder.

If the addiction counsellor turns out to be the only source of help for the patient with dual disorders, there is an obligation to become more familiar with factors known to trigger and maintain the binge-purge behavior, with variables potentially involved in the origin of the disorder, and with appropriate treatment strategies. The remainder of this chapter is meant to serve as an introduction to these topics. Recommended readings are provided for a more comprehensive understanding.

TRIGGERS ASSOCIATED WITH BINGE-PURGING

Severe bingeing seldom occurs "out of the blue." At the time, the person is typically experiencing some negative mood state (e.g., anxious, angry, bored, depressed, frustrated, lonely, rejected). Such negative mood states are associated with relapses into substance abuse as well (Marlatt & Gordon, 1985).

Dieting is strongly related to bingeing; the stricter the diet, the more severe the bingeing (Vanderheyden & Boland, 1987). Bulimics diet chronically, often skipping meals early in the day only to binge in the evening. At the time they binge they are usually obsessing about food – often their favorite binge food. In general, chronic dieters and those with bulimia nervosa have many foods they label as forbidden when dieting. Paradoxically, these "taboo" foods take on the power to trigger binges, since consumption of even small amounts symbolizes the breaking of the diet (Knight & Boland, 1989). It is of more than passing interest for addiction counsellors that alcohol consumption has been shown to disinhibit eating in dieters in much the same way as consumption of "taboo" foods (Polivy & Herman, 1976).

Increases in stress level or relatively sudden increases in concern over appearance are also observed to be associated with bingeing and purging. There may be other triggers uniquely associated with an individual's bingeing (e.g., a need to be impulsive, a need to punish one's self), but the above elements, either alone or in combination, are commonly observed.

PAYOFFS THAT HELP MAINTAIN BINGE-PURGING

As with alcohol or drug taking, consequences or payoffs from bingeing and/or purging help maintain the behavior. As with substance abuse, the positive consequences tend to be immediate, the negative consequences delayed. Initially, there is the anticipation, tasting, and eating of the rich "taboo" foods that the person craves, and normally excludes from the diet. There is at least a temporary satisfaction of hunger. Psychologically, there is usually a temporary relief from the tension and negative mood that helped trigger the binge. If the person was bored, eating is entertaining; if lonely and depressed, it becomes a source of comfort and pleasure. In effect the person is using a food binge much like alcohol or drugs – to serve some function, to achieve some effect.

As the binge progresses (the typical binge lasts 30 minutes), the negative consequences appear. There is a return of negative mood states and the aversive feeling of being out of control. Many bulimics go to bed disgusted and full of self-hatred. There is the fear of weight gain, and the pain, nausea, and bloating that eventually helps stops the binge.

The negative consequences lead to attempts to undo the binge by purging, usually by vomiting within 30 minutes. This tends to "lock in" the binge-purge cycle, as the purging is powerfully rewarded by physical relief of nausea and bloating, and psychologically, by reduction in anxiety over weight gain. Eventually, the purging comes to play a large part in controlling the bingeing, as the bulimic will often not binge unless there is an opportunity to purge shortly thereafter. Many purge even after "normal" meals. Even when they don't vomit, there is still the commitment to undo the binge by such methods as fasting ("I'm not going to eat anything tomorrow!"), strict dieting ("I'm going to stick to 600 calories a day for the next week"), or laxative abuse.

In a way, the person is setting herself up for the next binge. The negative feelings have returned, and the purging, in whatever form, recreates the state of hunger and the obsession with food. Given the ability of humans to rationalize, coming into contact again with "taboo" foods is probably the easiest trigger to reinstate.

It is possible that in some cases a physiological response to a binge on refined carbohydrates can contribute to maintaining the binge-purge cycle. Refined sugars are absorbed directly into the blood, causing an acute rise in blood glucose levels. In response, the body releases large amounts of insulin to bring the blood sugar level down by transporting it into cells. In binge-purgers who chronically diet, this process can serve as a stimulus to eat (Spitzer & Rodin, 1987). Also, since most of the calories consumed during bingeing are soon purged, there is a possibility of insulin overshoot, resulting in an acute hypoglycemic state that may contribute to instability of mood, and craving for more sugar.

Helping the person understand the triggers and consequences that help maintain her particular binge-purge cycle is very important for interrupting the cycle in the early stages of treatment.

CAUSES OF EATING DISORDERS

There are many things we don't know about the etiology of eating disorders. So far, research suggests that multiple factors are involved, and that not all factors need be present in every case. The repetitive pattern of bingeing and purging described above has some similarities to addictive use of alcohol and drugs. However, the reasons why this pattern develops in the first place are different in many respects.

The gender difference in the incidence of eating disorders suggests a strong socio-cultural component (Striegel-Moore, Silberstein & Rodin, 1986). Our culture has strong expectations of women from many sources (e.g., magazines, T.V., fashion) to be thin. Thinness is associated with success, femininity, attractiveness, self-control, and many other desirable characteristics; fatness with negative characteristics (e.g., lazy, undisciplined, unfeminine and ugly). Since females are generally socialized more than males to value appearance concerns, they are more likely to internalize this ideal of thinness, and to fear the anti-ideal of fatness. Perceived deviations from this unrealistic ideal are associated with body dissatisfaction and low self-esteem. Indeed, the perceived rewards for thinness are so great that no matter what the source of their low self-esteem (e.g., sexual abuse) or body dissatisfaction, losing weight is often seen as a solution.

Paradoxically, while women experience excessive cultural pressure to be thin, they are also more socialized to interact with food than are men, and to form functional relationships with food – i.e., to use it as a coping mechanism or for pleasure. Clients have often pointed out to me that T.V. shows such as *The Golden Girls* and cartoon characters such as Cathy display a typical pattern. Something doesn't turn out right, or some problem arises. Solution: go for the chocolate ice cream or the cheese cake! This is compounded by the fact that most food advertising is aimed at women – often in the same magazines that suggest ways to diet and avoid these very foods.

It is in this cultural context that many women start to diet. Their strong desire for thinness is motivated by all the perceived rewards associated with achieving their desired weight, and by avoiding all the perceived punishments associated with fatness.

Unfortunately this sets up a serious conflict with forces seeking to maintain the "status quo." First, the individual typically deprives herself of the very foods from which she derives most pleasure – high-calorie, rich foods. It is no wonder that their absence engenders the "poor me's," "the blues," and obsessive thinking concerning these foods.

Second, many use pleasurable foods as a coping mechanism, much like they might use alcohol or drugs. The mechanism is missed when dieting, especially in stressful situations that normally provoke eating.

Third, the induced weight loss often puts the person below a comfortable biological weight – the weight (whether lean or fat) that we can comfortably maintain without undereating or overeating. This weight is likely determined by a physiologically based "set point" mechanism that is influenced a great deal by genetics (Bennett & Gurin, 1982; Keesey & Powley, 1986). The body's "set point" response to weight loss is to seek to maintain its fat stores by slowing down metabolic rate. Bennet & Gurin (1982) and others maintain that the overwhelming failure of treatment for obesity – 95 per cent eventually gain back the weight they lose – supports a "set point" explanation. The main point is that the chronic, strict dieting seen in bulimic and anorectic individuals places them so far below their comfortable biological weight that their bodies react as if they were starving.

A study by Keys, Biozek, Henschel, Mickelsen & Taylor (1950) is enlightening in showing the extent to which semi-starvation in and of itself generates symptoms of eating disorders. The authors deprived 36 young, mentally healthy male volunteers of half their normal calorie intake for a period of about six months, until they lost about 25 per cent of their original body weight. These subjects were objectors to military service who had none of the motivations for losing weight seen in women with eating disorders. Nevertheless, as the dieting continued, these men became obsessed with food, (e.g., read cookbooks, collected recipes, fantasized about food, etc.). Their concentration suffered, their work capacity dropped, and there was an increase in depression, anxiety, irritability, and hypochondria. Their self-esteem grew more negative, they reported feelings of social inadequacy, and became more isolated and withdrawn.

In people with eating disorders, these same negative experiences are accompanied by illusory beliefs such as "If I diet even harder, these feelings will go away; when I reach 100 pounds, all will be wonderful." These and other irrational beliefs feed into the disorder (Garfinkel & Garner, 1982). Also, like those with eating disorders, many subjects in the starvation study showed body image disturbance, and developed a bingeing pattern, especially during the refeeding period. Some reported guilt over eating, complained of feeling fat, and vomited. Some of the disordered-eating symptoms persisted even after the individuals had gained back their weight. In summary, no matter what the motivation for strict dieting, the resulting conflict with normal biological and psychological patterns can generate major symptoms seen in individuals with eating disorders, and contribute to the maintenance of the binge-purge cycle described earlier.

Many factors known to be associated with bulimia and anorexia nervosa feed into the above process, and contribute to the development of abnormal attitudes towards food, weight, shape, and a pathological drive for thinness. For example, a career choice of ballet dancer or model is associated with increased risk of eating disorders, presumable because of the thin body shape they must achieve (Garner & Garfinkel, 1980).

Obesity is another risk factor. A high proportion of bulimics have a prior history of obesity. Such individuals would likely experience more punishment (ridicule, embarrassment, etc.) for fatness, and have more reason to believe that dieting would answer their problems (Loro & Orleans, 1981).

Some evidence suggests that family dysfunctions that discourage autonomy and a sense of personal control over life can contribute to eating disorders as well. For individuals in these families, weight and shape may be one of the few areas of their lives that they can control. Refusing to follow directives to eat can be a way of expressing autonomy. Unfortunately, this narrow attempt at control and autonomy becomes an anxious obsession with no general alleviation of feelings of ineffectiveness and low self-esteem (Bruch, 1977).

Juvenile diabetics have an increased incidence of eating disorders (Rodin, Daneman, Johnson, Kenshole & Garfinkel, 1986). In part, this may be due to their having to chronically restrict the rich high-calorie food that their peers enjoy.

Recent research suggests that individuals with a personality disorder are also at higher risk for bulimia, possibly because of poor impulse control (Piran, Lerner, Garfinkel, Kennedy & Brouilette, 1988). A similar case has often been made for an association between personality disorders and alcohol and drug problems.

Various other personality and family variables have been put forth as playing a causal role in the development of eating disorders. However, it is difficult to determine whether they are causes or consequences of the disorder. For example, although depression is strongly associated with bulimia nervosa (and for that matter, alcohol problems), it is likely that most depression is secondary to the bulimia, and is alleviated as the bulimic behavior decreases (Cooper & Fairburn, 1983). Similarly, although neurochemical abnormalities, especially those involving serotonin, can be associated with eating disorders (Fava, Copland, Schiveiger & Herzog, 1989), it is impossible at this time to distinguish whether they are a consequence or cause of the disorder.

In summary, a number of factors are known to be associated with an increased risk of developing bulimia. These factors may vary from individual to individual, and it is important for the counsellor to determine and deal with the particular factors that make their clients vulnerable.

TREATMENT CONSIDERATIONS

Only a small minority of bulimics require hospitalization, usually because of medical consequences (e.g., electrolyte imbalance), suicide risk, or because a severe binge-purge pattern cannot be brought under control with good outpatient treatment.

Addiction counsellors in an inpatient facility who work with clients who have been identified as having an eating disorder should be encouraged by Hazelden's report that in most cases, the course of treatment was similar for bulimic and non-bulimic chemically-dependent clients. Throughout treatment, the focus at Hazelden remained on chemical dependence with no insistence on total abstinence from disordered eating behavior. It would appear that counsellors arranged some education about eating disorders, helped patients identify factors associated with their bulimic behavior, supplied them with a food plan and helped them relax before meals. As part of their aftercare plan, bulimic patients were referred to a relevant support group or eating disorder treatment program. No information on treatment outcome was supplied.

Some outcome information is available on dual-problem women treated for their bulimia in a cognitive-behavioral program (Mitchell, Pyle, Eckert & Hatsukami, 1990). These authors found that the outcome of bulimia treatment in women with substance abuse problems was comparable to the outcome with bulimics without substance abuse problems (over 60 per cent free of bulimic symptoms and another 15 per cent improved at two- to five-year follow-up). In this program, individuals with a chemical dependency problem receiving treatment for bulimia must first undergo treatment for the chemical dependency.

Pharmacological treatments have been explored with bulimics and anorectics. The use of tricyclic antidepressants (e.g., imipramine, desipramine) have proven most beneficial, at least in the short term (less than eight weeks). In the long run (one to two years), it is difficult to keep patients on medication, with frequent changes of drugs required, a high dropout rate, and a high relapse rate occurring when medication is withdrawn (Mitchell, P.B., 1988).

A variety of psychological treatments have been explored with bulimic patients either on an individual or group basis, in either an outpatient, inpatient or day hospital program. Family therapy is also often useful, especially with young patients living at home. Excellent outlines of a wide variety of treatment approaches are presented by Garner & Garfinkel (1985), Brownell & Foreyt (1986), and Schlundt & Johnson (1990). Many therapists use an eclectic approach, borrowing a variety of techniques from different theoretical orientations.

Cognitive-behavioral approaches have received the most research attention and are associated with relatively good outcome (Fairburn, 1988; Mitchell, P.B., 1988). The approach concentrates on instilling self-control by changing maladaptive attitudes, beliefs, and behaviors to more adaptive patterns, and by increasing the person's problem-solving and other coping skills. Various combinations of cognitive and behavioral skills training have also been used successfully in the treatment of alcoholism (Hester & Miller, 1989), and the approach could serve as the basis of integrating treatment of both disorders.

THE SEQUENCE OF TREATMENT

The first one or two sessions are usually devoted to a general assessment of the client along with answering the client's questions about eating disorders. The Diagnostic Survey of Eating Disorders (Johnson, 1985) is a useful structured interview for gaining information on such matters as weight, dieting, menstrual history, negative consequences experienced, attitudes towards body, sexual abuse, drug abuse, etc. In these initial sessions the therapist might outline for the client the general strategy for treatment, emphasizing that it involves gradually increasing self-control and that change is the client's responsibility.

A thorough medical checkup complements a psychological assessment of eating disorders. Medical complications result not only from binge-purging, but also from the state of starvation or semi-starvation that individuals with eating disorders endure. Kaplan & Woodside (1987) give an excellent overview of these symptoms. Among the more common are tiredness, headaches and poor concentration. Dry skin and hair often result from dehydration. Dental cavities, bursting of veins around the eyes, puffy cheeks related to salivary gland enlargement, and cracks at the corners of the mouth are largely due to chronic vomiting. Purging also eliminates sodium and potassium, which could cause an electrolyte imbalance that could result in hospitalization. Deficits in potassium can produce symptoms such apathy, delirium, irritability, and mood swings. Electrolyte deficiencies affect nerves and muscles, sometimes resulting in abnormal brainwaves and serious heart irregularities. Low potassium levels, especially when aggravated by laxative abuse, can cause interference in the wave-like contractions of the gut and intestine that pass food through the body. This can result in stomach cramps and chronic constipation. Amenorrhea is a diagnostic symptom of anorexia nervosa. Possibly 20 per cent or more of bulimics also experience this problem, while at least half experience some degree of menstrual irregularity. Eating disorders tend to interfere with normal hormonal functions, especially when the person is below her comfortable biological weight. The evolutionary message is: if you're starving, this is not a good time to have children. Sexual desire usually drops with chronic dieting. As a result of purging, low intake, and the stress of dieting, calcium levels can become abnormally low, encouraging osteoporosis. Alerting clients to these and other potentially negative consequences of eating disorders (Schlundt & Johnson, 1990) can help them to change and better understand their disorder.

The general strategy for cognitive-behavioral treatment can be described in terms of a direct and indirect attack on the disordered eating. Early treatment directly focuses on the bingeing and purging. As these problems become reduced, the focus shifts to factors that indirectly contribute to the bingeing (e.g., poor coping skills, body dissatisfaction).

The direct attack has a number of components. Typically, between the first and second session, the client is asked to self-monitor her eating, purging, weighing, exercise, and other relevant patterns without attempting change. When does the bingeing take place? What is going on at the time? What kinds of thoughts and feeling accompany the binge? What is consumed? Which meals are eaten or skipped? When and how frequently does purging occur? In which situations are urges to binge or purge most likely to occur? Which situations appear safe? Answers to these and other questions supply useful information on current maintaining factors, and offer a baseline from which to judge the progress of treatment. In this context, some self-monitoring should be maintained (e.g., binges, purges). It is wise to encourage clients to keep a diary of their relevant thoughts, feelings, and behaviors throughout treatment. This will prove a continuous learning experience for both patient and therapist. Where normal self-monitoring is impossible because the patient has been placed in an inpatient setting, self-reports concerning the same material should be carefully gathered in as much detail as possible. As women with dual disorders report high similarity in factors precipitating both bingeing and drinking, it should be possible to integrate a functional analysis of dangerous situations associated with both disorders.

When clients first see you, they invariably believe, and fervently hope, that you can eliminate their bingeing, purging, and associated problems while they continue to diet and maintain unhealthy weight levels. However, given the strong relationship between dieting and bingeing, one of the first components of the direct phase is to normalize the client's eating – three planned meals and one or two snacks per day. Many bulimics do not know what it is like to eat normally, and have lost touch with cues of hunger and satiety. Stimulus control is useful at this stage (e.g., eating planned meals at the same time and place each day, limiting availability of forbidden foods, etc.). Of course, eating normally usually makes them anxious about weight gain, and it's important for the therapists to deal with this in a supportive manner. I start clients at approximately 1,800 calories and eventually work up, if need be, to a sensible caloric intake for that person (about 2,200 calories for the average woman). Some do gain weight because they must reach a comfortable biological weight that they can maintain without dieting or overeating. Some bulimics maintain their approximate weight throughout treatment, possibly due to eliminating bingeing. Certainly, in severe bingers who do not purge by vomiting, eliminating the bingeing is commonly associated with weight loss. One sensible guideline is a goal weight not less than 90 per cent of the highest adult weight ever attained by the client (Garner, Rockert, Olmsted, Johnson & Coscina, 1985). The key is to find a comfortable weight clients can maintain without dieting or bingeing.

Goal setting for bingeing, purging, weighing and exercise is very important. An agreement is struck between the client and therapist for the general reduction of bingeing and purging. For example, a client who binges every day might attempt to reduce bingeing to four days per week. Once this goal is accomplished she might reduce it to two days per week, and so on. I actually encourage clients to binge without guilt on binge days. This sometimes has the paradoxical effect of reducing bingeing on those days as well. As one client said "It's just not the same when you tell me it's okay to do it." Reducing weighing to once a week tends to reduce the obsession with weight. If this is done in the presence of the therapists, any anxiety caused can be used productively as a treatment topic. Eventually, weighing can be dropped completely. A common saying in self-help groups is "Scales are for fish."

If a patient is not exercising, I encourage moderate activity as it seems to help self-control. If the client is exercising obsessively, attempt to reduce it to less obsessive levels, and encourage fun activities rather than activities aimed at pure calorie reduction.

Laxative and diuretic abuse are very inefficient means of eliminating food from the body (Bo-Lynn, Santa-Ana, Morawski & Fordtran, 1983). They essentially eliminate fluids and are associated with many dangerous side effects. Most clients respond well to therapeutic attempts to give up these substances.

Friends and family can be helpful during this first phase of treatment. Eating with others, having them around at dangerous times (e.g., after meals, evenings), being able to call on them for support when urges to binge or purge are present, are all very valuable. This presupposes that the friends or family members will be supportive. In some cases it is necessary to involve a friend or family member in treatment, not only to specify how they can be supportive, but to resolve conflict and prevent sabotage of the client's efforts. When clients live at home with parents, this is very important and often needs special attention.

The therapist should help clients generate alternative behaviors, preferably pleasurable ones (e.g., a walk, a movie, talking to a friend, rewarding themselves with non-food purchases, etc.), which can distract them or help them cope with difficult periods. In the early phase of treatment it also helps to avoid some situations (e.g., staying home alone to bake double chocolate chip cookies when they are feeling lonely and anxious).

A client with a severe bulimic pattern will often claim that she has no control over her bingeing urges, that the urge and the binge are one. Some form of systematic urge control training is useful here, and would have direct relevance to drinking or drug-taking urges as well. Clients can be educated about urges. An urge is only the first link in the chain that leads to the bingeing or substance use. It is a lot easier to control the urge than it is to control the bingeing or drug taking. If not satisfied, urges will eventually decline in frequency, but not necessarily in intensity. Urges are a normal part of breaking a habit. The worst strategy for dealing with urges is to remain passive or to think negatively. An urge should be a signal to go into action, go on the attack (engage in distraction activities, call a friend, go to an AA meeting, etc.) I find it helps to have clients write down thoughts or ideas that they find helpful and to rehearse them when experiencing an urge. ("The more urges I extinguish, the less frequent they will get, the more control I will have. I will not be passive. I'll outsmart this urge by doing the following. I will call a friend, etc.").

Some clients find imagery techniques helpful (e.g., imagining an on/off switch that controls the urge and picturing themselves turning the switch slowly to off, feeling in control and coping effectively). It's useful here to introduce clients to cognitive therapy techniques for combatting discouragement, catastrophic thinking, perfectionism, and other self-defeating cognitive patterns (Garfinkel & Garner, 1982).

The net effect of all the strategies and techniques used during the direct attack phase is to greatly reduce or eliminate the bingeing and purging, and normalize eating.

As the person grows more confident in her ability to control the bingeing and purging, the therapist increases the time spent indirectly attacking the disordered eating. If the person uses bingeing to cope with anxiety and stress, then the therapist can teach anxiety and stress management skills. If the person binges in response to boredom, skills at structuring time may be required. If they are lonely and depressed, then social skills and mood control may need to be developed. I find it most useful to teach skills in a general problem-solving format (i.e., identify problem, generate solutions, choose solution, implement and evaluate solution, etc.).

Along with an increase in coping skills, and the increase in confidence that usually accompanies effective coping, clients should be gradually reintroduced to coping with "taboo" foods. As long as these foods are avoided they tend to have the power to elicit bingeing. The approach I like best is a graded exposure from least-avoided to most-avoided "taboo" foods, but some programs require patients to eat all food right from the beginning of treatment. This may be particularly suitable in an inpatient or day treatment program where monitoring and access to therapists are readily available. Careful planning and initial exposure to "taboo" foods in the presence of the therapist or a trusted friend is helpful. Remember, consumption of these foods generates anxiety, and in the past was almost invariably followed by purging. It is therefore especially important to avoid purging, and deal with any anxiety generated. Indeed, Rosen & Leitenberg (1982) make this exposure-plus-response-prevention strategy the central basis of their promising treatment of bulimia nervosa. If the avoidance behavior (purging) is blocked, then the anxiety response to the "taboo" foods should eventually subside, enhancing the client's sense of control.

During the indirect phase of treatment the therapist continues cognitive therapy to correct any myths or irrational thoughts the client has concerning food, weight, or shape (e.g., "I have to be 105 lb. to feel good. I can't be attractive unless I'm thin. It would be terrible if I gained any weight. I can't be happy unless I'm thin"). This emphasis blends nicely into general consciousness raising over how society shapes women's attitudes and behavior in destructive ways. Exercises such as critically evaluating women's fashion magazines, and contacting organizations such as HERSIZE, are useful. The National Eating Disorder Information Centre in Toronto can supply excellent handouts relevant to consciousness raising. A healthy dose of feminist-oriented literature, such as *Fat is a Feminist Issue* by Orbach, or *Making Peace With Food* by Kano, is highly recommended.

As the person gains control over bingeing and purging, the therapists also work to increase the client's self-esteem and body esteem. The general strategy is to broaden self-esteem beyond appearance and weight to other aspects of one's personality and behavior, and to encourage less judgmental, more accepting, and more positive attitudes toward the self. Often, the therapist and client together must work through negative attitudes towards body and self that stem from past sexual abuse or chronic criticism. Problems concerning sexuality and intimacy are commonly encountered. In clients with dual disorders, shame and embarrassment over events associated with an alcohol- or drug-abusing life-style also require a therapist's attention.

There are numerous exercises and homework assignments for improving body image (e.g., Butters & Cash, 1985; Wooley & Kearney-Cooke, 1986). The person is encouraged to get rid of clothes that don't fit, stop judging her body, make friends with it and discard beliefs such as "A flatter stomach and thinner thighs are the answer to school, job, family and relationship problems." The person can be encouraged to do now all the things she had planned to do on reaching her magical ideal weight.

The final stage of treatment concerns planning for the future, and relapse prevention training (Marlatt & Gordon, 1985). In an ideal world there would be no lapses after the end of treatment. Unfortunately, data from many areas of addictive behavior suggests that occasional lapses are the norm. The therapist is then wise to help the client not only to avoid lapses, but to prevent them from turning into full-scale relapses. Here, relapse-prevention training for substance abuse can easily be integrated with relapse-prevention considerations for bulimia nervosa. The latter involves teaching the client to recognize potentially dangerous situations (e.g., going home for Christmas), and to have a good coping plan for dealing with them. The problem-solving strategies used earlier are obviously relevant here. If a binge occurs, the client should have the attitude of learning from the mistake, reintroducing self-control strategies, enlisting the help of friends, etc. Going back to dieting will only encourage more bingeing, which in turn makes purging more likely.

If appropriate self-help groups for eating disorders are available in the community, the therapists might consider suggesting that the client join. The best groups are those that concentrate on problem solving and social support. I have now seen a number of dual-problem clients who also attend meetings of AA or Women for Sobriety. In general, while these self-help groups deal primarily with substance abuse, they have been rather helpful as they deal with many issues that are also relevant to recovery from eating disorders.

ACKNOWLEDGEMENT
The author sincerely thanks Joanne Trousdale for typing this chapter and for her expert editorial assistance.

REFERENCES

American Psychiatric Association (1987). Diagnostic and statistical manual of mental disorders (3rd ed.). Washington, D.C. : Author

Bennett, W. & Gurin, J. (1982). The dieter's dilemma. New York: Basic Books, Inc.

Boland, F.J. & Butt, J. (1989). Increased signs of eating disorders in women with alcohol problems. Paper presented at Canadian Psychological Association, Halifax.

Bo-Lynn, G., Santa-Ana, C.A., Morawski, S.G. & Fordtran, J.S. (1983). Purging and calorie absorption in bulimic patients and normal women. Annals of Internal Medicine, 99, 14–17.

Butters, J.W. & Cash, T.F. (1987). Cognitive behavioral treatment of women's body image dissatisfaction. Journal of Consulting and Clinical Psychology, 55, 889–897.

Bruch, H. (1977). Psychological antecedents of anorexia nervosa. In R. A. Vigersky (Ed.). Anorexia Nervosa, (pp. 1–10). New York: Raven Press.

Cooper, P.J. & Fairburn, C.G. (1983). Binge-eating and self-induced vomiting in the community: A preliminary study. British Journal of Psychiatry, 142, 139–144.

Fairburn, C.G. (1984). Bulimia: Its epidemiology and management. In A.J. Stunkard & E. Stellar (Eds.). Eating and its disorders, (pp. 235–258). New York: Raven Press.

Fava, M., Copland, P.M., Schiveiger, U. & Herzog, D.B. (1989). Neurochemical abnormalities of anorexia nervosa and bulimia nervosa. American Journal of Psychiatry, 146, 963–971.

Fairburn, C.G. (1988). The current status of the psychological treatment of bulimia nervosa. Journal of Psychosomatic Research, 32, 635–645.

Garner, D.M. & Garfinkel, P.E. (1980). Socio-cultural factors in the development of anorexia nervosa. Psychological Medicine, 10, 647–656.

Garfinkel, P.E. & Garner, D.M. (1982). Anorexia Nervosa: A multidimensional perspective. New York: Brunner/Mazel.

Hatsukami, D., Mitchell, J.E., Eckert, E.D. & Pyle, R.L. (1986). Characteristics of patients with bulimia only; bulimia with affective disorder, and bulimia with substance abuse problems. Addictive Behaviors, 11, 399–406.

Hatsukami, D., Owen, P., Pyle, R.L. & Mitchell, J.E. (1982). Similarities and differences on the MMPI between women with bulimia and women with alcohol abuse problems. Addictive Disorders, 7, 435–439.

Hatsukami, D., Eckert, E.D., Mitchell, J.E. & Pyle R.L. (1984). Affective disorder and substance abuse in women with bulimia. Psychological Medicine, 14, 701–704.

Hester, R.K. & Miller, W.R. (1989). Handbook of Alcoholism Treatment Approaches. New York: Pergamon Press.

Johnson, C. (1985). Initial consultation for patients with bulimia and anorexia nervosa. In Garner, D.M. & Garfinkel, P.E. (Eds.). Handbook of Psychotherapy for Anorexia Nervosa and Bulimia. New York: The Guilford Press.

Kaplan, A.S. & Woodside, D.B. (1987). Biological aspects of anorexia nervosa and bulimia nervosa. Journal of Consulting and Clinical Psychology, 55, 645–653.

Keesey, R.E. & Powley, T.L. (1986). The regulation of body weight. Annual Review of Psychology, 37, 109–133.

Keys, A., Biozek, J., Henschel, A., Mickelsen, O. & Taylor, H.L. (1950). The biology of human starvation. Minneapolis: University of Minnesota Press.

Knight, L.J. & Boland, F.J. (1989). Restrained eating: An experimental disentanglement of the disinhibiting variables of perceived calories and food type. Journal of Abnormal Psychology, 98, 412–420.

Loro, A.D., & Orlens, C.S. (1981). Binge-eating in obesity: Preliminary findings and guidelines for behavioral analysis and treatment. Addictive Behaviors, 6, 155–166.

Marlatt, G.A. & Gordon, J.R. (1985). Relapse Prevention. New York: The Guilford Press.

Mitchell, J.E., Hatsukami, D., Eckert, E.D. & Pyle, R.L. (1985). Characteristics of 275 patients with bulimia. American Journal of Psychiatry, 142, 482–485.

Mitchell, J.E., Pyle, R.L., Eckert, E.D. & Hatsukami, D. (1990). The influence of prior alcohol and drug abuse problems on bulimia nervosa treatment outcome. Addictive Behaviors, 15, 169–173.

Mitchell, P.B. (1988). The pharmacological management of bulimia nervosa: A critical review. International Journal of Eating Disorders, 7, 29–41.

Perlman, A. & McKenna, T. (1988). A comparison of bulimic and non-bulimic chemical dependency patients. Hazelden Professional Update, 7, 1–6.

Piran, N., Lerner, P., Garfinkel, P.E., Kennedy, S. & Brouilette, C. (1988). Personality disorders in restricting and bulimic forms of anorexia nervosa. International Journal of Obesity, 1, 589–600.

Polivy, J. & Herman, C.P. (1976). The effect of alcohol on eating behavior: Disinhibition or sedation? Addictive Behaviors, 1, 121–125.

Rand, C.S.W., Lawlor, B.A. & Kuldan, J.M. (1986). Patterns of food and alcohol consumption in a group of bulimic women. Bulletin of Society of Psychologists in Addictive Behaviors, 5, 95–104.

Rodin, G., Daneman, D., Johnson, L., Kenshole, A. & Garfinkel, P.E. (1986) Anorexia nervosa and bulimia in insulin-dependent diabetes melitis. International Journal of Psychiatric Medicine, 16, 49–57.

Rosen, J.C. & Leitenberg, H. (1982). Bulimia nervosa: Treatment with exposure and response prevention. Behavior Therapy, 13, 117–124.

Spitzer, L. & Rodin, J., (1987). Effects of fructose and glucose preloads on subsequent food intake. Appetite, 8, 135–145.

Striegel-Moore, R.H., Silberstein, L.R. & Rodin, J. (1986). Towards an understanding of risk factors for bulimia. American Psychologist, 41, 246–263.

Vanderheyden, D.A. & Boland, F.J. (1987). A comparison of normals, mild, moderate and severe binge-eaters, and binge-vomiters using discriminant function analysis. International Journal of Eating Disorders, 6, 331–337.

Walker, C.E., Bonner, B.L. & Kaufman, K.L (1988). The physically and sexually abused child: Evaluation and treatment. Toronto: Pergamon Press.

Wooley, S.C. & Kearney-Cooke, A. (1986). Intensive treatment of bulimia and body-image disturbance. In K.D. Brownell & J.B. Foreyt (Eds.). Handbook of eating disorders (pp. 476–502). New York: Basic Books, Inc.

RECOMMENDED READINGS

Any of the following three books would serve as an excellent general reference to all aspects of eating disorders and their treatment:

Brownell, K.D. & Foreyt, J.P. (1986). <u>Handbook of Eating Disorders.</u> New York: Basic Books.

Garner, D.M. & Garfinkel, P.E. (1985). <u>Handbook of psychotherapy for anorexia nervosa and bulimia.</u> New York: The Guilford Press.

Schlundt, D.G., & Johnson, W.G. (1990). <u>Eating disorders: Assessment and treatment.</u> Boston: Allyn and Bacon.

For a very readable and comprehensive summary of information related to eating disorders see:

Garner, D.M., Rocket, W., Olmasted, M.P., Johnson, C. & Coscina, D.V. (1985). Psychoeducational principles in the treatment of bulimia and anorexia nervosa. In D.M. Garner, & P.E. Garfinkel (Eds.). <u>Handbook of psychotherapy for anorexia nervosa and bulimia.</u> New York: The Guilford Press (pp. 513–572).

Popular non-technical books that are useful in therapy by both client and therapist:

Chernin, K. (1981). <u>The Obsession: Reflections on the tyranny of slenderness.</u> New York: Harper and Row.

Hutchinson, M. (1985). <u>Transforming body image.</u> New York: Crossing Press.

Kano, S. (1989). <u>Making peace with food.</u> New York: Harper and Row.

Orbach, S. (1982). <u>Fat is a feminist issue II.</u> New York: Berkeley Books.

Polivy, J., & Herman, C.P. (1983). <u>Breaking the diet habit: The natural weight alternative.</u> New York: Basic Books.

For family and friends of a person with an eating disorder, a particularly good book deals with identifying an eating disorder, and getting a person to treatment:

Seigel, M., Brisman, J., & Wienshel, M. (1988). <u>Surviving an eating disorder: New perspectives for families and friends.</u> New York: Harper & Row.

The following organizations can help by sending newsletters, and informing about therapists, self-help groups, workshops, and conferences on eating disorders.

The National Eating Disorder Information Centre. Toronto General Hospital, 200 Elizabeth Street 2–332, Toronto, Ontario M5G 2C4.

Anorexia Nervosa and Bulimia Foundation of Canada. P.O. Box 3074, Winnipeg, Manitoba, R3C 4E5.

Bulimia Anorexia Nervosa Association. c/o Psychological Services, University of Windsor, Windsor, Ontario, N9B 3P4.

HERSIZE. 223 Concord Avenue, Toronto, Ontario M6H 2P4.

BASH. (Bulimia, Anorexia, Self-Help) Magazine, 6125 Clayton Avenue, Suite 215, St. Louis, Missouri, 63139, U.S.A.

Radiance Magazine. P.O. Box 31703, Oakland, California, 94604–9937, U.S.A.

Special Needs of Particular Populations: Dual Disorders

GERRY COOPER AND CARL KENT

INTRODUCTION

Concurrent psychiatric and substance abuse disorders within individual clients have only recently become the focus of a growing body of scientific literature. Despite the impression one might have as a result of this literature explosion, the condition often generically referred to as "dual disorders" is not a new problem. For example, in Freed's 1975 article "Alcoholism and Schizophrenia," almost 200 references were listed, many related directly to this topic, including Kantorovich's "The effect of alcohol in catatonic syndromes..." and Minski's "Psychopathy and psychoses associated with alcohol," both published in the 1930s. Indeed, the association between psychiatric syndromes and alcohol abuse and morphine misuse respectively dates back to Rush in 1798 and Levinson in 1878 (Glass, 1989).

Several factors may account for the recent escalation in attention to dual disorders.

First, improvements to diagnostic instrumentation and procedures (both psychiatric and substance abuse) have greatly assisted clinicians in their ability to identify clients (Malla et al., 1987; Merskey et al., 1988; Schofield, 1989) and their respective problems (Powell et al., 1982; Rounsaville et al., 1987).

One example of the considerable advances in diagnostic classification is the DSM-III-R (American Psychiatric Association, 1987), which encourages clinicians to make multiple and differential diagnoses of their clients (El-Guebaly, 1990; Pedersen, 1990).

The second factor concerns the effects of psychiatric deinstitutionalization (Brown et al., 1989). This societal development created an entirely new group of clients who frequently encountered a set of community-based problems previously unknown to many of them: homelessness, unemployment, and easy access to psychoactive substances, to name a few (Ananth et al., 1989; Susser et al., 1989). Many in this group have been described by Bachrach (1982) as highly mobile "baby-boomers" who often tend to use services inappropriately due to their mobility: prior to the era of deinstitutionalization, many of these persons would likely have been permanently hospitalized – not multiple-service users. Not surprisingly, the duplicate use of resources by this newer group of patients has caught the eye of clinicians and system planners alike. In many instances, the system of care has been overwhelmed by such deinstitutionalized patients (Pepper et al., 1981; Cohen and Johnson, 1988); as a result (at least in the U.S.), "psychiatric chemical dependency and rehabilitative hospital care [programs]... are now booming" (Peele, 1990, p. 181).

Finally, several large federal funding agencies in the U.S. have co-ordinated their efforts with regards to this issue. American mental health, drug, and alcohol treatment systems have traditionally been separate (Gottheil et al., 1980); with dual disorders, these bodies are attempting to bridge the knowledge gaps by funding cross-over demonstration treatment programs and associated research projects (Brown et al., 1989). The influence these above developments have had in Ontario should not be underestimated; it is safe to say that all are paralleled here as can be seen by key government policy documents (Graham, 1988).

From the foregoing, two conclusions can be drawn: (1) there appears to be a very high prevalence of dual disorders among both psychiatric and substance abuse treatment system populations; and (2) the level of care provided to such persons has generally failed to respond to their unique treatment needs. Gottheil and colleagues aptly summarize this point: "Often these patients are shuttled back and forth, or they fall through the cracks of the system and are lost to treatment, or they are treated in both [psychiatric and substance abuse] clinics with conflicting methods and confusing effects" (1980, p. xii).

The remainder of this chapter will address the following issues: definition, prevalence, etiology, obstacles to effective treatment, and recommendations for treatment efficacy; a brief conclusion will follow.

DEFINITION

The reader should be aware that the term "dual disorders" is generic, used in other ways (for example, Fisher et al. [1989] use "dual diagnoses" to refer to persons with mental retardation and psychiatric comorbidity), and that it requires further definition. In many instances, it may be a misnomer since individuals often suffer from more than two (dual) disorders. A more accurate description to accommodate persons with several illnesses would probably be "concurrent" or "concomitant" disorders; however, since most of the literature refers to "dual", the remainder of this text will yield to the common term. For the purpose of this chapter then, dual disorders will be basically understood to be "two overlapping but discernable subgroups of patients. One subgroup has by DSM-III criteria both a major substance abuse disorder and another major psychiatric illness. The other subgroup uses alcohol and/or other drugs in ways that affect the course and treatment of [their] mental illness" (El-Guebaly, 1990, p. 261).

However, even when confined to these realms, arriving at a precise definition is no easy task since (1) there are no absolute or uniform definitions currently in use, and (2) both the acute and chronic effects of psychoactive substance use/abuse can either mask or mimic just about any psychiatric disorder (hence El-Guebaly's important qualifier that the symptoms satisfy DSM-III criteria).

The need for complete detoxification in order to better understand and respond to the client's presenting symptomatology is underscored by Miller and Gold (1989):

> "The need to observe and follow the clinical state of the [substance abuser] for a period of time during acute, subacute, and protracted withdrawal in the abstinent state is frequently necessary to establish another psychiatric diagnosis. Alcoholic hallucinosis, alcohol- and cocaine-induced anxiety and depression, and hallucinogenic-induced psychosis are examples of 'psychiatric symptoms' that may persist for weeks to months following cessation of use. Premature intervention with unnecessary treatment modalities may interfere with establishing the correct diagnosis and the institution of effective modalities" (p. 228).

Due to the persistence of some mimic-type symptoms, it is clear that proper assessment needs to be conducted on an ongoing basis and the provisional diagnosis, usually made at the outset of intervention, be adjusted accordingly as new and clinically significant information becomes apparent (Ananth et al., 1989). Universally accepted diagnostic classification systems (such as DSM-III-R) should be used consistently when addressing a client's problems, as they set out standardized criteria for rendering diagnoses (based upon observable symptomatology).

The diagnostic picture is further complicated, though, by even smaller subgroups within the dual disorders population. For example, the young chronically mentally ill person has been described as being "hypervulnerable – chemically, psychologically, and socially – to the effects of even mild or recreational use of drugs and alcohol" (Brown et al., 1989, p. 567). These individuals' psychiatric treatment often includes pharmacotherapy; even modest amounts of alcohol could interact with the medication(s) to produce a compounded effect; often to the person's complete surprise. Therefore, to make accurate diagnoses, clinicians may need to drop some long-held beliefs and stereotypic notions about substance abusers. Substance use and/or abuse, and not necessarily full-fledged dependence, may precipitate and exacerbate psychiatric problems in this particular subgroup (Schmidt, 1989).

PREVALENCE

Substance abuse among psychiatric patients and psychopathology among substance abusers seem quite common. Given the earlier warning by Miller and

Gold about the need for accurate post-detoxification diagnosis and the fact that many of the prevalence studies to date suffer from related methodological problems, it is difficult to establish just how common these phenomena really are.

Table 1 on page 386 outlines various efforts to identify the extent of the dual disorders problem among different populations. While this is not a complete inventory of prevalence studies, it is felt to be fairly comprehensive and quite representative of the literature. The majority of these studies examined substance abuse among psychiatric patients in treatment, but several also considered psychiatric problems among substance abusers both in treatment, and in the general community. Table 1 describes the research team, sample characteristics, sample size, and key findings of each study.

Due to the varied methodologies used therein to report prevalence, it would be inappropriate to compare each study directly to all of the others. For example, some studies conducted exhaustive assessment batteries with post-detoxification clients, while others merely conducted retrospective analyses of clinical records. Other factors affecting the reported epidemiology of this problem include: a) the definitions used by researchers (once again, these vary); b) treatment type and location: different kinds of services attract different presenting problems in their clientele (Glaser, 1988; Pedersen, 1990); and, c) the qualifications, attitudes, skill levels (Gottheil and Weinstein, 1980; Seixas, 1980) and diagnostic habits (Raistrick, 1989) of the staff at treatment programs. Suffice it to say however, that the percentages found for dual disordered clients throughout both the psychiatric and substance abuse systems, are indeed cause for concern by all those who staff affected programs.

The extent to which these statistics are indicative of the dual disorders problem in the general population is not known (although Weissman and Meyers [1980], Helzer and Pryzbeck [1988], and Schmidt [1989] give some measure of this from U.S. data). It may well be that due to the seriousness of debilitation, those with such problems eventually find their way into treatment (Woody et al., 1990); one would then expect their numbers to be high at treatment programs relative to unitary disorder patients who may have a different course of illness and treatment, and perhaps higher rates of natural recovery/self healing (Bukstein et al., 1989). What is not known are the characteristics of those who fall between the cracks and as a result are left out of study samples (Cooper et al., 1990a). However, even for those included in study samples, the predictiveness, generalizability, and applicability of the research findings must be questioned: these study clientele are usually quite distinct and it has already been noted that "dual disorders" is a catch-all term for many different conditions. In short, it is difficult to draw too many definitive conclusions about a population as heterogeneous as the dually disordered. Schmidt (1989) suggests that while her prevalence data indicate that the burden of comorbidity is not as great as that implied by other studies, such cases pose special problems to service providers.

Another possible explanation for the potentially inflated prevalence ratios in Table 1 concerns "the validity of such diagnoses when they are made at the point of entry into treatment, at a time when intoxication or withdrawal symptoms may mimic other psychiatric disorders" (Ross et al., 1988b, p. 1191). By way of illustration, some of the studies reviewed in Table 1 interviewed only post-detoxification clients while others did not; Ross and her colleagues (1988) interviewed three-fifths of their research subjects within three days of registration to an addictions treatment facility, at a time when one might expect to find at least some clients still in a state of withdrawal. This conceivably could elevate the prevalence of current psychiatric symptomatology, which might simply disappear with abstinence (Attia, 1988); in other words, a false positive finding contaminating the data pool. Fine (1980), for example, recommends that "the possibility of serious associated depressive disease be considered in all alcoholic patients [only] after a sufficient period of time (at least seven days) has elapsed after withdrawal from alcohol" (p. 136). Some have even noted the existence of "protracted withdrawal syndrome which can be seen in patients for up to a year or more following acute detoxification" (Wallen and Weiner, 1988).

Nevertheless, any question about over-inflated prevalence statistics must be tempered by the number of dually-disordered individuals who are served poorly or not at all, due to the inflexible status quo of many of the present treatment systems' structures (Carey, 1989a). Such clients are often denied treatment at substance abuse programs because of their psychiatric condition, and/or at psychiatric facilities due to their substance abuse problems. These people often receive less than optimal care, which results in their attrition from the helping system; hence the term "falling through the cracks." This rather bleak scenario has spawned some unflattering jargon such as "the patient shuffle" (Moss, 1990), "system misfits" (Moss, 1990), "ping-ponged" (Pedersen, 1990) and "pigeonholed" (Mee-Lee, 1990). To date, no published accounts provide comprehensive information about these people; anecdotal-type data suggest, however, that they exist in abundance (Willauer et al., 1990) and it is hoped that preliminary work in this area will provide some clues as to how their care might be improved in future (Cooper et al., 1990b).

ETIOLOGY

With respect to the cause of dual disorders, it appears that the jury is still out. Some claim that two-thirds of all such cases are a direct result of prior alcohol abuse (McEvoy, 1989), while others contend that substance abuse often results from psychiatric illness as individuals attempt to self-medicate. Hall et al. (1979) for instance, found as many as 50 per cent in one study where this was the case.

The self-medication hypothesis has received considerable support from other researchers. Reich et al. (1974) found that, contrary to the assumption that alcohol is used to counteract depressive symptoms, their subjects drank excessively primarily during the manic phase of bi-polar affective disorder, and did so to reduce their

TABLE 1
PREVALENCE RATES OF DUAL DISORDERS IN VARIOUS SETTINGS

RESEARCHER	SAMPLE CHARACTERISTICS	SAMPLE SIZE	KEY FINDINGS
1. Blumberg et al. (1971)	Young hospitalized psychiatric patients subjected to urinalyses.	332	60% covert drug abuse determined.
2. Cadoret and Winokur (1972)	Alcoholics interviewed from two St. Louis area hospitals.	259	50% exhibited additional psychiatric syndromes providing that secondary depression was included.
3. Crowley et al. (1974)	Consecutive patients admitted to an adult ward in a western U.S. university psychiatric hospital were assessed by bio-chemical markers and interview.	50	Over 33% had drug abuse (including alcohol) problems.
4. Reich et al. (1974)	Retrospective review of psychiatric patients treated in a Connecticut area inpatient unit and outpatient clinic for manic-depressive illness.	40	13/26 manic patients exhibited excessive drinking, 7/14 depressed phase patients exhibited excessive drinking.
5. Tyndel (1974)	Post-withdrawal alcoholic patients hospitalized at a Toronto addiction research centre (males to females 5:1)	1,000	"Some degree" of psychopathology identified in 100% of sample.
6. Fischer et al. (1975)	Interviews with consecutive admissions of psychiatric patients.	335 of 380 partic.	31% admitted to substance abuse of one or more drugs in lifetime (including alcohol); about 50% of this group currently using.
7. Westermeyer and Walzer (1975)	Young (15–25 years) psychiatric inpatients examined at a university general psychiatric unit in Minnesota.	100	49% found to be heavy drug users.
8. Fowler et al. (1977)	Diagnostic findings of all male admissions (under 65 years and in hospital at least 4 days) to a psychiatric inpatient service at a veterans administration (V.A). hospital in Iowa City, Iowa.	120	63 of 120 (53%) met research diagnoses of probable or definite alcoholism.
9. Hall et al. (1977)	Examination and urinalysis of all psychiatric outpatients attending medication clinics at a community mental health centre.	195 of 226 partic.	26 patients found to be currently using (non-alcohol) drugs and had a negative history of current or past drug abuse.
10. McLellan et al. (1978)	Male psychiatric inpatients randomly selected at a V.A. hospital near Philadelphia.	156	50% reported lifetime substance abuse prior to hospitalization; only 12% had revealed such to hospital staff.
11. Hall et al. (1979)	Interviews with consecutive admissions (prescreened to exclude substance abusers) at a large-city, university-affiliated, psychiatric research unit.	57	Substance abuse occurred in 58% of the population prescreened to eliminate its presence.
12. Weissman and Meyers (1980)	An entire community sampled in the rural New Haven, Connecticut area to identify rates of psychiatric disorders in alcoholics.	510	2.6% of entire sample identified as having a current rate of alcoholism, 6.7% had a lifetime rate of alcoholism, 24 of 34 (71%) of this latter group had at least one other psychiatric diagnosis.
13. Powell et al. (1982)	Interviews with successive male alcoholic admissions (thoroughly detoxed) from 5 V.A. inpatient medical centres.	565	63% had one or more diagnosable psychiatric disorders.
14. Rounsaville et al. (1982)	Opiate addicts administered a structured interview at a Connecticut treatment unit.	533	70% identified with a current and 87% a lifetime additional psychiatric syndrome.
15. O'Farrell et al. (1983)	Hospitalized psychiatric patients from 10 wards (excluding substance abuse) at a Massachusetts V.A. centre were examined.	309	Smoking was the most common addictive behavior (89%) followed by alcohol abuse (33%).
16. Ramsey et al. (1983)	Retrospective chart study of patients with psychiatric problems in an outpatient family practice clinic.	177	23% showed signs of possible alcoholism and 6% were identified as definitely alcoholic.

RESEARCHER	SAMPLE CHARACTERISTICS	SAMPLE SIZE	KEY FINDINGS
17. Hesselbrock et al. (1985)	Randomly selected post-detoxification hospitalized alcoholics from three treatment centres in the Hartford, Connecticut area were interviewed.	321	77% satisfied criteria of having one or more psychiatric syndromes.
18. Golowka (1987)	Psychiatric patients at a Maryland state hospital.	—	68% of all patients suffered some form of active drinking problem.
19. McKelvy et al. (1987)	Admissions to a state psychiatric hospital in Maine.	—	80% of admissions present drug and/or alcohol use as a complicating factor and 60% of all admissions show both mental illness and substance abuse problems.
20. Safer (1987)	Information obtained from treating clinicians and a case record review of young (19–39 years) unemployable chronic psychiatric outpatients at a Maryland community mental health centre.	41	30 of 41 patients (73%) had a substance abuse history (44% current and 29% lifetime).
21. Helzer and Pryzbeck (1988)	The largest ever personal interview survey of psychiatric disorder in the general population ever done; conducted in 5 distinct sites across the U.S.	20,000+	13.7% had a diagnosis of alcohol abuse/dependence, 47% of this group had another psychiatric diagnosis.
22. Menicucci et al. (1988)	Unit chiefs of various substance abuse and psychiatric units interviewed.	8 unit chiefs	Comorbidity found as follows: psychiatric units – three at 50%, two between 15 and 33%; substance abuse units – outpatient at 50%, inpatient at 30–50%.
23. Ross et al. (1988)	Patients seeking assistance with alcohol and other drug problems at an addiction research centre in Toronto were interviewed.	501 (52% male)	78% found to have had a lifetime prevalence of psychiatric disorder, and 65% a current psychiatric disorder.
24. Ananth et al. (1989)	Interviewed were patients (18–57 years) randomly selected from acute admission wards of a state psychiatric hospital in Los Angeles.	75 (52% female)	54 of 75 patients (72%) received a drug-related diagnosis even after excluding cases exhibiting occasional use.
25. Schmidt (1989)	Assessed for drinking problems via self-reports were equally divided community-based and inpatient mental health cases and a comparable interview with adults from the same U.S. county's household population.	406 clients 3,066 general population	18 to 25% of mental health cases identified as problem drinkers versus 2 to 6% in the general population.
26. Schofield (1989)	Patients consecutively admitted to three different wards of a general hospital in Cork, Ireland were assessed over 4 weeks.	331 of 407 partic. (54% male)	20% met the criteria to be a problem drinker; the greater the CAGE score, the greater the psychiatric morbidity.
27. Dobkin et al. (1991)	Voluntary participation of consecutive admission psychiatric patients (18–65 years) via interview and biochemical marker (GGT) in a North Bay, Ontario provincial hospital.	763 of 854 partic. (74% male)	56.7% tested positive on either or both of the screening tests and were therefore found to be possible alcoholics.
28. Olivera et al. (1990)	First admissions to an inpatient unit in Ohio specializing in the treatment of major mental disorders complicated by substance abuse were interviewed; all were illicit drug abusing psychiatric patients undergoing treatment with neuroleptic medication.	284 (99% male)	Tardive Dyskenesia (involuntary movements) were more likely in patients treated with neuroleptics if alcohol was chronically used (either alone or with cannabis).
29. Roy et al. (1990)	As part of an alcohol research program, alcoholic patients who had attempted suicide were interviewed in the Laboratory of Clinical Studies – NIAAA – Maryland.	57 of 298 had attempted suicide	Suicide attempters (19%) were significantly more likely to have had lifetime episodes of psychiatric disorder than non-attempters.
30. Willauer et al. (1990)	Directors of community and hospital-based substance abuse and psychiatric agencies and services throughout Northeastern Ontario were surveyed.	44 of 71 partic.	74% of respondents knew of clients on their caseload with a "formal" dual diagnosis; 92% "suspected" dually disordered cases among their clientele.

manic symptoms. McLellan et al. (1980) found that psychiatric patients routinely chose drugs with similar psychophysiological effects, as opposed to random drug combinations, and that specific disorders were related to drug type; they concluded that: "the progressive development of significant differential pathology as a function of drug pattern, are clearly suggestive of causality... that the regular, prolonged abuse of specific combinations of street drugs may have an active and direct role in the development and expression of psychiatric disorders" (p. 22). Ross and colleagues (1988) would eventually report a predictive relationship between the severity of substance abuse and the likelihood of psychiatric problems.

Some interesting gender differences have also been observed which may contribute to the etiological picture. Generally, women have been found to have a later age of onset of alcoholism than men (Winokur et al., 1970) and correspondingly, psychiatric problems frequently predate substance abuse in women (Fine, 1980); the reverse is true for men (Hesselbrock et al., 1985). It is difficult to know whether this has a cause/effect relationship regarding the higher prevalence of depression in women, and anti-social personality disorder in men.

Clearly, age of onset of substance abuse and/or psychiatric problems is a very important factor. It has been demonstrated that early onset of alcoholism and additional psychiatric syndromes are significantly related to a family history of alcoholism (Cadoret, 1978; Powell et al., 1982; Blankfield, 1987).

Other factors that should be considered include the absence of social support mechanisms (Lin et al., 1979) and stressors such as homelessness (Koegel et al., 1988); each of these issues have been found to exert significant influence upon illness symptoms and their prevalence.

OBSTACLES TO EFFECTIVE TREATMENT

It is not surprising that treatment services often fail to help the individual with dual disorders: unfortunately, it is quite common for these persons to go undetected (Robinson and Wolkind, 1970; Blumberg et al., 1971; Hall et al., 1977; McLennan et al., 1978; Hall et al., 1979; Menicucci et al., 1988 Anderson et al., 1990); to be mis-diagnosed (Schuckit, 1983; Pepper, 1984; Levy and Mann 1988; Woody et al., 1990); or otherwise improperly treated due to inappropriate staff attitudes and/or lack of competence (Panepinto et al., 1970; Gottheil and Weinstein, 1980; Carey, 1989a; Cooper et al., 1990b). An atypical response by substance abuse practitioners to their clients identified with psychopathology has been highlighted and keenly described by Raistrick: "Mental illness often has the unusual effect on clinicians of paralysing their normally prolific requests for [further] investigations" (1989, p. 177).

This latter point has been directly related to the absence of appropriate training in medical and other professional schools (Kamerow et al., 1986; Glass, 1989; Peyser, 1989). Very few programs attempt to identify and fully assess a client's psychiatric and substance abuse status; even fewer complement their findings with corroborative data from significant others and/or bio-chemical laboratory tests.

For those few who are correctly identified, there is an almost complete absence of specialized programs to refer them to, and those who do provide these services are usually not well known to most potential referral agents. Program directors who want to expand their service delivery base to better help the dually disordered will find very little treatment outcome research to assist with their task (Kofoed et al., 1986; Caragonne and Emery, 1987). Furthermore, the absence of any large-scale dual-disorders advocacy group that could influence policy makers, practitioners and administrators may also have contributed to this state of affairs (Kopolow, 1981). Until recently, there did not seem to be the necessary political will to alter this sad course: as stated earlier, traditionally the mental health and substance abuse systems have operated quite independently (Gottheil et al., 1980; Todd, 1980; McKelvy et al., 1987; Carey, 1989a). This has magnified all of the above problems.

Fortunately, this scenario is undergoing rapid change. The dramatic increase in the scientific and popular literature concerning this subject is having considerable impact. Dual-disorder self-help groups are being formed in many communities, clinicians are very predisposed to specialized training (Cooper et al., 1990b), and governmental position documents herald a commitment to change (Graham, 1988).

RECOMMENDATIONS FOR TREATMENT EFFICACY

Much work still needs to be done towards understanding the heterogeneity of dual disorders and empirically demonstrating the effectiveness of various therapeutic approaches; however, some consensus regarding relevant treatment principles seems to be emerging. What follows is a synthesis of this consensus, which is based on published program descriptions, case studies, and best advice models. Table 2 on page 388 presents the citations from which these principles have been deduced.

The reader may want to look at this list as a recipe for success in planning for dual-disorders interventions. Naturally, the degree to which these principles are implemented will affect the probability for consistently positive outcomes. However, it may not be within the mandate of any one person or program to enact each of these principles and hence, a systems approach appears to be necessary.

1. Complete detoxification, ideally from all psychoactive substances, should occur prior to assessment and treatment planning.
2. A comprehensive assessment of the client's presenting problems (both mental and substance abuse) and strengths (ie. support systems), should occur as soon as the client is free of intoxication and/or withdrawal.
3. The assessment should incorporate laboratory measures (such as urinalysis) and solicit corroborative input from significant others whenever possible.
4. A provisional diagnosis of the client's problem(s) and individualized treatment

TABLE 2

PUBLISHED ACCOUNTS OF DUAL DISORDER TREATMENT PROGRAM DESCRIPTIONS, CASE STUDIES AND BEST ADVICE MODELS.

TREATMENT PROGRAM DESCRIPTIONS	CASE STUDIES	BEST ADVICE MODELS
Weinstein and Gottheil, 1980	Druley et. al., 1980	Kopolow, 1981*
Chimera and Brinn, 1984	Pepper, 1984	Bachrach, 1982
Kofoed and Keys, 1988	Daley et al., 1987	Pepper and Ryglewicz, 1984
Levy and Mann, 1988	McKelvy et al., 1987	Caragonne and Emery, 1987
Wallen and Weiner, 1988	Kosten and Kleber, 1988	McKelvy et al., 1987
Carey, 1989b	Levy and Mann, 1988	Attia, 1988
Cliffside Staff, 1989	Schiff and Cavaiola, 1988	Beeby, 1989**
Kaufman, 1989	Wallen and Weiner, 1988	Brown et al., 1989
	Mann, 1989	Carey, 1989a
		El-Guebaly, 1990
		Smith and Birchwood, 1990**

* (re: how to increase client [or "survivor" as per Hurst, 1990] involvement in program design delivery etc.)

** (re: how to increase significant other involvement in program design, delivery, etc.).

plan should accompany this process; both the client and significant others should be involved as much as possible.

5. The provisional diagnosis should be reviewed periodically throughout the course of treatment and interventions should be adjusted accordingly.

6. When attempting to match interventions to the client's needs, it is crucial to adhere to several principles:
   • approaches need to be flexible
   • abstinence should usually be understood to be the most desirable goal of treatment
   • prior abstinence is not necessarily a requirement for treatment to begin
   • mental health and substance abuse interventions are employed as indicated
   • a holistic orientation is required
   • confrontational interventions may actually hinder the recovery process for many clients
   • treatment outcomes will likely be a function of the kind and severity of disorder present in the individual (however, the degree to which treatments are inappropriately matched to clients' needs will likely correlate with poorer outcomes)
   • a range of residential and non-residential options should be available
   • special attention may need to be focused on safe and supportive housing requirements of the client.

7. Treatment should concurrently address both psychiatric and substance abuse problems under "one program roof." Failing that, extensive communication between the various treatment components by one case manager (who takes the major responsibility for the case) is recommended.

8. The unified clinical team should ideally be comprised of professionally trained mental health and substance abuse staff (including physicians to administer and monitor pharmacotherapy), and supplemented by persons stabilized in their own recovery.

9. Treatment should be open-ended. Emphasis should be placed on ongoing care (aftercare), with extensive use of case management workers and rigorous outreach efforts.

10. Clients should be encouraged to use self-help programming, but should be carefully assisted by a member of the clinical team in "shopping" for a group where they are comfortable. In some cases, new groups with a special orientation to dual disorders may need to be facilitated and established.

11. Priority should be given to ongoing in-service education, where mental health and substance abuse staff train each other in their respective specialties. Staff may also need to advocate additional training from within their organizations and/or from accredited academic institutions.

12. Input by clients and significant others at a program advisory level is essential.

CONCLUSION

In the foregoing paragraphs, dual disorders were considered on the basis of five variables: definition, prevalence, etiology, obstacles to effective treatment for treatment efficacy. All five variables show clearly how this newly acknowledged, but old and familiar patient population is complex, heterogeneous and demanding of counsellor time, effort and creativity. It is hoped that a greater awareness of these patients and their special needs will lead to more regular identification, diagnoses and better treatment in the future.

As alluded to earlier when talking about a systems approach to treatment, the notion of a case manager who follows and co-ordinates the many treatment facets, during a crisis and over time, is crucial. After all, very often the problems of the dually disordered are chronic in nature and subject to setbacks. Change is likely to occur slowly and incrementally. Consequently, being the case manager for the dually-disordered client may represent a large commitment. Counsellors who are not working out of a specialized treatment setting for the dually disordered might be advised to seek administrative backing for this time- and energy-consuming task.

Clearly, this patient population demands and deserves more than the predominant short-term approach to counselling. The argument must be made that in the long run, only a long-term commitment to this client population will save money, effort, and staff time. It will also alleviate considerable human suffering, which is regularly caused by narrowly-defined, uninformed and unresponsive treatment systems.

ACKNOWLEDGEMENT

The authors wish to thank Ms. Angèle Vis and Ms. Egle Wennerstrom for the preparation of this manuscript.

REFERENCES

American Psychiatric Association. (1987). <u>Diagnostic and Statistical Manual of Mental Disorders –Third Edition</u> – <u>Revised</u>. Washington, D.C.: APA, 1987.

Ananth, J., Vandewater, S., Kamal, M., Brodsky, A., Gamal, R. & Miller, M. (1989). Missed diagnosis of substance abuse in psychiatric patients. <u>Hosp. & Comm. Psychiatry</u>, Vol.40(3):297–299.

Anderson, C.L., Jesswein, W.A. & Fleischman, W. (1990). Needs assessment based on household and key informant surveys. <u>Evaluation Review</u>, Vol.14 (2): 182–191.

Attia, P.R. (1988). Dual diagnosis: definition and treatment. <u>Alc. Treat. Quart.</u>, Vol.5(3/4):53–63.

Bachrach, L.L. (1982). Young adult chronic patients: an analytical review of the literature. <u>Hosp. & Comm. Psychiatry</u>, Vol.33 (3): 186–197.

Balcerzak, W.S. & Hoffmann, N.G. (1985). Dual treatment rationale for psychologically disordered and chemically dependent clients. <u>Alc. Treat. Quart.</u>, Vol.2 (2): 61–67.

Beeby, J. (1989). Involving families in planning for care of the psychiatrically ill. (An unpublished discussion paper by the Ontario Friends of Schizophrenics).

Blankfield, A. (1987). The position of psychiatry in alcohol dependence. <u>Drug and Alc. Dependence</u>, Vol.19: 259–264.

Blumberg, A.C., Cohen, M., Heaton, A.M. & Klein, D.F. (1971). Covert drug abuse among voluntary hospitalized psychiatric patients. <u>J.A.M.A.</u>, Vol.217 (12): 1659–1661.

Brown, V.B., Ridgely, M.S., Pepper, B., Levine, I.S. & Ryglewicz, H. (1989). The dual crisis: mental illness and substance abuse. <u>Am. Psychol.</u>, March:565–569.

Bukstein, O.G., Brent, D.A. & Kaminer, Y. (1989). Comorbidity of substance abuse and other psychiatric disorders in adolescents. <u>Am. J. Psychiatry</u>, Vol.146 (9): 1131–1141.

Cadoret, R.J. (1978). Genetic principles in the taxonomy of affective disorders and alcoholism. In: Akiskal, H.S. and Webb, W.L. <u>Psychiatric Diagnosis: Exploration of Biological Predictors</u>. New York: Spectrum Publications Inc., 1978.

Cadoret, R. & Winokur, G. (1972). Depression in alcoholism. Ann. N.Y. Acad. Sci (1972) Vol.233: 34–39 as cited in: Powell, B.J. et. al. Prevalence of additional psychiatric syndromes among male alcoholics. J. Clin. Psychiatry, (1982) Vol.43 (10): 404–407.

Caragonne, P. & Emery, B. (1987). Mental Illness and Substance Abuse: The Dually Diagnosed Client. Rockville M.D.: National Council of Community Mental Health Centres, 1987.

Carey, K.B. (1989a). Emerging treatment guidelines for mentally ill chemical abusers. Hosp. & Comm. Psychiatry, Vol.40(4):341–349.

Carey, K.B. (1989b). Treatment of the mentally ill chemical abuser: description of the Hutchings day treatment program. Psychiatric Quart., Vol.60(4):303–316.

Chimera, P. & Brinn, R.B. (1984). Project Adam – a new demonstration project for multi-disabled substance abusers with psychiatric disorders. Tie Lines, Vol.1 (July): 7.

Cliffside Staff (The). (1989). Cliffside: Four Winds–Westchester's program for psychiatric chemical dependency treatment. J. Subst. Abuse Treat., Vol.6:55–58.

Cohen, S.I. & Johnson, K. (1988). Psychosis from alcohol or drug abuse. Br. Med. J., Vol.297:1270–1271.

Cooper, G., Graham, D., Mainer, B. & Todd, L. (1990a). "Dual disorders" and the geographically remote individual: learning from service providers, service consumers, and significant others. Paper presented at the Second International Rural Mental Health and Addictions Conference, June 11–15.

Cooper, G., Graham, D., Hill, J.M. & Huneault, N. (1990b). Chronic mental illness and substance abuse: A needs assessment. Rural Comm. M.H. Newsletter, Vol.17(1):5.

Cooper, G. & Todd. L. (1990). Dual disorders in rural communities Network, Vol. 4(1):8.

Crowley, T.J., Chesluk, D., Dilts, S. & Hart, R. (1974). Drug and alcohol abuse among psychiatric admissions. Gen. Arch. Psychiatry, Vol.30:13–20.

Daley, D.C., Moss, H. & Campbell, F. (1987). Dual Disorders: Counselling Clients With Chemical Dependency and Mental Illness. Centre City, M.N.: Hazelden Foundation, 1987.

Dobkin, P., Dongier, M., Cooper, D. & Hill, J.M. (1991). Screening for alcoholism in a psychiatric hospital. Can. J. Psychiatry, Vol.36:39–45.

Druley, K.A., Baker, S., Blaine, J., Ottenberg, D., Carson, J. & O'Brien, C. (1980). Panel discussion: Treatment of the Substance abusing, psychiatrically ill patient (A case in point). In Gottheil, E.; Mc Lellan, A. T.; and Druley, K. A. Substance Abuse and Psychiatric Illness. New York: Pergamon Press, 1980.

El-Guebaly, N. (1990). Substance abuse and mental disorders: the dual diagnoses concept. Can. J. Psychiatry, Vol.35 (3):261–267.

Fine, E.W. (1980). The syndrome of alcohol dependency and depression. In: Gottheil, E.; Mc Lellan, A.T.; and Druley, K.A. Substance Abuse and Psychiatric Illness. New York: Pergamon Press, 1980.

Fischer, D.E., Halikas, J.A., Baker, J.W. & Smith, J.B. (1975). Frequency and patterns of drug abuse in psychiatric patients. Diseases of the Nervous System, Vol.36:550–553.

Fisher, W., Piazza, C. & Page, T.J. (1989). Assessing independent and interactive effects of behavioral and pharmacologic interventions for a client with dual diagnoses. J. Behav. Ther. and Exp. Psychiat., Vol.20 (3):241–250.

Fowler, R.C., Liskow, B.L., Tanna, V. & Van Valkenburg, C. (1977). Psychiatric illness and alcoholism. Alcoholism: Clin. and Exp. Res., Vol.1 (2):125–128.

Freed, E.X. (1975). Alcoholism and schizophrenia: The search for perspectives; A review. J. Stud. Alc., Vol.36 (7):853–881.

Glaser, F.B. (1988). Alcohol and drug problems: a challenge to consultation - liaison psychiatry. Can. J. Psychiatry, Vol.33 (May):259–263.

Glass, I.B. (1989). Psychiatric education and substance problems: a slow response to neglect. Int'l. Rev. Psychiatry, Vol.1:17–19.

Golowka, E. (1987). A Study of problem drinking in a state psychiatric hospital. Unpublished document 1987, as cited by Levy, M.S. and Mann, D.W. J. Subst. Abuse Treat., (1988) Vol.5: 219–227.

Gottheil, E., McLellan, A.T. & Druley, K.A. (1980). Substance Abuse and Psychiatric Illness. New York: Pergamon Press 1980.

Graham, R. (Chairperson) (1988). Building Community Support For People: A Plan For Mental Health in Ontario. Toronto: Ontario Ministry of Health, 1988.

Hall, R.C., Popkin, M.K., DeVaul, R. & Stickney, S.K. (1977). The effect of unrecognized drug abuse on diagnosis and therapeutic outcome. Am. J. Alc. and Drug Abuse, Vol.4 (4): 455–465.

Hall, R.C.W., Stickney, S.K., Gardner, E.R., Perl, M. & LeCann, A.F. (1979). Relationship of psychiatric illness to drug abuse. J. Psychedelic Drugs, Vol.11(4):337–342.

Helzer, J.E. & Pryzbeck, T.R. (1988). The co-occurrence of alcoholism with other psychiatric disorders in the general population and its impact on treatment. J. Stud. Alc., Vol.49 (3):219–224.

Hesselbrock, V.M., Hesselbrock, M.N. & Workman-Daniels, K.L. (1986). Effect of major depression and anti-social personality on alcoholism: Course and motivational patterns. J. Stud. Alc., Vol. 47 (3):207–212.

Hesselbrock, M.N., Meyer, R.E. & Keener, J.J. (1985). Psychopathology in hospitalized alcoholics. Arch. Gen. Psychiatry, Vol. 42 (Nov):1050–1055.

Hurst, C. (1990). Consumer or survivor? Network, Vol. 4 (1):16.

Kamerow, D.B., Pincus, H.A. & Macdonald, D.I. (1986). Alcohol abuse, other drug abuse, and mental disorders in medical practice: prevalence, costs, recognition, and treatment. J.A.M.A., Vol.255 (15):2054–2057.

Kantorovich, N.V. & Constantinovich, S.K. (1935). The effect of alcohol in catatonic syndromes; preliminary report. Am. J. Psychiatry, Vol.92:651–654.

Kaufman, E. (1989). The psychotherapy of dually diagnosed patients. J. Subst. Abuse Treat., Vol.6:9–18.

Koegel, P., Burman, M.A. & Farr, R.K. (1988). The prevalence of specific psychiatric disorders among homeless individuals in the inner city of Los Angeles. Arch. Gen. Psychiatry, Vol 45:1085–1092.

Kofoed, L., Kania, J., Walsh, T. & Atkinson, R.M. (1986). Outpatient treatment of patients with substance abuse and coexisting psychiatric disorders. Am. J. Psychiatry, Vol.143 (7):867–872.

Kofoed, L. & Keys, A. (1988). Using group therapy to persuade dual-diagnosis patients to seek substance abuse treatment. Hosp. & Comm. Psychiatry, Vol.39(11):1209–1211.

Kopolow, L.E. (1981). Client participation in mental health service delivery. Comm. M.H. Journal, Vol.17(1):46–53.

Kosten, T.R. & Kleber, H.D. (1988). Differential diagnosis of psychiatric comorbidity in substance abusers. J. Subst. Abuse Treat., Vol.5:201–206.

Levy, M.S. & Mann, D.W. (1988). The special treatment team: an inpatient approach to the mentally ill alcoholic patient. J. Subst. Abuse Treat., Vol.5:219–227.

Lin, N., Ensel, W.M., Simeone, R.S. & Kuo, W. (1979). Social support, stressful life events, and illness: A model and an empirical test. J. Health and Social Behaviour, Vol. 20 (June): 108–119.

Malla, A. & Merskey, H. (1987). Screening for alcoholism in family practice. Fam. Prac. Res. J., Vol.6 (3): 138–147.

Mann, D.W. (1989). Inpatient treatment of the mentally ill substance abuser: some medicolegal concerns. J. Subst. Abuse Treat., Vol.6: 19–21.

McLellan, A.T., Druley, K.A. & Carson, J.E. (1978). Evaluation of substance abuse problems in a psychiatric hospital. J. Clin. Psychiatry, Vol.39: 425–430.

McLellan, A.T., MacGahan, J.A. & Druley, K.A. (1980). Psychopathology and substance abuse. In: Gottheil, E.; McLellan, A.T.; and Druley. K.A. Substance Abuse and Psychiatric Illness. New York: Pergamon Press, 1980.

McEvoy, L. (1989). Alcoholism often goes undetected in psychiatric patients. The Medical Post, June 20, 1989, p. 40.

McKelvy, M.J., Kane, J.S. & Kellison, K. (1987). Substance abuse and mental illness: double trouble. J. Psychosocial Nursing, Vol.25(1):20–25.

Mee-Lee, D. (1990). Dual diagnosis (mental illness/addiction) – double trouble. Comm. Prog. Innovations Newsletter, Vol.7: 2.

Menicucci, L.D., Wermuth, L. & Sorensen, J. (1988). Treatment providers' assessment of dual-prognosis patients: diagnosis, treatment, referral, and family involvement. Int'l J. Addict., Vol.23 (6):617–622.

Merskey, H., Brandt, C.C., Malla, A., Helmes, E. & Mahr, V. (1988). Symptom patterns of alcoholism in a Northern Ontario population. Can. J. Psychiatry, Vol.33: 46–50.

Miller, N.S. & Gold, M.S. (1989). Suggestions for changes in DSM-III-R criteria for substance use disorders. Am. J. Drug Alcohol Abuse, Vol.15(2):223–230.

Minski, L. (1938). Psychopathy and psychoses associated with alcohol. J. Ment. Sci., Vol.84: 985–990.

Moss, H. (1990). Dual disorders getting closer look. The Journal, Jan. 1, 1990, p. 2.

O'Farrell, T.J., Connors, G.J. & Upper, D. (1983). Addictive behavior among hospitalized psychiatric patients. Addictive Behaviors, Vol.8:329–333.

Olivera, A.A., Kiefer, M.W. & Manley, N.K. (1990). Tardive dyskinesia in psychiatric patients with substance use disorders. Am. J. Drug Alcohol Abuse, Vol.16 (1 & 2):57–66.

Panepinto, W.C., Higgins, M.J., Keane-Daves, W.Y. & Smith D. (1970). Underlying psychiatric diagnosis as an indicator of participation in alcoholism therapy. Q.J. Stud. Alc., Vol.31: 950–956.

Pedersen, B.A.T. (1990). Dual disorders: psychoactive substance use disorder and non-addictive mental disorder. Paper presented at the Second International Rural Mental Health and Addictions Conference, June 11–15, 1990.

Peele, S. (1990). Research issues in assessing addiction treatment efficacy: how cost effective are Alcoholics Anonymous and private treatment centres? Drug and Alcohol Dependence, Vol.25:179–182.

Pepper, B. (1984). Director's column. Tie Lines, Vol.1 (July): 5–6.

Pepper, B., Kirshner, M.C. & Ryglewicz, H. (1981). The young adult chronic patient: overview of a population. Hosp. & Comm. Psychiatry, Vol.32 (7):463–470.

Pepper, B. & Ryglewicz, H. (1984). The young adult chronic patient and substance abuse. Tie Lines, Vol.1 (July): 1–5.

Peyser, H.S. (1989). Alcohol and drug abuse: unrecognized and untreated. Hosp. & Comm. Psychiatry, Vol.40(3):221.

Powell, B.J., Penick, E.C., Othmer, E., Bingham, S.F. & Rice, A.S. (1982). Prevalence of additional psychiatric syndromes among male alcoholics. J. Clin. Psychiatry, 43 (10):404–407.

Raistrick, D. (1989). Making treatment decisions. Int'l Rev. Psychiatry, Vol.1: 173–180.

Ramsey, A., Vrenburgh, J. & Gallagher, R.M. (1983). Recognition of alcoholic army patients with psychotic problems in a family practice clinic. J. Fam. Practice, Vol.17 (5):829–832.

Reich, L.H., Davies, R.K. & Himmelhoch, J.M. (1974). Excessive alcohol use in manic-depressive illness. Am. J. Psychiatry, Vol. 131(1):83–86.

Robinson, A.F. & Wolkind, S.N. (1970). Amphetamine abuse among psychiatric in-patients: the use of gas chromatography. Br. J. Psychiatry, Vol.116: 643–644.

Ross, H.E., Glaser, F.B. & Germanson, T. (1988a). The prevalence of psychiatric disorders in patients with alcohol and other drug problems. Arch. Gen. Psychiatry, Vol.45(Nov):1023–1031.

Ross, H.E., Glaser, F.B. & Strasny, S. (1988b). Sex differences in the prevalence of psychiatric disorders in patients with alcohol and drug problems. Br. J. Addiction, Vol.83:1179–1192.

Rounsaville, B.J., Dolinsky, Z.S., Babor, T.F. & Meyer, R.E. (1987). Psycho-pathology as a predictor of treatment outcome in alcoholics. Arch. Gen. Psychiatry, Vol.44:505–513.

Rounsaville, B.J., Weissman, M.M., Kleber, H. & Wilber, C. (1982). The heterogeneity of psychiatric diagnosis in treated opiate addicts. Arch. Gen. Psychiatry, Vol.39:161–166.

Roy, A., Lamparski, D., De Jong, J., Moore, V. & Linnoila, M. (1990). Characteristics of alcoholics who attempt suicide. Am. J. Psychiatry, Vol.147(6):761–765.

Safer, D.J. (1987). Substance abuse by young adult chronic patients. Hosp. & Comm. Psychiatry, Vol.38(5):511–514.

Schiff, M. & Cavaiola, A. (1988). The presentation of dual diagnosis in an adolescent chemical dependence unit. Alc. Treat. Quart., Vol.5 (1/2): 261–271.

Schmidt, L.A. (1989). Prevalence and correlates of problem drinking in a psychiatrically treated population. Paper presented at the Annual Meeting of the American Public Health Association, October 23, 1989.

Schofield, M.A. (1989). The contribution of problem drinking to the level of psychiatric morbidity in the general hospital. Br. J. Psychiatry, Vol.155:229–232.

Schuckit, M.A. (1983). Alcoholism and other psychiatric disorders. Hosp. & Comm. Psychiatry, Vol.34 (11): 1022–1027.

Seixas, F.A. (1980). A historical perspective on alcoholism. In: Gottheil, E.; McLellan, A.T.; and Druley, K.A. Substance Abuse and Psychiatric Illness. New York: Pergamon Press, 1980.

Smith, J. & Birchwood, M. (1990). Relatives and patients as partners in the management of schizophrenia: the development of a service model. Br. J. Psychiatry, Vol.156:654–660.

Susser, E., Lovell, A. & Conover, S. (1989). Unravelling the causes of homelessness – and of its association with mental illness. In: Cooper, B. and Helgason, T. Epidemiology and the Prevention of Mental Disorders. London: Routledge, 1989.

Todd, J.M. (1980). The mentally ill alcoholic. Maryland State Med. J., Vol. 29 (5): 21–27.

Tyndel, M. (1974). Psychiatric study of one thousand alcoholic patients. Can. Psych. Assoc. J., Vol.19:21–24.

Wallen, M. & Weiner, H. (1988). The dually diagnosed patient in an inpatient chemical dependency treatment program. Alc. Treat. Quart., Vol.5(1/2):197–218.

Weinstein, S.P. & Gottheil, E. (1980). A coordinated program for treating combined mental health substance abuse problems. In: Gottheil, E.; Mc Lellan, A. T.; and Druley, K. A. Substance Abuse and Psychiatric Illness. New York: Pergamon Press, 1980.

Weissman, M.M. & Meyers, J.K. (1980). Clinical depression in alcoholics. Am. J. Psychiatry, Vol.137:372–373.

Westermeyer, J. (1990). Treatment for psychoactive substance use disorder in special populations: issues in strategic planning. Advances in Alcohol & Subst. Abuse, Vol.8 (3/4): 1–8.

Westermeyer, J. & Walzer, V. (1975). Sociopathy and drug use in a young psychiatric population. Diseases of the Nervous System, Vol.36:673–677.

Willauer, S., Cooper, G., Graham, D., Todd, L. & Mainer, B. (1990). Dual disorders needs assessment: Phase I interim report. (Unpublished manuscript available from the second author).

Winokur, G., Reich, T., Rimmer, J. & Pitts, F.N. (1970). Alcoholism: III. Diagnosis and familial psychiatric illness in 259 alcoholic probands. <u>Arch. Gen. Psychiatry</u>, Vol.23:104–111.

Woody, G.E., McLellan, A.T. & O'Brien, C.P. (1990). Research on psychopathology and addiction: treatment implications. <u>Drug and Alcohol Dependence</u>, Vol. 25: 121–123.

Ziegler-Driscoll, G., Sax, P., Deal, D. & Ostreicher, P. (1980). Selection and training of staff to work with the psychiatrically ill substance abuser. In: Gottheil, E.; McLellan, A.T.; and Druley, K.A. <u>Substance Abuse and Psychiatric Illness</u>. New York: Pergamon Press, 1980.

AIDS and Substance Abuse

PETER M. FORD AND HANNAH KAUFMAN

INTRODUCTION

AIDS is a disease caused by the Human Immunodeficiency Virus (HIV). The virus is transmitted primarily by exchange of body fluids from infected to uninfected individuals. The body fluids most likely to transmit HIV are blood and semen. Maternal milk has also been implicated in mother-child transmission. Other body fluids such as sweat, saliva and urine are relatively non-infectious. Thus the major modes of transmission are:

(1) Injection with blood-dirty syringes, infected blood transfusions or infected blood products as in Factor VIII preparations for hemophiliacs.

(2) Sexual/anal intercourse, because of the trauma to mucous membranes lining the anus and rectum, is the most frequent sexual mode of transmission, but oral sex with ingestion of semen and vaginal sex are also capable of transmission. Indeed in the Third World, vaginal intercourse is the predominant mode of transmission, although at least in Africa, genital ulceration due to other sexually transmitted diseases seems to facilitate spread by this route.

(3) Maternal-fetal transmission may occur *in utero,* but probably most commonly occurs at the time of birth. Infants may also be infected by breast feeding, since breast milk of infected mothers may contain HIV infected lymphocytes.

Once an individual is infected, the virus enters a number of cell types such as lymphocytes, macrophages and cells in the central nervous system. *Once the virus has entered the cell, it inserts itself into the cell's nuclear material and may lie dormant for many years. Once infected, an individual will remain infected and potentially infectious until he or she dies.* The dormant period may last for from two years to more than 10 years. Indeed, 10 years after infection only about 50 per cent of infected individuals will be showing signs of disease. The remainder will be well, but are capable of spreading the disease to others.

TESTING

A number of laboratory tests can detect whether an individual has been infected with HIV. The commonly used ones depend upon the production of antibodies to the virus. These antibodies may take up to six weeks after infection to appear (in a few cases it may be as long as three to four months). *During this time, HIV screening tests will be negative, but the patient is capable of transmitting the infection* – this is the so called "window period." The main screening test is called the ELISA test, and while this test will be positive when antibodies to HIV are present, it may occasionally produce false positive results. Thus, if the ELISA is positive, a confirmatory test called the Western Blot Test (the name refers to the laboratory procedure) is usually carried out. The Western Blot is regarded as the gold standard. All positive tests should be repeated for confirmation.

When counselling either before or after testing for HIV, it is important to remember that if an individual has been exposed to risk within the previous three to four months, *they may be in the "window period."* This means that they may have been infected, but have not yet developed antibodies that would show up on testing. *They need to be tested again within six months.* Many injection drug users continue to expose themselves to potential infection and a single negative test will be meaningless; repeated testing will be required until risk behavior has ceased.

There is often confusion about the difference between being infected with HIV and having AIDS. Anyone with a positive confirmatory or Western Blot test is infected with HIV. They do not have AIDS until they actually become physically ill with some of the disease manifestations described below.

PROGRESSION TO AIDS

When the dormant virus is reactivated it proceeds to destroy the macrophages and the "helper" lymphocytes of the immune system. Both of these cells are involved in protecting the body against infection and the damage to them results in loss of immunity to a whole range of microorganisms, many of which never trouble people with intact immune systems. The decline in immune function occurs over several years and may be slowed by a number of drugs that inhibit viral growth, but unfortunately do not kill the virus. These drugs include Zidovudine (AZT), DDI and DDC. These drugs are relatively toxic and require regular monitoring. They are also expensive, although in Canada all are provided free.

As the immune system declines in activity and the risk of infection increases, it is possible to provide prophylactic therapy to prevent a number of the more common infections such as candida (thrush), herpes and pneumocystis (which causes a severe pneumonia). Ongoing care and monitoring is usually provided either by regional

AIDS clinics – which in Canada have been established in most major cities with provincial funding – or by interested family physicians. With close supervision, both the duration – *and quality* – of life can be improved. There is thus a positive incentive for HIV-positive individuals to seek appropriate medical care.

In addition to attacking the immune system, the virus also attacks the central nervous system and may cause dementia. This is usually only pronounced in the late stages of the disease and its incidence has been much diminished with the use of antiviral drugs. Dementia in the terminal stages of the disease may not only complicate management, but can also cause considerable strain and distress to care givers and patients alike.

An additional problem in AIDS patients has been the occurrence of certain tumors. These include Kaposi's Sarcoma, a tumor rarely seen other than in AIDS patients, intracranial lymphoma, and in females, cervical cancer.

AIDS AND WOMEN

Women and men with HIV show some differences in presentation and complications, although the survival times are probably much the same in similar socio-economic groups. Women may present with recurrent and persistent vaginal candidiasis and may also have recurrent problems with pelvic inflammatory disease. Also, as noted above, there appears to be an increased risk of cervical cancer. Because it is less familiar to physicians in Canada, HIV disease in women is often missed in the early phase, particularly when it presents as recurrent pelvic inflammatory disease. Although there has been some suggestion that AIDS is a more rapidly fatal disease in women than in men, this only appears to be so because more of the female cases come from the lower socio-economic groups. Women do no worse than males from the same groups. Male statistics are skewed by the fact that many of the homosexuals with AIDS come from the middle class with better access to health care and money to pay for treatment.

EPIDEMIOLOGY

When AIDS first appeared in 1981, it was initially recognized in homosexuals. Although it was also noted to occur in other groups, such as intravenous drug users and Haitian immigrants, for several years AIDS was regarded in North America as a "gay" disease. By the late 1980s, however, it had become clear that there was a second major epidemic of HIV infection in the IV drug-using population of some, but not all, U.S. cities. By the early 1990s it has become equally clear that there are now three epidemics of HIV infection: in homosexuals, IV drug users and the heterosexual population. While all three overlap to some extent, this is particularly true for the latter two groups. What is less generally appreciated is that the rates of spread will be different in all three groups. The slow rise of numbers among heterosexuals has given a false sense of security regarding this group. However, the chance of an individual becoming infected with HIV depends on how risky the behavior is, the likelihood of infection of the other partner and the number of partners the individual has. Vaginal intercourse with an infected male even without condom use carries a relatively low risk of transmission in the intact vagina and despite the impression given by the media, the average heterosexual does not have large numbers of partners. Female-to-male spread is less likely than vice-versa. Thus initially, infected females were drug users or sex trade workers or both. Non-drug-using partners of IV users then began to appear in the statistics and now heterosexual spread in the non-drug-using population is increasing.

INJECTION DRUG USERS

Once HIV entered a city's IV drug user population – in both the First and Third Worlds – it spread very quickly. For example, the incidence of HIV positivity in IV drug users in Bangkok in 1988 jumped from 16 per cent in the spring to 46 per cent in the fall and *more than 75 per cent were infected before the first case of AIDS appeared.* The current prevalence of HIV in injection drug users varies considerably in the Western hemisphere, being very high in such cities as New York and Edinburgh and low in cities such as Vancouver and Glasgow. Glasgow and Edinburgh make a fascinating and instructive comparison: at the beginning of the HIV epidemic, Glasgow already had in place a needle-exchange program because of concern about the spread of hepatitis. Edinburgh not only did not have such a program in place, but the police actually closed down the only pharmacy in the city prepared to sell clean needles and syringes to users. Thus in Edinburgh at the end of the 1980s, the prevalence of HIV in injecting drug users was over 70 per cent; in Glasgow it was around five per cent. There is now mounting evidence that needle-exchange programs coupled with education can reduce risk behavior and probably the spread of HIV. Such programs often provide the only point of contact for health care workers with this population. For a comprehensive and reasonably compact review of the subject of injecting drug use and HIV/AIDS, the reader is referred to Des Jarlais et al. (1992).

RISK OF INFECTION FOR HEALTH CARE WORKERS

HIV is not easy to catch except by one of the high-risk behaviors noted above. Health care workers of all types may be exposed to body fluids from clients, but generally speaking the only fluid of concern is blood. It is very unlikely that HIV-infected blood on intact skin can transmit infection. However blood on fresh cuts or on mucous membranes – such as the eye – may be capable of causing transmission, and of course blood on penetrating instruments such as needles can plainly cause infection. The risk of infection from normal physical contact is therefore zero. Friends and family members will often want to know their risk in the course of day-to-day contact. Such activities as kissing, sharing utensils, etc. are not potential methods of transmission. It should be remembered however that many HIV-infected individuals also have Hepatitis B, which is much more infectious. Relatives whose anxiety persists should be referred to the local Public Health department for further advice.

Health care workers who encounter spills of blood or other body fluids should wear rubber gloves as a precaution when clearing up. The virus is rapidly killed by diluted household bleach, which should be used to clear up blood spills. *Remember that the basic principle of universal precautions is to assume that everyone is infected and to take appropriate precautions with ALL blood and body fluids.*

It is also worth noting that HIV-infected individuals may be carrying more easily transmissible diseases; the most worrying of these now is tuberculosis. The recent rise in tuberculosis seen over the last five years in the U.S. – and now appearing in Canada – is mostly occurring in HIV-positive individuals, particularly injection drug users. Most worrying of all is that some of this tuberculosis is resistant to most drugs. All individuals working with clients who may be HIV-infected should have a Tb skin test. If the results are negative, the test should be repeated annually. All workers, regardless of skin-test results, should have an annual chest X-ray.

HIV COUNSELLING FOR SUBSTANCE USERS

HIV and AIDS raise many urgent issues for substance users and addictions counsellors. What is HIV/AIDS? How does one contract it? How is the substance user at increased risk of HIV infection? What does one do about their HIV status (either positive or negative)? When does a client need counselling? How do I provide counselling for someone who is concerned about HIV? How are appropriate medical care and support services accessed? What are the mental health complications of HIV infection combined with addiction? These questions are addressed in this section.

RISKS AND CONCERNS FOR SUBSTANCE USERS

Substance users are at increased risk for HIV infection because as a group they share key risk factors: needle sharing, compromised immune status, decreased inhibitions leading to unsafe sex and drug use practices, low self-esteem and poor access to HIV education and treatment programs. Any one of these factors can lead to HIV infection and related problems. In combination, the risk dramatically increases. The substance user may not be aware of the risk of transmission, or may not bring up the issue during substance abuse counselling. Because of these circumstances, all clients with a history of addiction require counselling about HIV/AIDS, its transmission, its prevention and its impact on the addicted individual and his/her family. Additionally, providing a variety of other HIV prevention programs can prevent an epidemic of HIV in a specific community, as well as stabilize prevalence of infection. These might include needle exchange programs, distribution of condoms and latex squares, peer education and HIV testing.

APPROACHES IN COUNSELLING

Counselling substance users about HIV/AIDS requires a multi-issue approach. People bring to HIV counselling all of their issues. Other issues such as psychopathology, addictions, and family or emotional problems do not fall away in the face of a concern about HIV infection. They may recede for a time, but will inevitably return. People who live with HIV don't necessarily change the way they live their lives. Although the issue of HIV infection may appear paramount, it also may obscure, exacerbate or transform other issues, such as physical and mental health problems, substance abuse, housing, finances, and family and relationships (Drucker, 1991). Counselling must be open to the usual issues relevant to the client, as well as to specific issues of substance use and HIV.

When providing assistance with concrete concerns such as housing and finances, the counsellor must be sensitive to the additional difficulties often faced by the HIV-infected person. In the event of anticipated deteriorating health, long-term housing needs such as accessibility, low cost and proximity to physician's offices and shopping are all considerations. HIV-positive people are often subjected to discrimination by landlords and tenants both. The counsellor may need to help the client make decisions about disclosure, and advocate on their behalf.

The goals of HIV counselling should include HIV education, life skills, awareness of and changes in attitudes and ultimately changes in behavior. Motivations, incentives and barriers to change should be explored and used in the counselling process, to enhance support systems and to minimize the avoidance of other major issues such as substance use.

HIV TESTING: PRE-TEST AND POST-TEST COUNSELLING

Pre-(HIV)test and post-test counselling are important parts of caring for an individual who is concerned about HIV. The primary rationale for this is clear: HIV testing requires informed consent. This may seem obvious. However, the risks and effects of undergoing testing are complex, as are the effects of receiving either positive or negative results. The actual act of being tested can produce anxiety and depression, suicide risk, uninsurability, and discrimination in the workplace and/or by friends and family. A positive test heightens these problems, and a negative test can lead to increased risk-taking behaviors and uncertainty. It is essential that the counsellor understand this complexity, and be knowledgeable about disease transmission. Lastly, the counsellor should feel comfortable talking explicitly about sex.

The primary role of the HIV counsellor is to help define the complex areas of concern to clients (Marks & Goldblum, 1990). The substance abuse counsellor must also understand the issues and the areas addressed during HIV testing. The purpose of this is two-fold. Firstly, the substance abuse counsellor can evaluate the services provided to their clients, ensuring they receive appropriate and complete counselling. Secondly, HIV counselling is rarely accomplished in one or two sessions. Additional assistance enhances information retention and behavior change.

The pre-test session involves:
• assessment of the client's knowledge level
• clarifying information about the mechanics and meaning of the test and transmission risks
• discussing relevant risk factors, the need for future testing and risk reduction strategies
• exploring the psychological effects of testing, including an assessment of individual coping mechanisms, support systems, and suicide risk.

The post-test discussion, if the test is negative, should include:
• identification of the client (to prevent mix-up of results)
• interpretation of the result (no infection or the need for retest)
• reinforcing risk reduction strategies.

DEALING WITH A POSITIVE TEST

A positive test result requires more involved counselling. This should include:
• identification of the client
• interpretation of the result (infected with the virus, not diagnostic of AIDS, and reassurance that a confirmatory test was performed to rule out a "false positive")
• discussion of issues important to the client
• discussion of coping and support systems
• assessment of mental status
• resource counselling (mental health agencies, support groups etc.).

Other issues to be explored during this or a following session are:
• partner notification
• expanding on transmission reduction strategies to include avoiding donations of blood, organ, tissue, sperm and breast milk, avoiding pregnancy, and protecting others from blood and body fluids (semen, vaginal fluid)

- medical follow-up
- discussion of health enhancement.

All clients, with or without problems of addiction, might be overwhelmed by a diagnosis of HIV infection. Newly-diagnosed individuals are prone to increased risk behaviors – such as needle sharing and unsafe sex – due to mental health complications, increased substance use and anxiety. Since denial is the psychic armor that allows for continued substance use, a challenge to that armor can result in suicide, depression or decreased acceptance of the diagnosis. Uncertainty about their health, life expectancy and the impact of HIV on everyday functioning can lead to attempts to assert maximum control over their lives. This can take the form of either seeking or avoiding knowledge about their illness, and either increased or decreased substance use (Weitz, 1989). Clients may be overwhelmed by illness, grief and a sense of loss. This powerful focus can result in overlooking or avoiding either the substance use or the HIV infection, again leading to high risk activities, anxiety, depression and suicide. The counsellor must be alert to these possibilities.

Counsellors in any setting sometimes fall into a "parallel process" with clients: sharing the avoidance and control behaviors they use to manage anxiety. The HIV or substance abuse counsellor, for example, may *unwittingly* enable the client's high-risk activities, especially increased substance use. It is important that the counsellor considers initially not insisting that the client totally abstain from what may be her or his only coping strategies. Insisting on abstinence often leads to an increased feeling of anxiety and loss of self-control. Prior to entering a formal substance abuse program, a goal of moderating his or her substance use may increase the client's motivation, and assist the counsellor with this more complicated engagement process. Counselling strategies that provide information – the equipment for behavior change – while enhancing self-esteem have been shown to increase the likelihood of behavior changes in coping strategies and in substance use as well.

FAMILY ISSUES

Families too may be overwhelmed by the HIV infection. They may experience feelings of helplessness and hopelessness, undermining the substance abuse treatment. This can take many forms: a withdrawal of personal and financial support for substance abuse treatment, a shift of focus to medical and emotional treatment for the HIV infection and a shift in focus away from the client, toward personal concerns regarding infection transmission and the ability to cope with yet another crisis. Rejection of the substance abuser and relationship breakdown can result from role changes, anger, prejudice, ignorance, and fear of infection and discrimination (Miller, 1987). Any or all of these issues can also compromise medical treatment.

PRACTICAL APPROACHES

A counselling session at a clinic or doctor's office before an HIV test might be the first contact an individual has had with the health care system. Although this provides a good opportunity for the client to begin to access medical care, it should not be the first opportunity to hear about HIV. Counsellors in treatment programs can and should introduce this issue into their programming. In particular, counsellors should ask about needle use, needle sharing and ask whether the client has a sexual partner who uses needles. Many clients may not be aware of the issues and the risks of transmission. Others may either think their concerns are irrelevant or experience embarrassment. The personal inquiry and weight given by the counsellor to HIV issues may raise the level of a client's awareness, which may have been compromised by denial or dulled by substance use. Intake sessions can include assessment of the client's risk factors for HIV, her or his concerns and desire to be tested. Other important areas to assess are the client's suicide risk, support systems, levels of anxiety and depression, and motivations and barriers to behavioral change. This information will allow the counsellor to provide services and referrals that are relevant and accessible to the client. The client may need referrals to medical facilities and community agencies specializing in HIV/AIDS, finances and housing. Clients and families living with, or at risk for, HIV can then have independent access to health-status monitoring and other services. Certainly many clients will be aware of their HIV status and other related issues. These clients require a different level of support and information. They may be dealing with issues of living with HIV, death and dying, family issues and so on. Their sex and needle-sharing partners may also have similar issues, especially if the HIV-positive partner continues with high risk behaviors.

Flexibility in substance abuse treatment plans and programming – to include, for example, self-esteem issues and HIV/AIDS-related topics for all participants – can increase behavior change for both clients and staff. Provision of HIV-related services and referrals, and a commitment to co-ordinated, co-operative care with other health care providers and agencies, can enhance all clients' level of well-being. Providing access to HIV-related support groups can help clients learn positive coping strategies and new information, and expand support systems to other agencies as well as affected and infected individuals. Care must be taken, however, when referring clients to community HIV/AIDS support groups. These groups are often perceived as "gay" or too radical, or may not be sensitive to substance use issues. Clients often will not attend such groups. Client education about, and actual contact with, such groups and their umbrella agencies often reduce some of the objections. Some communities can support separate groups for substance users. Lastly, referrals and linkage with community agencies, family doctors and hospital-based clinics can decrease uncertainty and increase the client's and family's ability to cope (Hilton, 1992). Again care must be taken to refer clients to services that are receptive to substance users.

Improved support networks can be a major breakthrough toward improved health and self-care for substance users who are marginalized and disenfranchised. This may be especially important for specific client groups, such as the HIV-positive clients who continue to use drugs or alcohol, or who are women and/or members of cultural and ethnic minorities. Individuals in these groups may be at increased risk for health care problems due to the substance use itself, minimal access to information, culturally insensitive programming, financial issues that affect purchasing medication, transportation and childcare, lack of medical and social research, and lack of emphasis on non-gay subjects. For example, society often considers women at low risk for HIV infection. This can lead to continued risk behavior, decreased access to HIV testing and health care, and insensitive HIV counselling. Society also reinforces women's lack of power in relationship with their male partners and in women's traditional roles. The result may be women placing their own well-being at the bottom of their list of priorities, and therefore not having the financial and emotional resources to look after themselves.

HIV CONCERNS AND THE COUNSELLOR

So what is a counsellor to do? First and foremost, counsellors must increase awareness of their personal attitudes regarding HIV/AIDS, such as homophobia, pity and denial. We must take responsibility to increase our knowledge base and begin to change our own behavior patterns. Personal awareness and professional knowledge about HIV can then complement our counselling skills and knowledge of substance use and addictions.

Many feelings are generated when staff face HIV issues. These feelings can either help or hinder the staff's and agency's provision of improved services and treatment. An agency that institutionally faces issues such as homophobia, AIDS phobia, and fears of transmission and death sets an example to all its staff, clients and the community. This can be a very painful and difficult process, but the payoff is enormous. Crises can be prevented or minimized, staff and clients can more freely voice their own fears and concerns, and adequate information and referral sources are more likely to be in place before they are needed. Staff tension and anxiety can be addressed more openly, and staff can work more efficiently.

Staff in residential treatment settings are often concerned about confidentiality, infection control, hygiene and condom distribution. These issues are best addressed, and policies written and activated, prior to the admission of a known HIV-positive client. Unfortunately, most programs will not have to wait long until that day comes, so the development of such policies should not be postponed. Addressing these issues is best done in consultation with other treatment centres, local health units, doctors and social workers in HIV clinics and agencies and ethicists. Non-judgmental processing groups and information sessions ensure that all staff have an opportunity to voice their concerns and fears, and to receive accurate information. It is helpful to involve staff when developing policies, procedures and operational systems.

NEEDLE-EXCHANGE PROGRAMS

Contact with a needle-exchange program not only helps reduce the risk of HIV infection, it may be a client's first or only interaction with a skilled advisor. Needle-exchange workers also provide information regarding HIV testing and education, referrals to treatment programs and health care agencies and access to latex products. The impact of such programs has been enormous, despite public outcry that they encourage and increase drug use. Drug use and high risk behavior have decreased in areas with these programs, resulting in reduced rates of HIV infection and, overall, improved health status.

PRISON ISSUES

Within correctional services, the efforts to slow the spread of HIV infection lag far behind the non-incarcerated community. HIV infection not only affects other inmates, but increases the level of risk in the wider community. In Canadian federal institutions, condoms are now available. However, inmates do not have access to clean needles, and adequate education programs and specialized HIV health care may be hard to deliver. Since at least 70 per cent of all inmates with Correctional Services Canada are identified as substance users, all services discussed in this chapter should be available to the prison population. Peer education and support groups, already in place in some federal institutions in Ontario, provide a valuable resource for inmates whose traditional distrust of institutional initiatives makes them avoid normal channels of counselling. These peer groups should become a model and provide the impetus for improvements in HIV health care throughout all federal institutions, so that AIDS can be regarded as a health issue rather than a security problem.

CONCLUSION

It is worthwhile in concluding to include some of the recommendations from the report of The Advisory Committee on Drug Treatment to the minister responsible for the Ontario Provincial Anti-drug Strategy (Treating Alcohol and Drug Problems in Ontario: a Vision for the 90s).

1) Treatment programs should develop a comprehensive HIV/AIDS program within their service, which considers the following key elements (depending on the population being served):
   a) information
   b) counselling regarding safer sex and safer drug use
   c) condom distribution
   d) sterile water and bleach kit distribution
   e) needle and syringe exchange.
2) Programs should review their admission criteria and make any necessary revisions to ensure that individuals who are HIV-positive have equitable access to treatment.
3) Programs should place special emphasis on behavior change that reduces the risk of HIV infection even when it is not accompanied by desirable reductions in drug use.

REFERENCES

Des Jarlais, D.C., Friedman, S.R., Choopanya, K., Vanichseni, S. & Ward, T.P. "International Epidemiology of HIV and AIDS Among Injecting Drug Users." AIDS 1992 **6:** 1053–1068.

Drucker E. "Drug Users With AIDS in the City of New York: A Study of Dependent Children, Housing and Drug Addiction Treatment" in The AIDS Reader: Social, Political and Ethical Issues. McKenzie, Nancy (Ed.). New York: Meridian. 1991

Hilton, Ann. "Perceptions of Uncertainty: Its Relevance to Life-Threatening and Chronic Illness" Critical Care Nurse. 1992 **12:** p. 70–73.

Marks, R. and Goldblum, P. "The Decision to Test: A Personal Choice" in Face to Face: A Guide to AIDS Counselling. Berkeley: AIDS Health Project, University of California, San Francisco. 1990, p. 54.

Martin, G.W. et al. Treating Alcohol and Drug Problems in Ontario: A Vision for the 90's A Report of the Advisory Committee on Drug Treatment. Toronto: Provincial Anti-drug Secretariat. 1990.

Miller D. in "Counselling" The ABC of AIDS. Adler M. (Ed.). London: British Medical Journal. 1987.

Weitz R. "Uncertainty in the Face of AIDS" Journal of Health and Social Behavior. 1989 **30:** p. 270–281.

GENERAL REFERENCES ON THE TOPIC

Adler M. (Ed.). The ABC of AIDS. London: British Medical Journal. 1987.

Dilley, James; Pies, Cheri & Helquest, Michael. Face to Face: A Guide to AIDS Counselling. Berkeley: AIDS Health Project, University of California, San Francisco. 1990.

King, A., Beazley, R.P., Warren, W.K., Hankins, C.A., Robertson, A.S. & Radford, J.L. Canada Youth and AIDS Study. Kingston: Queens University. 1987.

McKenzie, Nancy F. (Ed.). The AIDS Reader: Social, Political and Ethical Issues. New York: Meridian. 1991.

Miller R., Bor, R. with contributions by Dr. Christine A. Lee, Editor James W. Dilly. AIDS: A Guide to Clinical Counselling. Philadelphia & London: Science Press Ltd. 1991.

Ostrow, D. (Ed.). Behavioral Aspects of AIDS. New York: Plenum Medical Company. 1990.

Dealing with Probation and Parole Clients

CATE SUTHERLAND

*A*ddiction services are seeing increasing numbers of mandatory clients referred by probation and parole offices and the courts. This causes a bit of concern for some workers in the addiction field. Correctional clients are generally seen as unmotivated and more difficult to manage. In reality, this is not so. The purpose of this chapter is to: provide information that will increase your understanding of the situation; dispel the myth that it is difficult to deal with correctional clients; show that the management of these clients is only slightly different; and outline techniques that may help you deal with probationers or parolees and their referring agents. You will note that the terms probationer, parolee and correctional client are used interchangeably, as there is no significant difference between them. You may also notice that any references to gender are male. This is for the sake of simplicity and has no sexist implications or intent.

In recent years, there has been increased emphasis in the courts on alternate sentencing options that include rehabilitative conditions. As part of the sentence following a criminal conviction, a judge may order that the person accept help for a particular problem. The type of mandated help the person must accept is specified by a condition in a probation supervision order, by which the person has agreed to abide. The problem areas might include, for example, emotional health concerns or financial difficulties. The most common area of concern, however, is a person's alcohol and/or drug use. Much of a court's docket on any given day is comprised of alcohol/drug-specific offences or other offences that were committed while a person was under the influence of a substance. It is not unusual for such offenders to receive a probation order specifying that they must attend addiction counselling/treatment. The expectation is that such treatment will be provided by a community agency.

Traditionally, addiction agencies have only worked with clients who voluntarily seek assistance, and this influx of involuntary clients is disconcerting to some agencies. One problem may lie with an inherent belief in the addictions field – that you cannot help a person who does not want to be helped. The dreaded unmotivated client is often perceived as unco-operative and unlikely to benefit from compulsory intervention. This can be true in some cases – a few clients may choose to be unco-operative or close-minded and gain nothing from their involvement with your agency. But, remember this important fact: motivation is not a thing, but a *process*. It is possible for a person to begin that process at your agency. Further, we need to examine our definitions of voluntary and involuntary. Webster's Dictionary states that voluntary implies "freedom and spontaneity of choice or action without external compulsion." How many clients are truly voluntary by that definition? The vast majority of clients who present at an addiction agency are propelled by an external impetus – they have lost their job, family, health or are in legal or financial trouble. The external compulsion of court-ordered clients is just more obvious than that of other clients, and they may display some initial resistance. Still, with the right attitude and a little innovation, an addiction worker can create an environment in which a probationer is more likely to benefit from involvement with the agency. As a bonus, the addiction worker may find that working with mandatory clients can be challenging and satisfying.

First and foremost, it is imperative that a co-operative relationship be established between your agency and the local probation and parole office. While it is true that persons are ordered by the court to attend, the referral is generally handled by the probation office, or more specifically by a probation officer (P.O.). It is critically important that you meet with the probation office staff to clarify respective roles and expectations. This will make your job much easier in the long run and help prevent misunderstandings.

The Ministry of Correctional Services breaks the province into regions and those regions into different areas, each headed by an area manager. Your first contact should be with that person. In some cases, the area manager will designate a P.O. to work out the details of the working relationship, but usually you will work directly with the area manager. Be very specific in your discussions, and put your agreements and the results of your discussions in writing. Following are suggested topics that should be covered. In most cases, some advice is also offered.

• Who will make the actual referral, the P.O. or the client? I recommend that you arrange for the P.O. to make the referral and schedule the initial appointment. This arrangement helps reinforce for the client that it is the P.O., by way of the probation order, who is requiring his attendance. This helps the addiction worker maintain a neutral position. Another point: these matters sometimes end up back in court if the client unwisely chooses to not attend and is charged with failing to comply with his probation order. The evidence is clearer when the appointment times are given to the client in person by the P.O.

• Inform probation office staff of the type of information that your agency needs upon referral. It would be helpful to provide copies of your intake/referral form.

• Specify exactly the types of services that your agency can and will provide.

• What information, and how much, will be relayed back to the P.O.? Keep in mind that appropriate consent forms must be signed, and that the client may allow only certain information to be released. There is a rather grey area regarding the exchange of information when your agency is under contract to the Ministry of Correctional Services. In such an instance, your agency staff could also be technically considered employees of the Ministry and, as such, could exchange information with other employees without the written consent of the client. Still, this situation is open to interpretation and you are best advised to discuss the matter with your agency's legal counsel and the legal branch of the Ministry of Correctional Services.

• Will the information be conveyed verbally or in written form? A hint: giving most information verbally will save you and your agency a lot of work. Accurate note-taking of each conversation on the part of both the worker and the P.O. is, of course, crucial. Written reports may then only be necessary when the information is to be presented to the court. If the probation office insists that all communication be written, then compromise with form letters. For instance, a form letter from an assessment/referral centre might read:

> "Mr. Blank was seen on this date for a structured addiction assessment. The assessment indicates the presence of.... The following treatment plan was negotiated...."

• Who reschedules missed appointments? Again, you can save yourself some work by making it the P.O.'s responsibility to ensure that clients are aware of and attend appointments. If an appointment is missed, simply advise the P.O. by telephone – it is up to him to contact the client and arrange to reschedule. It is helpful to keep in mind that it is the P.O.'s job, not yours, to enforce any existing treatment conditions of the probation order. This will also help preserve your counselling relationship with the client.

• Insist that the P.O. take full responsibility for explaining to the client the reason for and the purpose of the referral to the addiction agency. Also, ask that the P.O. briefly tell the client what to expect when he arrives at your office. This should prevent people from showing up at your office for appointments without knowing fully why they are there or what is going to happen.

This list contains suggested topics, but may not include everything your particular agency wants to discuss. This subject is a good agenda item for an agency staff meeting. In all likelihood your agency has already had some past experience with probation referrals. Look at what worked, what did not, what needs to be changed, and how you would like to see things handled. Input from all staff – treatment and support – will be useful.

Once you have met with the area manager (or designate) and have ironed out all the details of the working relationship, ask to attend a staff meeting at the probation office. Ensure that everyone understands the guidelines set at your previous meeting with the area manager and explain the philosophy, policies, procedures, and services of your agency. Ideally, one P.O., through whom all referrals would flow, can be designated to act as a liaison between your agency and the probation office. It is not unusual for probation offices to break caseloads down by primary area of concern anyway. For example, one P.O. may deal with community sentencing orders, one with emotional health, one with substance use, etc. Using a liaison provides clear communication routes and reduces the likelihood of inappropriate referrals.

The probation staff meeting is also a good time to arrange for P.O.s to visit your facility to further familiarize themselves.

THE CLIENT INTERVIEW

Most agencies (or workers) have an accustomed format they follow in client interviews. Regardless of how you typically begin your interviews, there are three matters that I recommend you take care of first with correctional clients. First, make sure that the client understands why he is at your agency. Ask directly: "Can you tell me why your probation officer arranged this interview?" Hopefully, you will get a relatively accurate response, and can go on to the second matter. If not, carefully explain your understanding of the purpose of the interview. This will leave you with two options, depending on the client's attitude: if he is resistant, refer him back to the P.O., whose job it is to provide a proper explanation and enforce the treatment condition. If the client is compliant, proceed.

Second, determine how the client feels about having to attend. Again, be blunt: "How do you feel about being required to attend here?" Do not settle for vague answers, such as "It's okay." Take some time to find out how the client really feels – positive or negative. Should you receive a negative reaction, simply acknowledge it and perhaps empathize a little. For example, politely say "Thank you for being honest with me. I can understand how someone might feel that way," and then move on to your next item. This is a subtle, but very important point. From the beginning, it establishes that honesty during the interview is expected, and will not be judged or have any negative repercussions.

Third, declare your neutrality. Ensure that the client understands that it is not your agency that requires his attendance, and that you are not an extension of the legal system. Explain that your agency has a co-operative relationship with the probation office, but that your responsibility is to provide appropriate addiction services.

The last matter only needs discussing should you encounter negativity or resistance on the part of the client regarding mandatory attendance. To make the interview (and future sessions) productive, you must nullify the initial resistance. Appeal to the client's adult, and hopefully logical, sensibilities. Acknowledge that his attendance is probably not completely voluntary, but point out the advantages to complying and the disadvantages of not doing so. Consider the following example:

> *"I know it probably doesn't seem that you had a choice about whether to come here. But you could have chosen not to comply with the treatment condition, and to deal with the resulting legal charges. I realize that doesn't seem like much of a choice, but it's still a choice. The fact that you chose to attend tells me that you are able to make logical decisions that are in your best interest. Now you have another choice to make – you can just get through this and waste*

your time, or you can try to make the best of it. You may not consider your alcohol/drug use a problem, but it was an issue in court and resulted in your referral here. It might help to look at this as an opportunity to examine your drinking/drug use. The advantage to you is that this will help you find ways to prevent future problems."

If you feel comfortable doing it, you might inject a bit of humor at this point, i.e., "Just think, if you knew how to prevent alcohol/drug-related problems before, you wouldn't be sitting here now."

This, or any similar approach, should only be attempted if you can do it in a casual, sincere manner. Any hint of a patronizing, bored or condescending tone will be more harmful than helpful to the counselling relationship, and is disrespectful and insulting to the client.

Now proceed with the interview. It will be surprising to some workers that from this point on, the interview should be conducted exactly as it would for a referral from any other source. There are no tricks or special techniques needed to interview correctional clients. Typically, they are no different, no more or less truthful, forthright, or cooperative, than any other client. In fact, some people consider it easier to work with correctional clients because, in a sense, a treatment plan has already been set by the court. For example, a typical probation condition might read "Attend for, and be amenable to, alcohol counselling/treatment as directed by a Provincial Probation Officer." It's already decided that the person will attend something – the only thing left to decide is what. Obviously, the most logical approach is to assess the probationer to determine the most appropriate treatment services. If your area does not have an assessment/referral centre, the person will be referred directly to a counselling/treatment facility. Regardless, the addiction worker's job is simplified: you decide which services are most appropriate, ask if he is willing to attend, and make arrangements for the provision of those services. Remember: it is not your job to enforce the treatment condition. It is not up to you to convince the person that a problem exists or that he should participate in counselling or treatment. Yet it cannot be stressed enough that the worker's attitude sets the tone for the interview. Ideally, your goal is to create an environment in which the client can openly examine his attitudes and behaviors, start the process of motivation, and make personal, informed decisions about his alcohol/drug use. Fortunately, immediate emotional insight is not always necessary for ultimate therapeutic success. Sometimes simply exposing the client to a non-judgemental, positive counselling/treatment situation can precipitate constructive changes. An AA member of long-standing once used a cryptic analogy when asked his opinion of the benefits of mandatory attendance in treatment: "If you throw mud at the wall, some of it is bound to stick." Following this analogy, it would then seem that your job is to prepare the wall so that it is more receptive to the mud.

It is this writer's contention that many problems incurred by agencies when dealing with correctional clients stem from a lack of communication between them and the referring agent. Preparatory work must be done. Roles and expectations must be clearly defined. Other problems may be more the result of the addiction workers' attitudes than those of the clients. We tend to categorize, and make assumptions about, clients based on the referral source. We assume that the manner in which a client comes to us will dictate the level of motivation and success. This is fundamentally wrong. Each client presents at an addiction agency with his own agenda, expectations and needs. Addiction workers also have expectations when a client enters treatment. It's up to counsellors to determine whether those expectations are unrealistic or inaccurate, while attempting to meet the client's needs. Occasionally you can only expect that the client will attend as requested, be honest, and participate or at least not be disruptive. Correctional clients sometimes present with the expectation that the counselling or treatment will be boring and will not apply to them, but are still required to satisfy the treatment condition. In such cases, you may not be able to convince the client that his expectations could be more positive, but you can fulfil the immediate need by providing addiction services. It is quite possible to effect a secondary result, such as positive attitude change or increased awareness, from fulfilling the client's primary need to satisfy the probation condition.

In summary, effective management of correctional clients entails three factors: shedding preconceptions about such clients; developing a satisfactory relationship with the players in the correctional system; and a slight alteration to the orientation of the client. The numbers of correctional clients being referred to addiction agencies will undoubtedly increase with the ongoing trend of openness and awareness about alcohol and drug use. It will be productive for workers in the addiction field to look at this situation as an opportunity and a challenge to provide services to a group of people who, in many cases, would not have taken the initiative to seek assistance. While it may still be true that you cannot help a person who does not want help, it is also true that, with some planning and innovation, you can create a situation that will make it easier for a person to realize that help may be needed.

Testifying in Court

S.J. USPRICH AND R.M. SOLOMON

INTRODUCTION

Testifying in court does not rank very high on anyone's list of enjoyable activities. Nevertheless, being a witness fulfils an important function in our legal system. Aside from assisting the court process, a good citizen has a duty to the parties involved in a trial to ensure that the court's decision is based on as much relevant evidence as possible. In any event, a witness usually has no option. If you are subpoenaed as a witness in a trial or other hearing, you are obligated by law to attend and give evidence.

The experience need not be as intimidating or unpleasant as some people fear. Remember that you are not on trial. You are simply doing your duty by telling the court what you know in order to help the court arrive at a fair decision. The more you understand about the process of testifying and the better prepared you are, the less uncomfortable the experience will be.

PREPARATION

The best preparation for giving evidence begins long before you are informed that you may be called as a witness. Proper client records are not only of practical importance in your work,[1] they may eventually be of profound legal importance. There are various situations in which addiction workers may be required to testify about a client's treatment. Thorough and accurate records are indispensable to the witness.

First, the record serves as the basis for the reconstruction of the facts of the case. A trial often takes place several years and hundreds of clients after an event occurred. The record may be the only way the addiction worker can recall sufficient details about the case. Second, the record itself can be invaluable during the trial or hearing. A record that the witness made or approved close to the time of the event can be used by the witness while testifying.[2] Furthermore, the actual record may be admissible as documentary evidence, even if the addiction worker does not testify.[3] *This can be convenient, but at times it is vital.* For example, if the potential witness has died or is otherwise unavailable, the record becomes virtually the sole source of information and evidence.

Third, a witness's credibility in court or other legal proceedings may be influenced by the state of the record. A witness who faces the court armed with a complete record of facts and observations is in a strong position. If the record is accurate, objective, complete and contemporaneous, the witness will be perceived as organized, methodical and conscientious. Conversely, a sloppy record leaves the impression of a sloppy worker, whether or not that is actually the case.

Apart from these official records, it is often useful to make additional notes as soon as you are informed that you will (or may) be a witness. Litigation is a slow process and considerable time may elapse before the trial takes place. As soon as you know that you may be a witness, making notes of everything that you can remember about the relevant matters will help to preserve your memory of those events. Since these notes are made some time after the events in question, they will not be usable by the witness when he or she is actually testifying in court. Nonetheless, the notes can be useful at a later date to refresh your memory and help you to recall the events about which you will be testifying.

Once you learn that you may be called as a witness, it is sensible to advise the lawyer as early as possible concerning any dates on which it would be difficult to attend court. For example, you may have vacation travel plans that would make it extremely disruptive and expensive to attend court on certain dates. The earlier the lawyer knows this, the easier it will be to arrange a more convenient date. Similarly, if you receive a subpoena (an official document requiring you to attend court to give evidence) for a date that is unsuitable, you should inform the lawyer immediately. It may be possible to arrange a different date for your court appearance.

TALKING TO THE LAWYERS

Conventionally, each side in a court case will be represented by lawyers. If you are going to be a witness in a case, you will probably have been contacted by a lawyer for the side planning to call you as a witness. As part of their preparation, most lawyers try to meet their prospective witnesses to review the witnesses' evidence. Accordingly, you may be contacted long before the trial by the lawyer or someone else from his or her law firm to discuss your testimony.

There is no legal requirement for you to participate in this sort of discussion. In a strict legal sense, a subpoena obligates you only to appear in court and give evidence. Although you are not required to co-operate, you will nevertheless often wish to do so. In addition to being helpful to the lawyer, the pre-trial discussion can help you as a witness. You will know in advance the kind of questions that you will be asked when you testify. As well, if your employer is involved in the matter, you may be requested as part of your employment to co-operate.

The lawyer for the other side may also contact you to discuss the case and the evidence that you will be giving. You are not required to participate in any such discussion, but there is nothing improper in doing so. The side calling a witness does not "own" that witness; he or she is free to talk to the other side to the extent that the witness wishes. You may wish to seek guidance from your employer or from the lawyer representing your side as to whether and to what extent you should co-operate with the other side.

DAY OF THE TRIAL

Bring with you any relevant records or documents that you wish to have while testifying. These should have been discussed in advance with the lawyer. Also bring any personal notes that you have made, as suggested above, which you can review to refresh your memory prior to testifying. As a practical suggestion, it is useful to take along a book or magazine. You may sometimes have a considerable wait before giving your evidence.

When you arrive at court, let the lawyer know that you are there. If the trial is in progress, you should check with the court usher to see whether there has been an order excluding witnesses. At some trials, the presiding judge may make such an order at a lawyer's request. The effect of this order is that witnesses are not allowed to be in court to hear other witnesses prior to giving their own testimony. In that event, it would be improper for you as a witness to enter the courtroom. You can simply wait, or ask the usher to take a note to the lawyer.

PRELIMINARY MATTERS

When the time comes to give your evidence, your name will be called. Walk to the front of the courtroom and take your place in the witness box. If you were present during previous testimony, you will have seen other witnesses do this and know where to go. If you are not sure, the court clerk will direct you.

The usual procedure is for the witness to be "sworn" by taking an oath on the Bible. Canadian courtrooms typically have both Roman Catholic and Protestant versions available and you may be asked which you prefer. Since the Christian Bible contains the Old Testament, many members of the Jewish faith are content to swear on the standard Bible. If your religious beliefs require that the oath be taken in a different way, this is permissible. Whatever form of oath is in accordance with the witness's religious beliefs will be equally acceptable to the court. If the standard oath is not appropriate, you should inform the lawyer in advance so that proper arrangements can be made. For example, a Muslim may wish to take the oath on the Koran, which may not be routinely available. As well as informing the lawyer in advance of any special requirements, it may be simplest for the witness to bring along the appropriate holy book or other objects needed.

A witness may object to taking an oath or be unable to take it for a variety of reasons. His or her religious beliefs may make it inappropriate to swear an oath, the necessary objects may not be available, or the witness may not have any religious beliefs. Not wishing to take an oath does not disqualify the witness from giving evidence. Instead, the witness may simply "affirm."[4] This is simply a solemn promise,[5] without any religious connotations, to tell the truth. It is best if you advise the lawyer in advance that you intend to affirm, rather than take an oath.

GIVING EVIDENCE

After the oath or affirmation formalities have been concluded, you are ready to give your evidence. As you have probably seen on television or in the movies, the evidence of a witness is brought out through a series of questions and answers. The lawyer calling a witness goes first in what is variously known as "examination-in-chief" or "direct examination." Once the lawyer who has called you as a witness finishes asking questions, it then becomes the turn of the lawyer for the other side. This questioning is called "cross-examination." At the conclusion of the cross-examination, the witness is usually done. Sometimes, however, the original lawyer may ask a few further questions in "re-examination." The judge may also ask questions at any stage. Generally, you will be told by the judge when you are finished as a witness. Something along the lines of "Thank you, witness, you may step down" is often used.

In giving evidence, remember that a record is being made of all the questions and answers. Speak clearly and give your answers in words so that a proper record can be made. For example, answer "Yes" rather than nodding your head or grunting "Uh-huh." If you happen to respond with physical motions or gestures, the lawyer questioning you may describe your response by "talking it onto the record."

Q: How big was the knife?

A: About this long.

Q: The witness is indicating with her hands a length of about six inches.

Listen carefully to what is asked. Whether in direct or cross-examination, make sure that you understand the question before you answer it. If you are not sure, do not hesitate to ask for clarification. There is nothing wrong with asking that a question be repeated or explained. Similarly, if you don't know the answer, are not sure, or forget the information that you have been asked, don't hesitate to say so. There is also nothing wrong with taking a moment to think about your answer or to try to recollect a particular fact about which you have been asked.

In assessing a witness's evidence, the court often considers not only what you said, but how you said it. You should answer in a clear, straightforward manner and avoid being either hesitant or arrogant. Nevertheless, if you are unsure about something, it is not fair to anybody – including the *witness* – to answer with a confidence that you do not feel.

DIRECT EXAMINATION

The direct examination typically begins with mundane matters such as the witness's name and other relevant qualifications. Rather than the witness being asked questions to elicit this routine introductory material, the lawyer will often recite the information and simply expect the witness to agree.

> Q: You are Mary Smith and are employed as a youth counsellor at the Central Health Bureau?
>
> A: Yes, sir.
>
> Q. The Central Health Bureau is located at 123 Main Street in downtown Blankville?
>
> A: That's right.
>
> Q: I understand that in your professional capacity you were providing counselling to John Doe in May of 1990?
>
> A: Yes, he had been seeing me professionally from March through June of that year.

Particularly if you are being called as an "expert" witness, the lawyer may wish to bring out extensive details of your professional qualifications, such as education, training, experience, membership in professional bodies, and so forth. This is the sort of thing that should have been discussed well in advance of the trial so that the witness can be properly prepared with the appropriate information. Indeed, the lawyer may have requested a curriculum vitae or resumé for this purpose.

CROSS-EXAMINATION

There may be several goals that the other lawyer tries to achieve through cross-examination. The lawyer may try to get additional information from the witness that will help the other side, or additional facts that may weaken the evidence already given. The lawyer may try to get the witness to qualify a previously given answer, concede that there is some doubt on a particular point, or admit that an alternative explanation is possible. Sometimes, the lawyer may attempt to weaken a witness's evidence by discrediting the witness. There may be an effort to suggest that the witness is mistaken, biased, forgetful, or not credible for a variety of other reasons.

Although vigorous cross-examination may occasionally seem like a personal attack on the witness, remember that it is really the evidence that the lawyer is attacking – not you as a person. Try to avoid becoming angry or flustered by the questioning. The lawyer may be trying deliberately to provoke you. Don't argue, don't try to give "smart" answers, or engage in a battle of wits. Your job as a witness is simply to answer questions and give the court the relevant information you have in as honest and straightforward a way as possible. You are not trying to impress anyone with how clever you are, nor is testifying some form of test.

A common device that lawyers may use in cross-examination is to cut a witness off before he or she can give a full answer or a qualification to an answer. The result may be that a particular answer may be misleading because it is incomplete. If that should happen, it is permissible to ask the judge "May I explain?" Usually, the judge will then permit you to elaborate or complete your answer.

AWKWARD QUESTIONS

Although lawyers should not do so, sometimes they will ask "double-barrelled" questions. This is especially likely in cross-examination where the lawyer is permitted to ask leading questions that require only a "yes" or "no" answer. If you then simply answer yes or no, it may be unclear whether your single answer is in response to both halves of the question or only the last part. It is best to respond to such double questions by explicitly answering both halves. For example, a witness might be asked "Was the client intoxicated and did he attempt to attack you?" Rather than answering "yes," it is clearer if the witness were to say "Yes, he appeared drunk and attempted to attack me."

Another awkward form of question to watch out for is a question framed in the negative. For example: "You didn't see him do it, did you?" A simple reply of "no" could mean either "No, I didn't see" or "No, I disagree with you. I did see." Similarly, a "yes" answer could be equally ambiguous. Make sure that your answer is properly understood by responding fully: "No, I did not see."

FORMS OF ADDRESS

In speaking to the judge, you should call him or her "Your Honor" or "My Lord/ Lady." The correct terminology will depend on the level of court in which the trial takes place. You can ask the lawyer beforehand or simply listen to how the lawyers address the judge and copy their terminology. As an easier alternative, it is also appropriate simply to address the judge as "Sir" or "Ma'am (Madam)." If you should need to refer to the judge in the third person (where you would ordinarily say "he" or "she"), the correct form is "His/Her Honor" or "His Lordship/Her Ladyship."

In addressing the lawyers, use the polite terminology of ordinary conversation, i.e., "Mr." or "Ms. Smith" or simply "Sir" or "Ma'am (Madam)." Although it will rarely arise, you may occasionally wish to refer to one of the lawyers involved in the trial other than the one who is currently questioning you. Aside from referring to the lawyer by name ("Mr./Ms. Smith"), you may instead – especially if you don't know the lawyer's name – refer to him or her as "counsel"; e.g., "counsel for the plaintiff" or "counsel for [Mr. Jones, the hospital, etc.]."

MUST I ANSWER?

Generally, witnesses must answer all relevant questions put to them. Privilege is one of the few exceptions to that general rule.[6] The legal term "privilege" means the right to refuse to disclose confidential information when giving testimony.[7] Traditionally, the only professional relationship to which privilege applied was that between solicitors and their clients. In the absence of privilege, a person who refuses to answer a question when required to do so may be jailed for contempt of court.

Canadian law has no equivalent to the American device of "taking the Fifth." Under the Fifth Amendment to the U.S. *Bill of Rights,* a witness may refuse to answer a question that tends to incriminate him or her. In Canada, a witness would have to answer such a question. However, the *Canadian Charter of Rights and Freedoms* protects a witness from having any incriminating answer used against him or her in any other proceedings (except a prosecution for testifying falsely).[8] This protection automatically applies to all the witness's answers without the witness having to ask for it.

LIMITS ON TESTIMONY

Generally, a witness's testimony is confined to information within his or her personal knowledge. That is, evidence based on his or her own observations rather than on what other people may have told the witness. As a result, a witness is not usually allowed to give what lawyers call "hearsay" evidence.

The rule against hearsay means that you will often not be allowed to repeat what other people have told you. The hearsay rule is complex and not always easy to apply. First, the rule has many exceptions that permit hearsay evidence to be given. Second, hearsay evidence will not always be in the obvious form ("Charlie told me..."). For example, information that the witness obtained from someone else's notes may be hearsay. Third, repeating what someone else has said may sometimes *not* be hearsay, because the evidentiary issue may be the very fact that the other person made the statement. In this situation, the fact that the person made the statement is something that the witness has personally observed.

The important point is that as a witness you are not expected to be a lawyer with expert knowledge of the hearsay rule. In discussing your evidence with the lawyer before the trial, he or she can give you some guidance as to what conversations you may or may not be allowed to repeat because of the hearsay rule. If the issue arises while you are giving evidence and you are unsure whether, for example, you can repeat a given conversation, it is always appropriate to ask the trial judge whether you may say what someone has told you.

In situations where you are allowed to testify as to statements that other people have made, these statements may sometimes involve obscene or offensive language. There is no need to be embarrassed by this. The judge and the lawyers have undoubtedly heard such language before. Bear in mind that it is not you who used that language; you are merely quoting what someone else has said. The importance of the evidence might very well depend on the fact that the speaker has used that sort of language. While it is best to quote the speaker's words as accurately as you can recall them, you could instead paraphrase if you are truly uncomfortable in repeating the exact words. In that case, however, you should make clear that you are doing so. For example, you could say "He then used an obscene expression telling me to go away."

Another area where there are restrictions on testimony is in the witness' giving his or her opinions or conclusions. Only an "expert" witness, testifying specifically on a matter within his or her area of expertise, may give an opinion. An ordinary witness must testify only as to his or her observations, not the opinions or conclusions that the witness may have drawn from them. There is, however, some flexibility in this evidentiary rule so that a witness may give opinions concerning common matters on which, in a sense, everybody is an "expert." For example, a witness could testify that someone appeared drunk, was poorly dressed, was happy or sad, and so forth. Again, you are not expected to be a lawyer and to know all the fine distinctions. The lawyers and the judge will provide guidance as to what you may or may not say.

The lawyers and the trial judge have a shared responsibility to keep inadmissible evidence out of the trial. If some evidence that you are about to give is inadmissible because of the hearsay rule, the opinion rule, or for some other reason, you will often be interrupted and instructed not to give that evidence. Sometimes this interruption will take the form of an objection by the lawyer who is not currently asking you questions. He or she will interrupt by saying "Objection" or "I object." If that happens, you should stop what you are saying. The trial judge, after listening to both lawyers' arguments, will decide whether the evidence is admissible. The judge will then advise you whether you can continue with what you were saying. If you are not clear, do not hesitate to ask the judge whether you may continue.

CONCLUSION

Although testifying in court will never be a delight, it need not be a dreaded, anxiety-filled experience. Understanding what is expected of you as a witness will make testifying less intimidating. Good preparation is even more important. If you are adequately prepared, you will feel more comfortable and be able to give your evidence in a relaxed, straightforward manner. This will enable you to make a better impression as a witness and to leave court feeling that you made a significant contribution to the administration of justice.

ENDNOTES

1. Client records provide the basis for reviewing progress, planning client care, and communicating with others about the client. As well, accurate records are vital for teaching, research, audits, and accreditation. They are also important for effective time management, office administration, billing, and tax purposes.

2. See J. Sopinka and S. Lederman, The Law of Evidence in Civil Cases, (1974), pp. 489–496.

3. See Ares v. Venner, [1970] S.C.R. 608. For an example of a statutory provision, see the Ontario Evidence Act, R.S.O. 1980, c. 145, ss. 35 and 52. Note that s. 52 is limited to medical records.

4. See, for example, Canada Evidence Act, R.S.C. 1985, c. C-5, s. 14.

5. See ibid., s. 14(1): "I do solemnly affirm that the evidence to be given by me shall be the truth, the whole truth, and nothing but the truth." There are slight variations in the formulas recited under the various provincial Evidence Acts, but the wording is essentially the same.

6. For a comprehensive review of privilege, see P. McWilliams, Canadian Criminal Evidence, 2nd ed. (1984), pp. 915–924 and 963–976.

7. See the more detailed discussion of privilege in this book in Chapter 2, Section 2, Part (c).

8. Canadian Charter of Rights and Freedoms, s. 13.

A Counsellor's Practical Suggestions for Testifying in Court

CATE SUTHERLAND

When you deal with clients who are involved in the criminal justice system, you will inevitably be required to appear in court. There are a number of steps you can take that will help reduce your stress, and ensure that the image you present reflects the credibility and quality of your program. Providing testimony in an efficient, professional manner is an easily learned skill. This chapter gives advice on how to prepare for court appearances and tips on courtroom deportment, discusses what to expect in the courtroom and during the case, and lists typical reasons why addiction workers are asked to testify.

The courtroom can be an intimidating place. Criminal justice is serious business. The physical arrangement of the room is historical and deliberate; it sets the psychological stage for the proceedings. The defence and Crown attorneys are squared off across the room from each other. The judge is an imposing figure on his* elevated bench. The witness is isolated in a box. The procedures follow rigid guidelines, and business is conducted with the utmost propriety. For the layperson, appearing in court can be a stressful experience.

Preparation should start long before you are ever required to appear in court. Do some groundwork. If you have never been to court – go. Sit through some criminal proceedings and familiarize yourself with the procedures. Pay close attention to how things are done so that you will know what to expect. This will help eliminate the fear of the unknown.

Establish relationships with the main members of your local judicial system. Judges are much more approachable than you might think. Call the courthouse, ask to speak to the judge† and request an appointment to introduce yourself and your program. It's simple: "I'm Mary Smith from the Acme Addiction Program. Our agency is working with clients who have been referred by the court, and if I could have 15 minutes of your time, I'd like to schedule an appointment to come and tell you more about our program." Do the same with the Crown attorney.† When you attend the

---

*Please note that any references to gender are male. This is for the sake of simplicity and has no sexist implications or intent.

†Many areas have more than one presiding judge or Crown attorney. Concentrate only on those who refer to your program on a regular basis.

meetings, ask first if there is anything in particular they would like to know about your program. If not, explain only the basics – philosophy, objectives, program outline – in other words, the highlights of your program. Leave more detailed information for perusal at their convenience, and invite them to contact you if they wish further information or clarification. Keep in periodic contact – send your annual reports and a letter when you have made changes or additions to your program.

Taking the time to do a bit of public relations will go a long way for you if you must appear in court. First, you establish yourself as a professional equal. This may help reduce your nervousness, plus it usually prevents questions on the stand about who you are and what you do. Secondly, when the court is familiar with you and your agency your testimony will be more readily accepted, and challenged less.

After you have been subpoenaed (or requested) to appear in court, there are further preparatory steps to be taken. First of all, determine whether you are appearing for the Crown or the defence counsel (the client's lawyer). Then call that attorney and inquire about the nature of the information that will be expected from you. Don't hesitate to ask for examples of the types of questions that will be put to you. Knowing the direction that your testimony is expected to take will allow you to prepare mentally. Thoroughly reread the client's file, concentrating on the specific issues. Formulate what you would like to say. A word of caution: know the file inside and out and consider all aspects of the case. Sometimes the questioning can take an unexpected turn and you do not want to appear unprepared. For example, the Crown attorney may tell you that you will be asked to tesify on the client's poor attendance in the program, but on cross-examination the defence lawyer may ask about the subject matter of the sessions and the client's participation. Finally, envision yourself, as vividly as you can, on the stand, calmly responding to questions. You may find it helpful to have someone rehearse, or role-play, with you.

When the day comes, arrive at the courthouse a few minutes early. Seek out the attorney for whom you are appearing. The Crown is easier to find – he'll likely have an office in the courthouse. You will usually have to look around for the defence counsel – if you have never met, have someone point him out. Let the attorney know you are there. Ask if there are any last minute changes and briefly review your testimony.

When you are called to the stand, you will be sworn in before providing evidence. You state your full name for the record and then place your right hand on the Bible as the clerk asks, "Do you swear to tell the whole truth...etc." Witnesses who object to swearing a religious oath have the option of "affirming" the truth. Providing an affirmation of the truth instead of swearing on the Bible in no way affects your credibility as a witness.

Your credibility can be affected, however, by both your verbal and non-verbal presentation on the stand. Remember that the court is not only listening to your answers, it is also observing your demeanor and attitude. Following are a few hints that you may find helpful.

(a) Provide your testimony in a clear, well-modulated voice, loud enough to be heard by all. Mumbling or speaking inaudibly implies that you do not have confidence in the information you are providing, and makes it difficult for others to understand you. Take your time. Hurried answers are sometimes incorrect answers.

(b) Listen carefully to the question being asked and make sure you understand before you reply. Some lawyers have a tendency to ask convoluted questions (no offence intended) and it is sometimes difficult to understand just what they want to know. Do not hesitate to admit your confusion – simply say "I'm sorry, I do not understand the question. Could you please repeat it?" This forces the lawyer to rephrase the question in a clearer form, and has the added advantage of giving you a few extra seconds to formulate your answer. Don't be surprised, however, if after being asked to rephrase, the lawyer's next question has nothing to do with what you thought he was originally asking. This happens fairly often, and may be the result of the lawyer's realization that he was, in fact, not making sense before.

(c) Don't anticipate questions. Wait until the whole question is asked before replying. If the question is complicated, think about your answer first. It is better to take a few moments to reflect upon your answer than to provide muddled information, which could make you appear confused and incompetent.

(d) As a general rule of thumb, give very brief direct answers to direct questions. Do not elaborate unless specifically requested to do so and, even then, be as concise as possible. Consider the following example:

> *Lawyer: On what did you base your recommendation for residential treatment?*
>
> *Worker: On the findings of the assessment.*
>
> *Lawyer: Could you be more specific, please?*
>
> *Worker: The assessment indicates the presence of substantial alcohol dependence. Mr. Smith reports that he is unemployed, has no stable social supports, and no fixed address. He has been unable to maintain even brief periods of sobriety. It was my opinion that he might benefit most from the structured environment of residential treatment.*

(e) Do not allow yourself to get caught up in explaining the rationales of the field. Speak only about the particular client in his particular situation.

(f) Answer only what is asked of you. Do not offer information that is not asked, even if you think it is important. Remember, you are not there to tell a story, but merely to provide evidence. Defence lawyers love story-tellers; they will allow you to hang yourself by playing on conflicting statements.

(g) Speak directly to the person asking the question, and make eye contact. Call the person by name. Lawyers are addressed as Mr. or Ms.; the judge is always referred to as "Your Honor." Never address the defendant while you are on the stand.

(h) Do not address the judge directly unless he has spoken to you first. The only exception to that rule is when you need to refer to the file or your notes. Generally, you are expected to provide your testimony without looking in the file while you are on the stand. If it is necessary to do so, turn to the judge and request permission: "May I refer to my notes, Your Honor?" This is a formality and the judge will most probably give permission. However, testimony is supposed to be provided from memory, and if the witness must rely on notes rather than his own recollection, the attorneys have the right to determine whether the notes are reliable. This typically consists of a question or two about when the notes were taken, and reliability is usually established if you can state that the notes were taken during the interview or shortly thereafter.

A brief warning: a file can be taken from you to be entered as an exhibit if you use it on the stand. When you take a file to court, ALWAYS photocopy the contents beforehand and leave the copies in your office.

(i)   Do not allow the attorney who is cross-examining you to cut short your answer to his question. He may be getting an answer from you that he does not like and/or which will be detrimental to his case. To prevent you from finishing your answer, he may interrupt with a comment or another question. If this happens, firmly and courteously state, "Please allow me to complete my answer to your question." Often, however, the judge or the other attorney will intercede on your behalf, asking that you be allowed to finish.

(j)   Stand (or sit, if invited to do so) in the witness box as calmly as you can, without giving the impression that you are a mannequin. There is a very fine line here. You do not want to appear so relaxed that you seem indifferent to the proceedings; on the other hand, you do not want a ramrod posture to project an air of nervousness and rigidity.

(k)   Wear your "poker face" to court. Do not visibly react to what you hear. You should appear totally objective at all times.

(l)   Do not hazard a guess to a question when you do not know, or are not sure, of the answer. It is perfectly acceptable to reply politely "I'm sorry, I do not know the answer to that question."

There are also a number of other little tidbits of information that you should know that do not fall into specific categories. Some are definite rules (denoted by "always or never") and others are generally expected or accepted practices:

• Do not refer to the defendant (your client) by his first name, but as Ms. or Mr.

• Some judges do not allow anyone to enter or leave the courtroom during cases, only in between. To avoid the unnecessary embarrassment of being told to sit down, make sure to check this out when you are observing proceedings in your preparatory phase.

• Always dress accordingly. Courts generally have rather specific (unwritten) rules on what is considered proper attire – conservativism is the name of the game. This usually means suits, or at least a shirt and tie, for men, and suits or dresses for women.

• Never chew gum, or consume anything, in the courtroom.

• Some judges allow no talking during cases. If yours does, do so only in the most discreet whisper, but never when the judge is talking.

• Never stand with your hands in your pockets while testifying.

All courtrooms (read judges) have their own rules of protocol, which may or may not be on this list. Make a friend when you go to observe the proceedings and ask what you should know. Someone who is in the courtroom often, but not a court officer or lawyer, is your best choice. For example, look for someone in the front row who is taking notes.

Why are addiction workers usually called to court? The underlying purpose, of course, is to provide some type of information. Sometimes an addiction worker is called to clarify a point in his written report, or because the defendant disagrees with a portion of the report or with the recommendations. More often, cases involve "wilful failure to comply," more commonly known as a breach charge. These matters refer specifically to a client's attendance or participation, or lack thereof. This occasion arises when a client has been previously ordered by the court to attend for mandatory counselling/treatment, and has failed to do so. Your testimony in these matters is simple and brief: "Mr. Smith failed to attend scheduled appointments on..." or "Mr. Smith failed to complete the treatment program" or "Mr. Smith did not take part in any group discussion and was disruptive." What often happens in breach charges is that when the defendant sees the witnesses show up in court, he will change his plea to guilty, thus making it unnecessary for you to testify after all. Finally, a point to keep in mind. Sometimes cross-examination can get rough, and while it may feel like a personal attack, it is not. Remember, a lawyer's first obligation is to his client and it is his duty to test all evidence vigorously. While he may be aggressive towards you on the stand, you will probably find that this ends at the courtroom door, and he will otherwise be quite amiable.

All this probably seems like a lot of work for a few minutes on the stand, but the effort will be worth your while. Fortunately, required court attendance is a relatively rare occurrence, but as stated earlier, if your program is dealing with correctional clients, it is inevitable at some point. With adequate preparation and groundwork, however, your court appearances will not be a stress-provoking experience, and your calm, collected presentation will reflect the high calibre of service provided by your agency.

Note: Much of the information in this paper is the result of my agency's experience; bits were gleaned from lawyer friends. The rest may be attributed to a document entitled Ministry of Correctional Services, Probation & Parole Enforcement Manual, specifically the chapter called "The Courtroom Experience." The manual can be found in any probation office.

Alcohol, Drugs and the Workplace: Some Considerations for Counsellors

CHARLES PONÉE

INTRODUCTION

*T*he pedestrian perception of life problems is that some people are prone to them while certain others are totally immune. This notion that certain sub-groups within society are socially inoculated against the rigorous stressors of life and the health implications they hold should be put to rest; in reality, every individual will at times be personally tested by life's demands (Levinson, 1978). Births, deaths, mortgages, physical health problems, parenting problems, job complications, anxieties and all such passages affect us all (Sheehy, 1977, 1981). An "Annus Horribilis" does not befall the Queen of England alone.

Complicating life further for all of us in the 1990s is the fact that the Canadian workplace is undergoing profound and unremitting change as a result of alterations in traditional world-wide consumption and trade patterns, the removal of trade barriers, the globalization of economies, the phenomenal advances in telecommunications technology and information processing and the shift in core products from traditional raw materials to services (Crispo, 1992). Canadians are being called upon in the workplace to produce more and more efficiently, to be more connected to work than other aspects of life and to assume more responsibility and accountability for our work with ever decreasing supports and resources. The repercussions of this state of affairs are being soundly felt in both the private and public sectors, and more specifically in the general state of health and well-being of workers at all levels in organizations, and of their immediate families – today's families not being of the universal stereotype, but reflecting current trends and patterns in the demographics of Canadian society. Approximately half of Canadian workers are women, an increasing number of children are being raised by a single parent (usually the mother) and a portion of Canada's workforce is comprised of workers from cultures other than those of our founding peoples. (Bennett & Humpage, 1989). It is observed therefore, that the rapidly changing characteristics and dynamics of society and the Canadian workplace – with its vagaries, uncertainties and insecurities – all contribute to one of our major social challenges: that of addressing chemical dependency in society at large and at the plant, factory, shop and office in particular.

ALCOHOL, DRUGS AND THE WORKPLACE

There are varying statistics on the extent to which alcohol, prescribed drugs and street drugs are, or are thought to be, consumed by Canadians at large and at work. There are also varying estimates of how much alcohol and drug misuse cost Canadian industry. Obviously, such estimates are at best indicators, as data collection in this area is more an art-form than a science. This being said, however, most chemical-dependency professionals and observers of the issue at the workplace generally agree that, conservatively, between five and 15 per cent of Canadian workers at any one point in time have serious alcohol problems that are likely affecting job performance, and another two to seven per cent have problems related to other drugs. One American author recently stated the following:

> "The U.S. General Accounting Office has reported that approximately 5.3 per cent of the civilian (Federal) workforce suffers from alcoholism, and that each alcoholic employee is about 25 per cent less productive than non-alcoholic employees. Research shows that emotional problems cause annual productivity loss to U.S. business of about $17 billion and that 85 per cent of all industrial accidents are stress-induced. Findings also indicate that alcoholism is responsible for more than $40 million annually in costs to private industry. In the United States, three times more sickness and accident benefits are paid to employees with alcohol problems; lost productivity from alcohol abuse costs approximately $12 billion annually; and that alcohol abuse and smoking account for more than $60 billion annually in health costs (Brody, 1988)."

In 1990, William M. Mercer Ltd. (Mercer, 1990), the prestigious Canadian human resources consulting firm, conducted a survey of Canada's leading employers to determine the seriousness of substance abuse in the workplace in general, and within the surveyed organizations in particular. The survey sample was comprised of the chief executive officers of the largest Canadian companies, all first ministers and a sample of senior government officials – federal, provincial and municipal. Responses were received from 616 individuals and the survey findings were most informative. Of these workplace leaders, 92 per cent perceived substance abuse as a *serious problem;* 54 per cent saw it as a serious problem for their own organization; and 71 per cent saw it as a *growing* problem for Canadian society at large. They perceived that personal stress was one of three major generators of the problem. Interestingly, 24 per cent of the respondents saw *job-related stress* as a key factor in the problem. The addictions treatment community should note that 63 per cent of these respondents saw alcohol and drug treatment programs as a primary means of addressing such health problems.

But what did they perceive as the bottom line? The respondents to the Mercer survey indicated that between one and six per cent of payroll was lost to chemical-dependency problems and that one per cent would cost the Canadian economy 2.6 billion dollars annually. Absenteeism, short-term disability, long-term disability, wasted materials, down time, employer liability and the like were items included in these cost projections.

Finally, the majority of workplace leaders surveyed indicated that they would give the issue of chemical dependency priority in the near future, focusing on workplace wellness initiatives such as workplace alcohol and drug policies and Employee Assistance Programs (Mercer, 1990).

WORKFORCE WELLNESS PROGRAMS

Traditionally, established Canadian employers have provided for such employee benefits as: paid holidays, sick leave, maternity leave, health insurance, medical insurance, and dental plans. However, contemporary Canadian organizations, motivated in large measure by the health promotion philosophy and initiatives of the federal government – much of which was sparked by a 1974 issue paper by the then minister of health and welfare, Marc Lalonde – have assumed the responsibility to promote the health and well-being of their employees, and indirectly, that of the employees' immediate family members (Health and Welfare Canada, 1974). This direction was further supported in 1988 by Health and Welfare in a publication by the Honourable Jake Epp (Health and Welfare Canada, 1986). This altruism was also engendered and reinforced by leadership on employee wellness issues by labor organizations such as the Public Service Alliance and the Canadian Labor Congress, among others, which had predated management action on the issue by several decades. Again too, the "bottom line" for senior managers, in both the public and private sectors, has been a mobilizing force for employee health promotion (Warner et al., 1988). Not many companies in the affluent 60s and 70s took notice of the money that was bleeding away in reactive, tertiary intervention-level employee health measures; however, identifying and dealing with high cost health items brought organizations to the health promotion table. In the late 1980s, health promotion became a very significant method of reducing punishing workplace overhead costs:

> Long-term disability (LTD) costs by group plans have increased by 23 per cent from 1988 to 1990, according to the Canadian Life and Health Insurance Association (CLHIA). Short-term disability (STD) costs have increased by five per cent from 1989 to 1990. Many of these claims are due to stress-related illness. According to the Canadian Institute on Stress, it is projected that stress-related illnesses may increase Workers' Compensation Board (WCB) costs by nine per cent in 1992 (Coshan & Visser, 1992).

One U.S. study in 1985-86 found that a sample of large American organizations put an average of 0.11 per cent of net profits into health promotion programs, compared with 24 per cent of net profits expended on health insurance (Herzlinger, Schwartz & Calkins, 1985-86). Obviously this "penny wise and pound foolish" approach to the health of employees, and ultimately the well-being of the organization, would have to change.

Today, employers are changing their traditional human resource management approach and are striving to promote and maintain employee health – during difficult economic times to boot. In fact, most major organizations include in their "goal" or "mission" statements an organizational commitment to care, in practical ways, for the health and well-being of their employees. In the United States, for example, as far back as 1984, the *Hundred Best Companies To Work For In America* were deemed those that provided good work conditions, reasonable pay and benefits, had open communication, emphasized quality, and, most importantly, could meet the health needs of their employees (Levering, Moskowitz & Katz, 1984). Obviously, healthy employees give an organization a competitive edge. Employee health promotion is both morally and fiscally sound, more so than health-problem resolution. The old adage "an ounce of prevention is worth a pound of cure" applies well in this instance.

In the early years, workplace health promotion usually focused on tangible and readily deliverable initiatives such as: exercise and physical fitness programs, hypertension control, smoking cessation, workplace smoking restriction policies, nutrition and weight loss, stress management, motor vehicle safety belt programs, back injury prevention, and health risk appraisal. These programs were sometimes delivered singly at the workplace and sometimes in tandem with other compatible initiatives. On occasion these programs were well considered prior to implementation; more often than not they were an organizational impulse or the result of the lobbying of vested interest groups or individuals at the workplace. Many appear to have been effective and economically efficient; however, on a broad scale and over the long term, significant scientific evaluation of their objective value generally appears to be lacking (Warner et al., 1988). As a result, in recent years it became clear that a multi-faceted, holistic approach to employee health concerns was a more desirable option. This led to the contemporary concept of Comprehensive Corporate Health Planning.

COMPREHENSIVE CORPORATE HEALTH PLANNING

For organizations that are truly concerned about corporate wellness and employee wellness, at both the senior management and labor levels, models, methods and tools are now being developed and tested for the delivery of comprehensive health services to employees. Health and Welfare Canada, through its Health Promotion Branch, and the Addiction Research Foundation of Ontario, among others, are providing leadership and consultation on the subject to organizations both large and small. The question is: how does an organization set about establishing an effective, all-encompassing corporate health plan and related programming for its employees?

Today, when an organization commits itself to establishing a comprehensive wellness plan, it must take into account the continuum of care from health promotion to problem resolution. It is understood by the organization that a well-rationalized and equally well-implemented plan is the desired objective (Kiefhaber & Goldbeck, 1983). Generally the mandate for designing such a plan is given to a joint union/management committee with the understanding that the plan is to be *owned and operated* by and for employees. In most settings an external experienced health consultant is engaged to provide assistance, direction and generally to keep the planning process – and the key players – focused. Furthermore:

> "Such a comprehensive program should be based upon a clear and objective understanding of the worksite and workforce. As experience demonstrates, it should be developed by a delegated employee committee representing management and labor, men and women (Herzlinger, Schwartz & Calkins, 1985/86). Further, and most important, the program should be developed in such a fashion that, based upon identified employee health/social needs and preferences, it incorporates the reinforcement of existing worksite health and social initiatives and services that are deemed to be appropriate and desirable and the incremental introduction of new and innovative programs and services where needs dictate."

Obviously, human, material and financial resources predicate the extent to which a worksite can respond to employee health needs. Therefore, these needs will likely have to be dealt with in a priorized fashion. The challenge for an organization in clearly articulating its corporate health care program is to critique existing initiatives to ensure they meet identified health and social needs of employees, male and female, individually and collectively, and, if desirable, to generate required health programs/services where none currently exists. Conceptualizing in writing the rationale for these various "wellness" initiatives and clarifying the relationships among them are important components in this process" (Ponée, 1989).

Obviously, employee wellness activities – regardless of the extent to which they are rationalized, integrated, coordinated and implemented – will be of some value to employees at risk of chemical dependency. In some instances the value to such persons may be great but indirect (for example, nutrition seminars, cardiovascular risk reduction, hypertension control, time management, weight management, colorectal and breast cancer screening, fitness activities, communication workshops, shift-work-seminars). In other instances the value may be very direct (for example, AA meetings at the workplace, chemical dependency seminars, Adult Children of Alcoholics workshops, information sessions on prescribed drugs, addictions health check-ups, etc.).

The wellness program of utmost value to those employees who have, or are living with, a substance abuse problem is the Employee Assistance Program (EAP). In many organizations, EAPs have been the launching pad for other wellness programs and comprehensive corporate health planning. They set out a system for employee health care in one life problem area that all employees will likely support because of their positive intent and inherent sense of caring; their demonstrated dollar value in helping chemically-dependent persons who may not otherwise seek help at a given time; their demonstrated positive impact on morale; and finally, but very importantly, the model they establish for other health-directed partnerships between management and labor.

EMPLOYEE ASSISTANCE PROGRAMS

Interestingly enough, contemporary Employee Assistance Programs have their formative roots in occupational medicine, industrial social work, early labor self-help programs, enlightened management practice and last, but most significant of all, in workplace alcoholism programs. (Some early workplace alcoholism programs were developed at Eastman Kodak, Consolidated Edison, ATT and Caterpillar Tractor.) Sparked initially by the people and philosophy of the Alcoholics Anonymous movement, workplace alcoholism programs were essentially a reactive management-directed intervention to deal with employees whose blatant and advanced alcohol problems were obviously and seriously affecting the workplace. The cornerstone of such programs was *constructive coercion*: threatening employees with job loss unless they attended treatment. Although these programs were well intended and enjoyed some success – in fact, helped thousands of chemically dependent employees – they were often rooted in paternalism, manipulation, and covertness and attempted to deal with chemical dependency through treatment rather than prevention. They addressed the health needs of only a small percentage of those employees at risk of alcohol problems and, being AA influenced, tended to miss the needs of employees with other addictions problems. Also, they failed to meet the needs of senior level employees and female employees. Employee confidentiality was often compromised.

Contemporary EAPs have moved a long way from the workplace alcoholism programs of yesteryear. Today, EAPs are normally overseen and managed by a joint management-union committee and are usually solidly rooted in a workplace policy and procedures document (in which program philosophy, principles, roles and responsibilities are delineated) and are "employee owned and operated." (As of 1989, 16 per cent of all Ontario workplaces with more than 50 employees had an EAP [Dunbar, 1989].)

Originally offering counselling services through on-site counsellors (usually employees of the organization), volunteer referral agents and facilities, these programs now tend to provide professional and confidential off-site assistance and counselling to employees and their families for the full range of human concerns. The service provider usually has a formal contract with the employer, and is responsible for reporting related statistical data to the workplace EAP Committee program.

The provider meets the employer's EAP Committee on a regular basis to review the general operation of the program and to ensure that the program's services are meeting the expectations of both the organization and employees. The primary thrust of a progressive EAP is to have employees use the program's services *of their own volition* at the earliest possible stage in the development of a problem, when it may still be contained or solved through positive, constructive and attentive professional intervention. Reaching the greatest number of distressed employees in an organization is the challenge. Providing help for the "worried well" – as healthy employees with transitory but pressing problems are sometimes called – can lead an organization down the road to cost effectiveness. For example, one author has projected that such a program can return up to 185 per cent of the initial program cost in the first year, with a subsequent annual return of 485 per cent; the typical EAP cost being $30-$50 per organizational employee, per year (List, 1986). Canadian experience indicates that well managed EAPs will reach between three per cent and 20 per cent of an organization's employees in a given year. This is significant in that one study at Harvard University suggests that psychological treatment for individuals, such as that made available through EAPs, may cut subsequent health care visits by as much as half (Turkington, 1987).

CHEMICAL DEPENDENCY AND THE PROGRESSIVE EAP

An effective EAP has in place clear policies and procedures – and service quality control measures – for effectively relating to all forms of chemical dependency: alcohol and/or psychoactive drugs (street drugs, prescription and non-prescription drugs). (One research article indicates that between 10 and 25 per cent of all problems brought to counselling through an EAP relate to alcohol addiction [List, 1986]). There is usually a clear and comprehensive policy statement on chemical dependence, as a logical and natural extension of the EAP policy. This is usually based upon considerable specialist consultation. This statement should be rooted in the philosophy that chemical dependency is a progressively debilitating condition and that the employer will reasonably accommodate those employees so affected. It should also acknowledge that the workplace can also be part of the problem. As *denial* is often the response of the chemically-dependent employee, so too is it often the response of the workplace (Baltz, 1991). Therefore, such a policy should focus on abuse, not use; be integrated with other prevailing human resources policies; and acknowledge that chemical dependency is usually interrelated with other life problems and that assistance sought/provided should address this fact. Usually a workplace substance abuse policy relates to on-the-job and related behaviors and clarifies the nature and extent of the assistance that will be provided to employees with performance problems, the conditions under which assistance will be made available, etc. For example, clear measures of performance are developed for all employees and these are reviewed regularly with them. A discipline policy, and related proce- dures, should be developed and implemented and managers and supervisors should be trained, coached on it and be expected to implement it.

It is normally made clear in the chemical dependency policy that EAP ser- vices may be engaged voluntarily, and free of direct charge, by the employee. In such a situation, one's confidentiality is completely protected. However, if the problem affects performance and/or the organization, disciplinary action may be taken, the outcome of which may not assure the employee of total confidentiality with regard to his or her problem. (Studies have shown that around 50 per cent of those treated for alcohol and/or drug abuse will relapse within one year. By imple- menting follow-up programs for at least one year after treatment, the cost of dis- ability claims for substance abuse has been reduced in some cases by 31 per cent [Coshan & Visser, 1992].)

Community-based counsellors providing EAP services to the chemically dependent employee must be allowed to maintain neutrality in the counselling situation in order to be fully effective. Assistance, when requested by the employee, should be provided promptly and procedures should be in place to ensure this.

The professional training of counsellors, their professional experience in the addictions field and their general level of competence are all important issues. The employee client should be guaranteed, at minimum, a basic acceptable standard for counsellor qualifications and performance. Let us remember, counsellors must assume full responsibility for their actions, so it is prudent for them to be aware of their own professional limitations and to stay within their range of abilities. This is something that is often treated lightly (Rumsey, 1992).

EMPLOYER OR EMPLOYEE INTERESTS?

In providing EAP-related addictions counselling to an employee, one major question must be addressed by the counsellor: *Is my concern the well-being of the employer or that of the employee?*

Experience has clearly demonstrated that too many chemical dependency cases have "landed on the rocks" because of counsellors' ambiguity as to where their com- mitment lay. As many addiction counsellors come from dysfunctional families, this issue becomes even more challenging to resolve (McCabe O'Mara, 1992). For vari- ous reasons – a well-intended effort to bring all parties together at the counselling table, an ill considered appreciation of the procedural ethics involved, lack of fore- thought – confidences have often been breached and clinical mis-steps taken, with efforts at dealing with chemical dependency cases ending in failure, and worse.

It is important for the addictions counsellor to remember that employers –

especially those in the private sector – are primarily concerned with the organization's well-being as a whole and its profitability, and not with the health of an individual employee. On the other hand, the counsellor is more closely identified with the employee's needs and not those of the employer (Brody, 1988). The counsellor dilemma noted above sometimes becomes even more profound when the EAP client is an impaired manager, a senior level executive, a company partner, a family member (where the family owns and/or operates the company) and/or a high-profile "personality." This is especially true where the client is having a negative effect on his or her work group (O'Sullivan, 1992). When such is the case, the dynamics between the counsellor and the client, and the counsellor's interface with the workplace – human resources, health services, physician, associate, supervisor – are of utmost importance. In these cases of chemical dependency, as in all others, issues related to confidentiality must be taken fully into account throughout the helping process.

ISSUE OF CONFIDENTIALITY

Helping relationships are built upon the foundation of trust and mutual respect between the counsellor and the client. The client has the right to have his or her life situation protected against unauthorized release of information to others – individual or corporate – and the counsellor has the responsibility to protect client-related information and not to disclose willingly any part of it during or after the helping process. This matter must be of particular concern for, as helping systems such as EAPs become more common and the world becomes more litigious, the counsellor may at some point be called by law to account for his or her actions. A breach of confidentiality can lead to penal, professional and civic liability consequences.

An employee's greatest fear is to have information gleaned in counselling sessions passed on to his or her employer. This fear may be considerably greater for those in safety-sensitive or security-sensitive positions. For persons with chemical dependency problems this fear is usually quite acute.

Confidentiality is a cornerstone of the success of Employee Assistance Programs. A fully professional EAP is designed and implemented at every level to ensure that this principle is promoted and nurtured, which takes concerted effort on all parts. The most casual incident can lead to a breach of confidentiality and hence create significant problems for the counsellor, EAP service provider, the employee – and the EAP, per se (Solomon & Usprich, 1992).

In addition to their personal standards of ethical conduct, addictions counsellors are bound by statutory obligations and the code of ethics, performance standards and expectations of their particular professional associations. If they work within a health or social service agency – public or private – they can also be held accountable to standards of confidentiality espoused by their employers. In progressive and attentive settings, both experienced and new counsellors are asked to review the prevailing confidentiality policy and procedures and sign a statement agreeing to comply. Counsellors working for private EAP providers usually have very explicit policies and procedures regarding confidentiality. In addition, special and regular training sessions are held on the subject and regular meetings called to discuss it. They also receive professional supervision to ensure they practise what has been written in policy. (This matter may be more ambiguous for self-employed counsellors.) Support staff are routinely instructed and encouraged to ensure that their day-to-day work takes client confidentiality into account.

The general principle used in the EAP counselling field is that anonymity is to be guaranteed and that the employee's identity, as well as information related to any aspect of his or her contact with the counsellor, will not be revealed without the employee's voluntary written request, permission and consent. Usually, this written authorization is restricted to communication with an individual, regarding a single issue, on a single occasion and on a "need to know" basis, e.g. providing an opinion on "time for return to work." It should be noted that this working arrangement is normally reviewed by the counsellor with the client at the outset of the counselling relationship.

There are several circumstances when confidentiality can be over-ridden. They are, in brief:
• when the client is a threat to himself/herself and/or others;
• when there exists a clear danger to the public good (e.g., infectious diseases);
• when there are indications of child abuse.

If a counsellor is to override the principle of confidentiality, it is important that counselling supervisors/peers be consulted beforehand.

It is important for the counsellor also to understand that, in a court of law, it is not the actual decision made by the counsellor that matters but whether or not the decision was reasonable, competent and appropriate (Solomon & Usprich, 1992).

From a strictly administrative perspective, a number of practices can be instituted by a counsellor, or a counselling organization, to ensure that client confidentiality is maintained. They include:
• not leaving names, messages and telephone numbers at the client's home or place of work, with individuals, or on answering machine, without the client's written authorization
• not transmitting confidential information by fax or electronic mail
• appropriately maintaining records and record access, storage and retrieval
• secure maintenance and storage of client files on a day-to-day basis
• secure transportation of files outside the office
• ensuring that no client information is inadvertently released to a caller.

A word of caution: counselling agencies/counsellors should manage their relationships with corporate clients just as they manage their employee-client relationships. The same principles of confidentiality should apply.

"TIME OFF FOR TREATMENT", WORKPLACE RE-ENTRY AND RELAPSE

It is often disruptive and costly for an employer to have an employee take time off for health care. This is especially true for small or mid-size organizations that are more apt to feel the pinch of an absent employee for an extended period of time. It is also very true when the employee in question is a key player in the day-to-day operation of the business. However, it is clear from observation that most Canadian organizations are willing to invest in an employee in this manner – often absorbing most or all of the related costs – providing the employee is committed to the organization and demonstrates good faith in the care-seeking process. Sometimes too, unions are prepared to offset some treatment costs on a "one occasion only" basis, if requested to do so. Obviously, the patience and good will of the organization are tried when relapse occurs. Experience demonstrates that chemically dependent clients have a high rate of recidivism. This underscores the importance of responsive follow-up on such cases for a minimum of one year following treatment. Effective EAPs provide this type of monitoring and follow-up.

When the employer has extended support and/or assistance to a chemically-dependent employee, and the employee continues to perform below acceptable standards and/or relapses are ongoing, the employer may be required to take corrective action – based upon performance – and the employee may be called upon to cope with his or her problem without employer support. Ultimately, it is a matter of personal choice. Re-entry into the workplace can pose a major challenge for one returning from treatment. At this point, the employer and employer representatives should be most sensitive to the employee's requirements and consider such options as job modifications, work-load demands, transfers and other means of making re-entry more approachable for the client. Also, workplace education measures such as EAP awareness sessions can make clear to all employees that they have a moral, humanitarian and business responsibility to ensure that, at minimum, they are doing nothing to complicate the re-entry of the chemically dependent employee. When and where possible, family members should be assisted along with the returning worker. Supervisors, managers and shop stewards should have at their disposal coaching and consultation opportunities to assist them in facilitating worker re-entry.

OTHER ISSUES

As women comprise approximately half of the workforce, it is becoming increasingly more evident that alcohol and other drug problems in women can be expected to surface. Therefore, counsellors servicing employees must be attuned to chemical-dependency issues as they pertain to women; be sensitive to gender-oriented counselling; and be familiar with feminist counselling and the knowledge base and community resources that pertain to women. Comparable counsellor responsiveness to the older worker is also important as the Canadian population in general, and the workforce in particular, is rapidly aging.

Another EAP trend is that of servicing employees' immediate family members and dependents. This gives many more chemically-dependent or affected citizens access to helping services, and provides the addictions counsellor with tremendous scope and opportunity. Therefore awareness about such issues as family dynamics and the stress related to balancing job and family can prove significant in the helping process.

Well considered EAPs have broadened their scope of influence to include a broad spectrum of "enhanced services:" child care, elder care, legal, trauma, career and financial counselling, etc. The informed counsellor can skillfully ensure that clients use these enhanced services to optimize the possibility of containing or resolving an alcohol or drug problem.

Finally, addictions counsellors should be aware of workplace developments related to drug testing. The drug testing movement has, for the past decade, been developing a head of steam in the United States. It is being used for employee selection and performance monitoring in both regular and sporadic checks. By 1987, 50 per cent of the largest American corporations were performing employee drug testing of one type or another, for one reason or another (Henriksson, 1991).

The Canadian scene appears much different. The Canadian government proposed a program of mandatory drug testing in the transportation industry. However, as the scientific evidence on the benefits of drug testing remain unclear, there does not appear to be a great deal of support for this type of program. (For example, a 1986 attempt by Air Canada to introduce mandatory drug testing for its 22,000 employees worldwide failed.) Because of this, and privacy-related issues, the future of drug testing at the Canadian workplace remains uncertain. (Henriksson, 1991).

SUMMARY

Alcohol and drug problems are a major concern for all organizational leaders in the Canadian workplace. Well-considered and well-implemented comprehensive corporate health plans appear to be the most cost-effective way for employers to address these and other employee problems. A key workplace program, sometimes free-standing in an organization and sometimes part of a larger health programming package, is the EAP – which can offer optimal assistance to people with alcohol or drug problems – directly or indirectly.

The addictions counsellor should be well versed in workplace wellness programming, and EAPs in particular, and understand how he/she can best work with these health programming tools to the full advantage of the chemically-dependent employee.

REFERENCES

Baltz, E. (1991). Dealing with Denial. A paper of Corporate Health Consultants, Mississauga, Ont., 1991.

Bennett, P. & Humpage, K. (1989). Contemporary Issues For Women In The Workplace; A Sociological Perspective. In V. Carver & C. Ponée (Eds.), Women, Work and Wellness (pp. 39–47). Toronto: Addiction Research Foundation, 1989.

Brody, B. (1988). Employee Assistance Programs: An Historical and Literature Review. American Journal of Health Promotion. Winter 1988, 13–18.

Carver, V. & Ponée, C. (Eds.) (1989). Women, Work, and Wellness. Toronto: Addiction Research Foundation, 1989.

Coshan, M. (1992). Is an EAP an Employee Benefit? Employee Benefits Forum, Nov. 1992, 4.

Coshan, M. (1990). Enlarging the Concept of Employee Assistance. Corporate Health Consultants. Mississauga, Ont., 1990.

Coshan, M. & Visser, M. (1992). Spending to Save. Benefits Canada, April 1992, 59–62.

Crispo, J. (1992). Making Canada Work – Competing in the Global Economy. Toronto: Random House, 1992.

Dunbar, B. (1989). From EAP to Workforce Health Programs. Toronto: Addiction Research Foundation, 1989.

Gibbs, J., Mulvancy, D., Hanes, C. & Reed, R. (1985). Worksite Health Promotion – Five-Year Trend in Employee Health Care Costs. Journal of Occupational Medicine, 27, 11, Nov. 1985, 826–830.

Health and Welfare Canada (1986). Achieving Health For All: A Framework for Health Promotion. Ottawa: Health and Welfare Canada.

Health and Welfare Canada (1974). A New Perspective on The Health of Canadians – A Working Document. Supply and Services Canada.

Henriksson, L. (1991). The Unconvincing Case for Drug Testing. Canadian Public Policy. XVII, 2, 183–196.

Herzlinger, R., Schwartz, J. & Calkins, D. (1985/86). How Companies Tackle Health Care Costs: Parts I, II, III. Harvard Business Review. July/August (69–81); September/October (108–120); January/February (70–80).

Kiefhaber, A.K. & Goldbeck, W.B. (1983). An expansive view of worksite wellness. Marketing & Managing Healthcare, (37–54), Memphis: University of Tennessee Centre for Health Sciences.

Levering, R., Moskowitz, M. & Katz, M. (1984). The 100 Best Companies to Work for in America. Reading, Mass:. Addison-Wesley Publishing Co., 1984.

Levinson, D. (1978). The Seasons of a Man's Life. Toronto: Random House of Canada Limited, 1978.

List, W. (1986). Helping Out the Problem Employee. Report on Business Magazine, Sept. 1986, 68–76.

McCabe O'Mara, E. (1992). A Way Out For The Codependency For EAPS. EAP Digest. March/April, 1992.

McCallum, T. (1992). Shelter from the Storm. Human Resources Professional. Jan. 1992, 8–12.

Mercer Bulletin (1990). Substance Abuse in the Workplace: The Mercer Nationwide Survey of Canada's Leading Employers, 40, 10, Oct. 1990.

Naisbitt, J. & Avurdene (1985). Re-inventing the Corporation. New York: Warner Books Inc., 1985.

O'Sullivan, C. (1992). The Impaired Manager's Impact on the Work Group. EAP Digest. March–April 1992, 2–46.

Ponée, C. (1989). The Health of Female Workers: Worksite Programming Implications. In V. Carver & C. Ponée (Eds.), Women, Work and Wellness (pp. 103–126). Toronto: Addiction Research Foundation, 1989.

Rumsey, M.J. (1992). Making EAP Referrals Work, EAP Digest. July–Aug. 1992, 42–43.

Santa-Barbara, J. (1983). Productivity, Mental Health and Employee Assistance Programs. Canadian Manager, Dec. 1983, 4–6.

Sheehy, G. (1981). Pathfinders. New York: Bantam Books Inc.

Sheehy, G. (1977). Passages. New York: E.F. Dutton & Company Inc.

Solomon, R. & Usprich, S. (1992). Consent, Negligence and Confidentiality: A Legal Primer for Canadian Employee Assistance Programs. A paper prepared in conjunction with Corporate Health Consultants, Mississauga, Ont., July 1992.

Turkington, C. (1987). Help for the Worried Well. Psychology Today, Aug. 1987, 44–47.

Warner, K., Wickizer, T., Wolfe, R., Schildroth, J. & Samuelson, M. (1988). Economic Implications of Workplace Health Promotion Programs: Review of the Literature. Journal of Occupational Medicine, 30, 2, Feb. 1988, 106–115.

About the Authors

Helen Annis, Ph.D., is chief of the Behaviour Change and Relapse Prevention Clinic at the Addiction Research Foundation and professor in the department of behavioural science at the University of Toronto. She has published extensively over the past 20 years on the treatment of addictive behaviors, and has given workshops across Canada, the United States and Europe on relapse prevention counselling strategies for alcohol and other substance abusers.

Jane Baron, R.N., M.Sc., is the program coordinator for Lifestyle Enrichment for Senior Adults Program (LESA), Ottawa, a treatment program for people over 55 years of age who are experiencing social and/or health problems related to their use of alcohol or other psychoactive drugs. Jane has been advocating, through LESA, for a holistic approach towards seniors' drug treatment since the program's inception in 1981. Along with her program responsibilities, she also develops materials and provides training on how to identify and intervene with an older person with substance use problems.

Christine Bois holds a M.A.Sc. (University of Waterloo) in psychopharmacology and clinical psychology. Her experience in addictions includes treatment, research and education. She is currently the program director for the Addiction Research Foundation in Perth, the vice-chair of the Rideau Valley District Health Council, and a member of a provincial working group that is developing a Directory of Outcome Measures. Christine is also part of a team that is developing a Guided Format for Assessing Family Members.

Fred J. Boland, Ph.D., is a faculty member and former chair of clinical training in the psychology department, Queen's University. His major research interests include theoretical, treatment and relapse prevention aspects of substance abuse and eating disorders.

Richard J. Boudreau received his undergraduate degree from Boston College. While completing graduate work in Washington, D.C., he did specialized studies in clinical behavioral sciences at Georgetown University and the National Institute of Health. He also completed a diploma program with the department of psychiatry at McMaster University with specialization in family therapy, as well as an M.Ed. degree at the University of Toronto. He is presently a senior education consultant in training and education with the Addiction Research Foundation.

Doug Bullock received Bachelor of Arts (psychology and mathematics) and Bachelor of Education degrees from Queen's University and a Master's degree in social work from Carleton University. He has been involved in a variety of addictions-related activities, including program evaluation, treatment delivery, systems planning and public education. He helped the Ottawa-Carleton Independent Living Centre develop a peer support training manual, and is currently a member of the Centre's Peer Support Committee. As a member of the Addiction Research Foundation's Disability Issues Advisory Committee, he is active in advocating for the development of accessible addiction services in Ontario.

Gwen Carroll, R.N., is a nurse counsellor who worked with the Addiction Research Foundation from 1971 to 1993. As manager of the Residential Supportive Care Service in the Clinical Research and Treatment Institute, she was instrumental in the development of staff training programs in the management of intoxicated and disruptive behavior.

Virginia Carver, Ph.D. (psychology), has worked in the addictions field since 1974. She is currently a program consultant with the Ottawa Area Office of the Addiction Research Foundation, working mainly in the area of treatment service development. She has a special interest in the development of services for older persons and for women. She is co-editor of *Women, Work and Wellness,* a book about women and workplace health, published by ARF in 1989. Recently she has been involved in developing public information and training materials on substance use by older adults.

Blair E. Collins, B.A., B.TH., is presently in private counselling practice, and facilitates retreat and workshop presentations. He has worked for a number of years with people living with AIDS and HIV, and has a special interest in dealing with various lesbian/gay-related issues, including personal acceptance, psychosexual integration, and homophobia.

Gerry Cooper, M.Ed., has worked in the addictions field throughout Ontario since 1976. In 1984, he joined the Addiction Research Foundation, where he continues to work as a program director. His special interests include the areas of substance abuse/psychiatric co-morbidity and rural applications of treatment interventions such as detoxification. He also holds part time teaching posts at several post-secondary institutions.

Susan Cross, M.A.SC., is executive director of the Alcohol and Drug Referral Centre of Kingston. She was the research director for the project that developed the assessment/referral model of service that was adopted by the province of Ontario. She is particularly interested in the development of community services from a systems perspective.

Christine S. Davis, Ph.D, C.Psych., was a research associate with Dr. Helen Annis of the Addiction Research Foundation when their chapter on relapse prevention was written. She is now a psychologist consultant to oncology at Sunnybrook Health Science Centre and Toronto-Bayview Regional Cancer Centre.

Peter M. Ford, M.B., F.R.C.P.(C), is a faculty member in the department of medicine, Queen's University. He is director of the regional AIDS clinic that operates out of Kingston General Hospital and serves a wide area of both urban and rural Eastern Ontario, as well as providing services for the local penitentiaries. He has a research interest in the epidemiology of HIV infection within the penitentiary system and is currently organizing a prevalence study of HIV-infection in a male medium-security prison.

Kathryn Graham, Ph.D. (psychology), is a scientist with the Addiction Research Foundation. She conducts research in the area of addictions treatment evaluation, with particular focus on the areas of programs for older people, case management programs and relapse prevention. She has also completed work in the area of research and evaluation methods and women's issues.

Susan Harrison, B.A.(Hon), B.Ed., M.S.W., was a teacher for several years before pursuing a degree in social work, graduating in 1979. Her career since then has included experience in the fields of child welfare and school social work but has been primarily in addictions. Prior to her current position as regional manager, Community Programs department, Addiction Research Foundation, Susan was the director of a women's addiction treatment centre. She has given many workshops and presentations on addiction-related topics, her special interest and expertise being women and addictions.

Audrey Hill, M.A., Mohawk of the Six Nations Reserve, is a faculty member in the Native Community Care program, Mohawk College, Brantford, Ontario. She is working on her doctoral dissertation for a Ph.D. (psychology, specializing in chemical dependency). Her major concern in the addiction field is the development of culturally-appropriate services for native people.

Betty-Anne M. Howard, M.S.W., has worked in the addictions field for 12 years. She is currently a substance abuse counsellor at the Prison for Women, clinical supervisor of Employee Assistance Counsellors with Off-site Resources, and teacher at St. Lawrence College and Queen's University. In addition she has spent an equal number of years working with grass roots women's organizations addressing issues of violence against women and children, racism, classism, homophobia and ageism.

Deborah Hudson, M.S.W., Registered Trager Practitioner, is a psychotherapist and consultant in private practice in Kingston, Ontario. For the last 10 years she has specialized in work with survivors of assault. Her major interest is the body/mind connection and how this is effected by trauma.

Mel Kahan, M.D., C.C.F.P, F.R.C.P.C., is a physician scientist at the Addiction Research Foundation and assistant professor in the department of family and community medicine at the University of Toronto. He has a particular interest in the education of family physicians.

Hannah Kaufman, M.S.S., is a professional social worker at the Clinical Immunology Outpatient Clinic (HIV/AIDS) at Kingston General Hospital. Her particular focus is providing psychotherapy for individuals, couples and families during periods of high stress, such as a new HIV diagnosis, deterioration in health, hospitalization and family conflicts. She also provides case management and professional and corporate consultations and workshops.

Carl Kent, M.S.W., C.S.W., worked for a number of years in Ontario hospital and general hospital psychiatry and then switched to the field of substance abuse by joining the Addiction Research Foundation. At ARF he has worked in a variety of clinical settings. Presently he is a clinical program consultant with ARF's Community Programs department within the Metro Toronto region. He is interested in developing and promoting effective ways of treating the elderly substance abuser and the dually disordered; he has helped plan and organize several dual disorders workshops and conferences.

Edward Larkin, Ph.D., is a clinical psychologist who has worked in the addictions field for 25 years. He has held managerial and clinical positions with the Addiction Research Foundation. He has an interest in impaired health professionals and currently is involved in the development of treatment approaches for health professionals with dual substance abuse and other disorders.

Lynn Lightfoot received her Master's of Applied Science and her Ph.D. in psychology at the University of Waterloo. She was the research director of the Treatment Program Research Development Project, Queen's University for three years and then joined the Addiction Research Foundation for 10 years. Dr. Lightfoot is an adjunct assistant professor of psychology, Queen's University, Kingston, Ontario. She is the author of over 50 scientific articles, book chapters, conference proceedings and government reports in the field of substance abuse, and has specialized in the development and evaluation of substance abuse treatment programs for forensic populations since 1985. She has written and co-authored two treatment manuals and a staff training manual for Correctional Services Canada, and has conducted many training workshops and seminars. Dr. Lightfoot has worked as a consultant to Correctional Services Canada, and the U.S. National Institute of Mental Health, and was recently appointed to Ontario's Criminal Code Review Board.

Robert D. Murray, M.S.W., I.C.A.D.C., is a professional social worker and educator. He is currently a program consultant with the Addiction Research Foundation and co-ordinator of the Waterloo Region Alcohol and Drug Service. He has extensive experience counselling substance abusing clients and has a particular interest in the area of domestic violence. He provides group treatment to male spouse abusers, and has taken national leadership in developing and disseminating educational materials on domestic violence and substance abuse.

Charles Ponée, M.S.W., M.C.A., is vice-president, Corporate Health Consultants Ltd. (CHC), National Capital Region. He spent the first 24 years of his professional career with the Addiction Research Foundation. During that time he was involved in a broad range of addictions-related community development initiatives. One of his major interests is in the promotion, development and implementation of high quality Employee Assistance Programs that enhance the health of employees. He co-edited, with Virginia Carver, *Women, Work and Wellness.*

Martha Sanchez-Craig earned a Ph.D. in counselling psychology at the University of Toronto in 1972. She joined the Addiction Research Foundation in 1973, where she is a senior scientist. In a 20-year program of research with numerous colleagues, she developed a cognitive-behavioral approach for early intervention with alcohol and other drug use problems, which has been tested in parts of Canada, South America and Europe. The methods are described in numerous publications, including a therapist's manual for secondary prevention of alcohol problems and a self-help book, both published by the Addiction Research Foundation.

Wayne Skinner, M.S.W., has over two decades of experience in working with people with problems related to substance use. He has worked as a therapist, supervisor, trainer and manager. His interests include outpatient treatment approaches and family therapy. Currently, he is involved in developing programs for opiate users and mental health patients. He is assistant director, planning, at ARF's Clinical Research and Treatment Institute.

Terry Soden, M.S.W., C.C.P., I.C.A.D.C., is a psychotherapist and professional educator. He is principal of Soden & Associates, a treatment training and counselling service with its head office in Richmond Hill, Ontario. He has extensive experience in the field of addictions, including eight years with the Addiction Research Foundation as a therapist and senior education consultant. His major interest, in addition to psychotherapy, is training the helping professions in the competent use of treatment methods, modalities, strategies and techniques (including the use of self-help/mutual-aid process).

Robert Solomon, LL.B., LL.M., is a professor in the faculty of law at the University of Western Ontario. He has published widely in the last 22 years on various aspects of alcohol and drug law and policy. He has travelled extensively across Canada as a consultant and public speaker. In recent years, he has designed several professional development programs for counsellors in the addictions field.

Cate Sutherland is director of the Belleville ATAC Centre, an assessment service in southeastern Ontario. She is continuing her education on a part-time basis and is currently enrolled in a degree program at Queen's University. Areas of interest, during Cate's 15-year career in the addictions field, have been service provision to correctional clients and innovative program development.

Beryl Tsang is the senior program consultant for multicultural services at the Addiction Research Foundation. She holds a master's degree in East Asian studies and has worked extensively in the areas of international development, race relations and settlement counselling.

Darryl Upfold, M.A. (psychology), is director of the Young Adult Substance Abuse Clinic at St. Mary's General Hospital in Kitchener, Ontario. His clinical interests focus on applying cognitive-behavioral methods to addictive behaviors. He is the co-author of *Early Identification and Intervention for Students,* a training manual for school counsellors. He has consulted extensively with school boards and youth-serving agencies. He is an accredited trainer for the Health and Welfare Canada-Addiction Research Foundation skills training package, *Youth & Drugs.*

Syd Usprich is associate dean (academic) and a professor in the faculty of law at the University of Western Ontario. Specializing in criminal law and evidence, he combines over 20 years of teaching and research in those areas with several years practical experience as a part-time Crown attorney. In addition to numerous articles on criminal law and on alcohol and drug law and policy, he is co-author of *Evidence and Procedure in Canadian Labour Arbitration.*

D. Adrian Wilkinson obtained his doctorate in psychology at Oxford University. After post-doctoral studies at York University in Toronto, he joined the Addiction Research Foundation where he worked for 18 years. His principal research interests were treatment of substance abuse problems in youth and young adults, and the neuropsychological consequences of chronic heavy alcohol and drug use. In 1988, he left the Addiction Research Foundation and established a practice as a research consultant. He is currently director of research of Mensana Corporation in Toronto.